I0814501

PRAISE FOR *RESILIENT CITIZENS*

"Crucial topic and perfect timing considering today's challenging and dynamic threat landscape, especially in our homeland. The foundation of strategic deterrence is our resilience...[there's] no better person to articulate this than Dr. Chris Ellis."

—**GLEN D. VANHERCK**, General (ret), USAF, Former Commander, NORAD and USNORTHCOM

"Through scary field experience, rigorous research, and selfless public advocacy, Dr. Ellis has become one of the most important voices in the discussion around risk and resiliency in the 21st century. He and I have spent years teaching governments, media, and citizens about the fascinating history of preparedness, the nuances of 'mainstream preppers,' and why the old stereotypes and politics are doing you and your community a shameful disservice as we face a near future that is certain to be much more difficult than the recent past. This deep-dive study expands on [our] work, highlighting why the flaws of humans and our created systems deserve to be laughed at and critiqued—not preparedness."

—**JOHN RAMEY**, Preparedness Expert, Founder of The Prepared, Cofounder of the Defense Innovation Unit, Former Silicon Valley insider

"This is such a great book. I wish I had had a copy of *Resilient Citizens* when I started my journey to self-sufficiency five years ago; it would have saved me so much time, effort, and money. If you want to be ready—for anything at all—this book is the canonical starting point for the responsible preparation journey."

—**TUCKER MAX**, 4x *New York Times* Bestselling Author, Homesteader

"Illuminating—Ellis maps a fractured America where resilience isn't a hobby, it's a rebellion against a society that's forgotten how to save itself."

—**JAMES POGUE**, Author of *Chosen Country: A Rebellion in the West*

"A fascinating and definitive book on preparedness and resilience for a global audience. Written with humility, curiosity, and great insight, this is the book for right now."

—**DR. LUCY EASTHOPE,** Author of *When the Dust Settles*

"*Resilient Citizens* offers a uniquely high-level perspective on preparedness within the context of society as a whole. Dr. Ellis's personal experiences in situations of societal breakdown combined with his extensive research and personal connections provide unique insight. He goes far beyond the level of individual prepping to the necessity of building resilience for everyone in society. This is a must-read for anyone committed to the survival and continued thriving of our nation and civilization."

—**JONATHAN RAWLES,** Founder of SurvivalRealty.com

"I am obsessed with disaster preparedness. Maybe that's because I live in Los Angeles, where natural and man-made disasters do some of their best work. I've been a low-key prepper for years, but after reading Chris Ellis's essential book, I know I'm not alone. This book gives you the reasons you need for why you should always—as the Boy Scouts used to say—be prepared. We don't know what's coming. We just know it will. Highly recommended!"

—**PEACHY KEENAN,** Author of *Domestic Extremist: A Practical Guide to Winning the Culture War*

"Every American needs to be a 'resilient citizen.' This book is about much more than preparedness; it's an outline of how to approach life during these turbulent and unpredictable times."

—**SENECA SCOTT,** Activist

"For different reasons, and from different personal and political starting points, more people are embracing the need to build practical resilience bottom-up within their communities. Although it's a way of thinking that remains disreputable in mainstream narratives, Chris Ellis gives us a detailed and clear-eyed account of why it shouldn't. There are different ways to cultivate resilience, but it's striking how Ellis's emphasis on personal agency, community embeddedness, and spiritual connection resonates across so many of them. This is a timely intervention on a crucial issue."

—**CHRIS SMAJE,** Author of *A Small Farm Future* and *Finding Lights in a Dark Age*

"A must-read for understanding resiliency and the way forward in an increasingly risky world. Dr. Ellis's book is a meaningful framework for analyzing the how, the what, and the why now of preparedness. A book about doom and gloom? No. Hope, responsibility, and community are the true keys to survival."

—**DR. ANNA MARIA BOUNDS,** Associate Professor, Author of *Urban Preppers and the Pandemic in New York City* and *Bracing for the Apocalypse*

"Disaster could strike at any moment, and Ellis shows us exactly how to be ready. But Ellis gets something crucial exactly right: Real preparedness is valuable even if disaster never comes. By learning practical skills like first aid, growing your own food, or organizing drills with neighbors, you naturally become more capable, confident, and clear-headed. Better yet, these simple acts of cooperation pull communities closer together. As Ellis says, building genuine local connections create stronger neighborhoods—and the benefits of that are enormous. Everyone involved ends up happier, healthier, and less stressed, regardless of what the future holds."

—**MATT SMITH,** Founder of CrisisInvesting.com

"There's a lot of bluster and fearmongering in the preparedness space. Thankfully, we have Dr. Ellis to offer sane, measured, and actionable advice in an increasingly chaotic world."

—**JOSH CENTERS,** Editor-in-Chief of *The Firearm* Blog

"Dr. Ellis does us a remarkable service in reminding us of the paradox of disasters: awareness that will likely inspire us into becoming better people. More courageous, more skilled, more confident, more grounded into the landscapes and cultures we inhabit, and ultimately the need for the longer-term perspective. Preparation becomes stewardship of the cultures and places we love."

—WRATH OF GNON ON X, Traditionalist

"*Resilient Citizens* offers much-needed insight into how we understand the concept of what it means to be a 'prepper.' Dr. Ellis provides a clear and thoughtful taxonomy, coupled with deep expertise in disaster preparedness, delivering a well-rounded and timely perspective on the field. As I read, I found myself reflecting on my own resilience—shaped in part by a partially off-grid upbringing in rural Montana and further informed by my research as an artist exploring creative problem solving and artistic praxis. No matter [what] your political affiliation or personal background [is], this book is an important and thought-provoking read."

—KATE PARSONS, MA, MFA, Associate Professor, Pepperdine University, and Cofounder of Primal U

"Dr. Ellis is the real deal, a deep thinker with a lifetime of knowledge on one of the most important issues facing humanity: how to not only survive but thrive in a world that feels 'off.' If you're looking for guidance on why things feel so strange, why it feels as if 'the powers that be' don't want you to be independent or self-sustaining and what to do to become a resilient citizen, this is a must-read."

—GRAHAM SUMMERS, Founder and CEO of Phoenix Capital Research, and Author of *Into the Abyss*

RESILIENT CITIZENS

THE PEOPLE, PERILS, AND POLITICS OF MODERN PREPAREDNESS

DR. CHRIS M. ELLIS

Resilient Citizens: The People, Perils, and Politics of Modern Preparedness

I take the issue of plagiarism very seriously. This book contains a mixture of more than a quarter-century of my professional studies and experiences as well as hundreds, if not thousands, of articles, books, and other documents I have read and researched over the years. I have endeavored to meticulously cite any work that is not my own. Additionally, this book underwent multiple versions and revisions where, more than once, I found a footnote that was not transferred and had to be manually reinserted. All errors are mine alone.

Published by Forefront Books, Nashville, Tennessee.
Distributed by Simon & Schuster.

Library of Congress Control Number: 2025913311

Print ISBN: 978-1-63763-448-6
E-book ISBN: 978-1-63763-449-3

Cover Design by Studio Gearbox
Interior Design by PerfecType, Nashville, TN

Printed in the United States of America

25 26 27 28 29 30 [RR4] 10 9 8 7 6 5 4 3 2 1

DEDICATION

This book is first and foremost dedicated to my wife and children, who gave up time with me as I researched and wrote. Second, it is dedicated to my friends and colleagues who are actively serving as guardians or working to prepare us for the challenges and opportunities ahead.

TABLE OF CONTENTS

FOREWORD

Dr. Bradley Garrett

In a letter to the Stoic philosopher Seneca, penned almost two thousand years ago, his trusted friend Serenus writes that he is suffering from anxiety and seeks tranquility. Seneca replies, "It is too late for the mind to be prepared for the endurance of dangers after dangers have passed."[1] Seneca suggests that with proper preparation, moments of misfortune can be transformed into opportunities to demonstrate virtue.

The Romans were no strangers to disaster, and their pragmatism in the face of it often came to mind as I read *Resilient Citizens,* which treats disaster preparedness not as a quirky pastime but as a practical exercise in collective fortitude. In a time of political polarization, widespread misinformation, and relentless calamities, the book you hold in your hand is like an anxiety antidote for the "endurance of dangers."

As I get older, I find that I'm more attuned to those dangers. Awareness of mortality begins to creep in after close calls and loss. The wisdom of age makes clear that disaster is inevitable. Whether natural or cultural, existential or mundane, things will simply go wrong. If we accept this realist view, then what really matters is how we respond to it. As Dr. Chris Ellis argues here, that depends greatly on how prepared we are.

It turns out that we have been good at this for a very long time. Human beings have a unique intellectual capacity to speculate on imagined future scenarios. This ability to plan is a cornerstone of what has enabled us to survive as a species. It takes an enormous amount of cognitive power to assess your situation, run a mental simulation of everything that could upend it, and then put a mitigation plan in place to minimize a disaster's impact when it does inexorably unfold in front of you.

Much of the social and cultural stigma that was attached to stockpiling resources and general cynicism about the fragility of global supply chains was washed away by the COVID-19 pandemic. Those who had been mocked for decades were suddenly prescient. But as Dr. Ellis makes clear, prepping is as old as civilization. What is actually an anomaly is the small blip between the end of the Cold War and the present, when people forgot how important practical preparation is. The world is now experiencing a resurgence of interest in resilience, triggered by an increased awareness of our collective mortality. At the same time, we have access to all the information we could ever need to relearn how to become better prepared. But as Seneca suggests, the burden falls on us to act on that information prior to the arrival of the next disaster. If you seek that gentle encouragement, you need look no further.

While writing my own book, *Bunker: What It Takes to Survive the Apocalypse,* I had the opportunity to spend time in resilient communities across the world. In doing so, many of my preconceived notions about the "prepper" community were challenged.[2] Where I expected to encounter anxiety, I found solace; instead of homogenous beliefs, I discovered diversity; and where I thought I would encounter isolationism, I found community. But what truly surprised me, and what Dr. Ellis also makes clear here, is that prepping is about hope, not pessimism.

For social scientists, preppers are a tantalizing group of people to study. Most are charismatic and action-oriented. Many tend toward hyperbole and conspiracy, a by-product, I think, of circumspection around the idea that stasis is normal. They are also a notoriously difficult group to study, prone as they are to secrecy. As a result, only a small cadre of scholars has written about these practices. But none is more qualified than Chris Ellis. With a PhD specializing in disaster studies backed up by practical military experience dealing with actual crises—often in hostile environments—he is remarkably lucid in his scholarship and writing. He also has a rare ability among social scientists to give careful attention to hard facts and statistics, which you will find in spades here.

I have found myself, over years of radio and television interviews, citing Dr. Ellis's work—particularly his impressive use of publicly available FEMA data, which he has crunched to provide a holistic snapshot of contemporary preparedness in the United States of America. His data-backed observations—for instance, that as of 2023, there are twenty-three million Americans who can survive for thirty-one days or more without power, water, or public transportation—are now so well-cited that they are almost taken for granted. Having these data parsed and published in this book is invaluable.

The other key game-changing insight here is the development of a prepper typology. Given time, any group that becomes large enough begins to fragment. As Dr. Ellis makes clear, this is precisely what's happening to preppers, whom he now sees as cleaving into five categories. His snapshots of the Homesteaders, the Sentinels, the Interdependent, the Noahs, and the Faithful could only have been achieved through years of careful study and will forever change the way we think about preparedness practices.

At the same time, *Resilient Citizens* demonstrates how these diverse groups form a community. Dr. Ellis and I are both scholars at heart, but we were unlikely to meet if not for our shared interest in resiliency. He is a man of faith and family who works for the military. I am a vegan atheist with a horse ranch in the Mojave Desert. That he asked me to write the foreword to his book is a testament to the power of preparing as a methodology that creates bonds.

I, like him, am a Resilient Citizen, and as he writes, "Resilient Citizens represent the cross-section of American society and the world. They are your neighbors, friends, and family. They have differing motivations and focus areas on their preparedness, but they share a common goal to be resilient in the face of the unexpected." Both of us have been changed by our research and experiences, and although we might have different ideological frameworks that guide our lives, I am confident that I could trust him in an emergency, just as he can trust me.

What *Resilient Citizens* provides, ultimately, is something that has been sorely needed for a long time now: It is a holistic framework for understanding preparedness at every scale. For this reason, above all others, this book will be a staple reference for decades to come. This book is not a practical guide to teach you what to put in your bug-out bag; plenty of those are already out there. This book instead provides something even more valuable: It will leave you questioning how you see the world and how you act within it. It will pique your curiosity and, at the same time, challenge you to think about where you, your family, your community, and your nation fit into the story. And it may, just may, leave you better prepared to navigate the unexpected turbulence that life will provide us, allowing us to demonstrate our unique human virtue to endure.

Seneca would be proud.

PREFACE

Disaster is my first memory.

My youngest childhood recollections are from the 1980 Mount St. Helens eruption in Washington State. I remember being at my grandparents' house, and before I could go outside, I was required to wear a mask and told not to play with any gray snow. While growing up, television news told me that the only polar bears my children would see would be at the zoo because the ice caps were melting due to global warming. (Spoiler alert: The fuzzy death balls are doing just fine.) Sunday School told me that Jesus was coming soon and, with Him, the end of days. If you didn't live through the 80s, you missed out; we had the best music too.

I did not set out to be a disaster expert. Yet after a decade of counterinsurgency operations and nation-building, working at the ground level with real people who had real problems, I decided to shift my career in a different direction. Flash-forward to today. I have served in the United States Army for more than a quarter-century. A once-in-a-lifetime opportunity to attend Cornell University for a PhD allowed me to direct my final years in service toward a disaster focus. Terrorism, weapons of mass destruction, pandemics, full-scale nuclear war down to smaller-scale detonations, protecting the president of the United States, earthquakes, typhoons, genetically engineered pathogens, wildfires, cyberattacks, economic collapse, the US southern border—all and more have been within my purview in the classroom, the office, or at-home musings. I have read about or participated in more disaster exercises than I can count. Add to this many other scenarios, training events, conferences, and intelligence reports—plus my personal and professional readings on these subjects and my Christian faith—and you get a life highly attuned to calamities of all shapes and sizes—natural, supernatural, and man-made.

I have had my fair share of deployments in several of the world's hot spots. As a combat officer, I've had "boots on the ground" in areas of civil war and smelled the whiff of genocide. I have reacted to IEDs and rockets, pulled the dead bodies of execution victims out of sewers, observed massive institutional corruption, and worked my butt off to make personal connections with the locals to strengthen communities from the ground up. I have kick-started businesses and municipal services in Iraq, supported women's shelters in Afghanistan, and retrained former militants into disaster response officials in Kosovo. I have observed, firsthand, that the most resilient societies are those with rich, neighbor-level connections that maintain deep cultural, and often religious, traditions and that are not afraid to fight for what they believe in. And while these are no cure-all and exceptions abound, they do improve the odds.

Unfortunately, there are too many threats, too many vectors, and too many variables. God bless the service members, first responders, decent street-level bureaucrats, homemakers, volunteer organizations, and average Joes all laboring to keep things running throughout the world. But probability is an unkind companion. Small things will break repeatedly, but we still have the slack in the system to mitigate and absorb. However, as a civilization, we are coasting on fumes and have become unmoored from solid foundations. We are pitted against one another, and we focus more on what separates us than what unites us. We have lost much of what made Western civilization great. Larger breaks will come, cascading failures will come, and—like a man stuck inside an overflowing porta potty rolling downhill—the end result will be messy.

So why even write at all? *Because of hope.* We are living in the greatest time of human history ever. Recognizing where I started in life versus where I am today is the American dream.

My undergraduate degree from the University of Washington was in biology and focused on ecosystems, the interactions of species and earth.

I loved higher education and pursued several postsecondary degrees before earning my PhD.

My first master's degree was in public administration at the local level, how we shape and describe our communities and how best to govern them. My second master's degree was on insurgencies and counter-insurgencies. It looked at political and societal breakdown, which then resulted in terrifyingly intimate violence among neighbors and kin. My third master's degree concentrated on the military's interaction with history, politics, and doctrine. I learned how to interpret and interweave these inputs and create a strategy for pathways forward. In my fourth master's degree and PhD, as I mentioned, I focused on disasters at Cornell.

All these years of study have equipped me to approach disasters in a transdisciplinary fashion, trying to tease out specificities, commonalities, and points of divergence. I am also heavily influenced in my thinking by my military experience, my personal faith, and my brilliant wife, Kimberly, a professional teacher and horticulturist. Some of my writings here come from my dissertation and other published work I either produced or provided to journalists during interviews or for their articles. Much of it is completely new.

I have made innumerable mistakes along the way and am thankful for the opportunity for reflection on my faults and critiques of my actions from others, from farmers to four-star generals to brilliant academics and many others. This has made me better. If there is one thing this book is *not,* it is not a call to "*gaze upon my brilliance ye unwashed yokels.*" Nor is it another "prepper-for-dummies" manual. This is a book that focuses on the "why" of so-called enhanced preparedness. Why it is logical, why it is healthy, why it is *good* for society and our children.

This is a book about getting better, about improving yourself, your neighborhood, and your community. This is a book about resilience and how we all approach life's knocks in our own ways, but some reactions, contemplations, and strategies are far better than others. It is about recognizing your shortfalls and reaching out to others to help fill in the gaps.

It is also a book that reveals what both people and governments across the world are doing in the face of calamity. If you think prepping for large-scale disasters is only for crazy people, you may be shocked to see what the authorities are—and are not—planning for. Some are noble and reflect great foresight and a knowledge of risk and history. Others are fraudulent, abhorrent to the concept of natural rights or the rule of law, incompetent, or a combination of these traits. At least you'll be able to see some of what is going right and what is going wrong so that you can prepare your household accordingly.

Again, some strategies and approaches are far better than others, and no one is doing it perfectly.

Yes, there is hope. There will be pockets of societies, individuals, families, and communities that weather the maelstrom. Inspiration will come from unlikely candidates, and you'll meet some of them in the pages that follow. These leaders will be flawed and human as we all are, so if you are looking to criticize, you'll find plenty of ammo to do so. Most will not be particularly flashy or famous, and their concepts, rather than innovative, will be more of a return to past ways.

As for me personally, I draw my ultimate optimism from my personal Christian beliefs, and I am not ashamed to share them or write about them. My faith brings me a calming balm to the world's insanity—an explanation for what went wrong, how to fix it, and how it all ends. I need this. Due to the nature of my expertise, I deal with horrors, tragedies, and apocalyptic scenarios—both real and potential—habitually. Of note, the opinions and policy positions expressed in this book are mine alone. No opinions or positions should be construed to be endorsed by the Department of Defense, the Department of the Army, or any other military organization. For those reading this who come from a different faith or no faith at all, you will still find these pages illustrative of rigorous, fact-based information regarding catastrophes and resilience. I showcase various beliefs, cultures, and country examples.

This book took me three and a half years to write and reflects a lifetime of experience and study. I am still learning. Your journey will be just that, yours. But let's walk together for the next few miles.

CHAPTER 1

PEOPLE, PERILS, AND POLITICS

+ + +

You will never fully convince someone
that he is wrong; only reality can do that.
—Nassim Taleb

As it will be in the future, it was at the birth of Man
There are only four things certain since Social Progress began.
That the Dog returns to his Vomit and the Sow returns to her Mire,
And the burnt Fool's bandaged finger goes wabbling back to the Fire;
And that after this is accomplished, and the brave new world begins
When all men are paid for existing and no man must pay for his sins,
As surely as Water will wet us, as surely as Fire will burn,
The Gods of the Copybook Headings with terror and slaughter return!
—Rudyard Kipling,
"The Gods of the Copybook Headings"

+ + +

Lauren lives in the Rocky Mountains and was driving on the highway after dark to go pick up livestock. Without warning, the elderly couple in the car in front of her struck a moose at seventy miles per hour. An adult moose stands six feet tall and can weigh well over a thousand pounds. She recounted:

> It was like watching their compact car hit a brick wall. When I ran up on their car after getting my truck stopped, they were both slumped over. I thought they were dead. Luckily, they were just dazed and pretty cut up from the windshield glass but otherwise alright.[3]

The pictures are graphic. The front of the automobile looks like a smashed beer can. There is a massive antler jutting deeply through the windshield on the driver's side. Even worse, the moose was still alive. Lauren pulled out her pistol, apologized to the moose (she has animist leanings as her faith tradition), and then euthanized it on the spot. An incredulous bystander asked, "Do you just, like, always have a gun and a flashlight with you?!"

"Yes."

After law enforcement showed up, they asked her if she wanted to dress the animal and take home the carcass.

Lauren is a rancher, dairy farmer, and mother. Her parents lived in a teepee above ten thousand feet. She and her husband raise cattle on their nearly two-hundred-acre property. They met at a living history event where, along with others, they conducted extended camping trips and used primitive skills, tools, and equipment. He is originally from California and has a degree in computer science and artificial intelligence but did not think he could live a prepared lifestyle in his home state. Lauren and her husband intentionally build skills around preparedness and resilience, ranging from blacksmithing to field medicine, food preservation, and low-input farming. They have a massive barn, and their freezers are full of meat. Lauren says her family could last nearly indefinitely without outside government assistance. She enjoys deadlifting and carries her young children at her bosom as she traverses her property on her four-wheeler.

Lauren is a Resilient Citizen. She does not use this term to describe herself. For Lauren and her family, this is simply a way of life in a world of risk.

Perils follow a certain logic. Plane crashes, economic collapses, asteroids, landslides, viral outbreaks, house fires, wars, and even government failures and military blunders all trace the contours of mathematical or theoretical models, with ample historical predicates. Consequently, there is a corollary logic to disaster resiliency that experts and layfolk alike look toward as a counterbalance to life's threats. It is the association of cause and effect, potentiality and probability, surviving versus thriving. It is also one of trial and error and acceptance that one can better the odds but not become immune to them.

Preparedness is something you *do*; resiliency is the *result*.

Compare Lauren's experience to a far larger and more famous case. On March 11, 2011, the 9.0 Tohoku earthquake struck beneath the ocean near Japan's east coast, releasing enough energy to power Los Angeles for two hundred thousand years. Soon after, a massive tsunami, at points measuring over 120 feet in height, slammed onto the main island. The volume of displaced seawater was so significant that in certain areas the wave's impact extended as deep as six miles inland.[4] The devastation was immense. Cars, schools, airports, religious sites, homes, businesses, bridges, and other infrastructure were mangled or destroyed. Nearly sixteen thousand people died, and six thousand were injured. Almost four hundred thousand buildings were at least 50 percent collapsed, with another seven hundred thousand damaged. More than 4,000 roads, 29 railways, and 116 bridges needed repair; another 45 dikes broke.[5]

While the Fukushima Daiichi nuclear plant withstood the seismic disturbance, the wave cut both primary and backup power to three of the eleven reactors. This caused the cooling systems to fail and the subsequent meltdown and breach of their three cores. Explosions at the site released radioactive particulates into the air, prompting Japan's government to order residents' evacuation within 20 kilometers of the plant.[6]

This edict was later expanded to a voluntary evacuation request for those 20–30 kilometers away. Later, the government partially lifted the restrictions in certain areas, declaring them safe, but only after raising the international benchmark for radiation exposure by nearly 2,000 percent, from 1.0 millisieverts (mSv) to 20 mSv.[7] The United Nations cried foul, believing this to be a violation of human rights.[8]

Problems at the plant continue to the present day. Since the nuclear fuel has not yet been extracted, it remains at the base of the cracked plant. It is constantly cooled by groundwater seeping in and by injected water, much of which is in tanks that Tokyo Electric Power Company (TEPCO) constructed to keep up with demand.[9] In January 2020, TEPCO announced it would take another forty-four years to fully decommission the plant.[10] For the first time since the accident, in late 2024, a small robot extracted three *grams* of "molten fuel" out of a total of 880 *tons* remaining.[11] To date, it is the only incident other than Chernobyl to reach the highest accident level of seven on the International Nuclear and Radiological Event Scale.

The impact was not limited just to Japan. Within one week, Fukushima radiation clouds filled with radioactive and cancer-causing iodine-131 and cesium-137 were over the continental United States. Within eighteen days, these poisonous clouds had circumnavigated the globe.[12] In April 2013, a study published in the *Open Journal of Pediatrics* found that children born in five western US states (Alaska, Hawaii, Washington, Oregon, and California) in the immediate months after the Fukushima disaster had a 28 percent greater occurrence of congenital hypothyroidism (a loss of thyroid function) due to iodine-131 levels measuring 211 times greater than normal.[13]

Among the carnage of this entire ordeal was one incredible story of another child, a ten-year-old British girl named Tilly Smith, that led to what is known as the Miracle of Kamaishi. Tilly's story began years earlier on vacation. In December 2004, the third-largest earthquake ever recorded—the 9.1 Sumatran earthquake—triggered under the floor of the Indian Ocean with the power of over one thousand hydrogen bombs.[14] It spawned the deadliest tsunami in modern times, causing more than two hundred thousand fatalities.[15] The most significant direct physical and economic hits were for Indonesia, Thailand, Sri Lanka, and India. Fatalities as far away as Yemen and Kenya were attributed to it.[16] Many American and European tourist deaths occurred as well, and it was the worst natural disaster in terms of human life to affect Sweden and Denmark in over one hundred years. Sweden lost 543 (!) vacationing citizens and Denmark lost 46.[17] Nevertheless, Thailand's Mai Khao Beach did not register a single human life taken—because of young Tilly Smith.

Tilly had learned about tsunamis three weeks earlier in school and screamed at those on the beach to evacuate immediately. Her actions saved the lives of nearly one hundred people.[18] Japanese professor Toshitaka Katada surveyed Thailand's aftermath. Learning from Tilly Smith, he created a curriculum for schools in Kamaishi, Japan, a city with a long history of deadly tsunamis. Katada's instructions broke with tradition and taught children to act upon disaster warning signs even if adults around them were not. When the 2011 earthquake struck, because of Katada's teachings, students at Kamaishi East Junior High School began to run. Their action prompted nearby teachers and students of Unosumai Elementary School to flee as well. While other schools in the region had up to 80 percent casualties, these two schools did not suffer a single student death.[19]

Most likely neither Professor Katada nor Tilly Smith is a Resilient Citizen according to my classification system, but their behaviors are reflective of the primary trait every Resilient Citizen uses: agency. That is the capacity and ability to act, to identify and pursue goals effectively. Resilient Citizens inhabit the same world as all of us; an environment where People, Perils, and Politics interact. This interplay is illustrated by the following diagram.

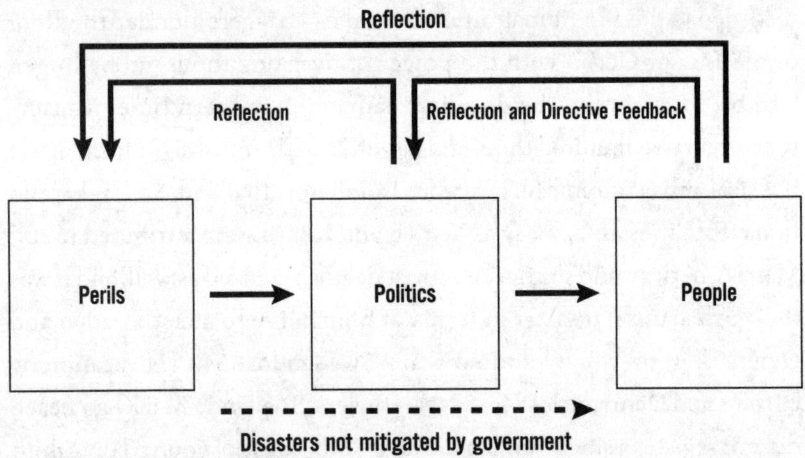

Figure 1: The Interplay of People, Perils, and Politics

Perils impact or threaten our lives all the time. Most are small, some are medium, and a few can be catastrophic, even biblical. They come in several types (meteorological, financial, societal, biological, and others) and have various warning timelines and overall durations. They have scales of impact from individual to global, vary in both frequency and repetition, and can often connect with other perils. Experts are often on the lookout for what are known as low-probability, high-consequence[20] disasters.

Our democratically elected—or *autocratically* selected—leaders may mitigate, prevent, or respond to these disasters in myriad fashions. Sometimes, they may even cause or negatively contribute to the calamity at hand. But governments cannot stop all perils; most things go straight to the populace. Therefore, both people and politicians reflect on the perils and internally process their response or nonresponse. Some do nothing, some do a little, and some do a lot. The interplay of this peer-reviewed model is the first of its kind to explain the full range of disaster readiness, from doing nothing at all to living in a former nuclear bunker.

Resilient Citizens occupy a portion of the "do a lot" group. They extend the logic of disaster preparedness to a level far more enhanced than most. Their characteristics are not a new phenomenon but rather the restoration of an older way of life and thinking.

This book examines—and promotes—the philosophy of resilience *and* citizenship.

WHAT SEEMS TO BE THE PROBLEM, OFFICER?

All disasters are local, but in the modern age, multiple threats are now universal. Once upon a time, we concerned ourselves with finding sustenance and keeping warm, fending off predators (both animal and human), and treating illness and infection. While some households were able to pull this off in pioneer fashion, across the vast swath of human history people showed better outcomes when they banded together in tribes and villages. Wolves hunt in packs, picking off the weak and separated. Likewise, we are safer when we are together.

Now we worry about terrorism, school shootings, foreign wars, transnational gangs, illegal immigrants, human trafficking, currency debasement, offshoring of jobs, supply chain disruptions, Frankenfoods, illicit drugs, the collapse of the fishing industry, depleted soil productivity, Lyme disease, hurricanes, online pornography, scam artists, corruption, and artificial intelligence. We also wonder whether we can trust our leaders, most of whom we have never and will never meet in person. There are those in some countries—such as America, Germany, France, Sweden, and the Netherlands—who treat elections almost as end-of-democracy existential events. At the same time, we would be hard-pressed to name our local mayor or sheriff.

It is not just these threats in isolation; so much of our life is now intertwined that we wonder if the entire *system* may come crashing down around us at any moment. Nuclear war? Check. Global economic collapse? Check. Open borders? Check. Pandemics? Check. Cascading failure is when an interconnected system snowballs downhill. It is very common in disasters and has become more so in a "flattened" world. The Fukushima meltdown began with an earthquake. The 2020s bout with global inflation ratcheted up due to COVID, which was itself caused by zoonotic spillover or the hubris of man or science, depending on what origin story you believe.

We also live in an era of *polycrisis*: "a cluster of related global risks with compounding effects, such that the overall impact exceeds the sum of each part."[21] Alternatively, polycrisis can be defined as "the causal entanglement of crises in multiple global systems in ways that significantly degrade humanity's prospects."[22] Add in a heaping tablespoon of generations of poor decision-making (e.g., debt levels, pollution, malinvestment) and you have the makings of Peril Soup.

This is psychologically and politically overwhelming, and many have not adapted—as individuals or societies—to cope with this reality. We thought we could nationalize and sometimes even globalize efforts to combat and respond to threats, but in the process, we forgot about the limitations of scale regarding the interaction of People, Perils, and Politics.

Nonstop angst is wreaking havoc on our health. "Climate anxiety" among the young is staggeringly high. A ten-country global study found 59 percent of those twenty-five and under were "very or extremely worried" about climate change and 75 percent thought "the future is frightening."[23] In America, the National Institute of Mental Health (NIMH) reports nearly one in four adults suffers from mental illness of some kind. NIMH reports rates are highest among the young, females, and those of mixed race.[24] Analysis of Pew Research data found correlating results and added ideology as a variable. Fifty-six percent of White, female liberals responded yes to the question: "Has a doctor or other healthcare provider EVER told you that you have a mental health condition?"[25] It has become cliché to mock snowflake millennials, but 90 percent of smartphone users feel real panic when their phone battery drops to 20 percent or lower."[26]

Heaven help us. Go touch some grass.

This constant bombardment of doomsaying disrupts our nervous and endocrine systems and our development. Kids cannot be kids, and adults do not fare much better. Too many suffer from *learned helplessness*:

> A psychological state in which an individual, after repeated exposure to uncontrollable negative events, believes they are powerless to change their situation, even when opportunities to do so arise. This leads to passivity, decreased motivation, and a sense of hopelessness, which can persist even when circumstances change and control is possible.[27]

We are robbed of our agency and our ontological security, two critical concepts that provide the foundation of this book's premises. *Agency* is the ability and will to take responsibility and to effect change. *Ontological security* is how one perceives how safe they are in their being. It is driven by—and satisfied via—agency or the care of others. If we choose not to exercise our agency, governments are all too often happy to step in and take control... often because we will blame them if they do not.

The problem is that politicians are human too. Not only do they have their own lives and families to worry about—and their own fears—but they also have the obligation and responsibility to help protect their constituents. Yet even these leaders are overwhelmed by disasters and disaster planning.

Paradoxes now abound. In an American context, we became atomized at the community level. Our financial riches and innovative wonders opened the door to possibilities of radical individuality. We prize extreme independence and therefore feel alone. The internet allows us to be connected to people across the world, and yet we feel isolated. Why do smartphones sometimes feel like one-part communication device, one-part instructional device, one-part wiretap, and one-part ankle bracelet? We have the world at our fingertips and doorstep via rapid advances in technology and transportation, but our civil engineering systems are now designed to prioritize cars and strip malls, not safe neighborhoods, further separating us from our traditional human bonding rituals and venues. We could be the freest of any time in history, but we have yielded much of our liberty to homeowners associations and to evermore centralized governmental power structures.

The same bureaucracy we entrusted to keep us safe now has the power to keep us subjugated.

We allowed this to happen. We forgot our responsibilities and obligations. We forgot our *duties,* something only humans possess. We also walked away from our faith. We demanded human saviors and instead got masters. We are the Little Pig, solitary and terrified in our house while the Big Bad Wolf comes knocking.

As varied and wondrously diverse as we are, though, not everyone is passive in the face of danger. Some people are rediscovering agency and taking steps to equip themselves and their families for what calamities may come. Most perils are low to moderate in severity but are frequent. Others are far more dangerous but blessedly uncommon. However, because the full scope of disaster is unfortunately present, some people have chosen to prepare at far higher levels than is commonplace. What these people are doing is reviving an ancient tradition of preparedness. This will take time and mistakes and false starts.

These are the people I'm talking about when I say Resilient Citizens.

WHAT IS A RESILIENT CITIZEN?

I first encountered this term while reading a chapter by Professor Chad Huddleston in a disaster compendium.[28] His context was in the study of preppers (individuals who take far beyond the normal steps to get ready for disasters) who wanted to help others get ready *and* desired to be mutually supportive of one another.[29] In my formal academic work, I broadened and formalized his portrayal and now expand it yet again in this book. For my purposes here, a Resilient Citizen is an individual who:

- Has the *foresight* to prepare for disasters;
- Has the *longevity*—via skills or ability—to survive in their community without government assistance for at least a month; and
- Espouses no extremist *creeds*.[30]

The term *resilience* has more than a dozen definitions, many of which are field-specific (e.g., engineering, psychology, or ecology). My definition is a slightly modified version of the Sendai Framework for Disaster Risk Reduction,[31] an international disaster-focused document. To me, *resilience* is

> the ability of an individual, household, system, community, or society exposed to hazards to resist, absorb, accommodate to, and recover from the effects of a hazard in a timely and efficient manner, including through the preservation and restoration of its essential basic structures and functions.

My definition of *citizen* is far simpler: "a productive and contributing member of a community."

Resilient Citizens do not believe they can plan for *everything* but do believe they can do *something*. They have an internal locus of control, one that emphasizes agency and personal responsibility to achieve ontological security rather than an external locus of control that yields blame and responsibility to chance or other actors. They do not believe in an all-or-nothing approach but often start out with a paired response to a specific threat. Over time, many adopt the concept of *generalized resilience*—like having a first aid kit—recognizing the commonality of many perils. They value preparedness, not prediction, but they do attempt to read some of the tea leaves. The best exemplars of Resilient Citizens take this a bit further by keeping the resilience but boosting the citizenship to a coequal position. Responsibility transforms into duty, and preparedness becomes an institutional or societal good. Every journey is different and so is every destination—but there are contours.

Most Resilient Citizens are rather private about their actions, but a minority shout from the watchtowers. Some are secular, yet a lot of them pray. There is no one "right way" to prepare, and just like learning a new sport, there are bumps and bruises along the way. Resiliency is neither primarily masculine nor feminine but a combination of the best of both. It is not restricted by age, education, income level, or race.[32] It is both ubiquitous and unique. Still, some common themes emerge. Most Resilient Citizens understand they cannot escape disaster—it is a part of life—but at a minimum, they try to insulate themselves as best they can.

Lauren's actions operate on the human scale and are relatable. We can picture ourselves in a similar situation: something frightening but manageable. The vast majority of us would be able to do something after the initial shock, even if it's only dialing 9-1-1. But without a bit of training, most people would struggle to act quickly on Mai Khao Beach as Tilly did. Only a fraction of individuals, including politicians and experts, would be able to process and respond to a Fukushima-level event. How do you mentally cope with 22,000 casualties? How do you prepare for 1.1 million buildings damaged? How do you calculate a rational plan to remove 880 tons of radioactive material? We are incapable of processing something of such magnitude. This resonates with Joseph Stalin's apocryphal aphorism, "A single death is a tragedy; a million deaths is a statistic."[33] Without training, our brains simply are not wired for that complexity and scale.

To be clear, this is neither a disaster book nor a prepper book. I will not spend an entire chapter on the Plague of Justinian or the Great Chicago Fire of 1871. I do not provide any advice on the best "Bug Out Bag" packing list (although I do recommend ThePrepared.com as a great resource). My approach is to understand the logic of Resilient Citizens and how they can work for the betterment of society. I look at the "who" and the "what" to help comprehend the "why."

THE STRUCTURE OF THIS BOOK

Holistically, disaster preparedness is best understood via the interaction of People, Perils, and Politics. I take it as a foundational fact that we are in a world of increasing risk and polycrises where paradoxes abound. While technology has enriched our lives in many circumstances, it has not eliminated risk or tragedy. While we have airbags, we still have car fatalities and a war on the streets regarding vehicle sizes. While we have antibiotics, we still have diseases and evolving resistance by germs. Safety is not a destination but a system of actions, reactions, and counteractions containing numerous variables, hazards, and response possibilities. Disasters are multifaceted and cascading, with higher than ever possibilities of contagion due to our interconnected world. What happens in Pyongyang can now affect life in Paris, Pittsburgh, or Prague. The good times of both the post–World War II and the post–Cold War eras are ending.

Part 1 begins with people. Chapter 2 focuses on the over fifty-year history of survivalists and preppers and attempts to count and describe their prevalence. Chapter 3 calculates the radical growth of enhanced preparedness membership in America from 2017 to 2023. Chapter 4 delves into a better way to distinguish groups and the logic undergirding the term *Resilient Citizen*. Chapters 5 through 9 then look at representatives and their incentive structures.

For part 2, I center the discussion on perils. Chapters 10 and 11 cover how we process risk from numerous threats, and then what we do—or do not do—about them. Chapters 12 and 13 examine perils and preparedness from the viewpoint of experts and governments. They are *very* concerned.

In part 3, I focus on politics. Chapters 14 through 16 are an in-depth case study of a large-scale catastrophic peril that the world still lives under—the specter of nuclear war. Here I rely heavily on archival research from the presidential libraries of Truman, Eisenhower, and Kennedy so you can read, in their words and those of their advisers, how they wrestled—and failed—to turn America into a nation of Resilient Citizens. In doing so, I come full circle, explaining the origins of most modern maligning of prepping. Chapter 17 discusses the realities of state failure and various interactions between people and politicians in the nexus of perils. I end with a few success stories from around the globe.

The conclusion ends the book with a return to everyday people. I discuss how material preparedness, or "preps," is at best one-fifth of true resiliency. Yet even many of the Resilient Citizens who possess the mindset and emotional regulation to exercise agency and feel a sense of ontological security have not fully attained what is required. My motto for the past several years is simple: Fight local, win local. We need one another. We need to once again human-scale our resiliency and embrace citizenship. We need to incorporate localism, interdependence, and neighborliness. I also reveal the number one prepping item every single home *in the world* requires.

PART ONE

PEOPLE

Part one of this book demonstrates that everyday people and their motivations are the focus of my examination of Resilient Citizens. Chapters 2 and 3 explain two opposing depictions of enhanced levels of preparedness and then prove that a greater number of individuals are (re)adjusting to the reality of perils. I showcase statistical analysis of the explosive growth of prepping in America from 2017 to 2023. Our current way of life is a historical anomaly. For most of human existence, long-term thinking about potential crises was a normal part of every culture. Unfortunately, prepping in the Western world has been denigrated for the past fifty years by academics and journalists. There is a heavy barrier to overcome to renormalize disaster resiliency at the household and community level, but a change in attitude is occurring.

After providing this context, I go a step further in chapter 4 and begin to classify Resilient Citizens in depth. They share common traits that allow for broad categorization yet are exceptionally diverse at the individual level. Chapters 5 through 9 illustrate five archetypes: Homesteaders, Sentinels, the Interdependent, Noahs, and the Faithful. They exist internationally and do not fit in a neat and tidy mold.

CHAPTER 2

THE PORTRAYALS OF PREPAREDNESS

+ + +

You probably imagined a prepper as a middle-aged white guy who fantasized about nuclear warfare in order to justify his gun collection to his wife.
—Josh Centers

When the whole world is running towards a cliff, he who is running in the opposite direction appears to have lost his mind.
—C. S. Lewis

+ + +

Any discussion regarding enhanced preparedness must discuss the phenomenon of preppers in the modern age and place the genre in the proper context. Since the term is widely known, I use it as a jumping-off point for the reader's understanding. Prepper depiction is more parody than reality, both in academic work and in popular journalism.

The organization of this chapter is threefold. First, I define prepping and preppers and how the movement attained its negative connotation in the 1950s and 1960s. I show how prepping went from compulsory to crazy in a short period. Politics and psychology explain much of this, as parts 2 and 3 further elaborate. Second, I speak to how practitioners of enhanced preparedness have been depicted since the 1970s. I provide an abbreviated overview of the two camps of thought, what I refer to as the Dominant narrative, which states preppers are uniform and crazy, and the Challenger narrative, which counters that preppers are more diverse and saner. Of course, if we cannot agree on what a prepper is, it will be very difficult to tally their prevalence. Third, I provide previous counting attempts to show the predicament. Overall, this chapter introduces the main problems addressed in part 1: stigmatization, classification, and quantification.

AN ABBREVIATED HISTORY OF PREPPERS

Broadly speaking, *prepping* (a verb) is the act of readying oneself or one's family via means of supplies, tools, plans, and skills for potential—often severe—future peril. Prepping is typically seen as a heightened form of normal household preparedness. In an American context, it is something that goes well beyond the three-day to two-week emergency readiness activities encouraged by the Federal Emergency Management Agency and American Red Cross, respectively. Citizens across the world engage in prepping. Some partake due to traditional or cultural practices (Australians in the Outback, Mormons), some because of recent events (the Taiwanese), others because of government regulations or encouragement (the Swiss), and still others due to a mix of these (Israelis, Latvians).

While there is no checklist or base requirement to qualify, *preppers* are those who undertake these extended steps, in many forms, such as (a) building bunkers; (b) purchasing large quantities of firearms and foodstuffs; (c) investing in alternative stores of wealth, such as productive land, precious metals, or Bitcoin; or (d) learning resiliency skills, including carpentry, foraging, animal husbandry, or medical training beyond first aid. There has never been an agreed-on definition or classification of preppers. Many preppers today do not like the term, nor use it to describe themselves, a fact that further muddies the waters.

Prepper is a relatively young label. According to a Google Ngram search, the term was hardly mentioned before 2008. Before this, the moniker associated most closely with the actions identified today as prepping was *survivalist. Survivalist* began a rapid ascent in book mentions in the late 1970s. It was popularized by the writings of author and survivalist Kurt Saxon in 1976 and received more than three times as many references as *prepper* in 2024.[34, 35]

Saxon noted some of the earliest negative media portrayals, stating, "Do not be surprised when you see survivalists portrayed as idiots and fear-crazed kooks."[36] This period (roughly 1976–1984) marks when nearly all future discussions of survivalists—and later, preppers—split them from the mainstream culture. The overwhelming majority of writing from 1984 and onward focused on prepared extremists. These individuals were often described as White nationalists, cultists, or psychologically unbalanced.[37] Lost or downplayed for decades were depictions of overwhelmingly non-extremist preparedness-minded individuals and their origins.

Why did extreme preparedness initially get such an ignominious reputation that spread throughout the world? The answer originates in the United States in the 1950s and 1960s. The "why" goes back to the psychology of personal security and the massive protests against the nuclear civil defense drills of that era. I cover this extensively in chapters 14–16, but here is a sneak peek.

Ironically, government successes and failures alike contributed both to citizens' distrust and disaster-readiness apathy. Prior to the atomic age, preparedness was exceptionally common among the masses, often by necessity, and part of the lore of Americana, for example the Pilgrims, the Oregon Trail, the Donner Party, and the Wild West. America began as an isolationist nation but slowly shifted to the philosophies of the Monroe Doctrine of the 1820s and then Manifest Destiny twenty years later. We remained in a comparatively isolationist (and rural) state until the attack on Pearl Harbor. After defeating the Axis powers, mainland America was virtually unscathed, and we emerged as the global hegemon. The war transformed us into an industrial production state with a far more powerful centralized government. Our economic boom was legendary, but the world was ours to police, with the Soviet Union as the ever-present foe. To the victor went both the spoils ... and the responsibilities.

During the mid-twentieth century, the US federal government and many state governments went all-in on getting the populace ready for a nuclear Armageddon. Bunkers were pushed as a solution for the masses, and civil defense drills became common. US states were threatened with loss of federal funding if they refrained from participating in these rehearsals. In some places, like New York, individuals could even be arrested for nonparticipation.

The problem was that the government pushed far too much doom and gloom while simultaneously taking action that would increase the levels of destruction if a nuclear war actually came to fruition.

Laypeople and prominent scientists alike argued the very idea of full-scale nuclear war was insane. The contention was that no rational democratic country should *ever* consider it as a viable option.[38] Therefore, this group was appalled by any action that made nuclear war more *probable* or more *acceptable* as a legitimate and moral government action to the average American. They particularly fought against anything that misled everyday citizens into thinking that they could resume their normal lives quickly after a nuclear winter—in as little as just a few weeks!

The government promoted mandatory nuclear drills and mass, country-wide construction of communal or private fallout shelters and it minimized warnings of health hazards from nuclear detonation testing. The antinuclear war crowd pushed back hard—not only against atomic weapons *but against anything even nuclear-adjacent,* including things such as backyard shelters. As people openly debated whether it was moral or Christian to shoot a neighbor who was trying to get into your underground fallout shelter, those pushing preparedness or following government instructions began to lose the PR war. Preparedness itself was branded as borderline genocidal or at least antisocial to a grotesque degree.

It became common to demonstrate against the US government concerning atomic weapon testing and fallout drills. Although it would take nearly thirty years for the government to fully abandon shelter and evacuation plans, the reputational damage was done. The pendulum swung too hard to one side, and preparation—*nearly all preparation*—was deemed bad. It became associated with mass death, and Americans don't like being reminded of their mortality.

The problem and the stigma were not caused primarily by the people but by the politicians.

Survivalists and preppers from that point forward were frequently denigrated because they reminded people that threats still exist. (Threats don't go away just because you stop thinking about them or because the government stops planning for your rescue.) The irony was that preppers of the day were reputed as crazy, but it was their *politicians* who were hell-bent on apocalypse. Unfortunately, the masses didn't want to just avoid thoughts of demise; they also wanted to avoid thinking about their own culpability and responsibilities. Therefore, much of the Western free world threw the resilient baby out with the radioactive bathwater and has only recently begun to discuss the rationality of extreme preparedness... in pockets... slowly.

HOW HAVE PREPPERS BEEN DESCRIBED SINCE THEN?

Who are these people who go to extreme levels of preparedness, and what do they look like compared to the rest of America? Personal and household preparedness levels for everyday emergencies have a rich legacy of theory and data. But academic work is comparatively lacking—"shallow and unreliable," as one author described it—in one area: that of extremely prepared individuals.[39] This is partially due to the topic previously being on the academic "fringe."[40] There is a common refrain among researchers on preppers that the literature is "thin" or "surprisingly understudied."[41]

These comments are true in two ways. First, the number of scholarly articles is notably low. Prior to 2020, most literature reviews commonly referenced a corpus of works of roughly twenty sources or fewer, many of whose units of analysis center on White, nonliberal males. The second is the type of research. With rare exception, unless the author is specifically referencing household preparedness studies, the methodologies common to almost all are small-scale and qualitative in nature, sometimes looking at just a few dozen people as subjects. That is, they are personal accounts, observations, or document research that involve a *very* small number of individuals.[42]

Ethnographies (i.e., cultural studies) lead the pack, followed by a smattering of netnography (i.e., research on social media), film and television review, journalism, and overall commentary. And, as the ethnographers have noted, writers of some of the more highly cited pieces have never even spoken with actual preppers.[43] Many of the remaining prepper "canon" pieces are short articles in media outlets such as *The New York Times, Newsweek,* and *Mother Jones* and typically exhibit heavy ideological skew.

The majority of literature, from peer-reviewed scholarly work to online commentary, is almost exclusively based on interviews, data gleaned from prepper websites, or by film and television reviews. Quantification is nearly absent, and theorization lacks comprehensive scope and agreement. This has led to massive confusion and conflation of terminology. Hoarders, preppers, survivalists, militia members, and hate groups are all commonly lumped together.[44]

This is not only inaccurate but also dangerous. Such caricatures can increase tensions between law enforcement and utterly nonthreatening citizens.[45] It has also prevented researchers' abilities to get these individuals to agree to be subjects of study, as many fear stigmatizations[46] or the unfair labels of being "selfish or 'tin foil hat wearing loonies.'"[47]

Regrettably, the fusing of prepper/survivalist/militia et al. has been the overriding position since the 1960s. This mixing is grounded in the fact that the groups can often share certain survival-based traits, thus causing overlap. But it is a classic example of the fallacy of composition: inferring to all the attributes of a few. It also relates to Fundamental Attribution Error: the overemphasis on personality explanations at the expense of environmental pressures.

There are two broad schools of thought in prepper classification, what I call the *Dominant* and *Challenger* narratives. The Dominant portrayal of preppers and their related forebears, survivalists, has been overwhelmingly negative. Dominants view the *extremely prepared* crowd as synonymous with *extremism* and rarely cite the history of why the phenomenon came about. Dominants also concentrate on American examples, and with a heavy ideological bias, they portray nearly all preppers as right-wing, potentially anti-government nutjobs.[48] Sometimes, this leads to amusing results. Relatively recent Dominant research has looked at left-of-center and even socialist preppers.[49] Whereas older Dominants derided these beliefs as an exclusively right-wing phenomenon, a newer generation of Dominants has found these same beliefs in far-left liberals—whom they praise for it.[50] The media largely falls into the Dominant camp. Depictions are clickbait in nature and skewed along political ideology. Most of my media interviews describing highly prepared individuals have fallen into this same rut of coverage. The opponents of the Dominants, the Challengers, are far fewer in number but have pushed back for decades—especially after 2010—on the reigning stereotypes. They seek to demonstrate that most preppers are qualitatively different from extremists. While they may share some characteristics in preparedness, the two are not the same in many beliefs or motivations. As one Challenger noted:

> Scholarship can be contradictory to prepper self-identity. The scholarly literature on survivalists and preppers has a noted bias

> against those who participate in these activities as being fearful of the world around them, fearful of the government and politics, right-wing racists, or religious kooks. Although the survivalist right is an undeniable part of the movement, they are an unrepresentative extreme. With self-sufficiency being the main unifying factor among preppers, it is impossible to class them as having a specific agenda of any type: political, religious, or social.[51]

Challengers acknowledge that extremist preppers exist, but the overwhelming majority of the highly prepared should not be considered extremists.[52] The historical cleavage, while using many terms, is one between "big-S" Survivalists (i.e., extremists) and "small-s" survivalists (i.e., preppers).[53]

Challengers say that preppers, as far as their aggregate composition goes, are closer to the mainstream. They can be soccer moms, college graduates, and ordinary people. Challenger research has far more international examples and fewer findings of ideological or anti-government motivations. They include greater themes of self-sufficiency, resiliency, and bonds of heritage or culture.[54]

One point of agreement between Dominants and Challengers is that most definitions of preppers and survivalists revolve around a single concept: a looming large disaster or threat—often with an extended duration of recovery—and then either personal skills or provisions (or both) to counter or mitigate that risk. Dr. Michael Mills gives a longer temporality to prepping that is more extreme than having a few boxes of toaster pastries and extra batteries for your flashlight:

> Prepping is thus distinct from ordinary short-term preparedness for hurricanes and other natural emergencies, being distinguished by its application towards manmade disasters as well as natural ones; medium- to long-term survival lasting weeks,

months, or even years; and violent social breakdown amidst collapse.[55]

Prepping is, therefore, for larger catastrophes. But this is where the agreement ends. With definitions in the eye of the beholder, one can only expect both counts and descriptions of preppers to be all over the map. And that's precisely what happens.

HOW HAVE THEY BEEN COUNTED?

Participants for examination were often discovered via prepper websites or at conventions. This lack of randomization leads to studies of clusters, not the breadth of the entire group. Sometimes data collection was a bit broader and thus could approach a representative snapshot of Americans. Academics and researchers must start somewhere, so please interpret my criticism here lightly. I learned from what others have done, their successes and shortfalls, and have attempted to add more clarity and accuracy.

On the higher end of calculations, one data point for the number of preppers that exist in America was conducted by the financial company *Finder*. Their 2017 survey of two thousand individuals indicated that, via extrapolation, 160 million doomsday preppers walked among us, with numbers dropping to 141 million in a follow-up survey in January 2020.[56] From the 2020 survey, 20 percent of Americans had purchased survival supplies in the past year. Broken down, 10 percent of respondents indicated they kept supplies due to concerns about natural disasters, another 5 percent because of political concerns, and the final 5 percent worried about both. *Finder* proclaimed another 35 percent of Americans would not need to go shopping in the event of a disaster since they always had "survival items on hand in case of emergency." This led the site to proclaim that "roughly 55 percent of American adults (141 million adults) ... are prepping for the end times."

However, when I dug into these numbers, the data indicated only common levels of "normal" household preparedness for the occasional—temporary—power outage. If anything, it showed a staggering *lack* of preparedness in the US populace during the times of the survey (2017 and 2020). The *Finder* surveys were repeated in 2021 and 2023, and the headline of the latter indicated seventy-four million people were preparing for a small-scale emergency but not "doomsday prepping" as the company's site would suggest.[57]

And yet the *Finder* surveys are a good source of descriptive information regarding the makeup of its paid survey volunteers. The top items Americans were buying were (a) food and water and (b) toilet paper. By dollar amount, the lead item was "investment into savings account" at an average of $1,057 per person. Men indicated higher preparedness actions than women and younger generations more than older. *Finder* also included a regional component, with residents living in the West preparing at higher levels (32 percent) than the lowest region of the Northeast (24 percent). Overall, the *Finder* surveys do provide value for generalized emergency actions conducted by Americans but not in *counts* of preppers.

On the lower side of prepper prevalence are estimates by Jon C. Ogg in 2013. His report, published on the online financial site *24/7 Wall St.*, indicated there were 3.7 million preppers.[58, 59] Yet Ogg lists no methodology or source for how he arrived at that number. In the same year, Dr. Mills, whom you read about earlier in this chapter, put the number at 5 million.[60]

More recent work from 2020 found 24 percent of respondents self-identified as either preppers or survivalists, which would equate to sixty-two million Americans. According to this data, statistically significant indicators of prepper self-identification were race and level of education. Age, gender, income, and political affiliation had no statistical impact.[61] However, the author noted the limitations and potential flaws of the study. First, the term *survivalist* was not defined; the survey population was free to interpret the question as they saw fit. Perhaps participants considered a week of emergency supplies as adequate, or owning a gun, or being the *survivor* of a previous crime or the victim of racism.[62] Second, it was noted that the sample is not nationally representative, so it is not possible to draw general conclusions from its results.

A survey from December 2023 of three thousand Americans and two thousand Canadians had mixed results. It reported 9 percent of Americans and 7 percent of Canadians (about 2.5 million Canadians, extrapolated) self-identified as preppers and broke down which states or provinces had the highest percentages.[63] The article showed the top four fears of Americans and Canadians were identical: natural disasters, economic collapse, pandemics, and then nuclear war. So far, so good.

But then, the article lumped in Canadian preppers with flat-earth believers.

The Dominant narrative strikes again.

The studies that do give clear annotations on the descriptive statistics of their population also suffer from selection bias and a lack of generalizability to the country as a whole. For example, with a sample size of just 248 people, one national survey from more than twenty years ago found survivalists were 89 percent male and 96.8 percent White. They were also educated, as 52.4 percent had a bachelor's degree or higher.[64]

With classification and quantification such a jumble, what is needed is both a defensible definition of extreme preparedness and then a random, large-scale sampling of a population to ascertain the prominence. If upper-end prepping is logical and confers an advantage, and if there is a general feeling of unease in the world that is also increasing, the occurrence of enhanced preparedness should be spreading beyond small microniches. I found such a large-scale national survey, one that was repeated annually, and discovered that prepping in America has exploded across a wide swath of people.

CHAPTER 3

THE PROMINENCE OF PREPAREDNESS

\+ + +

I wouldn't mind if the consumer culture went poof! overnight because then we'd all be in the same boat and life wouldn't be so bad, mucking about with the chickens and feudalism and the like. But you know what would be absolutely horrible. The worst?... If, as we were all down on earth wearing rags and husbanding pigs inside abandoned Baskin-Robbins franchises, I were to look up in the sky and see a jet—with just one person inside even—I'd go berserk. I'd go crazy. Either everyone slides back into the Dark Ages or no one does.

—DOUGLAS COUPLAND, *Shampoo Planet*

Survivalists do not accommodate themselves readily to favored methods of social science research—surveys, systematic standardized interviewing, and subsequent enumeration. Those who have sought to impose these approaches onto survivalism have been disappointed.

—RICHARD MITCHELL

\+ + +

This chapter is about solving the first problem common both to Dominants and Challengers: counting, with a clear and defensible metric, the number of people who prepare at enhanced levels. I pulled information from seven years of data collection, querying more than thirty thousand Americans from Guam and Puerto Rico to Maine and Arizona. This has never been done before at this scale. Since the dataset used contains demographic information, we will see a true portrayal of what Resilient Citizens look like collectively.

The purpose is to provide a powerful rebuttal against several Dominant myths. Furthermore, it gives Challengers a firm foundation for future research. Although this is the most statistically dense chapter, it is intended to be accessible to a wide audience.[65] If the numbers get to be too much, you can skip to the end of this chapter for a summary. And while Resilient Citizens have other traits besides physical supplies, I created a formal definition for numerical quantification and demographic observation.

Heavy statistical analysis was performed using four years of data (2017–2020) from the annual National Household Survey (NHS) from the Federal Emergency Management Agency (FEMA). A separate and less detailed analysis of the 2021–2023 data was performed due to numerous changes in the survey's structure. I argue that there were just under ten million Resilient Citizens in the United States in 2017, approximately fifteen million in 2020, and twenty-three million in 2023. Individuals are compared across a broad range of metrics. Demographically speaking, they are far closer to everyday Americans than typically portrayed. A resounding takeaway lesson is this: Enhanced preparedness in the US is far more common than predominantly believed.

HOW MANY PEOPLE ARE PREPARING AND TO WHAT EXTENT?

I've mentioned my preferred term, *Resilient Citizens,* several times already. Now I want to define it for you as clearly as possible:

> A Resilient Citizen is a private actor who can survive for thirty-one days or more at home without publicly provided power, water, or transportation.
>
> This gives a falsifiable marker, meaning an individual either meets the criteria or does not. Additionally, it is transferable, allowing researchers to count the number of Resilient Citizens in Singapore, Algeria, or Paraguay.

To count the number of Resilient Citizens in the US, I used the annual FEMA National Household Survey (NHS). FEMA asked interviewees, *"How many days do you think you could last in your home without power, running water, or transportation?"*[66] In 2018, 4.5 percent of survey respondents said they could last thirty-one days or more.[67] This extrapolates to 11.4 million Resilient Citizens in the US for that year.[68] This result is well below the high-end estimates in the previous chapter but two to three times greater than the lower estimates cited for preppers.[69] It is potentially an underestimation because the survey interviewed just one person from each household, and the average Resilient Citizen indicated 2.24 adults present in the household for 2018. Often, spouses and older children of Resilient Citizens engage in enhanced preparedness themselves, so this number could be twice as large as I indicate. However, to be conservative and consistent, I will stick with the 11.4 million Resilient Citizens in 2018.

As depicted in Figure 3.1, the distribution of individuals preparing is skewed heavily to the left, indicating the bulk of the population has less than two weeks of supplies. I can, therefore, classify those individuals with more than thirty-one days of preparedness as "extreme" in a statistical sense. This allows me to cleave Resilient Citizens into their own group. All others are considered "normal" based on commonly accepted statistical practices. For comparison, I use the term *Regular* for those with fewer than thirty-one days of supplies.

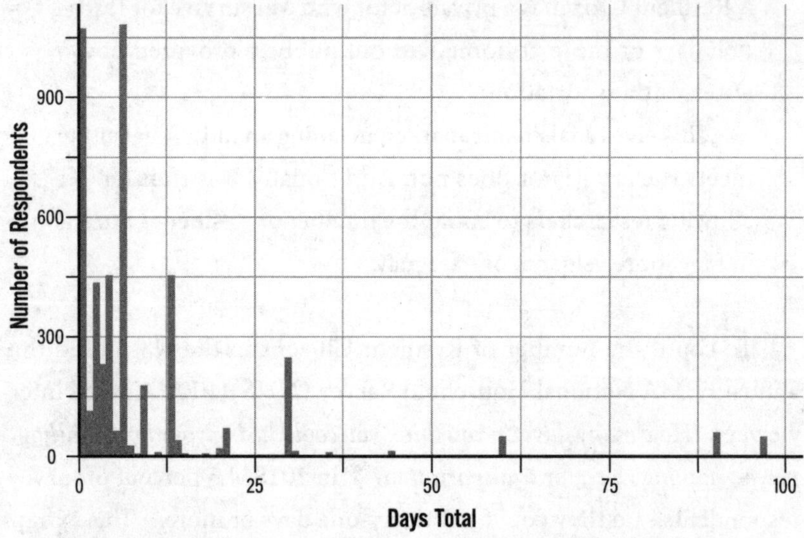

Figure 3.1: How Many Days Total Could Respondents Last at Home Without Power, Water, or Transportation? All Respondents in 2018.

But perhaps thirty-one days is not extreme enough. After all, some individuals are preparing for large-scale economic collapse, nuclear war, and pandemics. Does the composition of Resilient Citizens change if I include only those individuals who could last at home for ninety days or more? With the 2018 FEMA sample population, only 110 people out of roughly 5,000 surveyed met this cutoff. This amounts to 2.3 percent or roughly 5.8 million Americans. I call these *Highly Resilient Citizens*, or HRCs. Finally, there is the select group that indicated 97 days of preparedness or more. FEMA capped and coded all responses of 97 days or greater (e.g., 120 days, 365 days, and so forth) at 97. Therefore, some respondents may have indicated higher levels, but this information was not captured. In 2018, just 48 people told FEMA they could survive at this extended duration. This implies a little over 2.5 million people in the US are gearing up for disasters of epic proportions. I labeled those at 97 days as Ultra-Highly Resilient Citizens, or UHRCs.[70] Perhaps it is these latter two groups that come closer to the popular demographic portrayal of preppers?

With terms and time cutoffs thus explained, I can now show changes, year to year, from 2017 to 2020. Figure 3.2 depicts percentages in America, and Figure 3.3 shows the total number of Americans (in millions) for the same time frame.

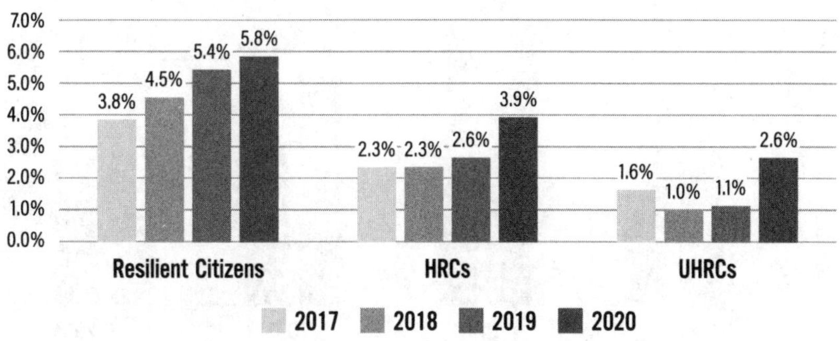

Figure 3.2: Percent of Americans Who Are Resilient Citizens by Category and Year (2017–2020)

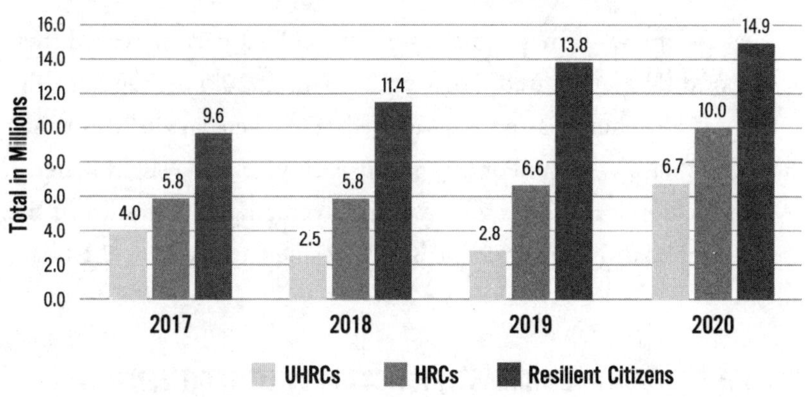

Figure 3.3: Resilient Citizen Population Growth (2017–2020)

The number of Resilient Citizens in America increased every year from 2017 to 2020. By 2020, Resilient Citizens increased approximately 50 percent from 9.6 million to 14.9 million Americans. Ultra-Highly Resilient Citizens (97 days or more of preparedness) jumped from 4 million people in 2017 to 6.7 million in 2020. While these are notable jumps, higher-level prepping was not "mainstream" during this period.

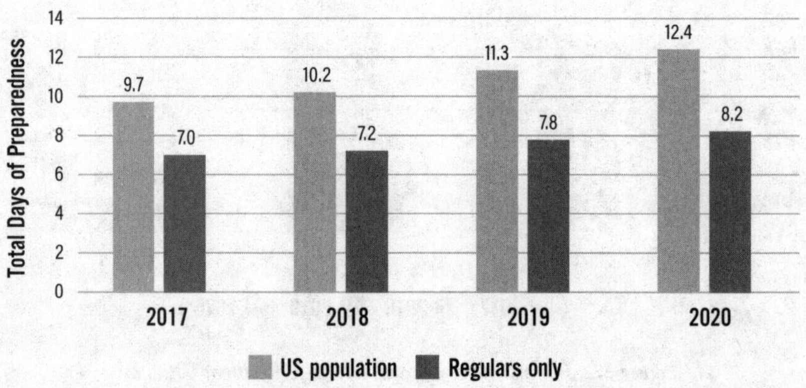

Figure 3.4: Preparedness Levels by Year and Category

As Figure 3.4 shows, Americans have collectively increased their levels of disaster preparedness from 2017 to 2020. For Regulars, the effect was small but measurable—an average of seven days in 2017 to just over eight days in 2020. For this group, each year saw a slight increase. When including Resilient Citizens and averaging all Americans, the mean jumped from just under 10 days of resilience in 2017 to 12.4 days in 2020.

THE COMPOSITION AND CHARACTERISTICS OF RESILIENT CITIZENS

How do Resilient Citizens compare to Regulars? Dominants declare that preppers are a monolith of White men living in the boonies. The facts show something quite different. Let me paint a more accurate picture of Resilient Citizens by analyzing eight metrics: gender, age, race, education, disability, neighborliness, finances, and where they live.[71]

Gender and Age

The speculation by both Dominants and many Challengers is that more men than women prepare at extreme levels. I found this to be true in all years of analysis. In 2017, of the Resilient Citizens who gave a binary gender response, 74 percent were men. By 2020, this ratio had steadily dropped to 69 percent male. However, both genders saw growth in their overall numbers, with men increasing by 35 percent and women by 75 percent. Ultra-Highly Resilient Citizens also saw overall growth in men and women when comparing 2017 to 2020, but there were down years in 2018 and 2019.

Age is an interesting variable that may impact other demographics such as income, disability, and location. The data indicate the average age of Resilient Citizens to be about fifty-three years old, just a year older than Regulars. Contrary to other reports, the young were *not* increasingly demonstrating enhanced preparedness. In fact, Resilient Citizens under thirty-five years old *dropped* from 20.6 percent in 2017 to 14.4 percent in 2020. Comparatively, growth in those aged thirty-six to forty-nine was flat and those fifty-plus saw a modest jump.

This is likely due to the expensive nature of American-style prepping. Older individuals have higher aggregate net worth and disposable income; therefore, they have the means to purchase more items for increased resilience.

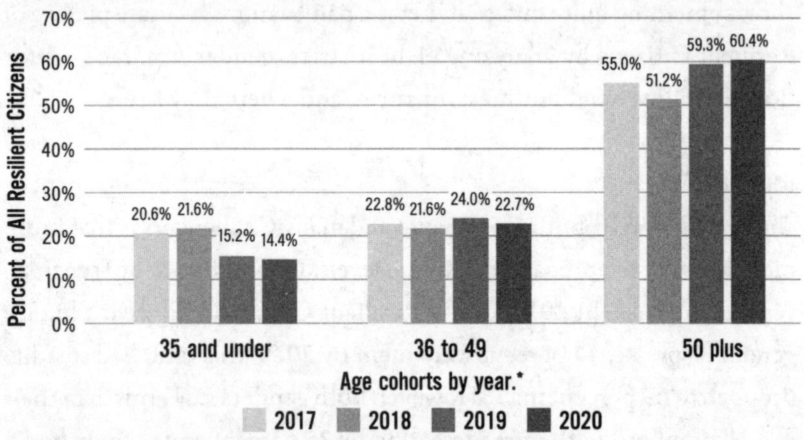

Figure 3.5: Proportion of Resilient Citizens by Age Cohort
**Note: Yearly percentages do not add up to 100 percent due to rounding and some missing data.*

Race[72]

Race is far more complex. Both Dominants and Challengers believe Whites comprise the bulk of preppers but to differing degrees. Dominants see preppers as nearly exclusively White, while many Challengers have a more diverse picture in mind. Both the US Census data and the FEMA survey use six categories for race, but each survey also includes mixed-race responses. Unfortunately, the FEMA survey split Hispanics into a separate question, and they were the only group by FEMA's methodology to include mixed race. This makes accurate tabulation difficult for Hispanics and generally leads to severe undercounting of that group. Because of this, racial totals will not sum to 100 percent.

Isolating a single year gives an illustration of the racial diversity among Resilient Citizens compared with the racial diversity of America writ large. As Figure 3.6 shows, Resilient Citizens are *not* a White monolith. Several interesting findings are notable.

First, from FEMA's survey, almost 25 percent of Resilient Citizens are *not* White alone, and the true figure might be higher since Whites are

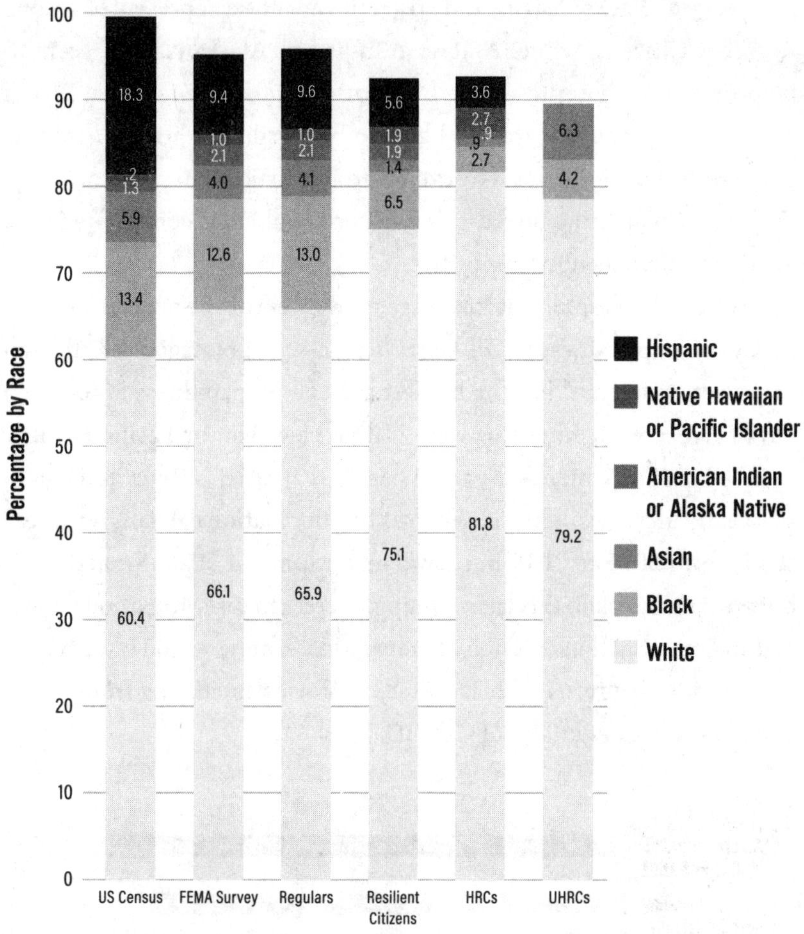

Figure 3.6: 2018 Comparative Racial Composition of Various Groups

oversampled by 6 percent. This would extrapolate to about 2.8 million non-White or mixed-race Resilient Citizens in the United States in 2018. While Whites comprise the preponderance of the Resilient Citizen population, it is a proportional difference of only 9 percent from the FEMA baseline of Whites surveyed. Whites are more heavily represented in the HRCs and UHRCs, but in no category do they garner more than 82 percent.

Second, Blacks, Asians, and Hispanics are underrepresented among Resilient Citizens, while "American Indian or Alaska Native" seem to be proportionally represented. I do not minimize the fact that Blacks, Asians, and Hispanics are less likely to be Resilient Citizens, but this could be heavily influenced by other variables, such as income or where they live. The missing mixed-race category could also contribute to the lower numbers seen for minorities.

Third, when looking at four-year aggregates for the average number of days of preparedness for *all Americans,* we see the category of "Alaskan or Native American" has the highest average preparedness at fourteen days (Figure 3.7). After this were Native Hawaiian or Pacific Islander, then White, Hispanic, Black, and Asian, in that order. Whites and Blacks saw yearly increases, while other races had fluctuations. Asians were very stable from 2017 to 2019 but saw a major jump in 2020. Several possibilities could explain this latter finding: increased discrimination, higher cultural or social transmission of preparedness, or news and information consumption patterns such as affinity to stories emanating from China and Asia at the beginning of COVID.

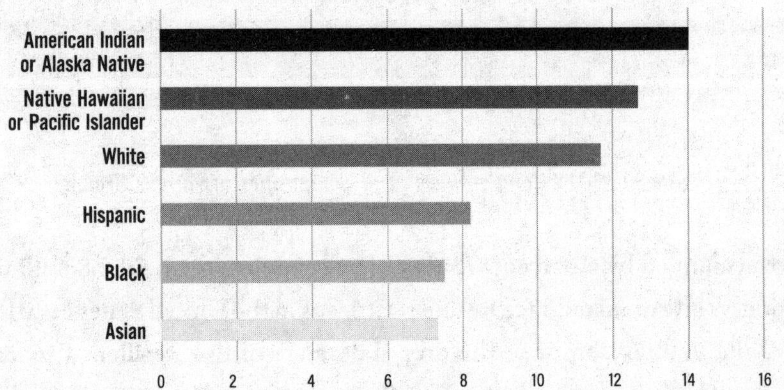

Figure 3.7: Average Days of Preparedness by Race (2017–2020 Aggregate)

Fourth, the story solely among Resilient Citizens is slightly different. For four-year aggregates, Hawaiian/Pacific Islander topped the list at 92 days, followed by Alaskan/Native American at 79 days, then Hispanic at 77 days, White at 76 days, Black at 71 days, and Asian at 65 days. A word of caution: There were not enough respondents in these categories for me to confidently depict any racial patterns, only general observations. Relatedly, when conducting multivariate analysis and controlling for things such as income, education, and an urban versus rural home location, the variable of race was a poor indicator of being a Resilient Citizen. The maximum observed impact across numerous calculations was only 2 percent.[73]

For further confirmation of diversity, I looked at the number of respondents who did not speak English as their primary language at home. Using this measure, 8.8 percent of all Resilient Citizens did not speak English as their primary language as compared to 15 percent of the Regulars in 2018, the first year FEMA included US territories in its survey. These Resilient Citizens had an average of 72.5 days of preparedness.

Roughly one-third of the non-English-speaking group were from Puerto Rico. If I remove the Puerto Rican responses and extrapolate to the rest of the United States, this still infers at least 580,000 non-primary English language individuals are Resilient Citizens that year. The years of 2019 and 2020 yielded slightly lower overall percentage, with 7.2 percent of Resilient Citizen households in 2020—down from 8.8 percent in 2018—not speaking English as their primary language.

Education

Researchers, particularly Challengers, conducting in-person field observations or interviews habitually point out that the education levels of Resilient Citizens are high. While there are some accusations by Dominants that people who prepare are less educated,[74] neither Challengers nor Dominants state any trend or hypothesis. The data support this ambivalence. FEMA's National Household Survey (NHS) from 2017 to 2020 asked about education on a seven-point scale where 1 is less than a high school diploma and 7 is postgraduate work/degree. For all four years, both Regulars and Resilient Citizens hovered around 4 on the scale, indicating "some college." Figure 3.8 shows this for 2018.

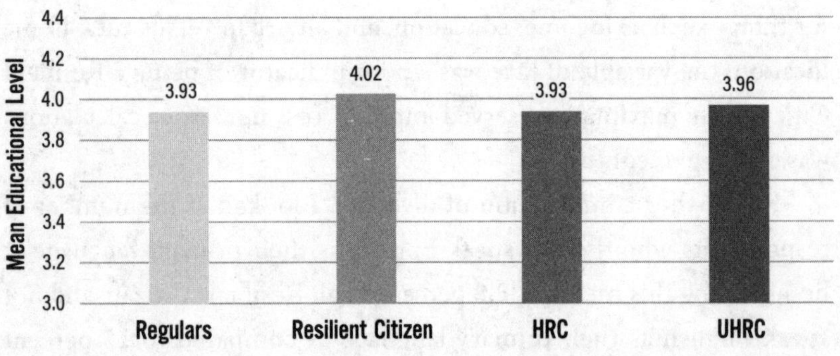

Figure 3.8: Mean Educational Level of Groups
Note: 3 = Technical/Vocational school, 4 = Some college, 5 = College graduate

Disability and Inclusiveness

The former head of FEMA, Craig Fugate, stated that at the time of Hurricane Katrina in 2005, 20 percent of Americans (roughly fifty-four million people) were living with some sort of disability.[75] The US Census estimate for 2018 was much lower at 8.6 percent, although they only counted those sixty-five years of age or younger.

To determine how many Resilient Citizens contend with disabilities, I used the following question from the NHS: "Do you have a disability or a health condition that might affect your capacity to respond to an emergency situation?"[76] Among Regulars, 17.7 percent indicated having a disability for the four years studied. Among Resilient Citizens, 17.5 percent. Oddly, HRCs and UHRCs saw even higher rates of reported disability at just above 19 percent for both.

Neither Dominants nor Challengers speak much about disability, but this finding is intriguing because it supports the notion that *prepared individuals are more like a cross-section of America.*

Looking at all four years, there was a curious jump in the number of Resilient Citizens with a disability. I noted a 50 percent increase from 2017 to 2020, even though the FEMA data indicated only a 3 percent rise in disabilities in the overall sample population during the same time frame. Perhaps this is merely a correlation with the higher average age of Resilient Citizens.

Neighborliness

Some Dominants claim that preppers are only out for themselves and will turn a blind eye to the suffering of others during a disaster. Others take issue with this depiction of callousness because preppers often make a distinction between those who *cannot prepare* and those who *refuse to prepare.*[77] Since people are far more likely to be rescued by a neighbor after a catastrophe than by a professional crew, it would be helpful to know if prepared neighbors are dependable for aid. In some instances, neighbors are *nine times more likely* to rescue you than a professional crew![78]

FEMA has an indirect measure to potentially answer this query. They asked if people would check on their neighbors after a disaster to "make sure they are okay." In the four years of data, Resilient Citizens were slightly more likely to check in with their neighbor at 69 percent compared to Regulars at 66 percent.

Finances

Maybe what most separates Regulars from Resilient Citizens is how much money they make. Academic literature proves that richer countries fare far better in disasters for a multitude of reasons, such as building codes, land use, and robust response capabilities. With more money, individuals can prepare at higher levels. Several questions from FEMA queried people along these lines. Combined, they paint a picture that shows Regulars and Resilient Citizens have roughly comparable levels of income, but concerning disasters, they handle their money very differently.

FEMA queried respondents for monthly household income based on a 12-point scale.[79] Over the four years of results, Resilient Citizens indicated a mean score of 7.7 and Regulars scored 7.2. This translates to an annual income of $56,400 and $50,400, respectively. For context, US Census data indicate that the average 2018 household annual income was just over $60,000. FEMA's surveyed population of both Regulars and Resilient Citizens, then, had an average household income slightly lower than the country as a whole.

This could be due to respondents' markedly lower feedback on this question. Nearly 30 percent of Resilient Citizens and 27 percent of Regulars failed to answer this question, which is not surprising as people often do not like talking about their income—especially for a government survey. Additionally, writings on high-net-worth individuals, especially in a prepping context, find them to be incredibly tight-lipped and clandestine.

Spending and saving patterns are interesting. In response to whether individuals *have emergency savings*, 79 percent of Resilient Citizens and 67 percent of Regulars said yes in 2018. In both groups there was an increase to 86 percent and 71 percent in 2020, respectively. Far more interesting, though, is the amount of money saved for emergencies. While the Regulars' emergency savings average *rose* from $9,300 in 2018 to $10,800 in 2020, the Resilient Citizens' average *dropped* from just over $15,000 to just over $12,000 (Figure 3.9). Why? My guess is that Resilient Citizens converted cash savings into preps. In February 2019, North Korean nuclear negotiations with the United States faltered, and COVID struck in 2020.

While this is speculation on my part, it does match some of the literature on the spending habits of preppers. They are far more likely to invest in their disaster-readiness preps than ordinary citizens.[80] Taken

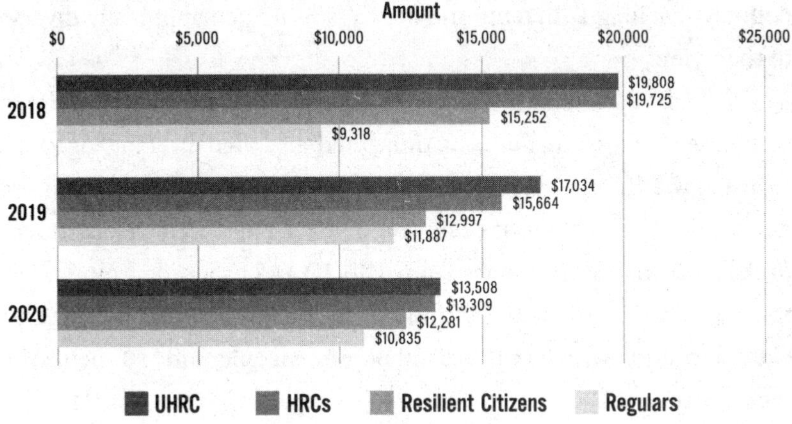

Figure 3.9: Average Emergency Savings, 2018–2020

collectively, the financial situation and choices of Resilient Citizens point to a group that considers—and then takes steps to mitigate—risk as it is related to disasters.

Where They Live

The common depiction is that preppers live in areas with lower population density. Sometimes, this is validated by research both domestically[81] and internationally, such as in Sweden[82] or Switzerland.[83] From the Dominant narrative, this is due to the belief that these individuals are quasi-separatists who reject the rest of humanity. However, an alternative explanation suggests a correlation in culture, activity, or skill sets of rural areas that overlaps more with the survivalist mindset. Hobbies such as hunting, fishing, camping, and raising livestock can all lower the barrier to longer-term prepping and are often more accessible to those living outside the city. In rural areas, "prepping" may be synonymous with farm life or getting ready for a long winter. These factors may also partly explain the racial and gender divides seen previously—that is, more men hunt than women, and Whites are more prevalent in rural areas than in metropolises. Challengers list examples both of city-dwelling and country-dwelling adherents and are thus more geographically diverse in their view.

To probe this divide, FEMA's NHS dataset indicated the zip codes of respondents. I took that information and then coded dwelling locations by using the Rural-Urban Commuting Area Codes (RUCA) from the Economic Research Service division of the United States Department of Agriculture.[84] RUCA goes from 1 to 10 and proceeds from largest to smallest—that is, with "1" indicating living in an Urbanized Area Core, a location with fifty thousand or more people, and "10" being the most rural.[85]

Approximately 75 percent of FEMA's survey members resided in Urbanized Area Cores, slightly under the US Census estimates of 80–81 percent.[86] Sixty-two percent of Resilient Citizens and 60 percent of Highly Resilient Citizens lived in these metropolitan locales as depicted in Figure 3.10. The graph shows the urban to rural average RUCA of each group, where a lower mean indicates a more urban domicile. The upper line shows the percentage of individuals living in an urban core, and the lower line shows the percentage of individuals living in a small town or rural place. Unsurprisingly, Resilient Citizens were almost twice as likely to live in small towns or rural areas (RUCA 7–10).

There are other interesting observations about this data. First, the majority of Resilient Citizens in the FEMA survey live in a city or suburb of a city. Challengers stated that Resilient Citizens are more geographically diverse, but this finding of such a high proportion living in or near cities is almost completely unexpected.[87] Perhaps the reason lies in how RUCA is calculated. Any zip code with fifty thousand residents gets a RUCA code of one, so people living in downtown Chicago are coded the same way as those who live in Terre Haute, Indiana.

A second interesting finding comes to light when analyzing RUCA codes compared with total days of preps. Neither Regulars nor Resilient Citizens had any discernible pattern. The inclination would be to expect

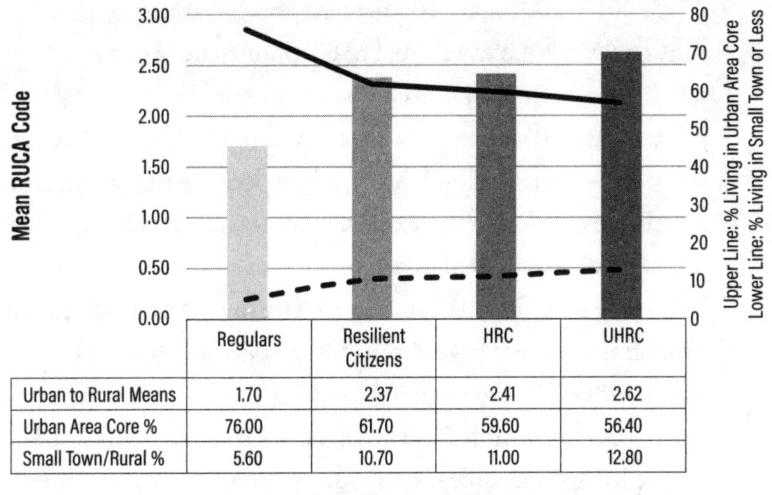

	Regulars	Resilient Citizens	HRC	UHRC
Urban to Rural Means	1.70	2.37	2.41	2.62
Urban Area Core %	76.00	61.70	59.60	56.40
Small Town/Rural %	5.60	10.70	11.00	12.80

Figure 3.10: Mean RUCA and Percentage Living in Urban Area Cores vs. Small Towns

more days of preparedness when the RUCA code increases in value from urban to rural, but this was not the case. There was no upward trendline in either group.

A SHORT ADDENDUM REGARDING THE 2021-2023 FEMA DATASETS

Toward the end of writing this book, I was able to conduct a preliminary analysis of FEMA's National Household Surveys (NHS) from 2021 to 2023.[88] Because this examination is rather raw and many changes were made to FEMA's survey methodology, I have far less analysis than I had for the 2017–2020 data.

Survey Changes

I must provide a few caveats before presenting the highlights:

- The number of Americans surveyed massively increased from five thousand per year in 2017–2020 to over seven thousand per year in 2021–2023.

- While 2017–2020 were 100 percent phone-based questionnaires, 2021–2022 were a mix of telephone and internet sampling, and 2023 was exclusively web-based.
- While 2018–2020 surveys were consistent in oversampling six disasters—tornado, flood, hurricane, wildfire, earthquake, and an urban event (a nuclear explosion)—the 2021–2023 questionnaire oversample of disasters *changed every year*.
- Beginning with the 2022 survey, FEMA sought nine additional demographic subsamples from "historically underserved communities." These included LGBTQ+, those over sixty years old, people with Faith-Based Beliefs and Religious Minorities, people living in rural areas, the socioeconomically disadvantaged, and others.
- FEMA no longer allowed respondents to indicate how many days they could last at home without power, running water, or transportation as a single question.

That last change is critical to understand. Rather than using the original phrasing, FEMA broke the question up into three separate parts:

- How long will the supplies that you have assembled last?
- How long could you live in your home without power?
- How long could you live in your home without running water?

Additionally, people no longer had the option to state their number of days openly but rather had a menu of option choices from *Fewer than 1 day, 1 to 3 days, 3 days to 1 week, More than 1 week, More than 2 weeks, More than 1 month, More than 3 months, Don't know,* and *Prefer not to answer.*[89]

Taken all together, these five methodological shifts make direct comparison to the 2017–2020 datasets quite tricky, as these former surveys were far more uniform. Consistency is best from a statistical standpoint when one is trying to compare annual data.[90] In order to still isolate Resilient Citizens from Regulars, I had to make a critical assumption: Those people who answered yes to "more than one month" or "more than three months" for *both* the power *and* the running water question are analogous to the Resilient Citizens of 2017–2020.[91] There were other impacts as well; for example, I can no longer separate out Ultra-Highly Resilient Citizens as there is no "97 days or more" response option.

Insights

First, did COVID-19 jump-start a radical increase in Resilient Citizens? The answer seems to be a resounding yes! If you recall, the 2020 data collected in the early months of COVID-19 saw a modest increase of 1.1 million more people prepping compared to 2019 for a total of about 15 million (Figure 3.3). By contrast, 2021 saw an explosion of over 5 million new Resilient Citizens, totaling more than 20 million Americans. A slight drop was reported in 2022, but 2023 saw a 3 million person rebound, totaling just under 9 percent of the US adult population, or 23 million Americans (Figure 3.11).[92] By contrast, Highly Resilient Citizens did not show any growth from 2021 to 2023.

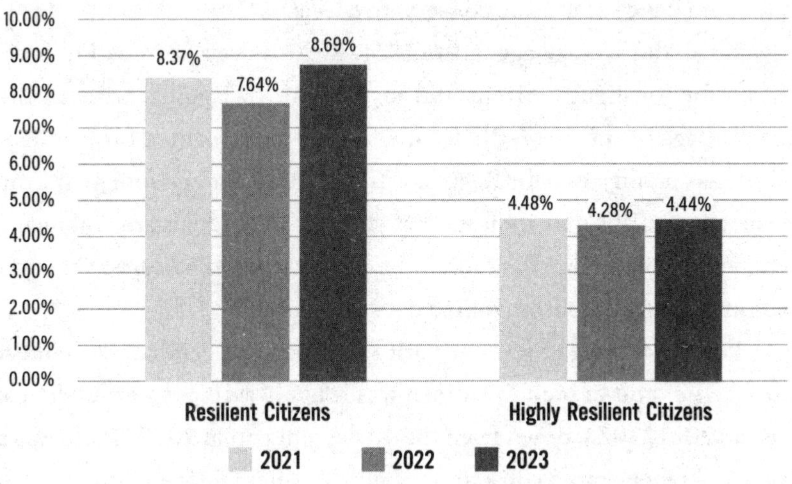

Figure 3.11: Percent of Americans RC and HRC by Year[93]

Second, should we expect to see continued growth in the Resilient Citizen population? There is no way to know for sure, but I speculate we may be hovering around the "16 percent chasm," also known as the diffusion of innovation adoption curve. Often used in technology or consumer economics studies, 16 percent utilization of a new widget (think smartphone or Tesla) or a new social practice (think mask-wearing) is the theorized psychological line in the sand for social adoption.[94] If just under 9 percent of Americans are reporting enhanced preparedness and a good bit of them are married with spouses participating, then we may be bouncing around 16 percent of the adult population in the United States practicing the traits of Resilient Citizens. If that is the case, then the true number of Resilient Citizens in America, based on a 16 percent extrapolation, would be more than forty million people in 2023. The 16 percent chasm could also explain the drop in Highly Resilient Citizens. Perhaps ninety days of preparedness is the new radical extreme, and a month of preps is more socially accepted. From previous studies of the diffusion of innovation adoption curve, we cannot predict what will happen. Enhanced preparedness could go mainstream and rocket upward or crash back into fringe territory. For this reason, I will keep my estimates at a far more conservative level.

Third, the average age in the 2021–2023 surveys dropped to forty-seven for Resilient Citizens and forty-eight for Regulars. Recall the average age in the 2017–2020 time frame was fifty-three for Resilient Citizens and fifty-two for Regulars. This is a six-year and four-year drop, respectively. This may indicate that younger individuals are embracing enhanced preparedness, or it may be a reflection of the surveyed population coming more from online data collection.

Fourth, it appears greater parity between the genders has continued.[95] The ratio of men to women was roughly a 10 percent difference across 2021–2023, down from the 40 percent gap in 2020. There was a slightly higher gender gap among Highly Resilient Citizens, but it is still a smaller spread than the 2017–2020 average. FEMA also added a Third

Gender/Other choice in 2021. In 2023, 1 percent of Resilient Citizens selected this option. See Figure 3.12 for a compilation of gender statistics.

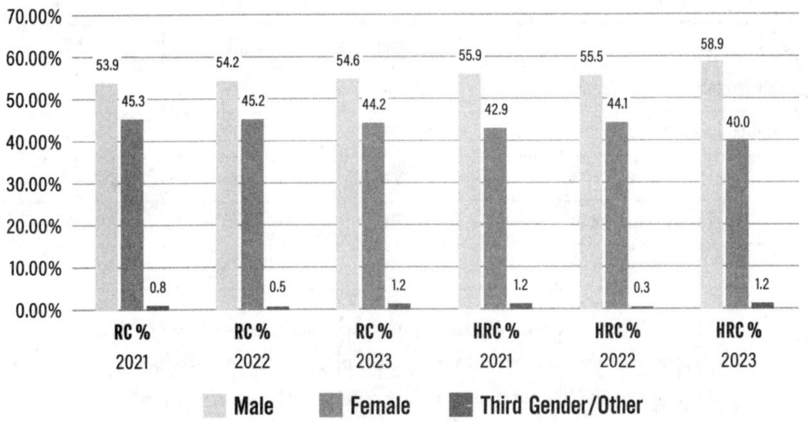

Figure 3.12: Percent of Resilient Citizens and Highly Resilient Citizens, Including Gender by Year, 2021–2023

Fifth, financial and racial data are challenging. For finances, FEMA's surveys had some issues with clarity that I was unable to remediate in time for this book. I hesitate to speculate at this point. As for race, FEMA tried, and succeeded, to reach more racial minorities in its questionnaires in 2022 and 2023. For example, for the overall survey, the number of American Indian or Alaska Native responses tripled, and the Native Hawaiians or Pacific Islanders queried in 2023 quadrupled.[96] This also means that fewer Whites were surveyed.

Still, the results specifically regarding Resilient Citizens are intriguing. While Whites show a precipitous drop in 2023, Black Resilient Citizen rates remained constant. Asian and Native Hawaiian/Pacific Islander responses *doubled* as did those who self-reported being two or more races. American Indian/Alaska Native responses nearly *quadrupled*. It will take two or three more years of data to get a clearer picture of just what is occurring.

Race	2021 RC %	2022 RC %	2023 RC %
White	72.55%	76.56%	59.76%
Black or African American	11.48%	12.82%	12.86%
Asian	1.16%	0.92%	2.42%
American Indian or Alaska Native	2.16%	2.20%	8.17%
Native Hawaiian or Pacific Islander	0.83%	0.55%	1.97%
Other	6.99%	2.75%	6.66%
Two or more races	4.83%	4.21%	8.17%
Hispanic	21.63%	14.47%	25.57%

Figure 3.13: Racial Composition of Resilient Citizens in 2021–2023
**Note: Numbers do not add up to 100 percent due to rounding and because Hispanics were polled separately from other races.*

People who did not speak English as their primary language at home remained flat for Resilient Citizens for the average of 2021 to 2023. The tally was 8.8 percent, identical to that of the previous four-year average.

Sixth, educational results are a bit more straightforward. The recent numbers show roughly 60 percent of Resilient Citizens have some college education or more. An average of 15 percent of Resilient Citizens have a graduate degree or higher across the three years of data (2021–2023).

Taken holistically, Resilient Citizens saw a jump in numbers above previous years. They appear to be educated and varied in their racial makeup. They are closer to a cross-section of America in terms of gender but a bit younger in terms of average age. COVID-19 introduced the phrase "out of an abundance of caution" to our lexicon. I think that approach is prudent when looking at recent information from FEMA. I am in wait-and-see mode before making any other claims as to the composition of Resilient Citizens in America from a quantitative viewpoint.

ATTENTION

If your eyes glazed over reading all these numbers, stats, facts, and figures, it is now safe to snap out of it! Here's where I put it all into plain English.

WHAT DOES ALL THIS MEAN?

I warned you at the start that this would be the most stat-filled, number-heavy chapter of the whole book. When attempting to correct decades of myths, it's important to "show my work," just so you know everything I'm presenting here is steeped in quality, quantifiable research conducted over many years using unbiased sources. But I also know it can be hard for many people to make heads or tails of all these surveys, stats, and charts. So let me end this deep-research portion with what I hope is a layman's summary to give you a clear picture of exactly who these Resilient Citizens actually are.

Neither journalistic nor academic endeavors over the course of four decades have accurately counted the number of extremely prepared individuals using a methodology that was reliable, representative, and falsifiable. This has led to significant trouble. The Dominant account of preppers is one of masculinity, racism, low education, and selfishness, among other unfavorable traits. The Challenger view, especially since 2010, picked away at some of these stereotypes by showcasing exceptions to such caricatures.

Based on the data collected by FEMA, Resilient Citizens are much closer to the average cross-section of Americans in several respects. Far from being total aberrations, Resilient Citizens are like commonplace Americans. They live in urban and rural areas, they have roughly equivalent incomes, similar levels of education, and a prevalence of disability when compared with their Regular counterparts. They are also just as likely to be concerned about their neighbors after a catastrophe. A greater preponderance of Resilient Citizens is men, but the gender gap is shrinking. While Resilient Citizens are more likely to be White, other racial groups exhibit sizable levels of preparedness—especially Native Alaskans, American Indians, Native Hawaiians, and Pacific Islanders. Financially, Resilient Citizens do act in ways that separate them from Regulars. They are more likely to have emergency savings, to save at higher levels, and to spend their savings on preps.

When it comes to ascertaining differences in levels of preparedness among various demographic groups, it is important to remember these are averages that allow us to peer behind the curtain. I am not arguing that race, income, and location are unimportant, but the critical point is that being a White male from the backwoods of Idaho does not automatically make one a prepper, and being a Hispanic female from Miami does not automatically disqualify someone from that description. Resilient Citizens are a diverse bunch and have been for years. Overall, these findings threaten the Dominant narrative. While there are undoubtedly groups of extremists among Regulars and Resilient Citizens, broad brushstrokes obscure the whole picture. While the Dominant view could have been accurate in a previous time frame, it does not hold for the years studied (2017–2023). The Challenger narrative is strengthened by these findings because Resilient Citizens do not fit the prominent descriptions. I stand with the Challengers. The global disaster of COVID-19 brought forth the logic and benefits of individual and household preparedness, even for longer-term and larger-scale events. This rediscovery of resilience may be transitory, but it may feed a growing trend of resilience. And while the number of Resilient Citizens *is growing*, most Americans are vastly *underprepared*.

Hopefully, these demographic data insights have left you with a far deeper understanding of just who is engaged in enhanced preparedness in America, and we can turn to the flesh-and-blood people behind these numbers. Their stories are varied and fascinating. They are as normal as you and me, and they could be your neighbors.

CHAPTER 4

THE PEOPLE OF PREPAREDNESS

"They're all going to laugh at you."
—Stephen King, *Carrie*

Global political economy is a field of study that deals with the interaction between political and economic forces. At its centre have always been questions of human welfare and how these might be related to state behaviour and corporate interests in different parts of the world. Despite this, major approaches in the field have often focused more on the international system perspective. A side effect of this has been the relative neglect of non-elites and an all-too-often missing recognition of ordinary individuals.
—Günter Walzenbach

Society has evolved beyond primitive man fearing a saber-toothed tiger in the bushes or a hostile tribe on the other side of the mountain. Today we're more concerned about an influx of, quite literally, global threats. There are many perils in a variety of areas: natural to man-made, individual to global, and acute to chronic. How people react is equally diverse, and some choose to take extraordinary steps.

But what's the difference between two people who both own shotguns and a hundred rolls of toilet paper? Why is one a hobbyist hunter but the other a Resilient Citizen? Why do some preparedness-minded individuals build bunkers, whereas others plant crops and raise goats? Over forty years of argument have not provided much clarity, so I propose a new way forward.

Chapter 2 introduced the first criterion for Resilient Citizens, *longevity* of thirty-one days or more of preparedness. I slightly modify that in this part of the book and explain the final two criteria: *Foresight* describes the actions and mindset well in advance of peril, and *creed* disqualifies extremists.

This chapter finalizes my classification of Resilient Citizens and then introduces the analysis of types. The five common types of Resilient Citizens I have studied or interacted with both domestically and internationally are the *Homesteaders, Sentinels, Interdependent, Noahs,* and *Faithful.* Their style pairs with their lifestyle, personalities, and the threats that most concern them.

YOU'RE EITHER WITH US...

My definition of longevity in chapter 2 was a bit more restrictive based on how FEMA worded its survey. It applied to that chapter alone to quantify Resilient Citizens and analyze their demographic data. For the rest of this book, I use the following definition, which enhances the role of citizenship:

> *Criterion one, longevity: A Resilient Citizen is a private actor who can survive for thirty-one or more days ~~at home~~ in their community without publicly provided power, water, or transportation.*

Now I can expand to my full classification of Resilient Citizens. Not all people who stock a month or more of food are Resilient Citizens, nor are all gardeners, gun owners, farmers, militia members, cultists, or billionaires, even though they may share some characteristics with the genre. Resilient Citizens must also have:

> *Criterion two, foresight: The private actor must meet criterion one (longevity) based on an assessment of disaster risk and a paired response to that risk that is executed well in advance.*

The *private actor* distinction is important. I do not include as Resilient Citizens those individuals whose position is within a government function and yet meets my benchmarks. That is, there are no "state actor" Resilient Citizens. For example, a naval submarine on a mission may have more than thirty-one days of food, water, and power while conducting traditional military maneuvers based on global threats. I would not—nor I doubt would any other researcher—consider this vessel to be full of preppers. At the same time, individuals on that crew, while at home and in their private capacity, could be.

Similarly, the vice president of the United States may have a secure location (a bunker) he relocates to in a crisis, but I would not count him as a Resilient Citizen in his official capacity. Crewmembers of the International Space Station may be self-sufficient for six months, but they have that capability not due to worries of a volcanic eruption or civil war but rather because of their job.

Also excluded are private actors who simply make an extra trip to the grocery store to stock up on goods for a specific, short-term emergency. Nervous citizens could bulk purchase granola bars, peanut butter, bottled water, and plywood a few days prior to the impact of a hurricane, but they would not be considered Resilient Citizens. Rather, Resilient Citizens engage in lifestyle choices more analogous at the very least to a serious hobby. It is not a spur-of-the-moment endeavor.

A criterion is needed to reflect this clarification that is robust enough to handle the variety. This is where paired response comes into play. The actions are taken against a threat or collection of threats to achieve a security of being, a concept called *ontological security,* which I explain in great detail in chapter 11. This may seem trivial, but it eliminates several types of people. A rancher might have one hundred cattle on her property with enough food on the hoof to live for years, but this alone does not make her a Resilient Citizen. The Amish can survive, both individually and as a community, for more than thirty-one days. Still, they are not conducting their actions primarily in preparation for a coming disaster, either physical or spiritual, though Mormons, by and large, are. Therefore, criterion two keeps many (although not all) Mormons but eliminates the Amish as a collective. As a final example, take a billionaire who has a ten-thousand-acre ranch, complete with an orchard, several stocked refrigerators, freezers, and pantries with back-up generator power, and a safe room tucked away in his estate house. Is this person a Resilient Citizen? Maybe. If his actions are predicated on concerns of social upheaval or other threats and not just a desire to have a well-supplied mansion, then, yes, even billionaires can be preppers (and many indeed are). Criterion two is, therefore, causal; the response (prepping) derives from a risk assessment that is acted on long before a peril approaches. This metric is paired; you do not plant tomatoes to ward off a home invasion. Ends must link directly to threats. It also cannot be a spur-of-the-moment impulse, like that which characterizes hoarders or panic buyers. These are not one-off shopping trips. It is also on the scale of the localized. These Resilient Citizens are not out to solve world hunger, just their own.

Now let's move on to criterion three, which is useful for separating out extremists. To my knowledge, it is the first attempt to use a regulatory measure codified under the power of the state to do so. While the spirit of criterion three is present in some publications on preppers (e.g., James Coates's big-S vs. little-s survivalism), my taxonomy uses official military policy—

Criterion three, creed: An individual must not participate in extremist organizations or activities as defined by the United States military.

I use *Army Regulation 600-20: Army Command Policy* paragraphs 4–12. This provides both clearly defined terms that explicitly prohibit multiple extremist ideologies and, by extension, gives the foundation for an abundance of military judicial and nonjudicial jurisprudence. Criterion three is thus legally codified in statute. It prohibits several individual actions regarding discrimination, intolerance, support for terrorism, and seditious or subversive acts. I argue that because the US military allows noncitizens to join its ranks, this criterion is robust enough to apply to non-Americans. Only within the combination of all three criteria does one meet the designation of Resilient Citizen.

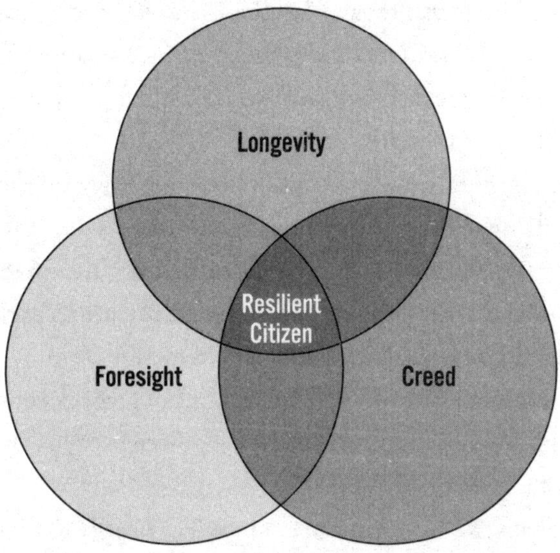

Figure 4.1: Visualizing Group Relations and Intersection

Figure 4.1 graphically depicts a way of visualizing the overlaps and should intuitively help explain why confusion on this topic is so pervasive.

Now that I have described who is and who is not a Resilient Citizen, I now propose a heuristic that lays out five typologies I mentioned previously: Homesteaders, Sentinels, Interdependent, Noahs, and Faithful. These are broad, not exact, descriptions, so it is common for many individual preppers to lean strongly toward one archetype while still embodying some aspects of the others. These groupings are rules-of-thumb, not set in stone, for one key reason: As people enter prepping based on an analysis of probabilities or because of cultural or institutional practices, they often interact with the community of other like-minded individuals or naturally discover the interconnected nature of polycrisis and general resilience. They can also learn of other disaster-readiness actions or disaster cascades (i.e., how one disaster can trigger another). For example, COVID-19 was a biological pandemic, but it cascaded into an economic crisis. People can start as Sentinels and later combine attributes of Noahs or Homesteaders. Shifts such as this are common. My own journey started in one category and then morphed into generalized resilience against a host of perils.

These examples are *not* representative of every possible type of Resilient Citizen—other variations are out there—but they do cover a wide swath in America and abroad. I settled on these five groupings based on the available survivalist and prepper literature, both academic and journalistic, as well as my personal interactions. You will see these groups are not merely a modern occurrence but go back centuries, even millennia. In every particular case, though, these people were driven by a desire for their security of being.

Additionally, *Resilient Citizen* is a moniker *I* apply to them. Outside a handful of academic references, I have never seen this term publicly adopted. If I mislabel someone, the error is mine alone.

CHAPTER 5

THE HOMESTEADERS

"A plague o' both your houses!"
—William Shakespeare, *Romeo and Juliet*

Oh, the Lord is good to me,
And so I thank the Lord!
For giving me the things I need;
The sun and the rain and the apple seed.
The Lord is good to me.
—Johnny Appleseed

For generations, productive farms and woodland areas have been associated with harvest, bounty, and often peaceful escape. Disease often decimated urban environments, and sustenance was more readily available, either on the hoof or from the root, closer to the wild. Homesteading is the original Resilient Citizen typecast. In the modern era, it is politically diverse and seems to contain a higher percentage of left-of-center adherents. Among practitioners, health seems to be the unifying constant.

PLANET EARTH

Homesteaders have been around for thousands of years, and America's first Resilient Citizens were the native tribes and later the Pilgrims in 1620. They prepared for a disaster called "winter" or "bears." Their modern counterparts are different in degree, not kind.

Jim and Susan have a sixty-acre ranch.

Dana runs a hobby farm to ensure she always has access to sustenance.[97]

Joanie and Graham fear genetically modified organisms (GMOs) and grow their own food for health fears and concerns. Joanie abhors guns and feels the freedom to farm is far more important than the freedom to own a firearm.

Galen is a retired twenty-year submarine veteran of the United States Navy with degrees in horticulture, electrical engineering, and theology. He maintains a small farm in Maine and is motivated to prepare for disaster mainly because of his grandparents' experiences of losing their farms during the Great Depression and the Dust Bowl.[98]

Jim, Susan, Dana, Joanie, Graham, and Galen are all Homesteaders.

The Abrahamic faiths teach that human life began in a garden—peaceful, bucolic, abundant. Throughout the world, wealthy individuals have summer homes out in nature. Presidents of the United States vacation at Camp David, located in a lush greenbelt in northern Maryland, far away from traffic or neon lights. In times of both relaxation and crisis, we tend to "head for the hills," seeking refuge. Savvy entrepreneurs in the early 1900s sold escape havens for "rural tranquility" and safety as a remedy for anxious city dwellers.[99] That practice—and the angst that underlies it—waxed and waned for decades yet continues in America and across the world even today.[100] While villages and towns are omnipresent in human history, large cities were far less common. Why? Two major reasons are apparent and continue to the current era: pestilence and food insecurity.

NOTHING TO SNEEZE AT

During the Peloponnesian War between ancient Athens and Sparta, a plague in the first city wiped out at least 25 percent of the population. Thucydides described the suffering of the victims. They had vomiting, convulsions, and pustules so painful that many preferred to be nude. Death came from diarrhea, and those who lived were often scarred with disfigured appendages, including their genitals.[101] Six hundred years later, smallpox reduced the Roman Empire by 10–30 percent. The city of Rome lost five thousand people per day.[102] Just before the time of Christ, Rome's denizens devoured six thousand tons of grain each week. After Rome fell, the next city in the world to match that level of consumption would be London in the 1800s.[103]

Cities are havens for various pathogens. Sexual contact, sewers, rainwater, spoiled food, and vermin are all vectors with plenty of hosts to choose from. The countryside, by contrast, is far more conducive to health and longevity. The chance of living past the age of thirty was more than double outside the city of Rome in the empire's heyday.[104] In the 1300s, the Black Death laid waste to a third of Europe, and cities were hardest hit. This does not mean disease is contained only in metropolises. China saw nearly *half* its population die from the Black Death outbreak and subsequent famine; disease and starvation are common brethren.[105] It took another five hundred years and the inventions and practices of such things as inoculations, handwashing, wastewater treatment, and refrigeration to make cities a viable option for high populations.

Modern epidemics can be from natural sources or man-made ones, either deliberate or accidental, and they are exceptionally costly. Isolating just a single year, the German reinsurer *Munich Re* estimated for 2020 that natural disasters alone, not including COVID-19, cost the world $210 billion.[106] Yet this is a drop in the bucket compared to the $10–30 trillion range estimates for COVID-19's fiscal devastation as provided by World Bank numbers[107] or the International Monetary Fund,[108] respectively. Data from the Bank of England show that 2020 was the United Kingdom's largest GDP plunge since 1709.[109] Expert testimony before the United Nations in December 2020 indicated an additional 270 million people worldwide dropped into the threat of starvation.[110]

COVID-19's origin is still hotly debated. Five agencies in the US intelligence community are on record for saying it was a natural pathogen, but the Department of Energy and the FBI both believe it was a laboratory "incident."[111] Robert F. Kennedy Jr., now the Secretary of Health and Human Services, and certain members of Congress suggested a more sinister explanation.[112] History is on the side of the doomsayers.

Chemical and biological warfare have been used for millennia. The Sumerians used poisons as far back as 4500 BC and were followed by the Assyrians, Babylonians, Egyptians, Indians, Native Americans, Scythians, Mongols, various African tribes, Romans, and Greeks—all the way to the relatively recent history of World War II when Germans, Japanese, Russians, and others partook in chemical and biological offensive weapons.[113] The United States researched an anthrax bomb for the war, and Britain tried to purchase five hundred thousand of them.[114]

Although bioweapons were banned by the 1972 Biological Weapons Convention, the Soviets continued research on them, such as anthrax in amounts from a single missile that would sicken or kill everyone living in New York City. In 1979, a lab leak from a weapons testing facility in Sverdlovsk killed more than a hundred people. Soviet officials first blamed a natural animal outbreak, and then the party line for the next twenty years was that food vendors had sold contaminated meat.[115] Sound familiar?

The Tokyo subway system was attacked by cultists using sarin gas in 1995, and anthrax has been mailed to members of Congress. In 2018, a former Russian spy living in the United Kingdom was allegedly subject to a chemical assassination attempt with the nerve agent Novichok. Although the former spy survived, the British government spent more than £30 million on the investigation, including medical care and sanitization of the site.[116]

Pathogen escapes from research institutes are ubiquitous throughout the world. "Mishaps" are up 50 percent since COVID-19 within the United Kingdom alone.[117] The Biden-Harris administration's National Biodefense Strategy of 2022 indicated lab leaks "may be increasing with the rise in the number of laboratories around the world conducting high-risk life sciences research and research with potential pandemic pathogens without appropriate oversight." It further states the "use of biological weapons or their proliferation by state or nonstate actors presents a significant challenge to our national security, our people, our agriculture, and the environment."[118] Artificial intelligence is making Franken-viruses easier to create. The same technology and university-level teaching that enables targeted therapeutic drugs can also be used for nefarious purposes.[119]

WHAT HAVE YOU GOT TO EAT AROUND HERE?

Food insecurity is a second major driver for many homesteaders. In the Western world, we no longer eat hand-to-mouth, and government programs and charities feed the impoverished. However, concerns still linger over childhood malnutrition and the health of our groceries.

Roxanne Ahern is a writer, Homesteader, holistic nutritionist, and permaculture designer who lives with her husband and five daughters in the South. Roxanne lived a middle-class suburban life and worked in real estate before having a family. Over the years, Roxanne began to become concerned about the quality of food she was eating and feeding her young family. Their family moved to Costa Rica for a brief period, and in that time, Roxanne was impressed by how the locals cooked whole foods from scratch. As is very common among the more holistic-minded mothers, the more she looked into our food system, the more she became concerned with the risks inherent in it.

Roxanne explains:

> It is expected that about 40 to 60 percent of agricultural lands are going to change hands in the next ten years, and who is going to buy that land? Is it going to be Bill Gates? Is it going to be foreign investors? Or is it going to be small family farmers? We need more hands in the dirt. We need more people working the land.[120]

Now, in her day-to-day life, she homeschools her five daughters, and their schooling includes home economics—from gardening to food preservation, baking bread, and even making small businesses on the homestead. "When you learn about the way agriculture is currently done versus seeing it up close and on a small scale, [and when you learn] what that means for the ecology of the place and the human health that is a part of that ecology..." she ponders, her words trailing off. "People don't want to hear it, but what we need is more people working in agriculture."

People are fascinated by this kind of American pioneer mentality, which has exemplars across our culture, for example, in the book and television series *Little House on the Prairie.* The popularity of modern shows such as *Homestead Rescue* and *Building Off the Grid* continues the appeal.

The most famous of the Homesteader's heroes might be Joel Salatin, who was highlighted in Michael Pollan's bestselling book *The Omnivore's Dilemma.* Joel is both a conservative and a Christian yet embraces "ecological stewardship" and has no problem excoriating Republicans who are beholden to "Big Agriculture," or "Big Ag" for short. Elsewhere Joel explains:

> I shudder when conservatives defend Monsanto's genetically modified organisms (GMOs) as the answer to food insecurity. I cringe when Christians say, "It's all gonna burn anyway. Haven't you read Revelation? Use it up, man. What are you waiting for?" In the same breath, they say it all belongs to God. Pardon me, but if I were God and I made something beautiful like the earth, I don't think I'd appreciate infertile frogs, three-legged salamanders, eagle eggs that won't hatch, and a dead zone the size of Rhode Island in the Gulf of Mexico. I'd call that a poor return on investment. And I'd blame humanity for the abuse.
>
> Unfortunately, because liberal Democrats own the environmental movement, Republicans feel compelled to make fun and crack jokes about caring for trees and earthworms. The

> liberal-conservative feud in this arena is tragic for our nation, for the soil, for healing.[121]

The Homesteader designation in the modern era has not changed much since Saxon first identified them in 1980 as "ecologists" or "back-to-the-landers."[122] Their connection with nature is strong because pollution and other hazards are viewed as an extension of pestilence. Forever chemicals, pesticides, fertilizers, hormone mimickers, and the presence of licit and illicit drugs and antibiotics in both land and water all have the potential to fall into their dread calculations.

Many are concerned with items at the grocery store, with their fears driven by contamination, sketchy ingredients, inflation, or outright shortages. In 2019, swine flu raged through China, as it has several times before. In that instance, 130 million pigs were culled in a country where pork makes up 70 percent of the average citizen's meat intake.[123] A multi-year European study surveying hundreds of thousands of residents of Europe saw a major spike in people "who consider food and water supply to be one of the biggest challenges." Nearly a quarter of 2023 respondents in France, the United Kingdom, Spain, and Italy were worried.[124]

Dr. Ashley Colby, trained as an environmental sociologist, was so worried about pollution in the environment and contamination in the food supply that she moved her family to Uruguay in South America to find a more pristine environment within which to build her nine-acre homestead. "We wanted to find a place where we could peacefully learn how to produce food for ourselves, where our neighbors were also people who were adept in food self-sufficiency, where we had control over the inputs such that I knew my kids would be eating clean and healthy."[125] For Ashley, it is not only about food free of contamination but also food access in the case of supply chain interruptions or disasters.

During the COVID-19 crisis, food insecurity quadrupled in the United States, and long lines at charitable donation sites became ubiquitous in both the first and second waves.[126] In 2024, America's beef cattle herd size reached its lowest point in more than sixty years.[127] Bird flu, foot-and-mouth disease, mad cow disease (bovine spongiform encephalopathy), and aquatic viruses and parasites in farmed fish are constant threats. Improper cooking and handling techniques have resulted in outbreaks of *E. coli* and salmonella.[128] Overall, 42 percent of Americans have either low or no "confidence in the government to keep food safe."[129] Farmers' markets are more popular than ever, but they face stiff competition from subsidized Big Ag.

GATHERING AROUND THE HEARTH

Food and health seem to cut across ideological lines with greater ease. You may think it is primarily farmers and ranchers who are responsible for grocery stores full of corn or steak or whole wheat bread, but it is largely Exxon and Saudi Arabia. Our modern food system is based just as much on *oil* as it is on *soil* and is grotesquely destructive. Governments are partially to blame, but so are we.

The British author, farmer, agrarian populist, and social scientist Chris Smaje writes that our current farming practices are deleterious to our environment and well-being via a "range of toxic and nutritional assaults."[130] He argues modern farming is incredibly extractive because it undercuts good farmers and healthy practices in the adaptation of an industrial model instead of an ecological one, and it bleeds massive levels of waste.

Approaching the situation from the opposite end of the political spectrum, John Klar argues for a return to smaller farms and an embrace of the humble family cow. "Local farms are supportive of local economies, but also of community culture, environmental stewardship, individual liberties, and national security."[131] He agrees with Smaje—as well as Joel Salatin and Michael Pollan—that industrial practices such as concentrated animal feeding operations (CAFOs) and monocropping (e.g., corn and soybeans) are oil-based operations and environmentally detrimental, not to mention bad for our health.

Klar argues industrialization is killing us via added sugars, corn syrup, trans fats, and other substances. His solution is to eat more grass-fed meat. He also believes manure, at the appropriate scale, is a critical solution for regenerative agriculture. Soil health has been an existential threat to societies for eons, and that certainly includes America. Personally, I rank our dirt and our debt as America's second and third most pressing and intractable earthly perils.[132]

Once upon a time, the US government actually pushed resiliency via at-home subsistence. Leading by example in World War I, the White House was home to forty-eight sheep "as a symbol of the president's commitment to the war effort and White House compliance to food and fuel conservation programs." In fact, the White House has seen vegetable gardens and fruit trees on and off from the time of John Adams in 1800 to Michelle Obama. During World War II, nearly a third of Americans had victory gardens in their backyards.[133] In a bright spot, gardening continues to be a popular pastime and has seen millions of new—and younger—participants join the ranks since 2020.[134]

Homesteaders share a desire to gain or regain self-sufficiency or resilience. One Challenger opined that this self-sufficiency—not extremism—is what linked groups together.[135] Other themes were escaping the city's rat race, including its concrete jungle and high cost; pursuing simplified living; and connecting or reconnecting with the land. This affinity to the dirt is often generational with some family farms or plots.

There are reasons that the Homesteader approach is most acceptable to left-of-center ideologies. One is the motivating factor of a belief in climate change.[136] There is a more than fifty-point percentage gap in America between Democrats and Republicans on this topic. In 2022, 78 percent of the first group agreed with the statement that "global climate change is a major threat to the country," whereas only 23 percent of the latter did. This divide is up more than fifteen points since 2010.[137]

A second reason is some Homesteader variants exist in population-dense settings where left-of-center demographics are more prominent.[138]

One example is urban homesteading, "a sustainable lifestyle movement that promotes household self-provisioning practices such as gardening, foraging, chicken and beekeeping, and food preservation."[139]

Dr. Anna Bounds wrote extensively on urban homesteaders in New York City and their successes and challenges due to COVID-19. She found a general feeling of government failure was pervasive in her interviews.[140] Dr. Ashley Colby found Homesteaders in Chicago were varied in motivations—fear of disaster, government incompetence, health, and a lack of corporate standards in food quality.[141] Urban gardens are often multiracial spaces—and ideologically varied—especially in the larger cities, and share food security concerns, which overlap with those of Resilient Citizens and Regulars.[142]

Among Homesteaders, there is also a strong sense of community, a trait shared with many of the other Resilient Citizen subtypes. In her ethnography, Martha James found that every individual she interviewed stated something to the effect that "they knew their neighbors in their off-grid neighborhood far better than they ever did living on the grid."[143] Perhaps when we integrate more with the land and take on a localized mindset, it encourages deeper interpersonal relationships.

Off-grid, tiny home, and cottagecore practitioners overlie some routines and beliefs with Homesteaders. They may share the aesthetics of the "tinkering" do-it-yourself culture.[144] Others focus on—or tie in—reduction in their carbon footprint or need for municipal services. The Canadian documentary *Life Off Grid* featured Lasqueti Island residents in British Columbia, who are disconnected from electric transmission lines or city plumbing and rely on assorted self-supplied power and water.[145]

With such a cornucopia of practices and diverse characteristics, where does one draw the division lines?

Those lines are blurry.

Take the nation's homeless, for example. While "off-grid," the homeless do not meet criterion one for thirty-one or more days of survival.

The same could be true for home gardeners, community gardeners, or urban foragers. While their hobbies are common to many Homesteaders, they cannot be considered Resilient Citizens without meeting the thirty-one-day criterion.

The Amish satisfy criterion one but do not live that lifestyle in anticipation of, or in mitigation of, a looming disaster, which is the requirement for criterion two. So, as a group, they are not Homesteaders.

In an analogous vein, certain indigenous groups such as Alaskan Natives, Middle Eastern Bedouins, and Kenyan pastoralists are living a lifestyle that provides them with thirty-one days or more of supplies while on the land, but it is derived from cultural and ethnic practices, not doomsday motivations. So they would not as a collective body be considered Resilient Citizens either.

And for criterion three, even though Ted Kaczynski, the Unabomber, lived off-grid in Montana and did so from anti-government motivations, he fails the creed test due to his support for terrorism.

There is, however, a group of Resilient Citizens who view risks of both government excess and absence of government as central to their motivations while still meeting all three criteria. They are Sentinels, which we will examine next.

CHAPTER 6

THE SENTINELS

The world is a dangerous place to live; not because of the people who are evil, but because of the people who don't do anything about it.

—Albert Einstein

Civilization begins with order, grows with liberty, and dies with chaos.

—Will Durant

Due to such shows as *Doomsday Preppers* and both Dominant and Challenger portrayals, Sentinels are the most common depiction of preppers in the popular imagination. Many own land, hunt, fish, or backyard garden. Some might appear to be Homesteaders or pair with the Homesteader motivation at first glance. But what separates Sentinels is their *primary* motivation: disasters caused by the government. Sentinels are the Goldilocks of the Resilient Citizen world. They are motivated by both porridge being too hot (that is, governments of tyranny, subjugation, war, or genocide) and porridge being too cold (that is, too little government, a scenario known as WROL [Without Rule of Law], in which society can quickly break down and lead to anarchy). In both cases, personal, household, and community security and survival become paramount.

JANIE'S GOT A GUN

Examples of porridge that is too hot are legion. War drums have been beaten since we first banded together in tribes. The Old Testament is littered with battles. The Great Wall of China was built to ward off foreign attackers—not lawn care solicitors or cookie-selling Girl Scouts. Various peoples across the globe have followed feelings of patriotism, religious fervor, bloodlust, dreams of riches, or state compulsion by impressments or drafts to conquer, rape, enslave, and loot.

Borders are not force fields, and walls can be breached—just ask the Thebans, Romans, Greeks, Carthaginians, Prussians, Polish, Austrians, French, Japanese, Vietnamese, Afghans, Yezidis, and Ukrainians. Even Washington, DC, was burned in the War of 1812 by invading Canadian and British forces.

A 2024 survey of Americans found 61 percent believed a world war would occur in the next five to ten years, and two-thirds thought nuclear weapons would be used. More than 10 percent thought America would *lose* this conflict, and a comparable survey in the United Kingdom found 21 percent of Brits thought Western nations would not be triumphant![146] Taiwan, China, Ukraine, Russia, Israel, and Iran have been multiyear nuclear and conventional weapons flashpoints. South Korea broke a six-year hiatus and reintroduced national civil defense drills in 2023 based on new "provocations" by North Korea.[147]

While some national and military leaders attempt to follow an ethical code of conduct such as the just war theory, other clashes have been for sport, pride, or sheer pugnacity. Yet winners, as they say, write history books. Countries and cultures enshrine their victors such as Xerxes, Alexander the Great, Genghis Khan, Napoleon, George Washington, Mao Zedong, and General George S. Patton. We teach their battles in schools and military institutes. We celebrate veterans in parades and on national holidays. America has had five Medal of Honor recipients aged nineteen and under. The youngest, eleven-year-old drummer boy William Johnston, served in the Civil War.

Sometimes the government, just like with Homesteaders and victory gardens, encourages or enshrines into law Sentinel-promoting behavior: *Si vis pacem, para bellum* (Latin for, "If you want peace, prepare for war.") Finland, Norway, Sweden, and Latvia all have a belligerent neighboring country in Russia, so their leaders are keen on maintaining a reserve force that is proficient in firearms and basic military maneuvers. During my deployments to Iraq, adult Iraqi males were authorized to possess one AK-47 at home. Switzerland mandates that healthy eighteen- to thirty-four-year-olds who have completed military training keep an assault rifle in their domicile. Consequently, the Swiss have one of the highest rates of gun ownership and exceptionally low firearm crime. The October 7, 2023, massacre by Hamas in Israel radically loosened gun rights laws in Israel. Israeli officials were approving upward of three thousand personal firearm requests per day after emergency legislation was passed.[148]

Of course, no country on earth comes close to the gun ownership levels of America. We are the only country to have more firearms than people.[149] However, *unlike* other countries, the US Constitution reasoned that these weapons were not primarily for hunting, household protection, or invasion resistance but for *countering the government itself.*

Our Founders feared the same type of government tyranny they had just fought to overthrow. In response, they created a federal republic and empowered the citizenry with the means of lethal resistance. Thankfully, America has had only one civil war and has never industrialized the slaughter of its own citizens. The same cannot be said for the Killing Fields of Cambodia; the liquidation of the Jews, gypsies, and other "undesirables" of Europe in the 1930s and 1940s; ISIS captives; Soviets under Lenin and Stalin; Chinese under Mao in the Great Leap Forward; and Uighurs today. After tallying the deaths due to wars and state-sanctioned internal slaughter, only disease has killed more people in human history.

PANIC EARLY, AVOID THE RUSH

Situations where porridge is too cold are Without Rule of Law (WROL) events that happen when the local or national government cannot or will not provide adequate security. Modern Sentinels, therefore, prepare for these events by owning and practicing with firearms.

Martial defense is their *primary* mechanism to achieve a state of physical and mental security. Sentinels are gun owners, and many prefer to live in areas with a prominent pro-gun culture. Often, these are rural areas where individuals can come together to achieve collective security.[150] While prevention of crime, such as home invasion, is an additional benefit, Sentinels are not primarily preparing for a one-off burglary attempt but rather for a sustained breakdown in the social order.

David and Abigail are a couple in their mid-thirties who work remotely in the software industry. They live in East Texas with their two small children. This couple has focused on firearms training, growing their own food, making their own repairs, having backup power sources, and enhancing security on their home in anticipation of a WROL event. Abigail explains:

> Similarly to how you hold a basket of assets that covers a variety of potential outcomes for the market—within a normal market future, index funds handle most of this for you—I believe in covering a variety of outcomes for civilization broadly. However, this has to include "everything continues on as normal," so the question is a combination of the following: What is the rough distribution of outcomes I think is likely? Is it 80 percent things continue on as usual within my time horizon, 10 percent of civil unrest ("troubles"), and 10 percent of very clear logistics decline? What is the minimum buy-in to prepare for different specific scenarios? Let's say I think there's a 10 percent chance of civil unrest within thirty years. Do I only put 10 percent of my assets towards that, or is it more due to the fact there's more potential downside?[151]

From the outside, David and Abigail seem like a relatively normal young family living in a suburban neighborhood. But they are thinking in a very measured way about potentialities and how to protect themselves in these unlikely, but possible, scenarios.

The Sentinel is a well-known brand of Resilient Citizen. Weapons are popularized and promoted in multiple television and movie accounts in the disaster genre. If the whole of society collapses, the fear is a return to the Wild West. Fictional disaster books such as *The Patriots* by prepper James Wesley Rawles describe a world after a devastating economic collapse when a band of highly armed friends must resist marauders and an illegitimate government's military incursion. In other movies and forums, zombies often substitute for the feared "others."

But even less extraordinary events can trigger this anxiety. Hurricane Katrina was a WROL event. Fifteen percent of the New Orleans Police Department—more than two hundred officers—deserted their posts in the aftermath and fifty-one were later fired for this.[152] The 2020 national riots that began in conjunction with the death of George Floyd while in police custody are related to—and therefore stoked fears of—WROL events. The United States Federal Bureau of Investigation (FBI) statistics indicate 2020 witnessed a 29.4 percent increase in murder and nonnegligent manslaughter.[153]

A well-known representative of the Sentinel is bestselling author Tucker Max. Tucker, most famous for writing about his sexual exploits in the fratire genre, has made a recent post-pandemic turn toward homesteading and preparedness. Now a devoted father of four, he spends a significant portion of his time setting up his property just outside of Austin, Texas, to be ready for myriad perils. Tucker had a major turning point during the 2020 Black Lives Matter protests:

> I was totally on board with the concept behind the Black Lives Matter movement. And I'm still on board with that concept, but f--- the evil Marxist clowns that run that organization, which is a very different thing. But then it turned into riots. Sure, there were some genuine, peaceful protests. But many others were

> outright riots, often planned and executed by domestic terror organizations like Antifa (yes, they are literal domestic terrorists). That's when my Special Forces buddies started raising red flags. Their message was clear: Coordinated psychological operations (psyops) were taking place here in the US, run against the US populace.[154]

One of Tucker's "Special Forces buddies" is Clay Martin, author of the prepper book *Prairie Fire,* which is much in line with James Wesley Rawles's writing. I have noticed authors of prepper books that deeply comment on guns are almost exclusively former military. Optimistically, it is our training and desire to warn and protect. Pessimistically, we see a dark future.

By 2021, Tucker was deep in research and fully convinced that the United States was on the precipice of rising inflation, supply chain issues, and widespread social breakdown. One aspect of his plan for a WROL situation includes self-defense. This includes not only training to use a gun under pressure but also physical fitness, knife skills, unarmed combat, home defense, and—for him most importantly—surrounding his family with the right community.[155]

Americans' trend of panic-buying guns is more fact than stereotype. An all-time high of 3.9 million FBI firearm background checks were initiated in July 2020 as civil unrest began. Before this, the onset of COVID-19 contributed to the 3.7 million background checks in March 2020. That month broke the previous record by more than 700,000.[156] Kareem Shaya says the "common thread is just uncertainty."[157] That is precisely what ontological security would predict.

These purchases were not just among Whites, men, Republicans, or previous gun owners. First-time buyer purchases were up nearly 70 percent from their two-decade average. Black American purchases were up nearly 60 percent, and female purchases were up 40 percent compared to 2019. There were also increases in sales to liberals and Democrats.[158]

The National African American Gun Association (NAAGA) reported that ten thousand people joined its roster in 2020 alone and that there was an "explosion in the number of black gun owners nationwide."[159] This followed large purchases of weapons by Asians at the beginning of the COVID-19 pandemic.[160] Calls to defund or abolish police forces across the nation, the saga of Kyle Rittenhouse, and the multiweek existence of the Capitol Hill Autonomous Zone (CHAZ) in Seattle fueled Sentinels' calculations that cities at best, or America at worst, were headed toward internal violence and strife.

While the jump in firearm acquisitions does not directly predict a rise in Resilient Citizens, this along with the combination of urban flight to less dense areas could open doors to positive experiences via social interactions at gun ranges or hunting excursions. The trend is bipartisan. Even before the turbulence of 2020, left-of-center preppers were arming up, but many kept quiet about it.[161] One concealed carry instructor at the time noted that he had received calls from unexpected sources asking him for private training because "they don't want anyone to know they're doing the training, let alone going to buy a firearm," adding that "I have seen the emergence of a new class of students seeking training: anti-Second Amendment liberals."[162] Liberal purchases of guns do not seem to be a fluke, but their secrecy, due to fear of scorn, mimics that of many preppers.

Several parallels exist. After the 2016 Orlando Pulse nightclub mass shooting, Pink Pistols, an LGBT pro-gun organization, saw its membership quintuple and—against liberal sensibilities—many have found more acceptance on gun ranges for their self-protection choices than for their gun ownership among their LGBT community.[163] Academics in criminal justice have linked victimization of crime—both actual and potential—to be a driving force for higher gun ownership rates.[164]

ENEMIES AT THE GATE

Two special types of fear combine to motivate Sentinels. The first is a concept referred to as anarcho-tyranny. At its core, anarcho-tyranny is when the state chooses *not* to protect you but does not allow you to protect yourself—and may even punish you for doing so. British police arresting and imprisoning people who make memes or call for the deportation of immigrant criminals, while at the same time ignoring foreign rape gangs, would be one example.[165] Punishing European women for carrying pepper spray to protect themselves from various crimes would be another. Prosecutorial discretion or governmental edicts that apply ideology over judicial neutrality, such as declaring some people *rioters* while others merely *protesters,* or picking winners and losers of which businesses could be open during COVID-19, are all additional examples. The justness or unjustness of these instances has a heavy ideological tilt.

The second type of fear motivating Sentinels is the threat of revolutions or civil war. In these circumstances, the rule of law can be eroded or replaced quickly, and at the same time, the heavy hand of the state or a rebel leader can crack down. The American Civil War divided the nation in short order. The Yugoslav Wars of the 1990s fractured Yugoslavia into six countries. Peacekeepers, some from the United States, are still in Kosovo as of 2025.

Mao Zedong once said, "Revolutionary war is an antitoxin which not only eliminates the enemy's poison but also purges us of our own filth."[166] Being on the wrong side can be hazardous to your health and liberties. Women in Iran after the 1979 revolution went from dressing like Westerners to wearing hijabs. Afghan women have it far worse now that the Taliban is back in power in that country.

The Bolshevik Revolution of 1921 saw torture and rape with fifteen million dead, most from famine and disease. The Mexican Revolution that began in 1910 and partially included a war against the Catholic Church saw over a million dead, half from starvation.[167] One of the more infamous examples is the French Revolution. After Louis XVI lost his head, many of his usurpers also faced a date with the "national razor." We get the terms *reign of terror* and *Thermidorian Reaction* from this historical series of events used to describe waves of reprisal killings, many sanctioned by the state. The chaos lasted for a decade and did not end until Napoleon became the ruler of France. Food insecurity was both a cause and an outcome of the French Revolution. Again, disasters often travel in packs.

Change can happen in an instant. President Trump had at least two assassination attempts against him in a matter of months during his 2024 campaign. In December 2024, the stalwart democracy of South Korea saw its president declare martial law to avoid political impeachment. Two senior police officers and the country's defense minister were arrested shortly thereafter, and the latter attempted suicide while in custody.[168]

I think much of the angst among Resilient Citizens and especially Sentinels comes down to issues of trust. A Rasmussen poll in 2014 found 54 percent of Americans "consider the federal government today a threat to individual liberty rather than a protector," a jump of 8 percent in just two years.[169] By 2021, the number had increased to 58 percent.[170]

Americans' anxiety about their government existed even pre-COVID-19. More than three-quarters of Americans stated their greatest fear is "corrupt government officials" at 77.2 percent in 2019. The government has been the top fear *for four years in a row*, rising 17 percent over that period and is 10–20 percent higher than the next greatest worry.[171]

The Economist reported in 2024 that America was trending downward for trust in national institutions as compared to other G7 countries. From 2006 to 2023, the United States went from tied for first place to dead last.[172]

The same magazine a month later wondered, "Is America Dictator-proof?"[173] A 2021 survey in America found 53 percent of voters believed "democracy in America will end in the next generation or so," with election integrity being a major concern.[174] Internationally, a 2023 survey of thirty countries found just 57 percent of those aged eighteen to thirty-five "felt democracy was preferable to any other form of government," with 42 percent of this cohort saying "they were supportive of military rule."

Experts across the globe report "erosion of social cohesion and societal polarisation" is rising as a chief concern.[175] Affronts to freedom and overall dread regarding government seem to be increasing as well. Hong Kong has been all but subsumed into China. The "one country, two systems" principle is practically erased. German courts repeatedly overruled the country's illegal COVID-19 lockdown edicts, and *Die Welt* found "the Interior Ministry hired scientists from the Robert Koch Institute and several universities to justify the country's strict lockdown measures."[176] That country had discussed putting quarantine breakers in detention centers, much like Australia had done.[177] In the US, a Democrat official suggested putting Trump voters in re-education camps,[178] and a Public Broadcasting System lawyer opined taking the children of Republicans for the same purposes.[179] Several academics warned that COVID-19 was pushing democracies closer to authoritarianism with mandatory surveillance and other tactics that are massive denials of basic human rights.[180]

Internationally, Europe's migration and terror crises, the latter of which is disproportionately a result of migrant criminal attacks, have pushed many citizens to stock up on guns, pepper spray, or stun guns. Firearm permits nearly doubled in Germany over two years from 2016 to 2017, primarily due to safety fears regarding "foreigners and refugees." Worries of violence from neo-Nazis or right-wing extremists were a far-distant concern.[181]

Not every person with a shotgun or a concealed carry permit is a Resilient Citizen Sentinel. But the types of people my taxonomic criteria do eliminate are state actors such as the National Guard, which, as a group, prepares for various scenarios where weapons are required. While in their official capacity these guardsmen are not Resilient Citizens, they are more likely to be prepared for disaster in their households.[182] Others that would be removed are groups such as militant separatists arming for a race war such as the Aryan Nation or the Black paramilitary group NFAC (Not Fu----g Around Coalition). Greater international research on individuals who meet the Sentinel criteria is ripe for further study.

From antiquity to the modern day, people's very lives have been threatened by neighbors, strangers, governments, and warring tribes or countries. Individual self-defense has always been one of the tools for counteracting this. Disarmament often precedes abuse or an abrogation of natural rights. This truth is the basis of the US Constitution's Second Amendment. In *Blackstone's Commentaries,* St. George Tucker famously wrote:

> This may be considered as the true palladium of liberty. . . . The right of self defence is the first law of nature: in most governments it has been the study of rulers to confine this right within the narrowest limits possible. Wherever standing armies are kept up, and the right of the people to keep and bear arms is, under any colour or pretext whatsoever, prohibited, liberty, if not already annihilated, is on the brink of destruction.[183]

Sentinels are fully justified in their underlying fears and mitigating actions. History showcases this, and our modern day reinforces the benefits of self-defense. And yet there is another way to achieve security, not as a stand-alone but as a stand *together*. This is the path of the Interdependent.

CHAPTER 7

THE INTERDEPENDENT

Though one may be overpowered,
two can defend themselves.
A cord of three strands is not quickly broken.
—Ecclesiastes 4:12 (NIV)

That men do not learn very much from the lessons of history is the most important of all the lessons that history has to teach.
—Aldous Huxley

If Homesteaders could be pithily summed up, they would be the food and health group. Sentinels would be the conflict and physical security crowd. Interdependent Resilient Citizens, by contrast, are the hardest to describe with any one collective adjective, as they are incredibly diverse.

Interdependent is defined by *Merriam-Webster* dictionary as "dependent upon one another: mutually dependent."[184] Synonyms come close to describing the genre: *synergistic, reciprocal, joined, complementary,* and *cooperative.*

Neither *communal* nor *neighborly* quite fit either . . . but they come a bit closer.

What primarily drives these individuals is not a *singular* low-probability, high-consequence disaster but rather *any* peril, big or small, that threatens the local area in which they live or an event that requires their skill sets in response. This is the concept of *generalized resilience* and gives this group an edge when it comes to polycrisis, as they recognize points of commonality and diversity in various hazards and are flexible in their response. Since smaller disasters are far more frequent, the Interdependent are, on average, more proficient and flexible. While they tend to lean toward preparing for natural disasters, they are the jack-of-all-trades and the neighbors you hope to have.

YOUR FRIENDLY NEIGHBORHOOD RESILIENT CITIZEN

Interdependent Resilient Citizens have two massive advantages in their column. First, they are not lone wolves but look to protect the pack. Their first similarity is a *community orientation,* and therefore they tend to have high trait overlap with libertarians and proponents of localism and/or small government. Their presence belies the argument that all preppers are insular and care only about their own protection. In some areas of the world, their actions are nearly indistinguishable from cultural, indigenous practices. The Interdependent often have strong roots where they live and can, therefore, call on decades—or even generations—of local lore, experience, and connections.

The second common trait is *antifragility*. When perils are personally experienced or befall others, these Resilient Citizens use them as training exercises or teachable moments. They also seem to harmonize these aspects into an infectious synergism that can become a cultural norm, balancing variables like an ecologist would for a healthy ecosystem and prioritizing sustainability over short-term gains. Intertwined with this—and their predilection for the community—is a predisposition to think long-term.

YOU SCRATCH MY BACK...

Jonathan Rawles is a young man living in the American West with his wife and young children. Jonathan is the son of James Wesley Rawles, whom I referenced in the previous chapter. Jonathan runs a survival real estate business, a company that focuses on selling homes and properties with preparedness enhanced amenities such as bunkers, off-grid power and water, food- and fuel-production capabilities (gardens, livestock, woodlands), and has written a book titled *Survival Retreats and Relocation* with his father. While Jonathan characterizes his dad as more of an "old school nuclear war collapse of civilization type prepper," he sees himself more focused on self-reliance, which he thinks of as a better term to describe his approach than the word *prepper*. Where his father's books often focus on a rapid and sudden collapse, Jonathan is more convinced that the reality is more like "a multitude of smaller collapses that happen on a daily basis." Ultimately, his approach ends up "being a question of being prepared to handle the catastrophes that come our way whether it's a personal one—illness or losing your job—or the long-term degradation of our society, natural disaster, or societal collapse."[185]

Together with his realty business and his community orientation, Jonathan's focus is on interdependence as preparedness. A central hub for community-making for Jonathan and his young family is their church, as he describes:

> We're members of a congregation here of about four hundred people. About half of those are under the age of eighteen. So, we're very child-friendly. We don't do children's church or separate nurseries, so it's a big crowd of adults and children and babies, and it's a fun time on Sunday mornings. I'm very optimistic in seeing the young people that are growing up in this community and knowing that there's, you know, many communities like this nationwide, just in our own little, tiny sliver of Christendom as it were.

Many members of the Rawles's church were brought to this location with preparedness and survival in mind, and they are intentionally building out a network in this area of other self-reliant families who share their values.

Larger Interdependent-minded prepper groups tend to come and go, and three years after COVID-19, most seem to have disappeared in the United States. But their fleeting existence still provides insights. The Zombie Squad, a prepper club from Missouri, was a representative typecast. Professor Chad Huddleston's research on this team denoted several participants as valuable members of society. Like the Zombie Squad, some work hand in hand with police, first responders, and disaster groups such as the Red Cross or Citizen Emergency Response Teams (CERTs).[186] Groups like the New York City Prepper's Network (NYCPN) or the Urban and Outdoor Survival Club practiced uniting together to increase resiliency within the team or to help others.[187] Among the unaffiliated, many members of the spontaneous Cajun Navy that pop up after natural disasters in the US could be part of this species as well as several residents of Hong Kong before the Chinese takeover.[188, 189]

The Interdependent seem to have the largest collection of vocal advocates who are public about their activities, contrary to the secrecy seen in other groups. Jason Charles, founder of the NYCPN, was often interviewed by national media outlets such as *The New York Times*. Their presence is also related—at least tangentially—to community resilience measures and activities.[190] That is, strong, socially bonded towns and neighborhoods are sturdy in multiple facets, including disaster preparedness. Their philosophy is that you are only as good as your weakest link. So raising your neighbors' level of resilience is a mixture of altruism and self-protection.

Public involvement in disaster preparedness might be one of the best ways to inculcate a spirit of togetherness. In a fascinating study, researchers brought together members of the local populace for a disaster tabletop exercise, a scenario-based operation common for planners from the local to the national level. Rather than beginning with a catastrophe, though, the researchers started by having people list community assets, things worthy of protection.[191] Instead of focusing on vulnerability, the members present were guided to look at their town's assets and strengths. Whether or not these exercises led to increased personal preparedness was not examined, but it is this same spirit that motivates the Interdependent.

SOME BAD IS GOOD

The second trait of the Interdependent is their *antifragility*. This is a term coined by Nassim Taleb, a former instructor of mine and a risk analysis expert.[192] Antifragility treats small- and medium-size shocks as growth opportunities, much like running or lifting weights causes small muscle tears and fatigue in the short term for overall positive gains in the long term.[193]

How does this apply to disaster prepping? A fascinating reality regarding many—but not all—disasters is their scalability and resemblance to one another. So a generalized resilience gained from preparing for *some* disasters helps us adapt to a multitude of *other* disasters.

Fires, floods, wars, epidemics, asteroids, earthquakes, and several other perils follow mathematical distribution laws. In your own life, you've probably suffered far more cuts and bruises than broken bones or amputations. Because of this, you have probably acquired heavy proficiency in using Band-Aids, hydrogen peroxide, and antiseptic creams but probably have lower proficiency in applying a tourniquet or splinting a fracture. However, if you view first aid and medical treatment as a continuum, you may be inspired to raise your abilities in the latter tasks after mastering the former, maybe even progressing so far as becoming certified as an emergency medical technician. Why? Because the best way to master a skill is to practice and teach it.

While generalized resilience is critical in disaster prep, both Nassim and I offer two points of caution. First, experience and built-up resilience to small and medium perils can improve your odds, but it will not make you invincible. A lightning strike or megaquake could end your existence regardless of whether you have an orchard in your backyard and a year's supply of antibiotics. However, broadly exercised, it does make your society more durable. Second, you don't get much choice on the order in which you experience perils or their frequency. The "big one" could hit early on near the starting line, or a series of misfortunes could come back-to-back. Life isn't fair, but you can enhance your chances for success.

Let's use the danger of house fires as an example to illustrate the power of antifragility among the Interdependent. You may be surprised to hear that the American Red Cross does not spend the bulk of its time reacting to larger scale events such as hurricanes or flooding. Of the roughly sixty thousand disasters they respond to in any given year, upward of 93 percent are isolated house fires.[194] By their metrics, home fires kill more Americans in an average year than all other natural disasters combined. Kitchen fires lead to an annual average of 170,000 visits by fire departments and $1 billion in damage.[195] When I was attending an American Red Cross workshop in New England, I was told by a representative that more than 80 percent of that office's disaster calls were for these emergencies.

The Interdependent do not root for these events to happen, but they do prepare for them. To react to a home fire, you need to know the difference among classes. Class A fires are solids based (e.g., wood, paper) and are best countered with water, foam, or powder-based extinguishers. On the contrary, a grease fire in your kitchen is a Class F or Class K and would be made worse by using a water-based extinguisher. Cooking oils are best put out with a wet chemical extinguisher. Scaling up, if your home were to catch fire, do you have an evacuation plan for everyone in the family? A rally point? Do you have an idea of what items you would save if you had time, such as birth certificates, your marriage license, a copy of your will, and a backup external hard drive with all your financial information and treasured photos?

This is how the Interdependent think, and they will be the first to your door when you face a crisis if one is your neighbor. Anecdotally, one of the common places to find these Resilient Citizens is at local volunteer fire departments, search-and-rescue clubs, and as members of the National Guard or in CERTs.[196] Other organizations such as Team Rubicon, the Red Cross, and like-minded disaster associations are prime hunting grounds, just like 4-H is for Homesteaders.

Now, let me scale up the peril of fire again. Wildfire severity, in terms of area burned, has shown a modest increase of just over 5 percent from 2021 to 2023 globally.[197] In the United States from 1999 to 2020, 65 percent of all acreage burned was caused by lightning strikes and resulted in no damage to buildings. However, when looking solely at fires that did burn buildings, total acreage from human causation is up over 50 percent when comparing decadal averages. The researchers found that, as a result, "of all the wildfires that destroy structures in the West, human-caused events typically destroy over 10 times more structures for every square mile burned, compared to lighting-caused [*sic*] events."[198]

These episodes can be incredibly costly, both in terms of property loss and lives. As I write this, the initial estimates of the damage caused by the 2025 Los Angeles wildfires are more than $250 billion. Wildfires sparked most likely by power lines in California in 2019 were so bad that the owning company, Pacific Gas & Electric, filed for bankruptcy after agreeing to pay $11 billion in claims.[199] According to the official report, the Maui wildfires of 2023, including the town of Lahaina, took the lives of 101 people and caused more than $6 billion in damages. Contributing to the severity were high winds, poor land use practices that created tinderbox grass fuels that were "crunching" under the feet of firefighters, and limited egress options for those in the fire's path.[200] The report noted that "generally, wildfire risks are greatly undervalued by the public and policy makers" and that "a challenge exists in the willingness of the public and policymakers to proactively address and finance wildfire actions upfront in preparation, mitigation and response, as opposed to dealing with the recovery costs and impacts of wildfires later on."

This apathy drives the Interdependent crazy.

How would things be different if societies adopted the Interdependent way of thinking? Knowing household basics for fires and at-home egress scales up to community efforts of preparedness, mitigation, and response via building codes, density restrictions, and societal norms.

Japan gives an exemplar of what communal response at scale looks like for volcanic threats and other perils. The Japanese, as a collective, embrace both community and antifragility. They need to. By one measure, Japan has more earthquakes than any other country in the world.[201] It is also subject to typhoons, tsunamis, threatening neighbors, and a multidecade debt problem. And while Mount Fuji is just forty miles from the suburbs of Tokyo, the most active volcano in Japan is Sakurajima, located just ten miles from the city center of Kagoshima, a city of nearly six hundred thousand people.

Before 2006, ashfall and ballistic debris landed on the citizens of Kagoshima about once every three days. From 2009 to 2015, the volcano was far more active and erupted 450–1,000 times per year![202] Therefore, the people have "building codes, ash removal practices and community attitudes and preparedness to facilitate continuity of societal functions during periodic volcanic episodes."[203] A combination of social norms and messaging from city administrators keeps protective action measures above 90 percent compliance, with residents asking for more information from these officials and the Japanese Meteorological Agency.[204]

Japan's capital is home to the Tokyo Rinkai Disaster Prevention Park, a center that serves a dual purpose of educating civilians and acting as a base of operations in catastrophes. Nationally, the first of September is Disaster Prevention Day, and participants range from everyday citizens to national leaders. The Japanese Self-Defense Forces also conduct large-scale drills at other times. I was fortunate enough to be personally invited to one of these drills by Japan's top military officer, General Koji Yamazaki, in 2022. I observed a professional military force absolutely dedicated to saving lives; it was all-in on disaster preparedness for the survival of the community.

Returning to America, another well-known example of an Interdependent might be Wendell Berry, a famous writer and farmer who focuses on local knowledge and power. Berry is most well known for his work on agricultural systems. His seminal work is titled *The Unsettling of America: Culture and Agriculture,* so you might think he would fit into the Homesteader category. However, the main thrust of his work is a commitment to place and people as a form of resistance and resilience. In one of Berry's most famous poems, "Manifesto: The Mad Farmer Liberation Front," he states the case for what he thinks are the worst aspects of modern life:

> Love the quick profit, the annual raise, vacation with pay. Want more of everything ready-made. Be afraid to know your neighbors and to die... Your mind will be punched in a card and shut away in a little drawer. When they want you to buy something they will call you. When they want you to die for profit they will let you know.[205]

Berry is sharp in his critique here of atomization, government, and corporate profit to the point that the population is seen as automatons meant to create profit at their own expense.

The alternative to this bleak vision, for Berry, is a kind of dualistic expectation of the end of the world and living in joy and interdependence with nature and community despite this:

> Put your faith in the two inches of humus that will build under the trees every thousand years... Expect the end of the world. Laugh. Laughter is immeasurable. Be joyful though you have considered all the facts. ... Ask yourself: Will this satisfy a woman satisfied to bear a child? Will this disturb the sleep of a woman near to giving birth?[206]

The power of Berry's observation on the duality of community and nature cannot be overstated. A healthy society integrates the people with its environment at a sustainable, local scale.

PLENTY TO WORRY ABOUT IN YOUR BACKYARD

Just like politics, all perils are local. Few places on Earth are at a low risk for natural disasters. We tend to comingle with threats by necessity and then adapt to our circumstances. Counting just natural hazards alone, the World Bank estimated 13 percent of the global population lives in a country with "high exposure to two or more hazards." Guatemala, the Philippines, and Ecuador had five each, and Taiwan, Chile, Costa Rica, and Japan had four.[207] In the United States, the Hazards Vulnerability and Resilience Institute at the University of South Carolina estimated in 2006 that 91 percent of all Americans lived in an area of moderate-to-high risk of at least one type of disaster such as an earthquake, tornado, volcano, or terrorist attack.[208] Worldwide, more than four hundred volcanoes are within one hundred kilometers of locales with more than a million inhabitants.[209] Seattle, Portland, Naples, Auckland, and Manila all sit in the shadow of destruction.

The Interdependent approach of community involvement and antifragility localizes these perils. With limited time and assets, it is better to prioritize threats that have higher probabilities. Some societies deal with them far better than others. Here are a few examples of hazards that have a major geographical correlation:

- In Australia, the collection of 2019–2020 "Black Summer" fires burned forty-six million acres, an area of devastation larger than the country of South Korea.[210] Dr. Bradley Garrett's research found fire figures prominently in the minds of Australian preppers.
- The Dutch have been fighting back the sea for centuries with dikes and dams. In contrast, Polynesians embrace the ocean,

drawing on it for sustenance and trade even in the face of tsunamis and typhoons.

- The year 2019 was an anomalous year for tornadoes in the United States. Five hundred tornadoes struck in a thirty-day period with a reported twelve consecutive days "of eight or more tornadoes."[211] Tornado Alley in the Midwest lives up to the hype, and some homes have basements or a reinforced interior room for just such an event.
- New England is no stranger to major winter storms. The Great Blizzard of 1888 dropped five feet of snow on New York, created drifts up to fifty feet high, impacted 25 percent of all Americans, and caused four hundred deaths. Half of the dead were in New York City and died from exposure—or burial—on the cold sidewalks. Many of the deaths outside the city were from those who disembarked trains stuck in the snow.[212] The threat of this peril drove much of the development of underground subways in that city.

And what about earthquakes, a persistent and deadly danger that looms over many, many parts of the world? Fifty-seven thousand people lost their lives in the February 6, 2023, earthquake that struck Turkey and Syria, and eighteen million people were impacted.[213] A year later, although officials provided more than two hundred thousand temporary homes, many families still lived in tents and blamed national and local governments for slow recovery efforts.[214]

America may not fare much better in the face of such a disaster. If a megaquake happened in Southern California, seventy thousand troops would be required to maintain order and provide an effective response.[215]

The Cascadia Subduction Zone off the western coast of Canada and America is of specific concern to scientists and disaster experts alike. The former FEMA region director for that area stated his "operating assumption is that everything west of Interstate 5 will be toast" in the event of a megaquake.[216] The 2013 Oregon Resilience Plan, a report to the 77th Legislative Assembly and written by the Oregon Seismic Safety Policy Advisory Commission, also portends a gloomy outlook. It assumes we'd have between one to ten thousand casualties and tens of thousands of damaged buildings in Oregon alone from a 9.0 quake and tsunami.[217] Recovery costs are estimated to be 20 percent of Oregon's GDP. Inland restorations to electricity, drinking water, and health care are measured in months and coastal repairs in years. The commission emphatically states, "Citizens, too, need to plan to be self-sufficient for far longer than the 72 hours commonly advised for disaster preparedness."[218] The impetus to create the report was, not surprisingly, the 2011 9.0 Tohoku earthquake in Japan.

The Interdependent are not opposed to specialization *within the community*. They realize that some places, such as California, face high risk from several perils. An earthquake as small as 6.5 in the Sacramento–San Joaquin River Delta could destroy six hundred miles of levees, wiping out nearly half of America's fruit and vegetable harvest and taking over a year to repair.[219]

The year 2020 brought a new term into the American disaster lexicon: gigafire. The 2020 August Complex fire in California burned more than one million acres, a landmass the size of Rhode Island.[220]

In contrast, weather patterns in the Pacific Coast cause a phenomenon called an "atmospheric river." The National Oceanic and Atmospheric Administration's (NOAA) Aircraft Operations Center conducts sorties off the coast to measure these events. When I visited their headquarters, they told me these atmospheric floating waterways can contain as much moisture as the Missouri River, and NOAA's job is to run measurements to predict if the state needs to release water from its reservoirs in anticipation of a coming deluge. This is no small threat. One of California's worst events was the flood of 1861–1862, which left portions of Central Valley under thirty feet of water. In 2008, a sophisticated model called the ARkStorm simulation predicted events like this would occur every one to two hundred years. Further analysis surmised a price tag of $1 trillion in damages if/when it happens again. This number was promptly ignored by several officials.[221] In 2022, ARkStorm 2.0 calculated a 50 percent chance we'll see a repeat of the 1861 flood by 2060 and that it would occur so quickly that the majority of the area's five to ten million inhabitants would not be able to escape in time.[222]

Something of this nature would be apocalyptic for a large swath of California residents. The Interdependent are not ignorant of such calamity, but neither are they fatalistic. Societies are robust... to a point. But what if we made the problem bigger—something national or even multinational in scale? It is these country killers that our next Resilient Citizens, the Noahs, fear.

CHAPTER 8

THE NOAHS

Destroy nine interconnection (transformer) substations and a transformer manufacturer and the entire United States grid would be down for at least 18 months, probably longer.

—Federal Energy Regulatory Commission

Var förberedd, inte rädd.
(Be prepared, not afraid.)

—A Swedish adage

The penultimate group of Resilient Citizens, the Noahs, have two things in common. First, they fear epochal events: nuclear war, an electromagnetic pulse, X-class solar flares, virulent pandemics, nation-destabilizing social unrest, and national collapse. Second, while they may own land like Homesteaders or own guns like Sentinels, they also own or have access to a bunker.

Bunkers aren't that uncommon among serious preppers, but to earn my Noah classification, these Resilient Citizens must "bunker up" as part of a community, even a small one. By contrast, other bunker owners can be seen as the antithesis of the Interdependent because they retreat to their fortified enclaves alone or with just their family rather than help the collective.

In some instances, this can be taken to radical, dystopian extremes. One author related his conversation with an extremely wealthy person, in which the man openly discussed his plan of bringing his compound guards—former Navy SEALs, no less—into his bunker with him if/when the need arose. He even considered outfitting each member of his private army with a sort of disciplinary collar—just in case the SEALs decided to revolt and take over the place![223]

ALL THAT'S MISSING IS THE MOAT AND DRAGON

Every category of Resilient Citizen can trace its lineage back hundreds if not thousands of years. Before backyard chickens and victory gardens, there were nomadic pastoralists and valleys full of hand-planted row crops. Before guns, there were swords and spears. Before bunkers, there were castles and fortresses.

Hohenwerfen Castle towers astride the Salzach Valley in Austria. It is flanked to the east by the Tennen Mountains and to the west by the Berchtesgaden Alps.[224] Hohenwerfen was built in AD 1075 to protect the city of Salzburg, roughly thirty miles to the north. It was garrisoned by military soldiers for much of its history. If you tour the grounds, there is a mural of a knight whose inscribed shield warns invading armies, "None shall pass unpunished."[225, 226]

Built around the same time and under the orders of the same man, Archbishop Gebhard, the companion castle of Hohenwerfen is Fortress Hohensalzburg in the town of Salzburg itself. Architecturally, the site was built to withstand a heavy siege, like many of its medieval equivalents. Fortifications boasted the latest heavy artillery on the bastions, and the eight-acre grounds contained a rainwater catchment that funneled precipitation into cisterns for the occupants.

Surprisingly, neither Hohenwerfen nor Hohensalzburg ever faced an external enemy in their nearly thousand-year history; however, both sites were attacked by citizens. The sixteenth century's German Peasants' War saw the commoners rise up against the ruling class across portions of modern-day Germany, Austria, and Switzerland. Although the peasants were crushed in the end, the people instilled fear in the aristocracy for a time. Portions of Hohenwerfen were set ablaze. In 1525, after three months of citizen blockade, Fortress Hohensalzburg began to run low on food. Down to their last cow, the garrison commander had an idea. One day, he marched the cow across the top of the battlements for all the angry commoners to see. The next day, he painted the same cow and marched it along the same route. As the story goes, the will of the attackers broke; they believed the fortress was well-provisioned for an extended period and soon abandoned their siege.[227]

Other strongholds and their denizens were not so lucky. In his outstanding book *The End of Everything: How Wars Descend into Annihilation,* Victor Davis Hanson traces how entire civilizations were decimated when their fortress fell. When the Romans sacked Carthage in 146 BC, it was the end of "seven hundred years of Punic civilization in Africa." In 1521 Spanish conquistador Hernán Cortés took a force of fewer than fifteen hundred troops, plus native allies, and obliterated the rulers of the four-million-strong Aztec Empire.[228]

The end—or cataclysmic altering—of societies is a common part of the historical record. Noahs fear such a societal fall happening again in their lifetime. That fear isn't entirely unreasonable. Despite our technological advances, our modern day is not immune. In fact, I can name three plausible catastrophes that Noahs could reasonably expect in the near future:

- Grid failure
- Economic collapse
- Nuclear war

Let's take a closer look at each one.

PLAUSIBLE CATASTROPHE #1: GRID FAILURE

One of the best locales to study large-scale calamities is to look at islands. Islanders can face systemic impacts from just a single event, one of near totality and no—or few—safe areas to flee to for the masses. Because of the magnitude of these disasters, the ability of the local and national governments is often completely overwhelmed. There are large-scale power outages, infrastructure damage, limited transportation avenues, and degraded communications. Based on the separation of hundreds, or even thousands of miles, help and recovery assets are not just physically distant but temporally distant as well.[229]

I saw firsthand the devastation that Hurricane Maria had wrought on Puerto Rico even six months post-landfall. Debris was still strewn on the sides of the roads, makeshift electrical connections were common, and several buildings were condemned but not yet demolished. Beyond the death toll of more than four thousand people and the $90 billion price tag,[230] Maria showed just how long recovery can take after a major peril. Just 17 percent of the country's 3.5 million residents had power a full month after Maria hit.[231] Although the governor had promised that 95 percent of the island's grid service would be back to normal by the three-month mark, not even half the island was covered by then.[232] It would take six months to restore nearly all water and cell service and eleven months before the entire power grid was restored.[233, 234]

But nothing like that could happen to a country as large as America, right? Wrong. William Forstchen's novel *One Second After* explores what could materialize if we had a national and sustained power outage caused by an EMP (electromagnetic pulse). His work was referenced in Congress in 2009 as a clarion call to protect America's electrical grid.[235] In 2013, National Geographic released a television series called *American Blackout,* which listed four potential causes of a nationwide outage: a cyberattack, an EMP, a solar flare, and a cascading grid failure.[236] The 2024 movies *Leave the World Behind* and *Homestead* both explore grid-down imaginations.

These fictitious works are based on fact. Experts from various professions openly discuss our precarious situation. The Homeland Defense Institute at the United States Air Force Academy warns:

> Among the sixteen critical infrastructure sectors identified by [Presidential Policy Directive #21], four in particular are called

> "lifeline" infrastructure because they form the basis on which all others depend. The four lifeline sectors are communications, energy, transportation, and water. The four lifeline infrastructure sectors are mutually dependent; take away one and the others cannot function. *Among these four, perhaps the most vulnerable and easiest to take away is the electricity subsector in the form of the North American Electric Grid.*
>
> The loss of electricity over a wide region for a long duration is called a "Black Sky Event." The loss of the North American Electric Grid would be an extreme "Black Sky Event." A nuclear strike on the US would likely cause a Black Sky Event, but it is not the only means of shutting down the North American Electric Grid. Russia, China, and [North] Korea have the ability to create a "Black Sky Event" using Electromagnetic Pulse (EMP) and Cyber-Attack.[237]

The study noted that the number one cyber threat we face is nefarious actors shutting down the grid.

The Electricity Information Sharing and Analysis Center (E-ISAC) is the watchdog of the American grid. It is a private enterprise that collaborates with the US Departments of Energy, Justice, Homeland Security, and Defense as well as Canadian and other international agencies, both private and public. Their 2023 end-of-year report indicated that the number of critical vulnerabilities was up 24 percent since 2019.[238] Every two years, E-ISAC is responsible for running GridEx, an exercise designed to test the resiliency of the US and Canadian power networks. GridEx VII in 2023 saw fifteen thousand participants across 252 organizations. In this scenario, a combination of cyberattacks and gunfire against substation transformers knocked out a majority of North American power for forty-eight hours.[239] Comparatively, this was a low-consequence result, causing just two days without power.

At the opposite extreme come findings from the Task Force on National and Homeland Security and the Secure the Grid Coalition. Their conclusions are far more in line with what Noahs fear: *abject and prolonged state collapse that results in the death of hundreds of millions.* These experts state "an EMP event causing a nationwide blackout lasting one year could kill up to 90 percent of the American people and that such a catastrophe could, figuratively and literally, turn out the lights across entire nations and be the advent of a new Dark Ages."[240] That is more than three hundred million dead in the US and Canada.

The aftermath is utterly bleak in their proposed scenario. There's no television or internet for receiving information or cell service to call for help. National Guard members stay home to protect their own families. Military bases, supplied overwhelmingly by civilian electricity, are dark. Ninety-two nuclear reactors melt down by the end of the first month, potentially exposing 120 million Americans to fallout.[241] Even in a smaller scenario, the Task Force mentions the 200+ ton transformers that undergird our grid take more than a year to build and install. The war in Ukraine is extending those timelines, as their demands for electrical equipment have skyrocketed due to Russian attacks, further exacerbating the global demand.[242]

And let's not forget that a malicious actor is not required to cause all this; a large enough solar flare would also do the trick. The Task Force cites NASA's predictions that our risk of something of this magnitude is *12 percent per decade.*

Interestingly, the report indicates preppers are the rational ones and calls for increased levels of at-home preparedness and a community commitment to resilience. (Sorry, Noahs, but the Task Force is on the side of the Interdependent.) In addition to grid-hardening measures, the Task Force recommends a rapid transition to microgrids both for civilian and military locations. In the meantime, you could increase your resiliency in the face of far more common winter storms by purchasing a small gas-powered generator and a humble backyard grill. Other options abound. Be your own microgrid.

PLAUSIBLE CATASTROPHE #2: ECONOMIC COLLAPSE

As a country, America is struggling financially. On the positive side at the household level, our real disposable personal income has increased steadily since 1959, and the years 2019 to 2024 saw its highest levels on record.[243] According to the Federal Reserve's annual household economics survey, more Americans have emergency savings or can handle an unexpected $400 expense in 2023 than in 2013.[244] Both metrics were in a general uptrend over the decade. By contrast, the same survey showed a large jump in the number of "adults doing worse off than twelve months ago," with the number twice as high (31 percent) in 2023 as compared to 2019. Credit card debt is skyrocketing, as are student and auto loans.[245] Tack on mortgage loans and "total household debt stands at $17.5 trillion," twice the level of 2003.[246] This averages to around $65,500 per adult.[247]

Can two things be true at the same time? Yes. Our cars and homes are generally worth far more than they were at the turn of the millennia. We own flat-screens and smartphones and recreational vehicles galore. But you can sense something is wrong under the fiscal hood.

Looking at municipal finances, the total debt of the seventy-five largest cities in America was $288 billion, and fifty-three were fiscally underwater. New York City fared the worst with a $177.6 billion budget shortfall, a burden of $61,800 per taxpayer in the metropolis.[248] For those unlucky enough to live in a town financially underwater, the future reckoning will come in the form of lower pensions, less money spent on services, higher taxes, and other undesirable choices.

As bad as things are for households and municipalities, our national situation is *far worse*. By the end of 2025, the US debt will hover around $38 trillion (or more). That math works out to more than $140,000 per adult. Crunching the numbers, what would it take to pay this off? Let me assume America wanted to eliminate its debt in fifty years and carried a historically low 4 percent interest. This means everyone aged eighteen and older would have to shell out $540 *every month for fifty years.* The Federal Reserve notes the median annual income for 2023 was about $42,000.[249] Therefore, this would be 15 percent of the median worker's income just servicing the national debt.

If you add in total household debt and assume (a) city and state debt are a mere $10,000 combined per home, (b) neither Social Security nor Medicare will need additional funds,[250] and (c) no more wars or economy-crushing disasters like COVID-19 for a half-century, then your overall debt burden per two-adult home is *only* . . . $421,000. If both adults are working and making the median income, they would bring in $84,000 each year—and send $19,500 right back out to debt service. That is 23 percent of your hard-earned money. Of course, you must still pay annual city, state, and federal taxes, plus balance the annual federal budget, so that is conservatively another 30 percent of your household paycheck.

Noahs look at these numbers and believe they are insurmountable. A look at history confirms this. President Franklin D. Roosevelt confiscated personal property less than a hundred years ago to deal with debt. The Weimar Republic, Zimbabwe, Yugoslavia, Britain, Hungary, Argentina, Venezuela, and Romans all experienced hyperinflation, and most went bust. When the Great Depression occurred, there was a belief that Western society was ending.[251] The professionals have noted time and time again that this time is no different.[252]

Got gold?[253]

PLAUSIBLE CATASTROPHE #3: NUCLEAR WAR

There is one reason above all others that most Noahs own bunkers or live in refurbished nuclear silos: nuclear fallout. Annie Jacobsen describes a fictitious account of what might happen in the event of an attack on

America in her book *Nuclear War,* which makes for incredibly sober reading.

Interestingly, there is a massive divergence of opinion as to the potential of nuclear weapons use. A November 2024 poll from the Ronald Reagan Institute of 2,500 Americans found 76 percent were concerned Russia would use a nuclear weapon on Ukraine and 70 percent worried Russia would use one on the United States.[254] This was close to a similar question and survey from the American Psychological Association in 2022.[255] The Bulletin of Atomic Scientists put the world at eighty-nine seconds to midnight in January 2025, partially based on the nuclear capabilities of the countries named, plus Iran and China.[256] Others found far lower conclusions. In another study "domain experts . . . assigned a median 5% probability of a nuclear catastrophe by 2045, while superforecasters put the probability at 1%." This investigation found that the public put the odds at 10 percent, far higher than the experts but much lower than the polls above.[257] However, it may have had to do with the definitions given in this survey, which defined a nuclear catastrophe as causing at least ten million deaths.

This level of carnage is within the realm of possibility. Princeton University estimated 91.5 million would die within an hour of a US–Russia conflict in a 2019 simulation.[258] Even though there are far fewer warheads today than at the height of the Cold War, the nuclear shadow still exists. In 2019, the United States and Russia both withdrew from the Intermediate-Range Nuclear Forces (INF) Treaty. In November 2024, Russia altered its nuclear doctrine and reduced the threshold for utilization.[259] Pakistan and India still eye each other warily and every so often discuss open nuclear use.[260] The year 2023 had the second highest record of North Korean missile tests, topped only by 2022.[261] Nuclear-armed countries have increased their spending on these weapons by an average of 34 percent from 2019 to 2023.[262]

Even false alarms and mishaps have nearly brought us to annihilation. US radars accidentally processed the moon rising over Norway as a massive Soviet attack in 1960. Four months later, a US bomber fractured in flight, plunging two live nuclear weapons onto North Carolina soil; the detonation switches remained turned off. Twenty years later, a *training* tape was inserted into the *operational* feed of NORAD at Cheyenne Mountain, followed by three additional false alarms at that location alone in the next few months.[263]

Oops.

These are just some US examples. Russia and other countries have had their own close calls with declassified accounts running up into 2007.

In 2022, the International Campaign to Abolish Nuclear Weapons (ICAN) released a report detailing the carnage from a single 100-kiloton bomb over various national capitals. Casualties ranged from the hundreds of thousands to the low millions. Paris, for example, would see 1.4 million injured, with twenty-one patients competing over each hospital bed and each doctor responsible for forty-seven patients. The entire city has only forty-four burn beds, and the entire country of France has approximately four hundred thousand hospital beds in total.[264] Triage would be staggering.

In preparation for a possible incident, the World Health Organization issued guidance on what medical supplies countries should stockpile for treatment. It cited best practices from the US, Russia, France, Korea, and even Brazil and Argentina.[265] Noahs seem a little less crazy now, don't they?

REAL-WORLD NOAHS

Of the five subtypes, Noahs are usually the hardest to interview and study, especially among the exceptionally wealthy. This is the primary reason I do not delve deeply into named examples. Journalists engaged in disaster clickbait often attempt stories regarding the extravagance and financial resources involved. One example is the massive bunker funded by Facebook founder Mark Zuckerberg at his Hawaii compound.[266] At this upper end, where money can buy security, some Noahs are the glampers of the prepping world. It is *Lifestyles of the Rich and Famous, Disaster Edition.* Survival Condo is a US site well known by both journalists[267] and academics.[268] It is a refurbished nuclear missile silo in Kansas with a swimming pool, shooting range, movie theater, and medical bay, a veritable "sword into plowshare" way of living. Accommodation here costs $1.5 million. It remains to be seen if this is catching on in both the US and internationally, with multiple venues being more hype than reality. However, Vivos xPoint in South Dakota achieved a measured amount of interest.[269]

A common trait of most Resilient Citizens, especially those of higher incomes, is emblematic of Nassim Taleb's convexity principle. Taleb states certain actions have a low downside but an exceptional upside.[270] Going over budget on a luxury home to add high-end security and preparedness features is not much additional money, comparatively speaking, but if there was a large calamity, those extra dollars would pay off handsomely. Yishan Wong, a former CEO of Reddit, stated it this way:

> Most people just assume improbable events don't happen, but technical people tend to view risk very mathematically. The tech preppers do not necessarily think a collapse is likely. They consider it a remote event, but one with a very severe downside, so, given how much money they have, spending a fraction of their net worth to hedge against this . . . is a logical thing to do.[271]

Among the Silicon Valley and Wall Street crowd, it could simply be a factor less of risk calculation and more of keeping up with the millionaire Joneses next door. Or it could be seen as a continuum. Panic rooms are for criminal break-ins and are part of the castle mentality among many rich,[272] but it is not a large jump to repurpose the concept to deal with several other disasters such as terrorism or social unrest.

Those with deep pockets can even pursue a *country-as-bunker* concept, fleeing their homeland for safer locales. New Zealand is allegedly a top choice, and some of the ultrarich build bunkers in conjunction with their refuge destination.[273] Silicon Valley billionaire Peter Thiel and multimillionaire Kim Dotcom[274] are two examples of prominent Noahs, both of whom have domiciles in New Zealand. Peter owns a 477-acre plot on the southern island but lives in California. Kim is a permanent resident. Peter treats his plans as an insurance policy, and Kim as an inevitability.[275]

For those with more limited means, several outfits like Vivos or Fortitude Ranch indicate spots are still available at places across America—some at former military areas that are now communal disaster locales.[276]

There is also a *region-as-bunker* concept. In America, the prepping community discusses the "American Redoubt," an area that includes Montana, Idaho, Wyoming, and the eastern halves of Washington and Oregon. These regions can be *far* smaller. Take Indian Creek Village, a tiny island just east of Miami dubbed "Billionaire Bunker." Amazon founder Jeff Bezos bought his third property there in 2024.[277]

For those not wanting to move, numerous companies (e.g., Rising S Bunkers, Atlas Bunkers, Hardened Shelters) all offer at-home bunker solutions with prices ranging from the low tens of thousands to the millions of dollars. Business has been flourishing.[278] Today's versions, to those who possess them, are modern-day arks, and the Noah analogy is habitually used to describe both the motivation and the response.[279]

Household bunkers are international, as many are relics of the Cold War and the continuing nuclear age. The most famous are in Switzerland, a country whose laws mandate personal possession of such a structure or a tax for a spot at a community shelter. But not all international bunkers are built for atomic fears. Israel has taken a Swiss approach to becoming a bunker-dense country. Israeli law stipulates new residential buildings must possess a *mamad* (a Hebrew acronym that translates into "residential protected space").[280] The authors who studied these mamads note that although shelter creation started in 1951, incidents such as the Gulf War and the Israel–Hamas war of 2014 keep the threat of disaster relevant. The 2023 Hamas invasion and continuing missile, rocket, and mortar attacks from Israel's enemies have only contributed to both fear and a requirement for ballistic protection at home.

Government inducement to build home bunkers is nothing new. Air raid shelters were commonplace in Britain during World War II. From 1939 to the end of the war, 3.6 million Anderson shelters were installed in the backyards of UK homes.[281]

In the late 2010s, even foreign elections induced a bunker desire. Canadians who were afraid after Donald Trump's election snapped up bunkers created by American builders... just in case.[282]

As for the taxonomy of Noahs, who does not make the cut? For criterion one and two, not every rich individual with a panic room and a month's worth of MREs (meals ready to eat) is a Resilient Citizen. Fearing a home burglary is one thing; fearing *The Purge* is another. Additionally, there needs to be at least a nod to community and not an every-prepper-for-himself mentality. Also excluded are state actors such as military personnel working at sites such as Cheyenne Mountain (NORAD) in Colorado Springs. On a lower scale, military residents of Fort Riley or Fort Leavenworth, Kansas, are provided at-home basements or shelter rooms for tornadoes, but these are provided due to the state actor position of the servicemember and not by individual private action—and *not* for Armageddon.

Globally, those who have protected enclosures for storm surges, burglaries, conventional ballistic attacks, and other traumatic events might own these structures for acute events that are over quickly. Still, without a thirty-one-day supply of goods, they would not count as Resilient Citizens by my criterion.

Just like every other archetype discussed, I do not find the underlying motivations or reciprocal actions of Noahs to be irrational, to a point. There is value in having some hardened physical security at your home and even a bunkered community mentality for certain situations. Large and long-lasting disasters do exist, and no country is immune.

CHAPTER 9

THE FAITHFUL

To one who has faith, no explanation is necessary.
To one without faith, no explanation is possible.
—Saint Thomas Aquinas

Yea, though I walk through the valley of the shadow of death,
I will fear no evil;
For You are with me.
—Psalm 23:4 (NKJV)

Not all fears originate in the physical domain; some are spiritual.[283] Ancient Greeks, Romans, Egyptians, and several other cultures offered animal sacrifices and libations to please their gods. The Aztecs ritually offered tens of thousands of human sacrifices annually.[284] The Canaanite deity Moloch was fond of child sacrifices. Looking across cultures, religions, and history, some of these dedications were to ward off disasters or for the promise of good crops and were witnessed on every continent but Antarctica.

Many Noahs and Faithful have some overlap in their "origin story" so to speak, that of Noah's Ark. However, their takeaway lessons differ. While the Noahs from the last chapter focus on building an ark and saving their skins, the Faithful focus more so on saving their souls. Both engage in disaster preparation activities, but not to the same desired (or feared) end state.

If you think of the Noahs as Sentinels on steroids as to fears, the Faithful take things to the next level. The Faithful believe not just in the future catastrophic destruction of the world but in a rebirth or renewal for the devout and, for some, eternal damnation of unbelievers. However, the Faithful do not believe that offerings of any type will stop what is coming. Divine wrath is imminent and unyielding.

THE END OF THE WORLD—PART ONE

The Ark Encounter in Williamstown, Kentucky, features a full-scale replica of Noah's Ark. Standing next to it feels like standing next to the world's largest wooden cruise ship. The Ararat Ridge Zoo nearby features camels, kangaroos, sloths, and various African animals, including porcupines, tortoises, lemurs, and the African crested crane to showcase how Noah saved *kinds* of animals, not individual species, according to the beliefs of Young Earth Creationism (YEC) science. When I was stationed in Indiana, I took my family to visit, partly out of curiosity and partly due to my infatuation with perils.

Inside the Ark replica in Kentucky is a museum dedicated to the account of Noah and his connection to Christianity, writ large. To be honest, I was expecting to see a little bit of pseudoscience mixed in with evangelism and out-of-context facts. I was wrong. Answers in Genesis, the parent company, has built up a reputation not of quackery but rather of rich academic rigor.[285] The exhibits inside the museum do contain a hefty dose of Christianity but also intellectual stimulus.

Regardless of whether you believe that the narrative of Noah was historical or allegorical, Noah is a prominent figure in Christianity, Islam, Judaism, and Mormonism, accounting for roughly 4.4 billion people or 56 percent of the globe's population. Therefore, "Noah as a prepper" is a religious backdrop common for half the world's religious practitioners. Add in well-read secularists—mainly of the English-speaking world familiar with scriptural stories—and the numbers jump to more than five billion people acquainted with the notion of an ancient apocalyptic flood.

In the story of Noah, God warns that humanity's actions have doomed the world. The biblical account of the first destruction of the entire planet begins:

> Now the earth was corrupt in God's sight and was full of violence. God saw how corrupt the earth had become, for all the people on earth had corrupted their ways. So God said to Noah, "I am going to put an end to all people, for the earth is filled with violence because of them. I am surely going to destroy both them and the earth. So make yourself an ark of cypress wood; make rooms in it and coat it with pitch inside and out." (Genesis 6:11–14 NIV)

No prayer or petition would change the outcome. And yet God chose a small group of individuals to survive. These individuals then prepare, obeying their Creator's heed that the storm cannot be avoided but it can be weathered. In a floating storehouse, they gather a collection of foodstuffs and a menagerie, hunker down for the ensuing deluge, and emerge on the other side alive. Millions (billions?) of others perish.

Various other faiths have similar accounts. The Great Flood is prominent in several Native American cultures. The Chinese goddess Nüwa is not only the original procreator of all humanity but also saved people from heaven's great rains. But all these narratives look to the past. The Faithful look to the future with a mixture of terror... and hope.

THE END OF THE WORLD—A SEQUEL

Eschatology is the study of the end-times. Different faiths describe a similar end-of-days scenario, times of tribulation for which true believers must prepare.

The Mayan Long Count calendar runs 5,128 years. The year 2012 was the restart date, leading some to believe the world would end that year.

We're told the fifth and final Buddha, Buddha Maitreya, will be presaged by a mass depravity of mankind and an abandonment of Buddhist teachings.

For Muslims, it is the sinfulness of the earth before the return of the Mahdi (the twelfth Imam) and his subsequent war against unbelievers.

The original Armageddon is, quite literally, biblical. For Jews, it is the coming of the Messiah and the war with Gog and Magog. For Christians, it is the rise of the Antichrist and his government. Central Bank Digital Currencies (CBDC) and artificial intelligence may be the system the Antichrist uses with his mark of the beast. *Left Behind,* the popular fiction series of the 1990s, embodies fears of this nature for Christians. Any time spent on some popular prepper websites (e.g., *SurvivalBlog, The Organic Prepper*) will quickly reveal Christian quotations, references, and mild evangelism.

This is why I split the Faithful from the Noahs of the previous chapter. To be ontologically secure in this life *and the next* requires both terrestrial and *spiritual* aspects of salvation. The Faithful store up preparations in dreaded anticipation of an end-times future of supernaturally induced disasters and potential government persecution against them and fellow true believers. Yes, the Faithful are motivated by the preservation of their flesh for a time but more so by the deliverance and redemption of their soul.

Caleb Jones lives with his wife and children on a remote island in Alaska. Motivated in part by events of the biblical end-times, they bought totally undeveloped acreage as modern-day pioneers. When referring to 2024's Hurricane Helene wreaking havoc on western North Carolina, Caleb quipped, "I don't think it's global warming or military tech. I think it's signs and warnings from God to a world staggering under the guilt of its wickedness. Birthing pangs."

For Caleb, disaster is a sign from God about the wickedness of mankind's sinful nature. He explains:

> Over the past three to four years, I've observed an acceleration toward technologies that are anti-human and a simultaneous erosion of morality in science and bioethics, a leaning-in toward utilitarianism disguised as transhumanism. The global push toward money, backed by all that exists and transacted only by individual biological markers, brings the totality of utilitarianism of man full circle. We are being reduced to mere matter and energy. Realizing that the Mark of the Beast prophesied two thousand years ago by the apostle John seems to be rolling out at a rapid rate drove me to move my family to a remote island in Alaska and return to my human roots. Technology is antithetical to life on Earth. It is an inverted pyramid, requiring exponentially increasing inputs with ever-diminishing returns. It is Ouroboros. But God's plan is fractal. The grass grows, the cow eats it, the cow calves over and over, the cattle fertilize the grass, and man, their protector and steward, takes his wages from the milk and meat while the tendrils of the spirals grow ever outward and upward with natural checks and balances. I brought my family out here hastily to return to the way God intended. I acted with haste because I believe time is short, and I wished to insulate my family and any who would join us from the hardships those dependent on impossibly top-heavy, just-in-time systems may soon face. I brought my family to a place where we won't need money, because we live simple and free. God won't call everyone to live this way, but we believe he's called us to live this way in this place for a purpose. And we get up every day pushing to complete a sustainable farm with the knowledge that each day the supply chains could collapse, the bank account could be empty, the solar panel could be fried.[286]

Caleb carries the hallmarks of a Faithful Resilient Citizen. He calls Alaska "one of the last free places in America," where he is free from what he calls "so-called property taxes," which leaves him "free to not participate in a system you don't want to participate in." In two short years, Caleb has built his family a small cabin, a woodworking shop that doubles as a barn, a smoker for fish and game, and a two-hole outhouse. He has cleared a half-acre of forest, installed livestock fencing, and built a small solar panel system for electricity. They live without running water, and Caleb's wife, Shay, does the washing in a nearby stream. They hunt bear and fish salmon for meat and just recently acquired a yak for use as a draft animal.

Caleb and Shay aren't only motivated by the negative, however. Part of their interest in moving to Alaska is to connect with Shay's heritage as a Native American. "We kind of settled on staying in southeast Alaska just because Shay's heritage is here. Her people have been here for four thousand years, and that's our children's heritage, too. They have rights to hunt marine mammals like seals and sea otters, and we wanted to be close to their culture so they can stay involved with it."

In the realm of religiously motivated preppers, the reigning champions in America for decades have been faithful members of the Mormon church. Writing for *The Guardian*, J. Oliver Conroy explains:

> The more sophisticated practitioners have always understood that prepping is a matter of both individual and collective well-being. The Church of Jesus Christ of Latter-day Saints ... operates a massive network of grain silos and food depots. People undergoing hardship receive food and household goods, for free or in exchange for volunteer service, at the church's Costco-style warehouses. The system is vertically integrated, with food supplied by church-owned farms. All Mormons are also encouraged to maintain emergency stockpiles in their home—not only for their own sake, but to assist neighbors when a hurricane or flood strikes.[287]

Preparedness is almost as central to Mormons as the faith itself. Each ward (a local unit) is required to have a natural disaster emergency plan, and ward leaders are equipped by the church with radios and satellite phones.[288] There is an unofficial LDS Preparedness Manual (one version is over five hundred pages long) that is routinely updated and distributed.[289] This book covers shelter, emergency communication, sanitation, terror attacks, and pandemics.[290] The manual gives a visual depiction of one year of basic food storage for one person consisting of simple foodstuffs such as grains, legumes, sugar, salt, and oil.[291] You could fit the entire purchase in two grocery carts. Membership association with the Mormon Church was statistically significant for higher levels of disaster preparedness in first responders such as police officers and firefighters.[292]

The Mormons have several reasons to prepare. Not only are they awaiting the end of the world or even commonly occurring natural disasters but they also have a history of government persecution. While the LDS Preparedness Manual contains several pages of firearms information for home and property protection and unabashedly supports the National Rifle Association, guns are not a vital aspect of the Mormon Church in its disaster preparedness actions. Far more common are its emergency response efforts to natural disasters, a task at which the church excels, often besting government efforts, as we saw after Hurricane Katrina.

Thomas Massie, a Republican congressman from Kentucky, could be a well-known example of the Faithful. Sharing traits of many Homesteaders, Congressman Massie lives on an off-grid estate in his district in Kentucky, which he built himself using materials from the land. When describing his land in a short documentary focused on his life called *Off the Grid with Thomas Massie*, he says, "This is the shire. I mean, look at it; it can't get any more beautiful than this. And it stands in stark contrast to what lies beyond those hills, eastward, is Mordor, I mean Washington D.C."[293] For Massie, the goal is independence from the whims of central government and a sense of self-reliance for himself and his family.

But Rep. Massie positions his Christian beliefs first and foremost. He is concerned with multiple technological risks and puts these concerns in terms of his faith. When it comes to the COVID-19 pandemic, for example, Massie stated:

> There's an explanation for why the U.S. government pushed the false narrative that COVD [*sic*] came from the wild and not a lab: COVID was created with U.S. funded technology. They were playing God with new viruses to create new vaccines. They gave us both. Stop funding the madness.[294]

By his account, the Promethean exploits of lab scientists are in stark contrast to the natural order, determined by God, not fallen men who should not be given godlike powers.

Using my taxonomy, who is excluded from the Faithful? Many religiously minded individuals may think that (insert name of messianic figure here) will return in their lifetimes, but not all have thirty-one days of preparations on hand. Just being a fervent tither at the local Church of Christ or being an imam or rabbi does not make one a Resilient Citizen. As indicated by many Dominants in their portrayals of preppers, multiple cults and White supremacist groups invoke religion in their manifestos and possess thirty-one days of disaster preparedness materials but fail my extremism criterion. Members of ISIS or followers of David Koresh (the Branch Davidians) would not pass the military screening restrictions; therefore, they and others like them would be eliminated. Thus, Resilient Citizens of the Faithful variety are nonextremist in belief and yet prepare at high levels in anticipation of their bodies' earthly oppression or for the calamities of the end of days.

To loyal devotees, their faith is the ultimate prep, but it also brings a great deal of resilience to smaller hazards and daily strife. Manna no longer falls from the heavens, though, so they recognize the need to store.

PART ONE: CONCLUSION

Part one of this book illustrates several issues revolving around the discussion of preppers. One issue is the slanted coverage by both the media and academics, those I call the Dominants. But if disaster preparedness, even at "extreme" levels, is both a public and a private good, increases resiliency, and contributes to peace of mind, then it is counterproductive to "other" preppers into an exaggerated negative typecast. How does creating a psychological wall against preparedness assist women or minorities? For example, by casting preppers as racists, scholars could push minorities and many others away from the benefits disaster readiness brings, such as healthy eating, community betterment, resiliency, and positive mental health. Damaging prepper stereotypes travel internationally. Clearly, extremists should be eschewed, but carte blanche dismissal of prepping is not beneficial.

To solve this problem, I provided two solutions. One was a count of those conducting enhanced preparedness measures, and the second was a system of classification. I provided real-world examples, primarily drawn from Americans but with some international depictions as well. I showcased Resilient Citizens as a very diverse crowd across multiple facets but I also typically paired their response—at least initially—with their motivational fear or concern. No one way is "the" answer, and many Resilient Citizens incorporate some—or all—of the five categories I exhibited, moving toward a concept of generalized resiliency. The reality of cascading disasters, polycrisis, or interactions with Resilient Citizens of different stripes may drive this.

One trend is clear: The further one goes from observation of actual highly prepared individuals, the more hyperbolically they are portrayed. For example, most scholars' film and television reviews are skewed to unfavorable portrayals, but on-the-ground embedded research is mixed or even positive. Many nonextremist preppers are exceptionally inclusive and readily encourage others to engage in that lifestyle. From David and Abigail, a middle-class suburban couple with young kids who have made rational calculations for worst-case scenarios, to Wendell Berry, who seeks an almost spiritual connection to land and community in the face of the impending ecological collapse, Resilient Citizens represent the cross-section of American society and the world. They are your neighbors, friends, and family. They have differing motivations and focus on different areas in their preparedness, but they share a common goal to be resilient in the face of the unexpected. They have skin in the game and are often community-oriented, and many have an end goal of increasing the resilience of others. Due to the ubiquitous nature of large-scale disasters and the interconnectedness of the world today, we should listen.

PART TWO

PERILS

Part one of this book strongly argued that Resilient Citizens are a cross-section of America and the world. I provided hard, objective evidence that the phenomenon of enhanced disaster preparedness is neither fringe nor abnormal. Now I turn to a deeper analysis of *why*.

Chapter 10 lays out the basic reasons—cognitively and emotionally—of why we do or do not prepare by looking at how we process risk. These are universal traits. Chapter 11 then expounds on what we *do* about these risks, if anything. I explain our agency and our ontological security. Collectively, these chapters show what is in our nature and what we glean from an analysis of perils. With this understanding, you will see that the actions of Resilient Citizens are both predictable and logical.

Enhanced preparedness is rational, but taking agency over our lives is difficult. I discuss common obstacles and how to surmount them.

Resilient Citizens overcome the psychological impediments inhibiting the masses, so knowing how they do it is critical to your own journey.

Chapters 12 and 13 then turn to how the experts analyze perils and how seriously they take threats and the wisdom of why more of us should be stocking up and working together. If you had any doubts about the seriousness of perils, then the problems they grapple with and warn about should convince you of the dangers that lurk... and motivate you to action.

This is done to counter an argument I already foresee based on comments regarding preppers: *Resilient Citizens may be good people, but they are misguided. And the world is safe enough to not require such "extreme" preparedness*. This fable is part of the stereotype that contributes to the derogatory *othering* of Resilient Citizens. *Othering* separates and allows for ostracizing based on false clichés and supports feelings of trepidation regarding the outgroup. You can counter this by exposing the truth.

Understanding something makes it less scary. Communicating risk clearly, by neither fearmongering nor underselling, allows people to make rational decisions in their lives for resilience. Resilient Citizens, in many ways, are simply doing what the experts say they *should* be doing. Alternatively, Resilient Citizens see what governments are doing and are either copying them at the household level or using those actions as a harbinger.

CHAPTER 10

THE PSYCHOLOGY OF PERILS PROCESSING

Research shows that enduring extreme stress and overcoming adversity leads to neuroplasticity—the brain's ability to form new neural connections. This enhances cognitive flexibility, resilience, and problem-solving skills. Neurosurgeons actually "see" the brain change from overcoming and finishing hard [s--t]. Living outside your comfort zone forces your brain to adapt to new and unpredictable situations, strengthening mental toughness and emotional regulation. Studies have shown that individuals who regularly challenge themselves have higher levels of mental resilience and are better equipped to handle stress in their daily lives.

—Joe De Sena, founder of Spartan Race and Death Race

In this chapter and the next, I explain more of the *why* of preparedness, both the logic of it and an explanation of the existence of mass variation. Preparation is an interaction of People, Perils, and Politics. Individuals reflect on the realities of the perils and politics around them while also looking inward at their own abilities. This chapter argues that *true* resilience does not begin with the purchase of your first case of emergency foods, a down payment on a bunker, or enrollment into your local Red Cross first aid class. Rather, the first two steps on the Resilient Citizen journey are not physical—they are mental and emotional. Resilience begins with a *mindset* that is fulfilled in a state of contentment and controlled *emotionally*.

What are these first two steps?

- Recognize and process the risk.

- Personalize the risk and then own your agency—that is, exercise your ability and willingness to take control.

To understand these steps, you need to see how you psychologically and physiologically process and reflect on perils and politics. I begin this chapter with two simple theories that bracket disaster preparedness: one on why we prepare and one on why we do not. After that, I disassemble and further explain how what we think and feel drives what we do. Chapter 11 continues this discussion and focuses on step two.

HERE COMES THE BOOM

With an over twenty-six-year career in the army, I have had good days and bad. My bad days have been awful; they involve flag-draped caskets. Death and suffering are part of the job description, so I am personally motivated to ensure the protection and growth of my own physical *and* psychological health and the health of those I lead. A soldier's mind can be damaged just like his body, but the scars and trauma are harder to see. I've seen more than a dozen formal models on how we do—or do not—get ready for and then act on resilience measures. My favorite is called Protection Motivation Theory (PMT) because of its simplicity and applicability.

At its foundations, PMT is simply a stimulus paired with a response. Originally designed in 1975 by Ronald Rogers as a model useful to test "fear appeals on health attitudes and behaviors" like cigarette smoking, PMT was expanded to test its explanatory power for natural disaster preparedness, such as earthquakes and floods.[295] There was a crucial change in the application of PMT after Rogers, though. Whereas Rogers looked at *stopping people from continuing a negative behavior* (e.g., smoking), later researchers observed the power of PMT also to *encourage proactive or preventative behavior*—that is, beginning to take action *before* an adverse event or lifestyle choice.

The main bifurcation of PMT is the split between *threat appraisal* and *coping appraisal*. The *threat appraisal* is an amalgamation of probabilities: the chance of an event happening and its severity on an individual. The evaluation is both emotional and cognitive and allows for various types of hazards ranging from low-probability, high-impact (e.g., a tornado) as well as high-probability, low-impact (e.g., a home power outage).[296]

The *coping appraisal* deals with response efficacy, the belief that taking action will truly mitigate or remove harm to self or others, and self-efficacy, the belief that one can perform the acts required for response. Some researchers found that a threat has to reach a certain tipping point before one is motivated enough to take action.[297] Still, many found an intervention such as risk communication via the government, health-care professionals, or private actors could nudge individuals in the right direction.[298] Indeed, this tipping point allowed the coping appraisal component to transform into habits of real change.

Between the two processes—threat appraisal and coping appraisal—the common finding is that the latter is the more powerful and is most supported by empirical data. This verdict is true in both health promotion and disaster preparedness articles.[299] Consistently, *acting*—alternatively called coping, protective responses, or response/self-efficacy—was most highly correlated in quantitative analysis with *behavioral modification*, a feeling or belief of greater control.

In her research on survivalists and preppers, one researcher found empirical survey evidence indicating that PMT's coping components regarding proactive self-protection were statistically correlated with survivalist identity in the context of terrorism and crime. She also noted that survivalists, compared to the rest of the population, are less likely to be motivated by fear and more likely to be motivated by uncertainty and the desire to be prepared for multiple future threats.[300] PMT also shows how the government can be a positive force in pushing for resilience. PMT has a significant link to lower levels of disaster preparedness as well.

Then there is the opposite issue—why people do *not* prepare. Here, the research is also vast, but there is a simple explanation from two people with deep disaster and risk expertise, Professors Robert Meyer and Howard Kunreuther. Previously, these men were codirectors of the University of Pennsylvania's Wharton Risk Management and Decision Processes Center. Their book *The Ostrich Paradox* lays out six biases that impair action or disaster preparedness: myopia, amnesia, optimism, inertia, simplification, and herding.[301]

Here is their argument in brief:

- **Myopia.** People think in short time horizons and have difficulty conceptualizing how current action now can mitigate risk later. There is a mental battle between the concrete now and the abstract potential future.
- **Amnesia.** People quickly forget the "hedonic impact of past losses." The authors cite the rapid rise in flood insurance purchases after Hurricane Katrina and then a drop to "pre-Katrina levels three years later." There is also an emotional cost to preparing coupled with a subsequent false alarm, or the "cry wolf effect."
- **Optimism.** Stated simply, this is a belief that an event will not happen or will not be severe enough to require mitigation. It is the "underestimation of cumulative risk" to an individual.[302]
- **Inertia.** Making "no choice at all" is maintaining the status quo, the "default option." Change is hard.
- **Simplification.** The human brain often equates doing *something* with doing *enough*. The authors cite the example of the FEMA recommendation to acquire "food, water for three days, extra batteries, and so on. Yet once the first action is taken, say, extra food secured, there will be a natural tendency for our brains to see the problem as having been solved."
- **Herding.** Humans follow the cues of those around them. It is challenging for individuals to buck social norms.[303]

Does any of this resonate in your personal life? Are there negative habits that erode your preparedness? Is there a small step you could take to feel more in control and unlock the positives of PMT?

RISKY BUSINESS

How we handle perils, both psychologically and physiologically, is very straightforward. Step one, as we've seen, is relatively easy: Recognize there is—*or could be*—a problem and then process that problem. In the language of PMT, this is the threat appraisal stage. Except for children, I do not think I have ever met somebody who does not worry about something. Maybe these carefree sprites exist, but if they do, they are a rarity. We all live in either awareness or fear—or at least deep concern—about something. Our survival instinct is a good thing.

We live our lives in anticipation of the bang; we just don't know when it's going to hit. Anxiety, up to a point, is rational and normal. Our neural and biochemical makeup is programmed to be on the lookout for perils, be they spousal abuse, snakes, home invasions, or bombs. Stranger danger, the monster under the bed, and our aversion to bitter-tasting foods[304] are all defense mechanisms designed to keep us alive and kicking. Psychologist Meg Jay notes, "Frightening events provide important information about staying alive and so negative emotional memories tend to be more firmly installed in our minds. This is because our brains are wired to keep us alive, not happy."[305] We continuously conduct risk analysis regarding our surroundings to this end.

Come with Me If You Want to Live

The first thing to know about risk is that, as biological organisms, human beings have a basic programming to live. The initial quick processing is done at the individual level, an elementary desire to continue existence.

Psychologist Daniel Kahneman, a former Princeton University professor, is a legend in the field of behavioral economics and how we engage the world both rationally and irrationally. Kahneman describes how we think both fast and slow. He asserts our "System 1" brain (intuitive, emotional) reacts to a rustle in the bushes as a bear rather than a squirrel because an overreaction is less deleterious than being wrong… and being eaten.[306] Unlike animals, though, humans do not rely solely on instinct but rather on reasoning, "System 2." System 2 is more taxing on the mind and takes longer. Thinking takes effort, however, and our brains like to operate efficiently. Food was not as prevalent to our ancestors as it is today, and our brains are ravenous. On a normal day, an adult will channel up to 25 percent of calories to the brain, and young children can use nearly two-thirds![307] We prefer mental shortcuts, even when they yield false conclusions, not because our brains are lazy but because of their energy demands.

One of Kahneman's contemporaries is psychology professor Paul Slovic, who has done voluminous work on how we process the risk of various perils. Slovic writes:

> The ability to sense and avoid harmful environmental conditions is necessary for the survival of all living organisms. Survival is also aided by an ability to codify and learn from past experience. Humans have an additional capability that allows them to alter their environment as well as respond to it. This capacity both creates and reduces risk.[308]

To negotiate a world in which we are both passive recipients and active participants, people use quick rules of thumb "to make sense of an uncertain world."[309]

In the late 1980s, Slovic created an *unknown risk* and *dread risk* matrix based on eighty-one different hazards ranging from nuclear weapons fallout to vaccines to home swimming pools. He discovered that groups of individuals rated the perceived risk of these hazards very differently. *Unknown risk* "is defined at its high end by hazards judged to be unobservable, unknown, new, and delayed in their manifestation of harm."[310]

By contrast, *dread risk*—a combination of items such as "perceived lack of control" and "catastrophic potential"—has far more of an effect on laypeople, whereas experts see the world in expected mortality calculation distributions.[311] He remarked that the accident at Three Mile Island in 1979 changed the face of nuclear energy globally.[312] Slovic stated that Americans thought risks in the future would be greater than in the present day, a finding echoed by others in industrialized nations.

This is not to bash System 1 processing or to say that we humans are always irrational when encountering items unknown or dreadful. We do it all the time, and it can be perfectly healthy. For instance, think back to when you first learned how to drive a car. You had been riding in vehicles for over a decade of your life, but now, behind the steering wheel, things got intense. Your System 2 brain was far more engaged. You focused on every other car on the road, drove slower, and braked more quickly. For some, the sensory inputs and fears were overwhelming to the point of delayed reaction or even freezing. Internally, your cortisol levels (a stress hormone) were probably elevated, your pupils dilated, your heart rate increased, and several other markers of "fight or flight" were activated. Why? You recognized the dangers of driving and wanted to live.

Now think about how you drive your car today. System 1 is in charge. You are mostly motoring along on mental autopilot. Unless it is gridlock, high speeds, or poor weather conditions, you are operating on passive processing. If driving was as stressful throughout your life as it was when you were sixteen, your body would start to break down from the constant stress. You would not be able to take such tension for very long, so your brain shifts to efficiency mode as your comfort level rises. The uncertainty and dread of driving is greatly diminished, so much so that you may be engaging in conversation, singing along with the radio, listening to a podcast, adjusting the air conditioning, putting on makeup, or even eating. Too many people even feel comfortable and competent enough to drive drunk. Drunk driving in 2022 was the cause of a third of all traffic fatalities, and distracted driving was responsible for nearly three hundred thousand injuries.[313] Such are the trade-offs in our peril processing.

Sweet Emotion

A second approach to thinking about how we process risk is that it can be computed *via emotion*. Risk is not purely a mathematical calculation isolated from other variables. Have you ever worried about being attacked by a shark *in fresh water*, hundreds of miles from the ocean? This seems absurd and irrational, but our brain says, *Better safe than sorry*.

Other researchers categorize risk as "a combination of three elements: scenario, probability, and consequences."[314] Stated plainly, we wonder what might happen (the range of options), how likely each of those events is (the range of possibilities), and then what the impact is (the range of consequences).

So far, this sounds just like Kahneman and Slovic because they both recognized emotions play a part in the equation as well. Bearing on our estimations, how we *feel* about scenarios, probabilities, and consequences can tip the scales of our preparations and reactions. Overriding our emotions is incredibly difficult and quickly tiring: "Self-control is an exhaustible resource."[315]

Returning to my car analogy: When a driver cuts you off, do you process that purely from a rational standpoint, or do you silently ascribe negative personality traits to the offending driver? If a police officer pulls you over for driving without a taillight, do you thank him or her for keeping the roads safe? What are your thoughts on speed bumps, stopping for school buses, and bicyclists on roadways? All of these involve the actions of others and decisions by officials on local rules and regulations, including the design and safety of transportation options. Civil engineers are trained to design roads with behavioral analysis in mind, looking at what people *actually* do versus what they *should* do.

Emotions play a major role in decision-making. You can check my work on this with a quick mental exercise. Take two crimes: rape and identity theft. What is your risk for either of these happening to you over the course of the next year, and what do you plan on doing about them? I have given you two scenarios; how will you process your probabilities and consequences?

Chances are, you calculate rape at a more emotional level given its brutal intimacy. Your gender will probably play the dominant role in your assessment. After that, factors such as your age, your income level, your neighborhood, and your family situation will figure into your individual risk determinations, all of which factor into the probability of the equation. Fears of sexually transmitted diseases, shame, pregnancy, and a host of other negative prospects will all enter your mind.

Now, what about identity theft? You are far more likely to be the victim of this crime over the next twelve months. You may lose some money and even take a reputational hit. However, it does not trigger nearly the emotional cascade as rape, does it?

All Together Now

Third, and complementing the previous findings, is the work done by Lee Clarke on disasters. Clarke brings out the *social* aspect of perils, how we process these events in an associational milieu with others. In fact, there is a strong argument that this social element—at play in various facets of our lives—could be *the* dominant variable in widespread disaster preparedness acceptance.[316] In his book *Worst Cases*, his "central argument is that disasters are normal parts of life—spectacular, but prosaic in their cognitive and institutional patterns."[317] He contends that people think about perils on a scale based on three attributes: "inconceivability, uncontrollability, and social identification."

The first two attributes relate to the uncertainty and dread dimensions that the experts mentioned earlier in this chapter have heavily researched. Clarke argues it is perfectly rational to think about disasters, even the worst cases, stating, "Doom, failure, and catastrophe are a part of ordinary life. They are normal."[318] He also believes this is even more logical today since we have built systems that are *more* vulnerable to certain perils. Where Clarke adds to our understanding is via the *social* aspect of these events.

This third attribute, social identification, connects to personalized implications and how we look at things as members of a greater society. The Space Shuttle *Challenger* explosion, while tragic, is not as individually significant or threatening as a regional famine. "People process calamities based upon social similarity," says Clarke. When something happens, we analyze it as: Could this happen to me? If you are not part of NASA, your connection level to the *Challenger* is probably low.

However, in far more common events—car crashes, wildfires, tornadoes, violent crime, an outbreak of *E. coli* at a fast-food restaurant—we can see ourselves, our loved ones, or people like our demographic makeup as victims in these scenarios. Ask a mother of young children how she processes a school shooting in another state or the increased prevalence of autism. When we identify with a casualty, we take things more seriously. The tragedy of others is instructional. Clarke argues that learning from your own failures and the failure of others can increase resiliency. Governments habitually do this and even plan to fail in some circumstances; therefore, individuals should likewise prepare for the *possibility* of various extreme events.[319]

Déjà Vu All Over Again

Fourth and finally, there is also the aspect of *repeat play*. There is not just one hurricane, one robbery, or one broken bone from a trampoline fall that people must overcome in their lives but rather a series of risks. For individuals, a single unfortunate event is all that is required for total devastation or death.

Nassim Taleb describes this in various formal theorems such as time probability, ruin, and fat tails.[320] Simplified, his insights regarding disaster are such that a person is not safe for the rest of their life due to avoiding a single flood. Those same individuals roll the proverbial dice or spin the roulette wheel over and over. Risk is cumulative.[321]

On the flip side, preparedness reduces the odds of ruin, and extreme preparedness is a version of stacking the deck in your favor. If you can experience small shocks and feedback mechanisms, Taleb argues you can become antifragile, something that grows more resilient over time. You can never reduce your risk from all perils to zero, but you can greatly improve your odds. This impacts not only your rational calculus but your emotional well-being. Habitual routine in preparedness has an anesthetic effect on fear. If done as a community, the positive impacts can be synergistic.

The United Nations Office for Disaster Risk Reduction recognizes this overall principle of repeat play and the benefits of antifragility. For example, they cite Australia's Aboriginal practices regarding land use. The Aboriginals conduct cultural fire burning of the landscape both for regeneration and as a disaster mitigation effort.[322] Allowing small, controlled fires to occur lowers the risk of larger-scale engulfment. The US Forest Service often does the same thing. Small shocks make larger shocks more bearable, to a degree. Thankfully, we can take a lot of scrapes and bruises . . . but we die only once.

Wanting to stay alive serves us rather well, but it isn't enough to turn us all into Resilient Citizens. In the lingo of experts, it is a necessary requirement but not sufficient. As the United Nations found:

> Research into decision-making has found *awareness* of risk is not enough to drive behaviour change. In fact, people regularly fail to reduce their personal risk even when they know in the abstract that such risk is real. This is because risk decision making is a process.[323]

Now that I've shown various ways in which we evaluate risk, I want to turn to the second step, that of agency.

CHAPTER 11

THE PSYCHOLOGY OF PERILS PERSONALIZATION

"Fear is the mind-killer."
—Frank Herbert, *Dune*

"Game over, man! Game over!"
—Bill Paxton, *Aliens*

Chapter 10 focused on step one: how to recognize risk and process it. This was the *threat appraisal phase* from Protection Motivation Theory (PMT). Step two is personalization—the coping appraisal phase from PMT—and is the centerpiece of chapter 11.

The foundational concept that undergirds step two is *agency*. Downstream of this is *ontological security*: how one perceives the safety of their being. It is driven by—and satisfied via—agency *or* the care of others. Babies cannot fulfill their ontological security; it must be provided by a caregiver. Most adults have the capacity to satisfy their self-security, but some choose either to supplement or outsource it or to surrender that responsibility entirely to fate or the actions of others—*including the government*. Paradoxically, many people choose to abandon their free will and then wonder why life feels out of control.

"I AM THE MASTER OF MY FATE. I AM THE CAPTAIN OF MY SOUL."[324]

Agency is the *ability* to take charge of your life and the *will* to do so. PMT calls this the *coping appraisal stage*. Nearly all research points to this second step regarding disaster preparedness as the most crucial. The correlation between *feeling* agentic and enhanced resiliency is staggeringly high. However, because variation is substantial, it is also extremely difficult to measure in a way we could all agree on.[325] The independent and confounding variables (risk perception, awareness of disaster, experience, confidence, geography, demographics, culture, and a host of others) are voluminous.[326]

As adults, we take in the risks around us and process them through our upbringing and status via things such as communal norms, experience, emotion, income, gender, religious beliefs, and so on. That's step one. Then we come to a crossroads, which is step two. How are we going to act or react? Will we do anything at all?

Some of this depends on innate traits, but the larger part of the equation comes from how we have been trained. Most of us can exercise our agency, even if our upbringing was troubled. That is, nearly all of us have the *ability* to act. We are far more robust than we give ourselves credit for. Dr. Jay, who was introduced at the beginning of the last chapter, titled her book *Supernormal* because her research discovered a whopping 75 percent of American children were exposed to some sort of childhood trauma and yet still progressed into happy, functioning adults.[327] The *will* to act is a bit harder and is highly dependent on individual conditioning, but thankfully, both ability and will can be trained.

Military experience is a testimony to this. Wars are won and lost on the dirt. You need only look at Afghanistan, Gaza, or Ukraine to see this fact has remained constant since antiquity. What you cannot learn from books, however, is the *mindset* required in battle. That must be learned by experience. It must be repeated. The will to act can manifest both in System 1 (thinking fast) or System 2 (thinking slow).

One example of a combat System 1 scenario is reacting to an enemy ambush. An ambush is just like it's shown in the movies. The enemy sets up in a location and attempts to achieve a complete surprise. In Iraq, for example, improvised explosive devices (IEDs) were the primary threat, sometimes followed by enemy gunfire. When being ambushed, there is only one rule: *Get out of the kill zone!* Psychologically, you must recognize that if you freeze, you die. It must become second nature to respond, a reflex more than a conscious decision. So you pick a lane of egress, often *toward the enemy*, throw grenades in that general direction, shoot anything that moves, and RUN! Even in college, with simulated explosions and gunfire, many cadets froze or were incapable of giving competent orders. It is a situation that must be rehearsed repeatedly so that your brain can ever so slightly increase your chances of survival and those of your soldiers. It is no mystery to me why nearly every Sentinel I have ever met or read about has some affiliation with the military. Many of us have learned the hard way.

The point is that we can train ourselves to be more resilient. A supportive community will supplement or even supercharge this. In this book's conclusion, I show you how you can increase your resiliency; no bombs are required. On the flip side, we can also condition ourselves—or be conditioned by others—to be helpless. Let me illustrate all of this.

What Are You Going to Do with Your Life? The Desire for Ontological Security

What does our brain want? As I explained in chapter 10, the brain first wants to stay alive and then be happy. Additionally, the brain prizes efficiency and therefore wants this at a minimum effort. Maslow's famous hierarchy of needs illustrates this concept, with his five levels consisting of survival items at the base and then items of greater fulfillment as you move up the pyramid.[328]

First, we require basic physiological needs: things such as air, food, and water. Second comes the need for safety and security. That is, we want to continue existing. Only with these satisfied, Maslow argues, can we then work to achieve higher-level needs such as love and belonging, self-esteem, and self-actualization. The concept of ontological security operates primarily—but not exclusively—at these higher levels. It relates more to "security as being" rather than "security as survival."[329]

Whereas *ontology* is the philosophical study of being, *ontological security* is the security of the self. Ontological security refers to a state of *perceived* being. Ontologically secure individuals "can take the 'knocks and bumps' of normal life," whereas those without it are "overwhelmed by anxieties" triggered by various events in the world.[330] Even foreign (geographically speaking) threats that have just a minuscule chance of any personal impact can still cause apprehension, both individually and collectively.

Researcher Jennifer Mitzen explains:

> Ontological security refers to the need to experience oneself as a whole, continuous person in time—as being rather than constantly changing—*in order to realize a sense of agency. Individuals need to feel secure in who they are,* as identities or selves. Some *deep forms of uncertainty threaten this identity security*. The reason is that agency requires a stable cognitive environment. Where *an actor has no idea what to expect,* she cannot systematically relate ends to means, and it becomes unclear how to pursue her ends. Since ends are constitutive of identity, in turn, *deep uncertainty renders the actor's identity insecure. Individuals are therefore motivated to create cognitive and behavioral certainty,* which they do by establishing routines.[331]

Mitzen further argues entire countries have a collective ontological security that impacts how state leaders act in both domestic and international politics.

When an individual *feels* ontologically secure, they have reduced uncertainty in life, manageable levels of anxiety, stability to maintain routines and resist change, and they can exercise their agency.[332] Catastrophic shocks can threaten one's ontological security, so it must be reinforced via repeated action and community.

Disasters can trigger these shocks to one's personal feelings of security. Maslow's basal two needs explain why people panic buy in the face of incoming peril. Their lizard brain is firing and screaming, "GO GET STUFF!" One could link hoarding to System 1 processing in our minds. Because we are herd creatures and social cues provide oversize stimulus, we follow the crowd. The closest thing to an iron law of social psychology is that people do things because they see others do them.[333]

COVID-19 gave a global example of both commonalities and diversity. Government edicts such as lockdowns left people "trapped in worlds which are familiar yet just different enough that they cling to the select few routines they consider essential to their identities." In this and related crises, "the English panic buy frozen chips, [the] Russians panic buy buckwheat, [and the] Americans panic buy handguns."[334]

The world often witnesses hoarding in times of peril. *Hamsteren,* previously a jovial Dutch word to indicate stockpiling as in "stuffing food into your cheeks like a hamster," during COVID-19 gained a negative connotation, much like the similar German word *Hamsterkaufen,* and was equated with selfishly over-caching needed supplies.[335] When the pandemic began in Asia, toilet paper hoarding started early. In Hong Kong, armed thieves robbed a deliveryman of six hundred rolls.[336] A widespread survey of twenty-two countries could trace 19 percent of the differences in toilet paper purchases post-COVID-19 to feelings of individual anxiousness due to the perceived threat.[337]

Yet hoarders react *after* a crisis hits—or immediately before, provided enough early warning—whereas Resilient Citizens make their purchases well in advance. Toilet paper hoarding happened again during COVID-19's second wave, as governments returned to lockdowns in America,[338] Germany,[339] and Britain.[340]

Cultural norms and pivotal events shape a great deal of our actions and reactions. It isn't just bunkers and bullets that go in vogue during a presidential election year, although that is quite common.[341] Many

Americans flooded retailers with requests for abortion pills in the immediate hours after President Trump won the 2024 elections.[342] Fear sells… and motivates. As Maslow argues, once we get our beans and bottled water, *then* we can focus on desires above merely staying alive.

We maintain our agency through our actions. We exercise this via our ability and will to achieve a feeling of control. Our job provides income for shelter, food on the table, and excess for savings and vacations. Through church or social connections or family, we are free to experience the fullness of Maslow's hierarchy. This does not mean our lives are free from struggle or disappointment, but life in modern Western society is by several metrics safer and more open to self-actualization than the overwhelming bulk of human existence.

And yet, for all that we are blessed with, perils still exist, even those of extreme consequence. We have made life better in some circumstances and worse in others. We have both pasteurization and pollution, health insurance and high-fructose corn syrup. We've split the atom for energy and for sheer destruction. The same plane that can take us to paradise can transport the next plague. It is important to recognize both sides of this coin, both the improvement in overall safety, including the general capacity to pursue meaningful existence, *and* the residual threats still lurking.

We all process this differently. Personal capability is diverse, given differences in culture, knowledge, class, locale, beliefs, income, gender, and a host of other factors. Therefore, the variation in preparedness is immense. Preventative measures for disasters resemble a two-sided scale. People weigh their risk, security, and ability on one side and then pair their preparatory actions in parallel fashion. Little pairs with little, big with big.

In the context of disasters, some people take little to no action. This could be due to several reasons, beginning with the belief that their risk is low, either because they believe that the scenario, probability, and consequences are unlikely or bear a negligible loss or that the government provides adequate safeguards or quick relief. Why worry about perils if the government will act in a manner consistent with your security needs? Other explanations for the cause of one's inability to act include financial restrictions, lack of knowledge, or other barriers to action.

Another reason is that some people freeze, acting neither in fight nor flight mode. Our efficient brain must process something completely out of the normal and can't quite cope. We default to social cues and leadership.[343] Screaming and profanity from someone in charge can break through the brain fog.[344] Military leaders know this, and the best know when to use it properly. Drill sergeants who scream at new recruits are performing an act of kindness—to a point. Knowing how your body reacts during extreme stress and learning how to still function, especially at a high level, takes time and repetition. There is an inflection point though, which I cover in the final chapter. Overall, those who do not act in the face of disaster comprise a group of individuals who will be ontologically *insecure*; more on them in just a moment.

In a second group, some households may have confidence that minimal steps are all that is required, such as homeowner's insurance, a small stash of emergency supplies, or an evacuation plan. For this group, their ontological security is sufficient because doing *something* is enough. Government mitigation, preparedness, response, recovery actions, and legal structures also come into play and serve as a variable in an individual's calculation of mitigation and preparedness activities. Often, it is a sense of government failure that prompts people to increase disaster resiliency.

Others take a far more proactive approach. In their risk calculus, *extraordinary* steps are required to achieve ontological security. In some cases, they believe governments will be powerless to halt or contain certain hazards—*or may even cause* such incidents.

Preppers and survivalists often point to the historical record or modern trends to predict potential events, ranging from the moderately disruptive, such as a winter blizzard that cancels school and drops temperatures below zero, to the cataclysmic, such as crushing national debt and hyperinflation. They typically focus on events that have already occurred and could, therefore, happen again with or without warning. Several sources consider personal experience with disasters, including crime, to be a driving force for individuals to get ready.[345] As one New York City prepper stated, "We are not crazy people. People need to understand that we are not preparing for doomsday and the end of the world. *We are prepping for tomorrow. Tomorrow.*"[346]

Because people and politics are imperfect, things can go awry—horribly so—in the psychology of disaster, so I turn now to a couple of the obstacles.

A Cry for Help

Our risk identification and processing begin at birth, and agency comes soon afterward. Ask any mother of a toddler in the Terrible Twos. In a healthy childhood, our parents first provided us with both risk protection and mitigation, teaching us about hazards along the way (threat appraisal, PMT). We are fed, clothed, bathed, and protected. This makes our brain very, very happy. It gets its survival and security needs met, and because others are providing this, it gets to do so on the cheap.

We are then free as children to move up Maslow's pyramid to the higher-level needs, those of love and belonging, self-esteem, and self-actualization. Again, our mother and father provide the environment for us to flourish. We get to dream of being pilots and doctors. We fantasize about marriage and having children of our own. We paint, sing, pray, pet the dog, run through the sprinklers, and play hide-and-go-seek. We get to feel in control. Life is good!

As we age, though, we discover life is not as safe and carefree as we thought. Be it from bullying at school, puberty, college, our career, or marital decisions, we start to get some hard knocks. In adulthood, life and its concomitant responsibilities become ours to navigate. Now we have a decision: How will we retain our ontological security? Who will provide that and to what extent? Is the locus of control internal or external?

Stop, Thief!

What robs us of our agency? The complications are both numerous and common, as I have already depicted. They can also be overcome. Sometimes, we overestimate the threats to our well-being, such as being attacked by a shark, and sometimes we underestimate threats, such as developing heart disease. We err on the side of caution—or fear—because our brain wants to keep us alive. Why we take some risks too lightly goes back to our brain's efficiency seeking. Two final examples will help, one from government and one from technology.

First, recall that Maslow says we initially seek to satisfy our physiological needs, then our safety, and then only the higher levels of love and belonging, self-esteem, and self-actualization. If someone or *something* promises to deliver this, our minds will lap it up. In many cases, governments have stepped up to the plate.

Part of this is due to the unique time in which we live. World War II saw democracy ascendant. The United States became the leader of the free world. Even better, in the late 1980s, the Soviet Union fell, and America stood triumphant. The West was able to trade some of its guns for butter—or so we thought—and America was so flush that it could afford both.

Several countries poured out their coffers into major social programs. Social welfare programs abounded, and governments slowly morphed into the parents that ever provided the blanket of ontological security. The "nanny state" was born, though, in Sweden, it takes on a masculine nomenclature: *pappa Staten*.[347] Some lived in Neverland, where nobody had to grow up. They became zoo animals, content with rejecting some of their wild nature for the siren song of a carefree life. They outsourced their safety at the cost of freedom.

This rejection of responsibility and perpetual adolescence is apparent in a host of social manifestations, such as hours spent online or playing video games, delayed ages for first sexual encounters and marriage, increased pornography consumption, and helicopter parenting. We are also having far fewer children, so the biological drive to keep the few we have healthy enough to reproduce is strong.

Regrettably, some have attempted to bubble-wrap life to such a degree that safety has become nearly oppressive. Witness the parents arrested for having free-range kids or the backlash at the beginning of the COVID-19 pandemic when people attempted to "question the science." For disasters in general, we expect officials to respond quickly and with near omnipotence. One collection of surveys found 81 percent of Americans and 72 percent of the National Guard presumed that first responders or other National Guardsmen would provide them personal assistance within twenty-four hours of a major disaster![348]

All of this contributes to the notion of learned helplessness I brought forth in the introduction of the book. It is a feeling of powerlessness. Just like we can learn to be resilient, we can also learn to be passive and hopeless. Part of our society is actively creating more who freeze rather than cope with unfamiliar or unwanted opinions or realities, especially among the young. Antidepressant prescriptions are up 66 percent for US residents aged 12–25 from 2016 to 2022.[349] We are "coddling the American mind."[350] So-called safe spaces on college campuses or cutting off relatives because of who they voted for are mere symptoms of this psychological personalization of threat and agency.

When agency is lacking, resiliency wanes and panic sets in. Panic requires three prerequisites: (1) the feeling of being trapped, (2) a sense of helplessness, and (3) an overpowering sentiment of isolation.[351] How often do you feel trapped, helpless, and alone? Even in these dark moments, though, the mind can be trained to find light in the darkness. The military runs several SERE (Survival, Evasion, Resistance, and Escape) schools for those more likely to be captured or find themselves isolated, such as pilots, special forces, or embeds. My experience at SERE school taught me more about myself than any other military education. It reinforced a basic human truth: *Resilience is a mindset.*

A second thief of our agency is often technology, especially our hyper-connectedness in superficial settings. Though it has provided numerous boons, it also has a darker side. On a positive note, some research finds media coverage of adverse events (e.g., Ebola, ISIS, and Hurricanes Katrina and Sandy) were *more* of an initial catalyst for preppers than personal experience with a disaster. Official government warnings and proclamations for personal preparedness were also driving factors.[352]

A little bit can be a good thing. But just like the Standard American Diet, we overconsume. An alternative is that, like cattle in a feedlot, we are force-fed a lot of junk food. The reality is a bit of both.

There is a reason why newspapers know that "if it bleeds, it leads" and why social media algorithms feed us tribalism and outrage: It works, it is highly seductive . . . and it is profitable. Every four years, the media in several democracies proclaims we are voting to prevent "Literal Hitler" from taking the reins of power. We are natural doomscrollers. This plays on every concept I previously discussed: our System 1 and System 2 processing, dread and uncertainty, emotions, scenario-probability-consequence analysis, and the intense desire to be socially connected. This is *incredibly* unhealthy at these levels of oversaturation. At certain levels of imbibing, "crisis, or disruptive events . . . will eventually produce a sense of anxiety and insecurity *about the future*—even without physically threatening the lives of the agents in question."[353]

Disasters habitually capture the public's attention. For 2019, Chartbeat analyzed the world's online reading habits and discovered tragedies featured prominently in the top ten stories.[354] Other years show similar results.[355] Disasters make our brains light up, and it is hard for us to look away.

Popular portrayals can also warp our risk calculations. Insights into how we process risk were not limited just to System 1 and 2 analyses. There are myriad biases, fallacies, and mental screw-ups we fall prey to, such as affect heuristic, crowd effect, self-rationalization, narrative fallacy, hindsight bias, outcome bias, and many others.[356] So much stimulus has turned far too many people neurotic.

We are built to worry about lions and tigers and bears *locally,* not globally. And while uncertainty is a critical component of crisis thinking,[357] fears of economic collapse, pandemics, conflict, despotic governments, and civil strife can be internalized even if they are thousands of miles away. This is true especially in modern countries where news, television, and the internet can make faraway hazards feel closer.[358]

This goes back to my point about making disaster preparedness more human-scaled, as Lauren does in chapter 1. Paul Slovic, from chapter 10, gave us the unknown and dread matrix, which helps us understand threat appraisal from PMT. He also coined the term *psychic numbing,* which plays into PMT's coping appraisal.[359] In short, if a fire ripped through your neighborhood elementary school and killed ten children, that would be tragic. But what if it was a hundred students? Would our brain process this as ten times worse? No. We reach a point of saturation where adding one more life, or a hundred more, or one million more, doesn't move our needle. Even more surprising, "psychic numbing begins when the number of victims increases from one to two"![360] I suspect that something of that nature may be playing out in our brains when we start increasing the number of daily perils that our brains must process. Part of this is protectively healthy, keeping us from debilitative worry.

SECURITY BLANK IT

The opposite of ontological security is ontological *insecurity,* which "refers to the deep, incapacitating state of not knowing which dangers to confront and which to ignore, i.e., how to get by in the world. When there is *ontological insecurity,* the individual's energy is consumed meeting immediate needs."[361] This feeling can be all-consuming and exceptionally destructive. Dr. Laing, who gave us both terms, studied both secure and insecure patients. His goal was to delineate the stages between "sanity and madness."[362] Here is an excellent synopsis of this comparison, taken from Karl Gustafsson and Nina C. Krickel-Choi's article, "Returning to the Roots of Ontological Security":

> For most people establishing a basic sense of ontological security does not require much effort. But for ontologically insecure people all their energy goes into maintaining a tenuous sense of self, to the point that they struggle with tasks that go beyond the mere defense of their being. When dealing with this constant existential anxiety becomes too much, some individuals will split themselves further and invent fake persons with which to face the world.... Importantly, while the nature of Laing's work means that he is largely concerned with individuals suffering from a pathological condition, he recognizes that ontologically secure people also feel anxious when they are misrecognized or when their needs for significance and genuine relationships are not met. However, their anxieties are different because they "do not arise with anything like the same force or persistence" as they do in fundamentally ontologically insecure persons.... Laing implies that ontologically secure and ontologically insecure persons experience different kinds of anxiety; the former experience it in a "normal" and temporally limited way, while for the latter anxiety is permanent and existentially threatening.

In other words, the term *ontological insecurity* was coined to help describe a pathological condition that is quite rare and that can lead to extreme coping mechanisms.[363]

The key insight is the "quite rare" finding. But is this still the case in the modern world? Perhaps not.

Worldwide, only half of residents of the globe consider themselves ontologically secure. From one study, just 52 percent "said there is anything they could do to protect themselves or their families from a disaster," with 36 percent feeling completely helpless.[364] I can see the argument for this in impoverished countries, but only three-quarters of Americans and Canadians answered in the affirmative. And just 51 percent from northern and western European countries said they felt secure. This fatalism seems to be widespread in the West and could be due to our overdependence on the government for an unreasonable amount of protection and our acute sensitivity to any disruption.

To end on a positive note, a 2024 global survey of nearly twenty-four thousand people in thirty-three countries found 65 percent of respondents thought 2024 "was a bad year for my country." This may sound a bit bleak, but it was the best response to that question since 2019 and down from a high of 90 percent in 2020. Even better, 71 percent thought 2025 would be an improvement. But once again, all perils are local. The Chinese and Swiss thought 2024 was great, but South Koreans and the Turkish thought it was terrible. Indonesians and Columbians were most optimistic for the new year, the French and Japanese ... not so much.[365]

SYSTEM... PROCESSING

We all recognize risk and process it differently, but within certain observed patterns. While each of us wants ontological security, not everybody exercises their agency to attain it. The goal of ontological security is to reduce uncertainty.[366] Those who feel overwhelmed or lost do not act for the future but are instead caught up continuously in the present. In contrast, those who act can achieve a sense of control over events and a robust psyche. This action is motivated by emotion but acted on via agency.

Naturally, then, routines are vital. Activities cannot be a singular, one-off event; they must become habitual. There is a community aspect as well, where "individual identity is formed and sustained through relationships. Actors therefore achieve ontological security especially by routinizing their relations with significant others."[367] These entities can provide, contribute to, or harm your ontological security. Ontological security acts as a "protective cocoon" and is a "pre-condition for resilience."[368] Overall, the pursuit and achievement of ontological security is healthy and comes from reason, emotion, and your community.

While our fears have shared origins and there are commonplace models in which these inputs come into our processing mechanisms, variance is still high. We use both threat appraisal and coping appraisal, but how we achieve personal security is diverse. This explains the range of Resilient Citizens.

Perils are real, and threats do exist in the world. Yet having the right vocabulary to describe them and contextualize these events assists us as we process them individually and as a collective. Words and definitions help us to bucket things intellectually but also help us grapple with how perils connect and separate.

CHAPTER 12

THE PARAMETERS OF PERILS

The purpose of models is not to fit the data
but to sharpen the questions.
—Samuel Karlin

Lloyd: "Swammi, Slippy, Slappy, Swenson, Swanson?"
Harry: "Maybe it's on the briefcase."
Lloyd: "Oh, yeah, here it is, 'Samsonite.' I was way off."
—*Dumb and Dumber*

How one thinks about something, the lexicon used, and the underlying philosophy will drive comprehension, solutions, and discourse. There are entire books written regarding the definition and use of a single word. Numerous academic disciplines as well as government and nongovernment organizations attempt, via different means, to classify key terminology regarding disaster. This chapter gives three common methodologies: (1) classification by scope and risk, (2) classification by relationship, and (3) classification by whodunnit (the primary actor and by what method: natural, technological, and man-made). Thankfully, the international framework currently in common use is not dogmatic, and extreme precision is not required in day-to-day use.

THE POWER OF DEFINITION

Words convey meaning. The field of disaster studies is massive, and debates, both esoteric and practical, abound as to how to categorize events, define terms, and prioritize dollars and workloads. These conversations swirl around the halls of universities, think tanks, nongovernmental organizations (NGOs), and governments. The topic is so broad that there are even articles published in professional academic journals that cover prepping in video games.[369] Defining or categorizing elements relating to disaster cuts across multiple dimensions. Definitions involve markers such as scope, impact, altering standard patterns of life, the area affected, the response effort required, and others.

For example, take the concept of terrorism. Is terrorism primarily a problem of crime (people breaking the law) or is it an act of war? In an American sense, if you believe predominantly that terrorism is a crime, then the Department of Justice, the Federal Bureau of Investigation, and the Department of Homeland Security should be some of the lead agencies to prevent—and respond to—acts of terrorism. Perpetrators would then be tried in a court of law, evidence weighed, and sentences passed down. On the flip side, if terrorism is an act of war, then terrorists are enemies, and the US military would be a better choice with far more lethal—and swift—options on the table if the offender is not a US citizen and is residing outside of America's borders. Of course, the answer can also be *both*. Presidents from both major political parties have used drone strikes *and* arrests in their prosecution of terrorism. How you think about a problem drives your response to solve it.

Academia is often pedantic with endless quibbling over minutia. While I will give you an overview of key terminology, these details are not needed to understand the basic arguments. As you will see in the following, there are myriad methods of categorization with heavy blending. Lines are blurred just like my People, Perils, and Politics categories.

For most folks, all you need to know is that the current international gold standard for definitions relating to disasters—and human interaction with them—is the Sendai Framework as promulgated by the United Nations Office for Disaster Risk Reduction (UNDRR). According to the framework, the terms *disaster, emergency,* and other words you'll find in your thesaurus are transposable.[370] This book shares this ecumenical use. Therefore, *disaster, catastrophe, calamity,* and nearly all other synonyms, unless expressly noted, are used interchangeably.

Another reason this broad application is justified is because those who engage in high-level disaster preparedness often do so in an attempt to countermand a plethora of threats. It is the concept of *generalized resilience* that can occur even among those people who live in the same city. New York City preppers ready themselves for various catastrophes because that city has been subject to events as diverse as terrorism, Hurricane Sandy, flooding, economic shocks, and infectious diseases even before COVID-19. "For these New Yorkers, prepping is a reality-based exercise rather than one driven by fantasy."[371]

BY THE NUMBERS: CLASSIFICATION BY SCOPE OR RISK

How would you categorize a car accident or someone drowning in a backyard pool? What about a house fire? The American Red Cross habitually responds to the latter and labels them disasters. Most experts, though, would group these as examples of *emergencies,* not disasters. According to Enrico Quarantelli, the founding director of the Disaster Research Center at the University of Delaware, *emergencies* are small-scale, often individual events but could involve several dozen or even hundreds of people, such as an airline crash or larger-scale mudslide.

Disasters, in contrast, are far more extensive, often affecting multiple subnational jurisdictions, with examples including multicounty flooding or the kinds of wildfires that last for days on end and make national news.

Catastrophes are larger still, involving massive damage across a large area. The central government or even international entities take part in recovery or reconstruction efforts.[372] COVID-19, larger-scale wars, and the 2010 Haiti earthquake would all be examples of catastrophes in this context.

Here, we're classifying events by the *scope* of the damage and disruption. Still, disagreements abound. Where should we place things such as obesity, drug overdoses, or the prevalence of autism?

Another way to categorize these tragic incidents is by *risk*. We do this by examining questions such as:

- What disasters are common in my area?
- How often do they occur?
- How much would one cost?

As I discussed in chapter 10, risk is defined as "a combination of three elements: scenario, probability, and consequences."[373] They are applicable at scale, from the individual to the city to the state to the nation. Together, they provide interested government stakeholders with crucial information to prioritize funding, training, mutual aid compacts, and insurance requirements, among other needs, to set policy.

Once a policy is established, public staffers can devise disaster mitigation strategies. Mitigation is exceptionally cost-effective. One study found a seven-to-one cost advantage of preparedness to response.[374] For individuals, understanding risk levels is critical for one's agency. A helpful tool then for both households and public servants alike is accurate and accessible data regarding both scope and risk.

One resource used by professionals and researchers around the world is the EM-DAT (Emergency Events Database). EM-DAT, located in Belgium, is a consortium between the Centre for Research on the Epidemiology of Disasters (CRED) and the World Health Organization (WHO). EM-DAT officially codes something as a *disaster* if it meets at least one of the following four criteria:

- Ten or more people have died.
- One hundred or more people have been affected.
- A state of emergency has been declared.
- There has been a call for international assistance.[375]

EM-DAT has cataloged natural disasters since 1900. Figure 12.1 shows that starting in the 1960s, the number of disasters has risen dramatically. The reason for this is hotly debated. Various explanatory reasons include but are not limited to more accurate reporting methods (including technological means), higher global population, climate fluctuations, and the fact that more people are living in or near hazardous areas such as flood zones.

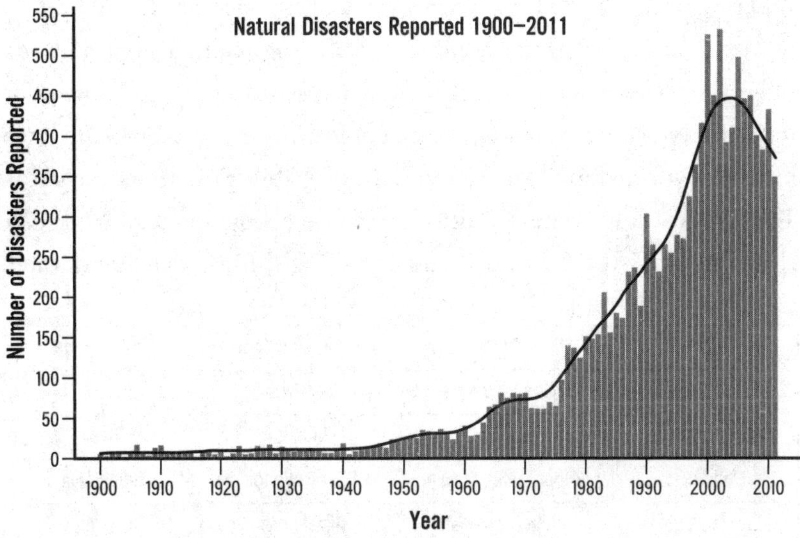

Figure 12.1: Rise of Global Natural Disasters from 1900 to 2011[376]

Another database is the Spatial Hazard Events and Losses Database for the United States (SHELDUS).[377] SHELDUS is owned and operated by Arizona State University's Center for Emergency Management and Homeland Security (CEMHS). It compiles information from several sources such as the National Centers for Environmental Information's *Storm Data and Unusual Weather Phenomena* and their *Global Significant Earthquake Database*, the United States Geological Survey's *Landslide News & Info*, and various other federal entities, including NASA, the

Census Bureau, and the Department of Agriculture.[378] In the past twenty years, SHELDUS has been featured in more than a hundred academic publications, theses, or dissertations. More than one hundred counties and US states have integrated SHELDUS into their hazard or emergency planning documents.[379]

SHELDUS sorts information in its database by location, dates, hazard or peril type, and various losses. Its data provide a measurement of a specific scenario and its consequences from multiple angles: human suffering or death, the length of an incident, and a financial toll both to residential and commercial holdings as well as agricultural impact. It also offers a scale or magnitude of that data to assist in proper planning for response efforts or insurance needs. Furthermore, SHELDUS provides historical information to understand the probability of various scenarios. To show just how minutely disasters can be deconstructed, Table 12.1 shows how SHELDUS categorizes just a single disaster element: water.

Avalanche-Snow	Flood-Lowland	Marine Incident	Storm Surge
Coastal	Flood-Riverine	Mud Flow	Surf
Dam Failure	Flood-Rural	Mudslide	Swell
Debris Flow	Flood-Small Stream	Poor Drainage	Tidal Wave
Erosion-Coastal	Flood-Snowmelt	Rip Current	Tide-High
Erosion-Lakeshore	Flood-Tidal	Rip Tide	Tide-Low
Erosion-Unspecified	Flood-Urban	Rock Slide	Tide-Rip
Flood-Coastal	Flooding	Rockfall	Water Damage
Flood-Flash	Freezing Spray	Seiche	Wave Action
Flood-Ice Jam	High Seas	Sinkhole	Wave-Rogue
Flood-Lakeshore	Landslide-Slump	Snow-Slide	Wave-Sneaker

Table 12.1: A Sample of Hydrological Perils[380]

Unfortunately, neither EM-DAT nor SHELDUS is very user-friendly to the layperson. However, there are nonsubscription-based, easily accessible alternatives, at least for America. The United States Federal Emergency Management Agency (FEMA) has two websites, both of which are publicly available and easy to use. Each approaches disaster risk in slightly different fashions. The first is FEMA's Disaster Declarations for States and Counties data visualization website.[381] This resource is a compilation of every federally declared disaster since the first one in 1953.

There are three types of federally declared disasters. The first two (Emergency and Major disaster) are made by the president of the United States and are subject to political influence. Therefore, the sampling does have bias.[382] The third is a Fire Management Assistance declaration. States submit requests to FEMA, which decides to approve or deny aid.[383]

FEMA's disaster declarations website combines all three types. On this site, you can enter your state or county, specify a time range, and then view the number and types of disasters. Using Washington State as an example, a few years ago when I queried the nearly two hundred disaster declarations made in the past seventy years, roughly 70 percent were wildfires. Not surprisingly, nearly all these declarations were in July, August, or September—peak fire season. For people desiring to know their historic risk levels in conjunction with federal support, this is a good resource.

In my opinion, a far better risk analysis repository is FEMA's more popular website, the National Risk Index.[384] This is a graphically and informationally rich warehouse of information, both for professionals and individual households. People can find their relative risk compared to the entire country or within their individual state at the county and census tract levels. The census tract data are incredibly fine-tuned and, in some areas, such as cities, can pinpoint information down to specific neighborhoods.

One can see their risk index overview, which includes expected annual loss, social vulnerability, and community resilience scores. You can also find up-to-date data on which hazards are likely or unlikely to affect your family in this region. When I looked up Washington State University, which is in Whitman County, the county had a national score of 23.83 out of 100 (higher is worse).[385] Key hazards include cold waves, wildfires, earthquakes, and landslides. By contrast, the University of Washington in King County has a national score of 99.65, with avalanches, earthquakes, volcanoes, and killer whales all vying to snuff out your life.

If you take only one action after reading this chapter, I highly recommend it be to check out FEMA's excellent National Risk Index website.

CONNECTIVE TISSUE: CLASSIFICATION BY RELATIONSHIP

Just as People, Perils, and Politics intersect, so do words such as *disaster, vulnerability, hazards, capacity, resilience,* and *preparedness*. Each of these is defined and (endlessly) debated as to meaning. I will *not* give you an exhaustive rundown of each of these here; I will simply give the basics.

Let's start with the big, overarching term. A *disaster*, according to the International Federation of Red Cross and Red Crescent Societies (IFRC) is:

> [A] sudden, calamitous event that seriously disrupts the functioning of a community or society and causes human, material, and economic or environmental losses that exceed the community's or society's ability to cope using its own resources. Though often caused by nature, disasters can have human origins.[386]

In this characterization, there is physical and economic harm, an inability to prevent said harm, and a component of overwhelming impact.

As for other terms, the United Nations Disaster Risk Reduction's (UNDRR) 2015 Sendai Framework is the current baseline document for the United Nations and is widely adopted across the globe.[387] The definitions UNDRR provides for resilience, vulnerability, hazard, and capacity are used here.

Vulnerability is characterized as "the conditions determined by physical, social, economic and environmental factors or processes, which increase the susceptibility of a community to the impact of hazards."

Hazards are "a potentially damaging physical event, phenomenon or human activity that may cause the loss of life or injury, property damage, social and economic disruption or environmental degradation." The UNDRR further notes that hazards might "include latent conditions that may represent future threats and can have different origins: natural (geological, hydrometeorological and biological) or induced by human processes (environmental degradation and technological hazards)."

Capacity is defined as "the combination of all the strengths, attributes and resources available within an organization, community or society to manage and reduce disaster risks and strengthen resilience."[388] Now let's see how these terms interact and intersect. The relation of these terms can be depicted using this IFRC model:

(Vulnerability + Hazard) / Capacity = Disaster

Hazards are man-made and natural threats that may or may not interact with humans. A mudslide in a remote area is a hazard. Some hazards, however, do interact with humans. Various models then classify *vulnerability* or *capacity* as abilities to resist that hazard. For example, a community in Iceland may have low vulnerability and high capacity to prevent deleterious effects from a snowstorm. A hazard becomes a disaster when it overcomes an individual or community's vulnerability level or capacity to resist.

And finally, we have two related concepts: *resiliency* and *preparedness*. According to the Sendai Framework, *resilience* is "the ability of a system, community or society exposed to hazards to resist, absorb, accommodate to and recover from the effects of a hazard in a timely and efficient manner, including through the preservation and restoration of its essential basic structures and functions." Having adopted this definition in my work, I would add "individual or household" to the list of entities to which it pertains.

Several academic fields look at resilience through different lenses. Holistically, I incorporated their overall philosophy. For example, there are engineering, emotional, ecological, and socioecological definitions, which describe resiliency in terms of "bouncing back" or "adaptive capacity."[389] Whereas vulnerability is an attribute that exists only *prior* to a disaster, resilience incorporates features *before* ("resist"), *during* ("absorb"), and *after* ("accommodate to and recover from") a disaster.

Preparedness is related to resiliency. Both terms infer both a proactive stance (something done well in advance of an event) and a probability component. The UNDRR defines preparedness as "the knowledge and capacities developed by governments, response and recovery organizations, communities and individuals to effectively anticipate, respond to and recover from the impacts of likely, imminent or current disasters."[390] Individual, municipal, or state preparedness is, therefore, a component of resiliency. Higher preparedness correlates to higher resiliency.

Adding to the disaster vocabulary, some agencies such as the (now defunct) United States Agency for International Development (USAID) have other definitional additions, bringing in other aspects such as a temporal component or other variables to calamities. Events that unfold quickly are *Rapid Onset Disasters* such as earthquakes or flash floods. Conversely, slower events such as famines or multiyear droughts are called *Slow Onset Disasters*. If martial conflict worsens a natural disaster—or creates the disaster—USAID refers to these as *Complex Emergencies*. This matters a great deal to some nongovernmental organizations, such as the Red Cross. For example, the International *Committee* of the Red Cross (ICRC) exercises its humanitarian mission in areas of "war and internal violence." Compare this with International *Federation* of Red Cross and Red Crescent Societies (IFRC), which responds to natural disasters and health emergencies.[391] What jumps out from these entities is that they recognize disasters can be natural or human-caused and can interact with one another.

Other buzzwords and catchphrases abound. The United States government includes terms and definitions such as *catastrophic incident, national security emergency,*[392] *incident, catastrophic event, complex catastrophe,* and *major disaster*[393] and implements them via executive orders, legislation, and practice. Numerous other analog descriptions exist such as those for mental health[394] or crime.[395]

Confused yet? You needn't be. Keep it simple with disaster and the steps you, your community, and your government can take to increase resiliency, all in the common and everyday understanding of the terms.

BLAME GAME: CLASSIFICATION BY WHODUNNIT

Finally, I turn to one final way in which disasters are commonly subdivided: that of the causal agent. Catastrophes are often categorized in three broad ways: (1) natural, (2) technological (accidents), and (3) man-made (everything from war to economic shocks).[396] Just like the preceding terminologies or the interplay of the 2011 Japanese tsunami from chapter 1 (i.e., earthquake, tsunami, nuclear accident), these categories can overlap and cascade on each other. Disasters can be individual or collective and exist in the full spread of chronological occurrence from acute to chronic.[397]

FEMA, while it prepares for a host of challenges, has only fifteen specified National Planning Scenarios. These plans ready the federal response for a mixture of natural, technological, and man-made disasters, several of which would require *months* of response and recovery—for example, a pandemic or a small-scale nuclear detonation.

Natural Disasters

Natural disasters, or "acts of God," as they are often referred to in legal and insurance circles, are the easiest to relate to and consist of events such as blizzards, heat waves, diseases, cyclones, solar flares, sinkholes, and other occurrences that arise as the result of geological, astrological, or related phenomena. Other planets in our solar system exhibit natural disasters, although most experts today would classify earthquakes on Mars as *hazards* rather than *disasters* since no humans are affected. The SHELDUS database tracks only natural disasters.

Technological Disasters

Technological disasters are the next category. While no lives were lost, the greatest environmental catastrophe in modern Spanish and Portuguese history occurred when the *Prestige* oil tanker broke apart in 2002, wrecking local beaches and commercial fishing operations. An echo was the *Deepwater Horizon* spill in the Gulf of America. The shadow of Chernobyl still lingers in discussions of atomic energy in Europe. Thirty years later, Norway has reindeer that register raised radioactivity levels.[398]

Another example is the massive North American blackout that occurred in 2003 when trees fouled up three high-voltage lines. Fifty million Canadians and Americans were without power, and cost estimates were at $6–10 billion.[399] Pacific Gas & Electric, a California power company, had to file for bankruptcy due to the costs of lawsuits and expenditures related to numerous fires caused by high winds damaging its infrastructure.[400] A further case is the Camp Fire, which obliterated the town of Paradise, California. It was the most expensive disaster in the world in 2018 and killed more than eighty people.[401]

Technological disasters and those natural disasters that have more of an overlap regarding human agency, such as certain diseases, might be in a separate psychological and political category. No one can halt a solar flare, but people can receive flu vaccinations.[402, 403] Viruses will continue to mutate, but the spread of hoof-and-mouth disease can be prevented by import/export inspections on livestock. We cannot stop earthquakes, but we can design buildings in a fashion that takes earthquakes into account.

Man-Made Disasters

And finally, there are *man-made disasters*. They differ from technological disasters because those are considered accidents, whereas man-made disasters are more volitional. They can be big or small and be committed via dogged determination or callous neglect.

War, genocide, and the 9/11 terror attacks are considered man-made disasters, as is the 2013 Boston Marathon bombing. Though any loss of life is tragic, no isolated act of violence or terrorist's rampage can compare to the deadly potential of sovereignties. If your metric is deaths in a single day, a low estimate for the US atomic attack against Hiroshima in 1945 was seventy thousand.[404] On July 1, 1916, the British Army attacked the German trenches in the First Battle of the Somme and lost nineteen thousand soldiers.[405] Scholars estimate between several hundred thousand and one million Tutsi were killed in the Rwandan Genocide of 1994, representing the loss of approximately 80 percent of Rwanda's Tutsi population.[406]

Deforestation, pollution, hyperinflation, and obesity are all examples of man-made disasters.

Then there are also odd duck outliers. Violent crimes, including mass shootings or murders, are *not* officially depicted as man-made disasters (or any other type), even though they weigh on the minds of people in ways similar to terrorism or government harassment. The world has seen ethnic cleansing, slaughter, and enslavement against the Yezidis by ISIS and oppression directed at the Rohingya by Myanmar or Uighur Muslims in China.

The category is quite confusing and has fuzzy edges. Cancer kills more than twenty-seven thousand people per day worldwide, and cardiovascular disease takes nearly twice that at roughly fifty-one thousand daily deaths.[407] Should we count medical ailments in our man-made catastrophe calculus if they come from lifestyle choices or poverty? What about suicides? What about mental health issues, fears of climate change, or the converse fears of climate alarmism?[408] What if a giant meteor doesn't wipe us all out, but something far more mundane such as the "birth dearth" or fertility crisis does?[409] Do these all count?

Well, maybe. Most disaster experts would not lump in heart attacks with tornadoes, but since this is a book looking at resiliency, it doesn't make much sense if you have forty acres and a panic room if you die from a chili-cheese-fries-laden diet in your forties. Either way you slice it, we humans are rather adept at killing one another—and ourselves.

The connection between government and disaster can also be viewed as one of neglect. As Professor Anna Bounds said, "The stereotype of preppers is that they're paranoid and think that the government is coming for them. . . . Whereas people in the city, preppers of color, prepare because they think that government isn't coming for them."[410]

For many citizens, the distinctions and categorizations are irrelevant. Government action or indifference still causes fear. The story of Peanut the Squirrel went viral just before the US 2024 presidential election, when the state of New York confiscated and then euthanized the animal due to anonymous complaints. Prior to this incident, the squirrel and his owner were minor internet sensations. Social media was abuzz with memes, but comments quickly moved to talks of government tyranny. Joe Rogan, who hosts one of the largest podcasts in the world, discussed Peanut with the world's richest man, Elon Musk.[411]

We live in strange times indeed.

As a final example of man-made disasters, there is a concern about economic shocks or even an implosion of the system. The world has seen at least three major economic hits after the year 2000 (the Dotcom bust, the 2007–2008 Great Financial Crisis, and the COVID-19 crisis). The last two, and especially the COVID-19 response, saw massive monetary injections into the system, resulting in rampant inflation. Bitcoin, which had a value of zero dollars when it was introduced in 2010, shot up to $100,000 at one point, as people either sought refuge from eroding currency purchasing power or engaged in crazy speculation. Premiums for physical gold and silver are several percentage points larger than their typical spread.

Long-time investing gurus like Stanley Druckenmiller sounded the alarm several years ago regarding US debt. In one interview, he noted that "three months in 2020 we increased the deficit more than the past five recessions combined," and the "Fed in six weeks bought more treasuries than in ten years under Bernanke/Yellen."[412]

As I write this, the US Department of Government Efficiency is attempting to streamline the national budget via cuts to spending and personnel. President Trump's "Liberation Day" tariffs caused a panic in the markets, with major indices dropping thousands of points in short order. Risk abounds, and how you process these events will be heavily shaped by your vulnerability and capacity (as well as your ideology).

NO EASY ANSWER

As I hope you have noticed, the dividing lines among events from mundane to catastrophic are not clear-cut. Take flooding, for example. Hurricane Katrina's destructive and financial impact was increased by levee failures and the building of expensive coastal homes and businesses supported by underpriced US federal flood insurance. Rich and poor alike were impacted. One can see how terms such as *hazard, capacity,* and *vulnerability* help describe things, but that's probably cold comfort to someone standing outside their demolished home.

Wildfires can be caused by lightning strikes, arson, and the carelessness of an untended s'mores fire. If COVID-19 was a naturally occurring zoonotic,[413] that places it in the natural disasters category. If it was a gain-of-function lab creation, it is a man-made catastrophe.

How would you determine whether a tragic event was technological or man-made? Whether it was a disaster or catastrophe? Or perhaps it was none of these and instead the result of shady business practices. For example, the US government allows the heavy use of synthetic herbicides such as glyphosate. It also subsidizes the production of ingested seed oils for nutrition. And yet these elements contribute to a host of deleterious health problems across the country. Is this a disaster? If so, is it man-made or technological? And where should we place malnutrition, racism, debanking, and cancel culture? Do these rate as disasters too? How do we know? How do we decide?

Don't feel bad. Experts grapple with—and argue about—these same issues. Let us look at what they are saying.

CHAPTER 13

THE PROBING OF PERILS

You are allowed to lie a little, but you must never mislead.
—PAUL HALMOS, MATHEMATICIAN

I tried to follow the science, but it was simply not there—then I followed the money; that's where I found the science.
—DR. MIKE YEADON, FORMER VICE PRESIDENT OF PFIZER

Academics and professional organizations approach thinking, modeling, and describing harmful events with as much fervor as many Resilient Citizens. The language is of a higher caliber ... or wonky, depending on your view. Specialists use descriptors such as Zipf's law or Feigenbaum constants and explain low probability/high consequence events as experiencing "higher kurtosis than the Gaussian" when "fat tails" would suffice.[414]

But if the big shots and the experts are treating extreme disaster scenarios seriously—and sounding the alarm—should not the populace listen ... and respond to the warning? If the call is coming from inside the house, would that not indicate the threat is real? If the alerts and premonitions are originating not from a single source but from a wide assortment of consortiums, universities, and public officials, should we not pay heed?

I also recognize that money, power, prestige, and politics are at play. I showed in chapters 10 and 11 how ordinary citizens have some distortions cognitively, emotionally, and socially on how they process perils. Experts, unfortunately, have their own related problems. You may think you are getting "The Truth" or "The Science" free from bias. Sadly, the structures at play distort how authorities and professionals communicate with—and think about—perils and people. Sometimes we get propaganda, and part of the fault is our own.

MEET THE PROFESSORS

Looking at catastrophes *holistically* across the entire spectrum, there is not a nice and tidy scholastic home. Several universities have a physics department, an English department, and an art department. Similarly, *singular* disaster studies exist within discrete disciplines; seismologists look at earthquakes, marine biologists study depleting fish stocks, soil scientists track soil health decline, and virologists investigate pathologies. Fortuitously though, the intersection of People, Perils, and Politics does come together in some of the social science departments.

I earned my PhD in International Relations with a heavy concentration in disaster studies from Cornell University. My coursework included Policy Issues in Disaster Prevention & Recovery in the Public Policy School, a class called Disasters and Human Rights and another titled Cybersecurity Law and Policy at Cornell Law School, and classes on international security and political economy in the Department of Government, among others. Additional offerings at the university that I sadly did not have time for include:

- Going Nuclear: The Spread of Nuclear Weapons and Energy
- Civil War
- Risk and Disaster
- Sociology of Disasters
- Risk and Society
- Sustainable Energy Systems
- Histories of the Apocalypse: From Nostradamus to Nuclear Winter

These classes came from the fields of political science, sociology, science and technology studies, biological and environmental engineering, and history.

This is merely a snippet from a single college. Syracuse University, in its top-in-the-nation Public Administration and International Affairs Department, offered Challenges in Crisis & Disaster Management and several options for studying Homeland Security. Johns Hopkins, UC Berkeley, Harvard, Oxford, the University of Auckland, the University of British Columbia, the University of Washington, Princeton, and dozens of other top schools across the world all have studies in disasters within their course rosters. These classes are in fields as varied as those I just listed, plus economics, public safety, civil engineering, medicine and public health, psychology, geology, and a host of others.

Some of these schools are looking at smaller-scale incidents such as building collapses and local fisheries. Others study larger events that are habitual and typically lower on the destruction scale, such as tornadoes, assassination of political rivals, landslides, chemical spills, and plant rusts. But they also look at the big ones, up to and including planet killers. Among the more apocalyptic scenarios are deforestation, chronic disease, crop failure, soil health, pollution, megaquakes, Category 6 hurricanes, tyranny, and genocide.

Niche studies abound. There is no all-encompassing *Department of the Apocalypse and Bad Things* in the hallowed halls of academia, but some departments come close. Samples of collegiate think factories geared toward catastrophes, mitigation, and public outreach include the Center for Emergency Management and Homeland Security (CEMHS) at Arizona State University, which

> addresses ongoing risk reduction challenges characterized by complex social, economic environmental, cultural, and technological interdependencies and conflicting objectives. Through

> projects, education and outreach CEMHS engages critical communities of practice, such as planning, community development, governance, defense, human welfare, and climate change adaptation.[415]

Like other institutes of higher learning, they offer degrees from the bachelor's to the doctorate level for those eager to pedigree in preparedness.

The focus of Columbia University's National Center for Disaster Preparedness is to "ENHANCE system readiness for disasters; EDUCATE and train the workforce to build resilience from catastrophic events; FOSTER community preparedness and engagement; UNDERSTAND population vulnerability; and ANALYZE strategies to improve disaster recovery [capitalization in the original]."[416]

The University of Pennsylvania's Wharton Risk Management and Decision Processes Center is an excellent example of how one organization attempted to integrate the heterogeneity of disaster explorations. Their 2018 annual report states the center

> has focused on understanding how individuals, communities, private firms and public sector organizations make decisions with respect to low-probability events that can cause significant losses and disruptions when they occur. *We are committed to research that leads to public policies that encourage relevant parties to invest in cost-effective protective measures that reduce catastrophic losses.* Over the past 35 years, the Wharton Risk Center has conducted research and held conferences *on topics ranging from chemical safety to natural disasters and terrorism,* bringing together key interested parties in a neutral forum. We have also created partnerships with organizations who share our view that it is important for residents and businesses in risk-prone areas to undertake protective measures now rather than waiting until

> the next disaster occurs. *Research in psychology and behavioral economics has found that human decision-making is often guided by biases that impede our ability to make good decisions about how to prepare* for low-probability, high-consequence events.[417]

What a bunch of nutjobs, right? There sure seem to be a lot of proto-preppers in the Ivy League and Ivory Tower![418]

Even existential studies are not uncommon. Perils have happened since the dawn of time. Geologists and evolutionary biologists will argue five mass extinctions have occurred within Earth's history. The oldest of these "Big Five" was the End-Ordovician extinction of 444 million years ago that wiped out 86 percent of all species on the planet.[419] The common explanation is a series of glacial alterations and shifts in Earth's plate structure.

The determinants of the other mass extinctions ranged from the spread of land plants, volcanic activity (both terrestrial and undersea), and asteroids. This later event is believed to have been responsible for the fifth of the Big Five, the Cretaceous extinction of sixty-five million years ago, which doomed the dinosaurs.[420] Some of my classmates along with one of my professors published a peer-reviewed article on asteroids and planetary defense.[421] In a previous work, the lead author noted an asteroid only eighteen meters in size hit Russia in 2013 "with the force of 30 atomic bombs," with far larger strikes possible.[422]

Every two years, the International Academy of Astronautics holds a planetary defense conference. The 2021 conference simulated a large impact on the Czech Republic.[423]

Apocalyptic climate and atmospheric studies have for years racked up a tremendous amount of research interest... and dollars, which unfortunately skews the data as grant money often has a thumb on the scale for what the "right" outcome should be. I once met a Princeton PhD student looking at sea level rises based on variables from the 2016 Paris Climate Accords. His dissertation adviser was a pillar in this field of thinking, and money poured in. Comparatively, my colleague studying asteroids gets pennies.

Pandemics are big fears and big money as well. The not-so-subtle title coming from the journal *Homeland Security Affairs* in 2023 blared "Global Pandemics Are Extinction-Level Events."[424] Academia and government institutions are made of human beings who are not immune to the temptations of power, fame, or money. Due diligence requires thought before accepting research conclusions.

Another face of TEOTWAWKI (The End of The World as We Know It) among the expert class is Jared Diamond, a professor at the University of California, Los Angeles. His most popular book is *Guns, Germs, and Steel: The Fates of Human Societies*. The book details how Eurasia conquered most of the globe. A follow-up work of his, *Collapse: How Societies Choose to Fail or Succeed*, showcased common reasons why past societies went belly-up. Whether your entire society is decimated by an outside force or from poor internal choices, the result is the same: There goes the neighborhood.

A CORNUCOPIA OF WATCHMEN

There are also some very big fish in the ocean of perils research, both public and private. Governments, for their part, have a vested interest in protecting their electorate. Mass death typically does not do well for favorability ratings and reelection odds. Additionally, public, private, and nonprofit disaster-focused organizations are legion. Their variation comes in scope, size, location, and composition. Private charities provide aid, think tanks publish studies, and nearly everybody in these various groups either advises leaders directly or lobbies public officials or both. What are these groups saying?

The US Government

After 9/11, the US government believed its intelligence apparatus was too stovepiped. A new position was created, the Director of National

Intelligence (DNI), who was charged with fusing information from the United States intelligence community, such as the CIA, FBI, and Department of Defense, and reporting to the president of the United States. The DNI is a cabinet-level position, and the occupant serves on both the National Security Council and the Homeland Security Council.

The DNI's 2024 *Annual Threat Assessment of the US Intelligence Community* opens with this claim:

> During the next year, the United States faces an increasingly fragile global order strained by accelerating strategic competition among major powers, more intense and unpredictable transnational challenges, and multiple regional conflicts with far-reaching implications. An ambitious but anxious China, a confrontational Russia, some regional powers, such as Iran, and more capable non-state actors are challenging longstanding rules of the international system as well as U.S. primacy within it. Simultaneously, new technologies, fragilities in the public health sector, and environmental changes are more frequent, often have global impact and are harder to forecast.[425]

Did you catch that? The top intelligence adviser to the president openly stated the rules-based international order that has governed the globe since the end of World War II is under severe pressure. The implication is that it may not survive much longer. The report covers several areas of concern, including war over Taiwan; nuclear, chemical, and biological weapons; North Korea; Azerbaijan; Kosovo; fentanyl; financial crimes; cybercrime; human and sex trafficking; terrorism; and malign influence operations. It also discusses disagreements regarding the true origin of COVID-19; some say it was natural, others a "laboratory-associated incident."

Congress is acutely aware of the dangers. Members of the House of Representatives Committee on Homeland Security recorded more than one hundred pages of testimony and statements in just one hearing alone in November 2022. Witnesses included the secretary of the Department of Homeland Security, the director of the Federal Bureau of Investigation, and the director of the National Counterterrorism Center. Cybersecurity, violent illegal immigrant gangs, natural disasters, extremism, guns, and misinformation were all discussed.[426]

The Federal Emergency Management Agency (FEMA), which would be the senior nonmilitary entity responding to a large-scale event in the United States, is also facing challenges. Former FEMA Administrator Dianne Criswell declared the organization is under stress. In the FEMA 2022–2026 Strategic Plan, she wrote, "Ten years ago, we managed an average of 108 disasters a year. Today, we are managing 311."[427] In 2023, one policy analyst testified to Congress that FEMA was "trying to handle a new disaster declaration every three days on average."[428]

Expensive disasters, such as Hurricanes Helene and Milton, can quickly drain the coffers of FEMA. Alejandro Mayorkas, the former Secretary of Homeland Security, under which FEMA is organized, stated FEMA "will need more funds" based on the impact of those two catastrophes.[429] One tally by a climatologist from the National Oceanic and Atmospheric Administration quipped, "In the 1980s there were about 3 months between billion-dollar disaster events, but over the last decade we are experiencing them every 3 weeks."[430] But it isn't just snowstorms and hurricanes that FEMA and the Department of Homeland Security (DHS) are preparing for; they are also researching apocalyptic scenarios. The Global Catastrophic Risk Management Act of 2022 charged FEMA and DHS to look at global catastrophic and existential threats for the next thirty years. The first report was delivered in 2024 and gave the top six possibilities: supervolcanoes, asteroid or comet impacts, severe pandemics, rapid and severe climate change, nuclear war, and artificial intelligence.[431] Some scenarios had casualty counts in the billions. (Hello, Noahs.) What did the experts recommend for dealing with these calamities? Generalized resilience and working together.

So here you have several examples of high-level entities acting in their official capacities and giving warnings on potential and actual risks that Americans face. These functionaries are also openly discussing the fear of their own departmental (and systemic administrative) failures as government entities.

The US Military

Every year, the United States government purposefully detonates a nuclear bomb in a major metropolitan city in the homeland. Buildings are destroyed, casualties climb into the tens of thousands, and a radioactive plume stretches for hundreds of miles. The response effort is massive. Thousands of soldiers; nuclear experts; professionals from national agencies including FEMA, DHS, and the Federal Bureau of Investigation (FBI); and first responders and state-level disaster teams descend on the scene in HAZMAT suits, radiological detectors, and search and recovery assets.

While the US military is typically not the Lead Federal Agency due to legal restrictions placed on armed forces operating stateside, they can provide thousands, or even tens of thousands, of response forces. This responsibility is often borne by USNORTHCOM's land component, US Army North, and three of its subordinate units: Joint Task Force Civil Support (Fort Eustis, Virginia), Task Force-76 (Salt Lake City, Utah), and Task Force-46 (Lansing, Michigan).[432] Although "America's worst day" does make the news, you have probably never heard about a single one of these detonations even though they have occurred annually for over a decade.[433] This is because each of these is a *simulated exercise* called Vibrant Response. I have personally supervised three of these events and dozens of other nightmare scenarios, acting as an exercise controller and referee.

Sometimes, the military mixes things up, adding in or supplementing a nuclear attack with a chemical, biological, or radiological scenario. Collectively, the military's actions for these events are known as the Defense Chemical, Biological, Radiological, Nuclear (CBRN) Response.[434] Thousands of uniformed professionals under various command structures serve as the disaster reaction or prevention vanguard.[435]

Numerous government agencies conduct their own CBRN Table Top Exercises (TTXs) on a regular basis, adding up to dozens—if not hundreds—of simulations per year. In America, as elsewhere, these larger planning events are incredibly complex due to the nature of the incident; various local, state, tribal, territorial, and federal laws; the alphabet soup of responder agencies; and the psychological weight of training for disasters.

As for Vibrant Response, the military training and maneuvers are often conducted at Camp Atterbury, Indiana, for the computer simulation portion and at Muscatatuck Urban Training Center, Indiana, for the hands-on training.[436] Muscatatuck is "a 1,000 acre urban and rural landscape with more than 190 brick-and-mortar structures with roughly 1.5 million square feet under roof, [and] 1.8 miles of subterranean tunnels."[437] It is one of the military's largest urban training environments and is quite impressive to see in real life. Walking through the complex, one can view a typical suburban housing area under several feet of floodwaters, a collapsible (hydraulic-powered) parking garage simulating an earthquake, a subway station, and an apartment building utterly ravaged by a hurricane or other large catastrophe.

What else are the top leaders of the military concerned with? General Gregory Guillot, the commander of both the North American Aerospace Defense Command (NORAD) and Northern Command (NORTHCOM), is the senior officer responsible for tracking and countering several of the military dangers against the homeland, including terrorism, Chinese balloons, Russian warships, and certain threats against the president. In his 2024 Senate testimony, General Guillot spoke of risks to the Defense Critical Infrastructure, China's growing nuclear capabilities, hypersonic glide vehicles, and transnational criminal organizations, among a multiplicity of other fears.[438] NORAD and NORTHCOM spend *billions* of dollars on homeland defense.

Institutional Players

Many—although certainly not all—academic experts play in the realm of the theoretical. There are other professionals with their proverbial—and often literal—boots on the ground. I will not catalog every organization on the globe that looks at disaster, but a short list should prove the point. Some work exclusively on pre-disaster prevention and mitigation activities. Others work on post-disaster actions response and recovery. Some do a mixture of both. Here are several by name and a short description in no particular order. I have visited, supported, and conducted operational planning with or used data and reports from nearly every one of these organizations.

United Nations Office for Disaster Risk Reduction (UNDRR): UNDRR is the lead proponent of the United Nations for the Sendai Framework, an international document that seeks to lower disaster risk across the world.

World Health Organization: The WHO ostensibly serves as a sponsor, monitor, responder, and provider of global health care. It focuses not only on diseases such as Ebola or the reaction to COVID-19 but also on cancer and diabetes. It advocates for universal health care, abortion, nutrition and fitness, and safe communities.[439]

World Vision: World Vision is a Christian organization that works on the chronic disasters of poverty and injustice. At its core is a community focus, and it has a heart for children. There are hundreds of private charity organizations in America and around the world that work to combat calamity. Other examples include Jaco Booyens Ministries, Samaritan's Purse, Mercury One, Doctors Without Borders, Team

Rubicon, and the Bill & Melinda Gates Foundation. Several are secular, and many have a religious foundation. They feed and clothe "the least of these" before and after all manners of disasters such as responding to drug abuse, child sex trafficking, natural disasters, and conflict.

The Nature Conservancy (TNC): TNC's key concerns are climate change and biodiversity loss. As one of its solutions, it buys major tracts of land and marine areas to keep them undeveloped. And when I say major, I mean gargantuan. TNC's 2030 stated goals are to conserve 10 billion acres of ocean and 1.6 billion acres of land globally.[440]

US National Hurricane Center (NHC): If you live along the US East Coast, in a Gulf of America state, or are a Weather Channel aficionado, you have probably seen the "cone of uncertainty" charts produced by NHC. Its various branches provide watches and warnings on tropical cyclone activity for America. This includes the continental United States but also Alaska and the islands of Puerto Rico, the US Virgin Islands, Hawaii, Guam, and American Samoa.

National Center for Disaster Medicine and Public Health (NCDMPH): You can think of NCDMPH as an educational center for various US federal departments such as Defense, State, and Homeland Security. It "advance[s] the Nation's medical and public health readiness for disasters ... [leading] federal efforts to develop and propagate core curricula, research, and training related to medicine and public health in disasters" as well as "maintaining the Nation's joint disaster medicine and public health science and education program for all executive departments."[441]

Administration for Strategic Preparedness and Response (ASPR): ASPR is like the FEMA of public health emergencies. It watches over the health-care industrial base—everything from the manufacture of rubber gloves to blood plasma, pipettes, vaccine development, and CBRN response—and oversees the Office of Medical Reserve Corps (health-care workers). ASPR also owns the Center for the Strategic

National Stockpile, which contains a massive inventory of medical goods from drugs to ventilators.

Plum Island Animal Disease Center and the National Bio and Agro-Defense Facility (NBAF): Plum Island, off the coast of Long Island, New York, hosts some of the nastiest livestock diseases we know of, such as African swine fever, foot-and-mouth disease, and rinderpest.[442] Historians blame rinderpest, a disease that decimates cattle and other ungulates, for contributing to the collapse of the Roman Empire.[443] Plum Island is under decommissioning and will be replaced by NBAF in Manhattan, Kansas, a cutting-edge biosafety level-4 (the highest level) facility to continue research into threats and protective measures concerning zoonotic diseases and animal pathogens. Fun fact: "NBAF's location in Manhattan, Kansas, places it within the Kansas City Animal Health Corridor, the largest concentration of animal health companies in the world."[444, 445]

Pacific Disaster Center (PDC): Located in Hawaii, PDC studies disaster data using large-scale analytics and artificial intelligence. Check out its publicly available Disaster Alert program (live and historic disaster information) and its national disaster risk profiles, which look at variables such as resiliency, vulnerability, and coping capacity.

Center for Excellence in Disaster Management and Humanitarian Assistance (CFE-DM): Also located in Hawaii, it trains military forces in the Pacific on humanitarian crisis response. CFE-DM also produces top-notch case studies on previous disasters, factsheets on the catastrophic risks to select Indo-Pacific countries, and handbooks regarding a country's vulnerabilities and disaster management capabilities.[446] This tiny organization punches well above its weight in output.

Risk mapping entities: Relatedly, there are several organizations dedicated to showcasing disaster risk, some down to street level. **US Drought Monitor** maps both current drought conditions and forecasts.[447] **HazardAware** allows people living in the Gulf area to input their home address and see what threats are likely to hit their house, related costs, and if they are likely to be reimbursed from the federal government.[448]

Other Big Fish

BlackRock Inc. is the world's biggest asset manager, dwarfing even giants such as Morgan Stanley, Goldman Sachs, and Deutsche Bank.[449] Billions of dollars are at stake, so you should expect their advisers to have a keen interest in analyzing risk and future outcomes. BlackRock's 2024 Global Outlook investment playbook does not disappoint.[450] What did the advisers predict for the next few years? In a word: volatility.

Inflation, recession, shrinking workforces, and geopolitical fragmentation were all cited by BlackRock's analysts. High US debt levels were seen as a drag on the economy, with predictions that interest on this debt would soon eclipse spending on Medicare. They nailed that one. The report was published in 2023, but by the end of 2024, debt payments exceeded Medicare payments by at least $150 billion.[451] Structural changes to the international system were seen in artificial intelligence, climate resilience, and aging populations in the world's larger economies.[452] Perils abound, but according to BlackRock, so do profits.

Another entity scoping out calamities is the World Economic Forum (WEF). Much like BlackRock, it publishes an annual report, but this one focuses less on investments and more on hazards. Its 2024 Global Risks report is a survey of roughly fifteen hundred stakeholders in the fields of (1) civil society, (2) international organizations, (3) academia, (4) government, and (5) the private sector.[453] Additional commentary comes from two hundred specialists in the risk and insurance sectors.

What do these leaders foresee in the next ten years? Nothing good. Shockingly, a full 91 percent of those questioned thought that global politics would be upended within ten years with only 9 percent believing in a continued "US-led rules-based international order." In a separate question, thirty-three of the thirty-four global risks queried were assessed as increasing in severity (either frequency or intensity or both). Three-quarters of respondents indicated a moderate (29 percent) or elevated (46 percent) risk of global catastrophes. Another 17 percent assessed this risk at the highest possible rating. Said another way, not even one in ten global experts had a "calm or stable" outlook for the world in the next ten years.[454]

How did WEF survey participants rank various risks? Table 13.1 showcases all thirty-four in order. They are grouped into five categories: Economic (Econ), Environmental (Env), Geopolitical (Geo), Societal (Soc), and Technological (Tech).

1st	Extreme weather events (Env)	13th	Concentration of strategic resources (Econ)
2nd	Critical change to Earth systems (Env)	14th	Censorship and surveillance (Tech)
3rd	Biodiversity loss and ecosystem collapse (Env)	15th	Interstate armed conflict (Geo)
4th	Natural resource shortages (Env)	16th	Geoeconomic confrontation (Geo)
5th	Misinformation and disinformation (Tech)	17th	Debt (Econ)
6th	Adverse outcomes of AI technologies (Tech)	18th	Erosion of human rights (Soc)
7th	Involuntary migration (Soc)	19th	Infectious diseases (Soc)
8th	Cyber insecurity (Tech)	20th	Chronic health conditions (Soc)
9th	Societal polarization (Soc)	21st	Insufficient public infrastructure and services (Soc)
10th	Pollution (Env)	22nd	Intrastate violence (Geo)
11th	Lack of economic opportunity (Soc)	23rd	Disruptions to critical infrastructure (Econ)
12th	Technological power concentration (Tech)	24th	Adverse outcomes of frontier technologies (Tech)

25th	Disruptions to a systemically important supply chain (Econ)
26th	Biological, chemical or nuclear hazards (Geo)
27th	Unemployment (Soc)
28th	Economic downturn (Econ)
29th	Labour shortages (Econ)
30th	Asset bubble bursts (Econ)
31st	Illicit economic activity (Econ)
32nd	Inflation (Econ)
33rd	Non-weather-related natural disasters (Env)
34th	Terrorist attacks (Geo)

Table 13.1: World Economic Forum 10-Year Global Risks in Order

A couple of items are notable from this list. First, the first four risks are environmental. It is no surprise that climate change and related fears would figure prominently in the minds of global experts. Second, in contrast to BlackRock, not a single economic threat cracks the top ten, and two-thirds of economic concerns are in the bottom ten risks. This shows even experts disagree, and radically so. I believe this is a clear indication of the impact of bias and ideology in the expert class, or at the very least how incentives or perceptions can skew beliefs. BlackRock is in the business of *making* money, and many of the WEF participants are in the business of not *losing* it. Both entities are enticed by the lure of power and prestige as well.

This should not come as a major surprise. Even rational risk calculation will yield differing results. For example, Table 13.2 shows WEF's top five risks in very different countries over the next two years.[455]

While "economic downturn" is on every list, its placement varies. Three of the five risks in Iraq are unique among the seven countries featured here. Countries near conflict zones such as Japan and Poland fear war. States have variance just like those who undergo enhanced disaster preparedness. Risks are localized.

Australia	Brazil	Ghana	Iraq	Japan	Poland
Economic downturn	Economic downturn	Unemployment	Economic downturn	Interstate armed conflict	Inflation
Inflation	Inflation	Public debt	Water-supply shortage	Labour shortage	Economic downturn
Household debt	Public debt	Inflation	Energy supply shortage	Economic downturn	Interstate armed conflict
Energy supply shortage	Censorship	Cybercrime and cybersecurity	State fragility	Non-weather-related natural disasters	Use of biological, chemical, or nuclear weapons
Extreme weather events	Inequality (wealth, income)	Economic downturn	Interstate armed conflict	Extreme weather events	Public debt

Table 13.2: WEF 2024 Top Five Risks over Two Years by Country

ELITE PSYCHOLOGY AND CONTROL

Before I move on, remember these authorities and specialists are people too. That is, in the People, Perils, and Politics model, they are *within* the matrix, not impartial observers *outside* of it. Academics, leaders, and professionals come with their own heuristics and biases. I am one of them. I come to the table with my own life experiences that shape how I process disasters, risks, and what I believe are appropriate mitigation actions.

Politicians across the world have the following options to deal with perils: (1) they can *pretend* to solve the issue, (2) they can *pass* responsibility to experts or other politicians, (3) they can amass more *power* and use the heavy hand of the state to address issues, and finally, (4) they can *prioritize* and *portion* disasters, actioning some threats at higher levels than others and sharing responsibility and blame with other jurisdictions and citizens themselves. Leaders pick and choose among these alternatives based on their personal skills and experience, their culture, their circumstances, and their form of government. Like the archetypes of Resilient Citizens, they do not fit in tidy buckets but rather blend.

One of the foundations of elite psychology boils down to one word: control. This should come as no surprise. As I stated in previous chapters, agency is the ability and will to take responsibility and to affect change. It is done to have a *feeling* of being in charge—or, for experts and politicians, to give off the illusion of it. Since elites are people, they will want to fulfill the same requirement, a desire for control.

Farming It Out and Faking It

The term *fantasy document* appears often in academic works looking at government disaster plans.[456] Members of Congress or Parliament do not sit down and personally type out how their country will deal with a catastrophic earthquake; they outsource to staffers, the administrative state, think tanks, and universities. Many times, the professionals tasked with writing the reports or sitting in official hearings are very honest and say things to the effect of, "We cannot predict the future; however, this is our best guess." The Global Catastrophic Risks report of 2024 from earlier in this chapter is stuffed with assumptions, caveats, and clear statements of conjecture. Other reports, from asteroids to hurricanes to pandemic modeling, do similar things. Fantasy documents do *not* refer to these good-faith efforts. Prediction is hard. But they do give cover to both the expert class and the political class that the elites are "doing something."

Fantasy documents are more analogous to TEPCO's plan for the Fukushima reactors. A thirty- to forty-year plan to remove 880 tons of radioactive material punts the solution to the far future, to some other person's term of office or another chief executive officer. Prognosticating rosy economic forecasts, anticipating when victory will be achieved in a war, assuring the public that two weeks will slow the spread... these are habitually the product of fantasy documents.

Fantasy documents get worse as the peril grows larger. Again, experts are human, and they have an upper limit to the number of variables and carnage one can imagine. A year before the 9/11 attacks in the United States, the Pentagon rejected an exercise that had the exact scenario of that fateful day, deeming it "too unrealistic."[457] But at least these documents are an initial stab. Sometimes, governments do not even want to acknowledge a hazard exists, such as floodplains and earthquake zones; it is bad for businesses... and therefore the tax base.[458]

Two additional factors are cost and who gets the credit. Preparedness measures and stocks are not free. They are a budget item that must be justified as a "what if" against things that are here and now. Voters and interest groups both engage in future discounting. Politicians respond to this and are seldom rewarded for what they do before a disaster but heavily favored for their performance after the boom (more on this in a moment).

Are You Positive?

Control has many aspects. A positive dimension is that control can mean *to manage* or *to regulate*. In other words, *predictability* or *stability*. As citizens, we like this! We want our tap water and electricity to turn on, the speed limit to be the same for everybody on a given stretch of road, and our schools to operate on the same schedule. We have efficient brains that like stasis so we can stay in our comfort zones.

What we typically do *not* like is change. This is why election season is so tumultuous. We debate over whether daylight saving time should exist—a worthy debate, by the way, given the twice-annual ritual is harmful to our health. We do not like volatility in our 401(k)s, home values, or bank accounts; we prefer a steady increase over wild stochasticity. We do not like being told by health officials that eggs are bad for us in even years but good for us in odd years.[459] We do not like shock and surprise. Ontological security is intimately intertwined with routines and agency, both of which are forms of control.

Therefore, we overwhelmingly ask our elites to provide us, or at the very least assist us, with this kind of control. Generally speaking, we receive benefits from the work of good elites. We ask our political officials for regulations and laws that we prefer and give them the power to enforce compliance. We tell our investment advisers how much risk we can tolerate so that we can avoid bankruptcy. We want real science to give us treatments for cancer and engineering designs for car airbags, and to keep poisons out of our food supply. We want experts to save lives, provide warnings, and promote health.

The mature among us know that life is rather complex, there are no silver bullet solutions, and sometimes "it depends" is the right advice. *This is normal.* Real science often changes as new information, or new ways of looking at information, come about. Real science loves inquisition and debate, and it is not hate speech to proffer alternative hypotheses.[460] Real science is messy and knows that a lot of "The Science" is often balderdash.[461] As to politics, it involves compromise. You can't please all the people all the time.

But we are fickle. When things go south, we clamor to be saved, even if we were the ones to make poor decisions. Bailouts, student loan forgiveness, obesity drugs, search and rescue of stranded hikers, consumer protection warnings that tell you not to iron your shirt while you are wearing it, flood or fire insurance cheaper than it should be, and on and on. We tell our leaders, "Don't just stand there, do something!" And they are happy to oblige.

Elites, just like us, do not enjoy failure; they like stability too. And we certainly do not want to be inconvenienced. You cannot simply cast *all* blame on politicians for our national debt or billionaires for income inequality. We keep electing the first group and buying the stuff of the second.

When our applecart is upset, Maslow's hierarchy dominates. Recall that safety and stability are second only to base needs such as food, water, and air. When a disaster strikes, we naturally incline ourselves to a leader who takes charge. This attribute is understandable. We dislike leaders who appear afraid. Recall from chapter 11 that screaming and brute force hierarchy can save lives and assuage fear. Control can bring calm. As one report phrased a common saying, "There's an Unwritten Law in Government of 'Thou shalt not panic or upset the American people.'"[462]

Feelings of favorability rocket upward for politicians who give an aura of control in a crisis. When President George W. Bush stood among the rubble in New York City after 9/11, much of the nation was calmed, and his approval rating went from 51 percent to 90 percent.[463] When Donald Trump survived an assassination attempt in 2024 and rose to the podium—bloodied ear and all—to proclaim "Fight! Fight! Fight!" it caused even his detractors to praise him.[464] Javier Milei of Argentina and Nayib Bukele of El Salvador imposed . . . shall we say . . . unorthodox methods that earned them devoted followers in their extreme approaches to economic insolvency and gang violence, respectively.

One Ring to Rule Them All

You can see the problem. The issue that arises is that we have a large variation in how much control we want and of what type. We do not agree on which cultural and social norms are acceptable. We don't agree on the level or what laws and regulations should be. We are vastly diverse in our levels of agency and ontological security. Too often, we regress to the lowest common denominator, putting our agency in the hands of others. Therefore, control in a negative connotation, that of *power over others,* comes into play. For elites, the default setting is . . . *more.*

You want less crime? OK, you will get more police.

You want safety from belligerent neighboring countries? OK, we will have a larger military force.

You want the problem to be fixed immediately? Sure, we'll pass a law or a regulation for that.

You want protection from viruses? OK, you will get vaccine mandates and masks. Oh, and noncompliance or even disagreement will be met with fines, monitoring, imprisonment, loss of credentials, job loss, shadow banning, deplatforming, debanking, and having your children taken from you.[465]

As the saying goes, "A government big enough to give you everything you want is a government big enough to take away everything that you have."[466] And this negative type of control is often expanded during times of disaster or crisis, both real and imagined. Never let a crisis go to waste, as they say. Such is the interaction of People, Perils, and Politics.

The 2024 World Economic Forum survey I mentioned earlier in this chapter provides another illustration of this tension. There is an interesting chemistry in the survey between (a) *misinformation and disinformation* and (b) *censorship and surveillance*. Misinformation and disinformation jumped from sixteenth place to first place in 2024's two-year outlook. Tellingly, it was also recategorized from a societal risk to a technological one.[467]

Part of the recategorization may have been influenced by the number of national leadership elections worldwide in 2024. Misinformation was ranked the top short-term risk in India, sixth in the United States, eighth in the European Union, and eleventh in both the United Kingdom and Mexico. Contrast this to the rise of censorship in the risk survey. The category of *censorship and surveillance* was not even listed in 2023 but came in at fourteenth in the rankings for 2024's ten-year list.[468] What are we to make of this?

Again, the default setting of elites is to maintain control. Often the media is a willing accomplice in the censorship department, either because it is an official or unofficial arm of the state or because it ideologically aligns with the state leadership.

Elon Musk purchased Twitter in the autumn of 2022, roughly a year prior to the WEF's 2024 global survey, conducted in 2023. Musk uncovered heavy partnerships between Twitter's old guard and the federal government to censor viewpoints antagonistic to or divergent from the official narrative. The year 2022 also saw a furor over the Department of Homeland Security and its Disinformation Governance

Board, which—depending on your ideological affinity—was either an important obstacle to misinformation or a freedom-squelching entity. In 2024, Mark Zuckerberg, owner of Meta and Facebook, claimed pressure by President Biden's administration to censor certain perspectives as well. Europe is undergoing similar discussions of censorship (authoritarianism?) as well. Like the old adage about Congress, "Throw the bums out, but not my bum," our attitude seems to be *billionaires have too much power over government and information . . . but not my billionaire.*

Department of Hurt Feelings

Simple disagreement becomes problematic in the context of negative restrictive control. Globally, free speech is on the decline. One report showed that in 2023, of the twenty-two democracies analyzed, 78 percent of new polices were restrictive in nature.[469] A study in late 2024 found three-quarters of Germans self-censor out of fear of repercussions.[470] There is a massive political angle in all the preceding examples, with those right-of-center more restricted than more left-leaning expressions.

Self-censoring and speech restriction are also prominent on college campuses worldwide. In the United States, those who attend Ivy League and other elite institutions—and their counterparts internationally—are the next generation of world leaders. The left-leaning bias is overwhelming. By one estimate, 60 percent of professors self-identify as liberal and just over 10 percent as conservative.[471] Another noted "radicals, activists, and Marxists" enjoy a 10:1 advantage over conservatives.[472] A 2022 survey of Harvard faculty found 82 percent were liberal, and just 1.46 percent characterized their political leanings as conservative.[473]

University professors and academicians have other related issues that revolve around *groupthink* or *wrongthink*. In the publish-or-perish world of academia, the pressure is on. Given that academics (in the case of professional journals) and bureaucrats (in the case of grant money or other funding) tilt significantly in one political direction, your research needs to toe the party line if you want it to be published or funded. For some experts, the most frightening disaster is a rejection letter from an editor or a budget cut.

Shaming is another social control tool. For example, public health officials monitoring certain diseases that are spread more readily in the gay community feared accusations of homophobia or racism if they dared suggest a moderation in high-risk activities.[474]

Unfortunately, when classrooms and research become this biased, we get a snowball effect of "The Science," which transforms into something closer to propaganda. For example, cigarettes were once considered healthy, and doctors even recommended them. Heterodox or iconoclastic thought is shunned and even punished. Our political tribalism, not the underlying morality or ethics of the issue at hand, skews whether we support or oppose whatever dictate comes from on high. Control—of the negative kind—is rewarded. I have personally witnessed this on numerous occasions and settings.

If academics are prominently skewed leftward in their ideologies, they are likely to reject actions and opinions that are categorized as politically associated with right-of-center beliefs. Resilient Citizens who have Sentinel or Faithful tendencies are most likely to feel this, but as I showed in part one of this book, the Dominant depiction writ large of those individuals preparing at far greater levels casts them as crazies. Climate change will be seen as an acceptable fear for Dominants, but not vaccines, gun confiscation, or the Antichrist.

Everybody, Calm Down

There is a final consideration in elite psychology. It is called *elite panic*. A stubborn belief among the elites—and therefore contained within catastrophe documents or emergency response operating procedures—is that in major perils, the populace is going to go feral. Officials believe that we are one major earthquake away from a *Lord of the Flies* scenario.

Sadly, many prepper forums and books have said the same thing for decades. Society is only "nine meals from anarchy" or YOYO (You're on Your Own) when crisis strikes. Several wealthy individuals fear social strife at scale as a high-probability event. Sentinels fear these Without Rule of Law scenarios, and those who prep in the Noah fashion desire bunkers or bolt holes in their survival planning.[475] Thankfully, societal panic is extraordinarily *uncommon*. What is far more common—and heavily documented—is how communities come together post-crisis. Score one point for the Interdependent.

The term *elite panic* was coined in 2008 by two professors at Rutgers University. Their findings indicate "one of the most robust conclusions in sociology [is]: panic is rare."[476] So why is the belief so persistent among the ruling class? "Politically, the problem of panic endures because . . . it resonates with institutional interests. [And] such an approach advances the power of those at the top of organizations." Said another way, panic is a useful tool for those who desire to maintain control. "The powerless, not the powerful, are said to panic. Arguably one reason for the rhetorical distinction is that the term panic is pejorative, usually coupled conceptually, if not literally, with claims of 'irrationality.'"[477]

Now you have a greater appreciation of the psychology of the elites, including politicians, and their interaction with ordinary citizens. You should realize our ruling class has incentives to provide for the common good but also be responsive to our (sometimes irrational) demands for safety and security, which often trend toward perverse outcomes. The blanket of security to some is a straitjacket to the agency of others, but too many of us feel snug wrapped up so tight.

Blame and responsibility are in tension; Maslow strikes again.

WE ARE ALL IN THE SAME BOAT

Remember, my goal is not primarily to convince you these various authorities are accurate, all-knowing, all honest, or all dishonest. I am also not arguing that you must take their various problems and solutions at face value or that each of these organizations is crying, "The sky is falling!" to secure continued funding or reelection. Rather, my goal is to demonstrate the overwhelming number of voices, from large to small, specialized or catholic, who are blowing trumpets and issuing prognostications of threat and doom, even if they are staffed by imperfect people.

If you dismiss the preparedness actions of Resilient Citizens as preposterous, then you must also sweep away the claims of those in charge, those advising the ones in charge, and those studying *what has been* and *what could be.* To be intellectually consistent, you must also dismiss the vast sums of money spent on disaster preparation and mitigation as just as harebrained.

You cannot have it both ways. Either disaster preparedness is rational for everybody or irrational for all.

I argue the former is true. In this book's final chapter, I tell you what you can do increase your personal resilience and agency.

CONCLUSION OF PART TWO

Perils abound and are highly varied, as are our responses. This pairing of disaster to resilience is nothing new. At the most basic level, our interactions—individuals, experts, and politicians—are about stimulus and response. What differs among us is our agency, influenced by our inherent traits, our position, our surroundings, our social milieu, and our conditioning. Thankfully, we can improve our average survival rates and end up physically and mentally healthier from doing so.

PART THREE

POLITICS

The last national American attempt to truly inculcate a deep level of resilience ended in failure. So many of the psychological concepts (protection motivation theory, agency, ontological security, psychic numbing, elite panic, and so forth) and the interfaces of People, Perils, and Politics I covered in part two leap off the page in the following chapters, which form a case study we can learn from today.

A large percentage of chapters 14–16 comes from my archival research at the Truman, Eisenhower, and Kennedy presidential libraries. These repositories contain hundreds of thousands of documents, not just from the presidents themselves but from senior officials, both civilian and military. Of the thousands of pages of information on civil defense, I perused only a fraction.

Nearly every example I read fell under the shadow of a catastrophic nuclear attack by the USSR. There are records from the National Security Council, staff papers, intelligence records, policy papers, White House Central Files, Cabinet meeting notes, and personal diaries of senior staff personnel, among many other official documents. Several of these were once classified "Secret" or "Top Secret," with declassification occurring as recently as 2013. Portions of some are still redacted, maintaining their classifications as recently as 2019 to 2024 when I explored the collections.

The specter of nuclear war changed the presidency and America. The intersection of People, Perils, and Politics is manifest in the following pages in an unfortunately all-too-possible apocalyptic scenario. Whereas I previously discussed the threat of nuclear detonation, the next three chapters are an immersion into history, drawing out the debates, the disagreements, and the horrifying realities of full-scale nuclear war.

The negative perceptions of modern-day preppers have their roots in the atomic era. Preppers did not need nuclear war to justify their enhanced preparedness actions, but the presence of these weapons is sufficient as a stand-alone validation.

Chapter 17, the last chapter of part three, zooms out to government actions, perceptions, incentives, and disincentives regarding preparedness. You may (or may not) be surprised at some of the recurring themes.

CHAPTER 14

THE PRELIMINARIES OF PREPAREDNESS

An evil man will burn his own nation to the ground to rule over the ashes.

—Falsely attributed to Sun Tzu (true author unknown)

Against stupidity the gods themselves contend in vain.

—Friedrich Schiller

We may tend to think of extreme preparedness in this day and age as an anachronism. However, our relative levels of *unpreparedness* are the actual anomaly. Survival from existential threats traces back to antiquity. Even relatively modern examples are abundant, such as the existence of border walls, fortifications, and military garrisons. We, as a species, often like to "bunker up."

This chapter kicks off by explaining the mentality of Fortress America that we inherited from our European lineage and how it was ripped away in World War II and its aftermath. I trace the birth of the Cold War and the plans enacted in the era of atomic weapons—plans that even presidents believed would make the US Constitution a dead letter, plans that presuppose tens of millions of dead and the annihilation of our current way of life. I show how seriously senior leaders took the logic of enhanced disaster preparedness.

Note: All dollar quantities are left in their original amounts and not adjusted for today's inflation.

THE GOLDEN AGE OF CIVIL DEFENSE FOR AMERICA

Hohenwerfen Castle, which I discussed in chapter 8, is a relic of the realities of ancient and medieval Europe. But an ocean, a continent, and several centuries separate Hohenwerfen Castle from an entirely different fortress, Fortress America.

After the Mexican-American War of 1846–1848, the United States faced no existential foreign enemy. Within a few decades, the West was "won," and American Indians were placed in reservations. This created a radical cultural shift, far different than that exhibited during the time of America's founding. Our walls were not made of concrete but of saltwater: the Atlantic and Pacific Oceans.

Not since the War of 1812 was the United States ever seriously threatened by adversarial powers... and now the British and Canadians are our allies. World War II came close to shattering the myth of Fortress America with the wake-up call of Pearl Harbor; however, this was an attack on an island far away, not the mainland. It was instead two different types of conflict, the Cold War and the Korean War, which first penetrated the walls of the American psyche, particularly of the military and civilian leadership.

The 1950s and 1960s should be considered the golden age of civil defense for America. The birth of that epoch came out of the death of the prior. It was midwifed by a single man, President Harry Truman (term of office: April 1945–January 1953). It was Truman who made the final decision to drop two atomic bombs on the Japanese, effectively ending World War II. It was Truman who, first through Executive Order 10186 and then via the Federal Civil Defense Act of 1950, established the Federal Civil Defense Administration (FCDA), a recognition of the beginning of the Cold War. After the conclusion of World War II, Truman faced a host of challenges. America was transitioning from a major war footing back to normal. Foodstuffs and other materials were still under heavy rationing. Meat and sugar were luxuries. Inflation hit 50 percent (!!) and remained in the double digits for years.

And yet it was not the US nuclear attack against Japan in 1945 that spurred renewed interest in US homeland preparedness. In fact, the Office of Civilian Defense, in operation since 1941, was shuttered two months *prior* to Hiroshima and Nagasaki. Instead, it was bookended by two events. The first was the Union of Soviet Socialist Republics (USSR) detonation of Joe-1, their first successful nuclear weapon test in August 1949, and then the entrance of the Chinese into the Korean War in October 1950. Both actions were nothing less than strategic surprises. US intelligence agencies believed the Soviets were *years* away from a functioning nuclear bomb. Similarly misguided, the US military and political establishments thought it inconceivable that China would ever enter the Korean War. American elites came to realize the walls of Fortress America could be breached.

NSC 68

Between these two events came perhaps the most seminal strategic document ever produced by the United States: *The National Security Council Report, Number 68: United States Objectives and Programs for National Security*. It is more popularly known by historians, political scientists, and military officers as NSC 68.[478] Philosophically, the report reached back to America's founding, intertwining Christian imagery and patriotic fervor. Its writing influenced presidents, politicians, and pundits for decades afterward. NSC 68 is still taught in the US Army War College in the Department of National Security and Strategy and is discussed frequently by professors who work there.[479]

This top secret document was declassified in 1975 by Henry Kissinger, but its origination came on January 31, 1950, when President Truman directed that the Secretary of State and the Secretary of Defense "undertake a reexamination of our objectives in peace and war and of the effect of these objectives on our strategic plans," as it became more likely that the Soviet Union would develop fission and thermonuclear bomb capability.[480] But the document went far beyond considerations involving just the Soviet Union. It set the foundations of a new global order. If Fortress America were no longer secure, based on its relative geographic isolation from the world, then the US would have to act beyond its borders and contain those who would threaten it.

NSC 68 cited as its justification the collapse of nearly all other major players on the world stage except for the US and the USSR. It noted that within thirty-five years, the world had been consumed by two global wars and had been rocked by two massive revolutions, the Russian and the Chinese. "It has also seen the collapse of five empires—the Ottoman, the Austro-Hungarian, German, Italian, and Japanese—and the drastic decline of two major imperial systems, the British and the French," the document added. "During the span of one generation, the international distribution of power has been fundamentally altered."[481] For several centuries, there had been no global hegemon, and nations had worked together (and against one another) in coalitions. But in the wake of World War II, a superpower would have to emerge.

The United States would become that hegemon, the leader of the free world. Had I not told you this report came from a *Democrat* administration more than seventy years ago, you could be forgiven if you thought it sounded like a speech from President Ronald Reagan or a "Christian Nationalist" from 2024.[482] Defining freedom and then spreading it throughout the world was the underlying argument of the text, which read, in part:

> The fundamental purpose of the United States is laid down in the Preamble to the Constitution: ". . . to form a more perfect Union, establish justice, insure domestic Tranquility, provide for the common defence, promote the general Welfare, and secure the Blessings of Liberty to ourselves and our Posterity." In essence, the fundamental purpose is to assure the integrity and vitality of our free society, which is founded upon the dignity and worth of the individual.

> Three realities emerge as a consequence of this purpose: Our determination to maintain the essential elements of individual freedom, as set forth in the Constitution and Bill of Rights; our determination to create conditions under which our free and democratic system can live and prosper; and our determination to fight if necessary to defend our way of life, for which as in the Declaration of Independence, "with a firm reliance on the protection of Divine Providence, we mutually pledge to each other our lives, our Fortunes, and our sacred Honor."[483]

In contrast, the Kremlin was portrayed as the embodiment of pure evil. Whereas Americans were good and God-fearing Christians, the USSR was a "slave state" and a "slave society" where the "system becomes God, and submission to the will of God becomes submission to the will of the system."[484]

Benjamin Franklin once suggested the phrase, "Rebellion to tyrants is obedience to God" be placed on the Great Seal of the United States. NSC 68 channeled that belief two centuries later. The terms *values* and *rights* fundamental and inherent to individuals are mentioned no fewer than thirty-one times.

Americans possessed not just the knowledge of—but the free expression to have—natural rights; and all the world should share in this. However, NSC 68 noted America should spread freedom across the world by consent rather than by compulsion. The United States would not seek to destroy the USSR but rather bring it into international norms. Critically, the document noted that under this framework, the global order was not "inflexible" and not necessarily peaceful: "It will consist of many national communities of great and varying abilities and resources, and hence of war potential."[485] NSC 68, therefore, set the stage for an epic contest between the self-proclaimed forces of good (America) and those of evil.[486]

The writers of the text believed the Soviets would employ a clandestine counteroffensive, targeting the opinions and will of the American people. They observed that the Soviets operated through infiltration and intimidation and thus sought to turn the institutions of American society against their own purposes—threatening labor unions, civic enterprises, schools, churches, and media with subversive opinions to corrode their material and moral strength.[487]

If you wish to understand one reason why US presidents and members of Congress of both political parties have sought to spread democracy throughout the world, why there were roughly 750 US military bases in eighty different countries in 2023,[488] and why there is such animosity against modern-day Russia, part of the answer lies in the spirit of NSC 68. As Dr. Patrick Garrity notes, "If the Soviet Union had been principally responsible for the origins of the Cold War, the United States seemed to bear the onus for having radicalized, militarized, and globalized the conflict."[489] The theoretical roots of such terms as *misinformation, disinformation,* and *malinformation* flow through the report as well.

To combat such an evil Soviet empire and make the world safe for democracy, massive increases in US military spending would be required. While the writers of NSC 68 proposed four "possible courses of action," including a continuation of current policies or a doctrine of isolation, a radical expansion of US power was the preferred route. The recommendation was:

> A more rapid building up of the political, economic, and military strength of the free world than provided under a, with the purpose of reaching, if possible, a tolerable state of order among nations without war and of preparing to defend ourselves in the event that the free world is attacked.... A program for rapidly building up strength and improving political and economic conditions will place heavy demands on our courage and intelligence; it will be costly; it will be dangerous. But half-measures

> will be more costly and more dangerous, for they will be inadequate to prevent and may actually invite war.[490]

Of course, this would also necessitate increased taxes on the American people. But such is the price of freedom because "budgetary considerations will need to be subordinated to the stark fact that our very independence as a nation may be at stake."[491] How much of an increase on defense did NSC 68 recommend? A near quadrupling. The 1950s defense baseline was $13 billion; NSC 68 would raise this to $50 billion.[492]

President Truman initially balked at the hefty price tag. In a note to James Lay, executive secretary of the National Security Council (NSC), Truman asked the NSC to "provide further information on the implications of the Conclusions contained" and noted costs needed to be further studied.[493] Truman's prescient concerns came to light under his successor, President Eisenhower, a few years later. In the meantime, fate would intervene. Two months later, in June of 1950, the Korean War erupted. Before the year's end, US and Chinese troops would clash on the peninsula.

Fear is a motivating force. And just as ontological security is at the heart of many individual motivations, it also heavily influences states and their leadership.[494] While NSC 68 acknowledged the Soviet Union's Gross National Product was a fraction of the US's (roughly 25 percent), the nuclear shadow loomed large. NSC 68 stated that should a war with the Soviets occur, "it must be anticipated that atomic weapons will be used by each side in the manner it deems best suited to accomplish its objectives."

America in 1950 was not yet immersed in the Mutually Assured Destruction (MAD) way of thinking, but nuclear war and fallout were clearly concerns. Indeed, billions would later be spent on Continuity of Government investments and nuclear bunkers for key military positions as well as senior members of the executive, legislative, and judicial branches of the federal government. Fortress America was vulnerable. But what about its citizenry?

After the Chinese entrance into the Korean War, Truman had seen and heard enough—too many surprises, too many prophesies of impending doom, too many hardliners on his staff. Truman reacted with Executive Order 10186, issued on December 1, 1950. It authorized the creation of the Federal Civil Defense Administration, whose chief executive would be paid the princely sum of $17,500 a year.[495] Afterward, in a time span of less than six weeks, Congress passed and Truman signed the Federal Civil Defense Act of 1950. The act put forth a "basic framework for preparations to minimize the effects of an attack on our civilian population, and to deal with the immediate emergency conditions which such an attack would create."[496]

At the Truman Presidential Library on the outskirts of Kansas City, Missouri, Civil Defense and the specter of nuclear holocaust feature prominently. There are photos of pupils conducting "duck and cover drills" at schools, pamphlets on civil defense aimed at wives and children, and numerous examples of backyard construction plans for fallout shelters.[497] The possibility of nuclear annihilation was promulgated from the president of the United States down to *Popular Science* magazine. Truman deserves credit for his work on introducing extreme disaster preparedness as conventional to the average citizen, but it was his successor who husbanded the next evolution in preparedness, both for the federal government and the people.

MATURATION

Along Interstate 70, a few hours' drive west from Truman's presidential library, is Abilene, Kansas, home of the presidential library and museum of Dwight Eisenhower, who took office on January 20, 1953, and served until 1961. During President Eisenhower's tenure, the production of nuclear weapons in the United States increased exponentially. The nuclear stockpile under Eisenhower, supervised by the control of the

Atomic Energy Commission, jumped to more than twenty thousand warheads of various yields, from tactical to strategic. Although a few years behind, the USSR ramped up their production as well. The arms race was on, peaking at *sixty thousand* nuclear weapons (possessed by the US and USSR) just before the collapse of the Soviet Union.

If the immediate period following World War II was the genesis of America's shift to a global hegemon, NSC 68 and its implementation was the puberty stage for America's "military-industrial complex." Eisenhower oversaw a massive expansion in arms production, which to that point was uncharted territory for the United States.

NSC 162/2

What prompted Eisenhower to resist some of NSC 68's starker recommendations? Part of the answer lies in a National Security Council report presented to him in his first year in the Oval Office, NSC 162/2.[498] NSC 162/2 reads as a more somber, clear-eyed assessment of US strategy, and its bravado is considerably muted as compared to NSC 68. The end state remains the same—the defeat of the Soviet Union with an emphasis on a strong US military with a large nuclear arsenal—but real and sizable constraints are considered. The document reflects a still threatening USSR, hard lessons learned from the Korean War that ended just a few months earlier, economic reality, national self-interests of allies and potential allies, and the mood of the American populace.

Three points illustrate major shifts.

First, money is a finite constraint. The avoidance of "seriously weakening the U.S. economy" is listed front and center as one of the "Basic Problems of National Security Policy." Economic growth, the avoidance of a recession, inflation, the federal budget, deficits, overall federal debt, wasteful government spending, revenue, and repressive taxation are all mentioned as vital issues in their regard to impacts on policy and strategy. NSC 162/2 reflects the fiscal constraints of governmental choices regarding spending (e.g., guns versus butter) and soberly recognizes that allied industrial output would be essential for the Soviet containment strategy to be successful.

Second, NSC 162/2 shows that being the "leader of the free world" and having allies, even staunch allies, is not the same as having carte blanche power over those same nations' spending and their foreign and domestic decisions. Other parties have their own national interests, their own constituents to answer to, and their own opinions on interactions with the Soviet Union. Trade is trade, and many sins can be forgiven...if the price is right. And, just like after World War I, many European countries were loath to be dragged into another major conflict. While not mentioned by name, the fresh specter of the Korean War had to be on their minds. Third world countries, described as "underdeveloped areas" in the document, were also discussed more respectfully and rationally. Overall, the change in the attitude of America toward other nations can be summed up by the declaration in NSC 162/2 that going forward, the goal would be to "retain the cooperation of our allies" and "seek to win the friendship and cooperation of the presently uncommitted areas of the world."[499] This is a marked departure from the hubris of NSC 68.

Finally, and perhaps most tragically, is the trap the writers of NSC 162/2 found themselves in: that of overextension and pride. It identified the fact that "the armed forces of the United States are over-extended" but that *any* withdrawal from "Europe or the Far East would be interpreted as a diminution of U.S. interest in the defense of these areas."[500] Nuclear weapons, though, would remain a key strategic asset and deterrent against the Soviet Union. By reciprocity, Fortress America would remain vulnerable to nuclear attack.

Civil Defense Under Eisenhower: The National Plan

If NSC 68 focused America outward, another classified document focused it inward. Labeled *Mobilization Plan D-Minus* and presented by the Executive Office of the President, Office of Civil and Defense Mobilization on May 1, 1957, it highlighted actions required by the government and the citizenry if a USSR atomic attack were to occur. The purpose of *D-Minus* was to give the government a game plan after such an attack "to survive, to prosecute the war, to maintain Government, to maintain the unity of the free world."[501] The plan was significant in that it anticipated a surprise atomic attack "delivered in the immediate future." It assumed a near certainty of a nuclear attack, and it outlined in detail the characteristics of nuclear weapons and how they cause damage.[502]

D-Minus presupposed that American Air Defense Operations destroyed 50 percent of incoming USSR bombers but none of the submarine-launched missiles. It assumed 25 million Americans would be killed in the onslaught with another 25 million injured but with the possibility of recovery. Note that this was out of a 1957 total US population estimate of 167 million people.[503] Therefore, planners were guessing 30 percent of America would be killed or injured in this scenario.

Just dwell on that assumption and its implications for a moment. Is it any wonder that it states that this "would require that the remaining human and material resources be organized and directed toward concerted action"? What would be your rational conclusion based on this? Martial law? Seizure of private property? Drafts for the military and forced conscription for industry?

Plan D-Minus was updated in 1959. One of the key changes was the *increase* in the death toll to 48 million but a decrease in the injured to 12 million. Overall casualties were still an increase of 10 million from just two years prior. The updated 1959 version (renamed the *Federal Emergency Plan D-Minus*) is a somber read regarding the balance of government power and natural rights. In some locations, it describes community resilience and bouncing back, with manpower requirements and supplies—including skilled labor—heavily varied across the country. It relies on state and local governments for localized action along with federal assistance. This includes military assistance "upon request."

D-Minus takes a very authoritarian tone in Part II—"Major Federal Policies."[504] Numerous entries prove the point. First, "The President, under his constitutional and statutory authorities . . . will take or direct whatever actions are essential for national security and survival."

What steps are deemed constitutional? Point 12 under "Maintenance of Government and Order" states, "A Federal order will be issued imposing immediate ceilings on prices, wages, salaries, and rents, and steps will be taken to ensure equitable distribution of essential consumer goods." Point 15 declares, "Censorship will be imposed including implementation of the voluntary Censorship Code for public media." The "Survival of the Population" section states, "Restrictions will be imposed on population movement." In context, this appears to be a restriction on spreading radiological fallout, but the document does not limit movement restrictions to this alone.

The "Use of Resources for Essential Purposes" states, "Federal controls will be imposed on production, construction, distribution, manpower, medical services, food, housing, transportation, communications, fuel, power, and water resources."[505] Interestingly, the document also mentions the importance of American gold holdings. In the end, the president can assume "authorities" in the interest of "national security" *even if Congress has not granted that power.*

Please note, this document was created under a *Republican* administration in the 1950s. While President Eisenhower may have reviled and warned against the military-industrial complex in his 1961 farewell address to the nation, his policies were instrumental in establishing total government control and codifying it into established practice during an emergency, a fact Eisenhower painfully recognized and *D-Minus* demonstrably proved.

D-Minus and Preparedness

The first twenty-five pages of the 1959 version of *D-Minus* offer insights of perennial interest in preparedness.[506] There are key planning assumptions that, while not identical to today, are conceptually linked to principles of preparedness (both routine and extreme) that all citizens (regardless of their country) should be made aware of.

First, some areas will be damaged and others will not. Estimates from another document of the time were 169,000 square miles burned, or an area 6,000 square miles larger than the state of California, and 50 percent of the nation covered in radiation, with some pockets persisting for up to two years.[507] This might seem like a commonsense observation, but it explains why it is logical to evacuate if given a warning of an impending threat, such as a typhoon, tidal wave, or the outbreak of war or imminent economic collapse. It is often beneficial to "panic early and avoid the rush." Your stuff is replaceable, you are not.

In catastrophic scenarios involving major physical damage, communication lines will often be down or strained. Businesses will most likely not be open. You can expect local governments (including first responders) to operate at no or low capacity and transportation options to be limited by capacity, debris, or ongoing fires (think of the Lahaina fires in Hawaii in 2023 or Hurricane Helene in 2024). *D-Minus* indicates "weeks, months and in some cases years, will elapse before remaining facilities can be safely used." *D-Minus* also indicates people's morale in the damaged and fallout areas will be very low.

Second, hospitals in the affected area may be destroyed, or their workers may be among the casualties. Health-care facilities away from the center of the disaster will most likely be overrun by the injured. Demand for medical care will dramatically outstrip supply, including medical drugs like narcotics. The planners writing *D-Minus* assumed "several million people will die [from their injuries] who otherwise might have recovered."

Those sickened or injured by the nuclear attack will not be the only victims in the following days, weeks, and months. *D-Minus* predicts hundreds of thousands of tertiary medical demands will be present. Why? Because sanitation will be lower, stress levels will be higher, and "malnutrition and overcrowding" will increase. Additionally, "communicable diseases," including those transmitted by insects and rodents, would be common. Under the heading "Long Term Effects of Radioactive Fallout" in the *Report of the NET Evaluation Subcommittee*, the Atomic Energy Commission estimated genetic effects on 2.8 million pregnancies and live births, a reduction of life expectancy of survivors by 800–1,600 days, and an additional 9.8 million incidences of cancer.[508]

In today's America, the University of California, Berkeley, reported in 2021 that one in six Americans was on anti-depressants.[509] As many as 22 percent of Americans use tobacco products like cigarettes or vaping, according to a 2021 National Institutes of Health report.[510] In that same year, the Centers for Disease Control and Prevention stated that 13 percent of Americans used illicit drugs.[511] How would these groups fare while undergoing withdrawal symptoms?

On top of that, 38.4 million Americans in 2021 had diabetes, representing 11.6 percent of the population.[512] Seven million of them use insulin, and 14 percent of those users reported they "spent at least 40% of their postsubsistence income—what is available after paying for food and housing—on insulin."[513]

In 2022, more than a million Americans stated they rationed their insulin because of cost.[514] Add in the number of people who are obese, and I surmise our modern-day populace would have a far greater demand on medical treatment that could not be met over a very long time horizon after a nuclear attack.

Not mentioned in *D-Minus*, but observed across the world after COVID-19, and applicable in any large-scale disaster, is the number of future illnesses or deaths caused by a lack of normal medical care and screenings. By one estimate, restrictions to health care caused by COVID-19 mandates prevented 9.4 million cancer screenings in the United States just for the year 2020.[515] When we see government predictions and estimations on potential future disasters that seem far-fetched, actual events prove some of them could be very realistic... or frighteningly even underestimates. Separating hype from rational calculus is difficult, though.

Stress and a loss of healthy habits will also contribute to negative well-being. Harvard Medical School discovered from patient data that 39 percent of people gained weight during the lockdowns, 10 percent of which saw increases of more than 12.5 pounds.[516] An American Psychological Association survey reported 42 percent of Americans gained weight, with an average increase of 29 pounds![517]

The third area mentioned in *D-Minus* revolves around food production and consumption. The authors of this federal emergency plan believed food access would be varied across the country, with distribution issues and radiological contamination contributing to shortages in some areas. While they believed home food stocks would generally be enough to meet immediate needs and nationally there would be enough food for the populace in the intermediate term, this latter assessment was only because 30 percent of Americans would be recently deceased as an immediate consequence of the disaster. Additionally, the government assumes that:

> Rationing has been instituted by local authorities in many areas and will be instituted nationally as quickly as conditions permit... [and] [n]ational control is being established over all production, processing and shipments of food products to be used outside the immediate area in which they are produced.

Under *D-Minus,* capitalism is abandoned, and any food destined beyond the local area would be controlled entirely by the federal government—a new twist on the idea of farm-to-fork.

D-Minus notes potable water may become a luxury, both because fresh water is contaminated in the attacked areas and because power systems to deliver it have been knocked offline or destroyed. In some areas, it will be "necessary to employ makeshift and primitive methods of supply and treatment."

Housing is another area discussed. While the Third Amendment to the US Constitution prohibits the government from quartering soldiers in your house, *D-Minus* allowed it to place survivors there or in your business without your consent under the title of "enforced billeting measures."

Banking in damaged areas would be nonexistent, and even in some undamaged areas, the planners expected "financial transactions ... to reach a standstill."

Communications would be subject to relentless strain as well as continued enemy attack. Undersea cables could be cut, and electronic jamming could impact other methods of information transmission. More than sixty years later, our modern world is just as vulnerable to satellite jamming (or destruction), cut cables, and cyberattacks knocking out nodes of communication. The internet is highly susceptible to these latter two risks.

Electric power needs in 1959 were "most acute ... for refrigeration, hospital operation, community water systems, heating, and mass feeding." *D-Minus* assumed there would be enough for the nation's minimal needs, but the repairs would be "slower than in cases of natural disaster" due to a lack of available manpower and the danger of irradiated areas. Twenty percent of US industries would be destroyed, with 60 percent "denied by radiation for periods varying from two weeks to one year."[518]

Transportation hubs and spokes will be under "severe disruption." *D-Minus* assumes heavy damage to several ports, warehouses, and "related facilities." International trade and travel to and from the US is also assumed to be heavily curtailed. Cargo ships and tankers will rarely have military escort.

While most of the nation's trains and trucks will be spared, fuel shortages will bring heavy restrictions, as supplies are diverted to military assets and items deemed essential. The plan states, "Idleness will be forced upon more and more of the prime movers in all forms of transportation" because of fuel shortages, including for essential purposes such as food production and engines for water supply, hospitals, and sanitation. Thankfully, the United States has a plentiful amount of local production of oil, natural gas, and coal mines, so *D-Minus* anticipated shortages and disruptions lasting several months and not years.

Because communications will be limited and much of the population will be dead or dispersed, and because of the overriding desire to contact loved ones and return home, *D-Minus* assumes manpower requirements for recovery and rebuilding will be heavily limited initially. What is not mentioned but could be assumed in 1959—and perhaps today—is the drain on manpower if a military draft were reinstated and hundreds of thousands, if not millions, of people were pressed into uniform to go to war or, at a minimum, provide additional defensive capabilities.

Every Resilient Citizen archetype I described would find a defense for their actions by reading *D-Minus*.

Let me pause here to summarize the planning factors that *D-Minus* took seriously. In the event of a nuclear attack, 30 percent of Americans would be killed and several million more injured and dying in the coming days. Blessedly, numerous locations across the country would not be impacted, but the national aggregate demand for food, water, power, medical supplies, fuel, and communication would vastly outstrip supply. While some areas would remain under local control and have enough to get by for the short- to medium-term, several areas of the country would come under strict federal governance. Much of what little excess there was would most likely be diverted to a war effort, with the military and the government taking the first cut.

During the time frame in which documents such as *D-Minus* were created, the US government understood all of this. The federal bureaucrats knew they could not possibly succeed in acting strictly at the federal level. They had to do something.

And, as we will examine in the next chapter, the household preparedness messaging, which began under Truman, took on renewed vigor under the Eisenhower administration.

CHAPTER 15

THE PINNACLE OF PREPAREDNESS

The Virgil Couch papers in the archives of the Dwight D. Eisenhower Presidential Library contain a "large volume of civil defense publications put out by private organizations, associations, businesses, corporations, and individuals. Private groups developed specialized materials to educate their members, and businesses and industries created manuals and information kits to prepare their employees for atomic attack or natural disasters. The U.S. Chamber of Commerce put out a brochure on family fallout shelters, and the Western Electric Company printed manuals on fire fighting and the work of a civil defense warden. These materials document the extent to which the entire nation became involved in the subject of civil defense and in the drive to prepare for nuclear attack." Holistically, "the materials contained within the Couch Papers reflect U.S. Government activities having psychological impact on the American people."

—The Dwight D. Eisenhower Presidential Library

Our Homeland Is Not A Sanctuary

—Posted at the entrance of the North American Aerospace Defense Command and Northern Command

The concept of civil defense, including nuclear shelters for the average American, took shape under the Federal Civil Defense Agency. Both public and private options were heavily debated, including discussions regarding lives saved and price tags.

Tiered response is the concept that government response to disasters starts locally and then builds upward. Tiered responsibility is the concept that everyone has a role to play in preparedness, including the individual. The Eisenhower years were the public blitz for shelters and tiered responsibilities in a paradigm of nuclear war.

For the reader's awareness, several quotes or references were taken from my archival research notes in the Eisenhower Library. I annotate the name of the documents for sourcing and citation. Unless noted, they are all a part of the Virgil Couch collection.

CULMINATION: THE PINNACLE OF CIVIL DEFENSE

Mobilization Plan D-Minus and its derivatives were not created by a fringe group of lunatics. This was not a position paper crafted by a few Senate staffers, a think tank on K Street, or a random low-level staff officer in the military. Instead, these were products of rational officials working at senior levels of government reflecting the common zeitgeist of the country and the analysis of classified intelligence from US and allied sources. *D-Minus* was distributed to every federal agency: the Departments of Transportation, Defense, Commerce, Agriculture, and Labor as well as the Federal Aviation Administration, the Federal Deposit Insurance Corporation, the Federal Reserve System, the National Aeronautics and Space Administration, and several others.

These plans and policies were assembled for approval by the president of the United States and presented to key Cabinet and Pentagon-level officials by some of the most brilliant minds of the day. One of these men was Virgil Couch.

Couch began working in the Federal Civil Defense Agency (FCDA) the same year in which Truman created it, 1951. He served in a variety of roles during his twenty-one-year career, even as the organization morphed over time and changed its name and structure.

Born in 1907 in Princeton, Kentucky, Couch would later graduate from the University of Kentucky with a degree in commerce.[519] After a five-year stint in the oil industry, he joined the US federal government, working in a series of farm-related jobs from 1935 to 1948. In 1948, his life took a radical turn. That year, Couch became the director of personnel in the Economic Cooperation Administration, which oversaw the Marshall Plan rebuilding war-torn Europe. Three years later, he would move over to the FCDA, serving in a variety of top roles, where he remained until his retirement.

Couch's influence on civil defense was voluminous. Within the Eisenhower Presidential Library, the Virgil Couch Papers make up 15.2 linear feet of shelf space comprising more than thirty thousand pages of "reports, plans, speeches, charts, guides, articles, memoranda, booklets, bulletins, notes, outlines, and periodicals."[520] The Eisenhower administration worked on civil defense in secret and yet pushed information to American households at an intensity far higher than even Truman's respectable effort.

His impact was so great that in October of 1961, Couch became the first career federal employee to ever grace the cover of *TIME* magazine. He was the literal face of the agency, earning the nickname "Mr. Civil Defense." While this public-facing effort was used to sell disaster preparedness to the American people, the classified reports undergirding the campaign were kept far from the public eye.

The July 1, 1957, *Report to the National Security Council by the Special Committee on Shelter Programs* was previously marked as Top Secret.[521] It was declassified in 1999. We now know the 1959 *Federal Emergency Plan D-Minus* estimated forty-eight million Americans would be initially killed in a nuclear attack by the Soviets with another twelve million injured. The defense budget in 1950 was $13 billion. The NSC *Shelter Programs* report aimed to calculate the cost-benefit of a massive nationwide fallout shelter initiative. Effectiveness was determined both by "the number of casualties which could be prevented and the cost per casualty prevented."[522]

Eight options were presented, with the level of US civilian protection ranging from partial to full and at a cost of $5.1 to $70 billion. Estimates for cost and casualties were forecast to a 1965 scenario, which presupposed a larger American population and took into account the predicted growth of the USSR's nuclear arsenal. If approved, construction would begin in 1958 and would last eight years.

While only tangentially mentioned, the envisioned construction time took into consideration the demands on raw materials and labor. In the year prior, Eisenhower signed the Federal-Aid Highway Act of 1956, which enabled the construction of an approximated forty-one thousand miles of interstate highway. This endeavor would compete for the same resources, causing a sharp increase in demand.[523]

Writers hypothesized the public would have just a fifteen-minute warning window before incoming detonation and that anyone who could use a shelter would, in fact, use it. Based on the new assumptions, a 1965 Soviet attack against an unprotected America would cause *67–116 million casualties, representing 35–60 percent of the populace.* Under the lowest possible protection plan under consideration, these numbers could be reduced to a casualty level of 52–93 million (27–48 percent of the population). Using the highest considered fallout shelter construction plan, nuclear casualties could be as low as 2–15 million (1–8 percent of the population).[524]

Shelter Programs created a list of 361 potential target areas and classified them based on two variables: population and military-industrial targets. *Shelter Programs* envisioned two types of constructed protection: fallout shelters and blast shelters. Fallout shelters provided radiation and thermal (heat) defense and were estimated to cost less than $120 per person in 1965 dollars. These were construction costs only, not maintenance fees, which added $1.33 per person per year.

By contrast, blast shelters are designed to additionally provide a safeguard against overpressure (the shock wave that occurs in an explosion, measured in pounds per square inch, or PSI). Blast shelters were far more robust (and costly). Under the plan, blast shelters rated up to 30 PSI would cost $172 per person, whereas those at the maximum level of consideration (100 PSI) would cost $528 per sheltered person. Unfortunately, from a cost and threat perspective, blast shelters would be in heavier demand in high-density metropolitan areas and at critical defense nodes, where Soviet missiles would likely strike, causing considerable direct damage. Fallout shelters could be built in the suburbs and countryside, where the indirect and transient effects of radiation would disperse based on debris scatter and wind patterns.[525]

Under the guidance of *Shelter Programs*, locations for construction would be in public areas such as schools, parks, subways, highways, and basements of several buildings. There would also be private shelters, to be constructed under homes or in backyards. As noted previously, under the most expensive and comprehensive option, a full fallout and blast shelter construction program for America would cost roughly $70 billion—$20 billion more than even NSC 68's $50 billion military budget.

Six weeks after the *Shelter Programs* report was published, the president's Council of Economic Advisers, with assistance from the Treasury Department, the Bureau of Labor Statistics, and other agencies, poured cold water over the costs involved and the economic impact on the nation. Their rebuttal, a declassified Top Secret document titled *Economic Implications of Alternative Shelter Programs* (hereafter referred to as the *Economic Implications Report*), listed several concerns.[526] One was the federal budget.

Under the four out-years studied by the council (1959–1962), the US budget was predicted to have a *surplus* of $4–11 billion per year. Under the scenarios studied, some of the lower-level protection plans envisioned by *Shelter Programs* could be built without turning a deficit. However, the authors noted this was only if the construction industry, now ramping up to build a new interstate highway system, had the excess capacity to build, which it did not. Inflationary pressure of both the highway system and the shelter plan would spike costs upward of $2.7 to $5.2 billion per year on top of the baseline figures.

Manpower was another sticking point. As the report notes, "the rise in construction outlays, if shelter program [Option 3] were carried out, would virtually double the growing demands on the construction industry."[527] The *Economic Implications Report* calculated the "Percent of Increase in labor force" required just for the *Shelter Programs'* building requirements would be 5–35 percent. In the key demographics of males aged 20–54, the increase needed would be 62 percent!

The economic adviser council did try to squeeze out ways to make the *Shelter Programs* plans a bit more fiscally palatable. One option was cost sharing, with the federal government providing 60 percent of funding. A variation on this was via tax incentives. However, the authors listed troubles with this idea as well. One proposal was to encourage businesses to construct dual-use buildings for their employees that could serve both as nuclear shelters and as business spaces. However, the authors of the *Economic Implications Report* did not think companies would find "an apparent commercial advantage to be gained."[528] Tax incentives to individuals were also explored. But the cost-benefit analysis was prohibitive, and the Treasury Department was opposed.

National Deliberations on Shelter

The years 1957 and 1958 were bumper years for classified papers to President Eisenhower on nuclear shelters and warfare. Discussions and opinions within the National Security Council varied on the implications, conclusions, and recommendations of the NSC *Shelter Programs* document. One of the more famous documents among historians and political scientists was the Gaither Report, named after one of the senior advisers, H. Rowan Gaither Jr.

This formerly Top Secret November 1957 paper, formally known as *Deterrence and Survival in the Nuclear Age,* was created by the Security Resources Panel of the Science Advisory Committee and opined that the homeland was at risk.[529] This was no surprise, given the panel consisted of a who's who of the defense-industrial complex and included roughly ninety people from think tanks and government defense contractors (Brookings Institution, Institute for Defense Analyses, RAND Corporation), industry (Bell Telephone Labs, Shell Oil Company, Chase Manhattan Bank, Raytheon), academia (Massachusetts Institute of Technology, University of California, Columbia University), and other government agencies (Central Intelligence Agency, US Information Agency, United States Air Force). The Soviets had launched Sputnik only a month prior to the Gaither Report, and public opinion was high on fear.[530]

The report proffered several concerning points:

- The US military was the "main protection" against the Soviets, but it might not be a sufficiently deterrent force against a nuclear attack.
- Gaps in radar coverage and their vulnerability to electronic countermeasures were a real worry.
- The US Navy required more research and development to counter adversary submarine-launched missiles, and the military needed better "air and ballistic missile defense systems."
- The Soviet Union was making rapid economic and military strides forward, including the possession of at least fifteen hundred nuclear weapons.

The panel was very supportive of a "nationwide fallout shelter program" and stated it had "been unable to identify any other type of defense likely to save more lives for the same money in the event of a nuclear attack."

The panel believed, with proper planning and training, citizens could "come out of the shelters and survive" after an attack. Stocks of food and water should be "six to twelve months," and medical research to increase survivability should be undertaken. The panel emphasized that a shelter program would demonstrate the country understood the urgency of the threat, was willing to face it with strength, and, most importantly, "It would symbolize our *will to survive*."[531]

It continued that America's foreign policy should be "in accord with the enlightened self-interest of the United States," and we should let our allies know we would not "retreat to 'Fortress America.'"

Despite the benefits, however, the panel did *not* recommend "major construction" of blast shelters. Cost concerns and internal beltway bureaucracy were listed as hindrances in "Management of Defense Resources." Written just a few months after *Shelter Programs*, the panel's analysis annotated a full-blast shelter program would not cost the $70 billion envisaged by previous estimates but rather $100 billion—roughly eight times the cost of the entire 1950 defense budget.

Over several months, the National Security Council debated commentary in the Gaither Report. These conversations included discussions on bombers, radars, missiles, costs, the steps the Soviet Union was undertaking in its own national shelter program, and active and passive US defense measures, including the construction of blast and fallout shelters.[532]

The Gaither Report was so seminal that nearly twenty years later, both the original report and a multipage commentary section were printed for members of Congress on the Joint Committee on Defense Production. Vice-Chairman William Proxmire stated it was "as great an influence on American strategic thinking as NSC 68" and several other documents from that period.[533]

Interestingly, his commentary noted the several predictions that the Gaither Report got wrong, including the "missile gap" that failed to materialize, the impacts of arms control treaties, and smaller requirements of air defense. But none of this was known in 1957 or 1958. Therefore, the Gaither Report stated, "We must act now to protect, for this and succeeding generations not only our human and material resources, but our free institutions as well." After deliberation, public messaging to the American people on the importance of fallout shelters went into overdrive.[534]

A Nation Prepares: Tiered Responsibility

By March 1958, the NSC was at the phase of prototype shelter analysis. *NSC 5807: Measures to Carry Out the Concept of Shelter* listed detailed proposals with costs. Under research, the government would:

- Test shelters' "radiological defense measure," including "exposure of animals to weapons' effects."
- Design "various prototype shelters," including "architectural designs and specifications for new types of multiple-use shelters which will be attractive as well as practical." The government would also award "grants to schools of architecture and engineering" to "stimulate curriculum development" and "training of new students."
- Fund studies "dealing with psychological, emotional, educational, and morale problems" to determine "tolerance limits under emergency conditions." This would include "medical, food, and water requirements ... and sanitary controls."[535]

Implementation would be a paltry $25 million. Under this concept, just under a hundred prototype shelters would be built. They would range from single-family residence basement shelters to those in hospitals, industrial plants, schools, underground parking garages, and subways. Each would house anywhere from only four people to as many as five thousand.

Another $25 million would be spent on public education. "Bomb phenomenology, especially the nature of gamma radiation" was a critical message to be delivered to the populace so they would know of the importance of immediately using shelters. However, and this is vital, "the public must be convinced that the problem is not hopeless, but can be dealt with effectively through provision of fallout shelters."

Citizens would be encouraged to build their fallout shelters at home. US states would provide "adult education programs" titled "Problems of Living in the Nuclear Age" with both general and technical support. The report called for finding neighborhood leaders to professionally "organize a community shelter effort." Another $100 million would be spent on shelters in federal and military locations.

Although government officials had recommended fallout shelters to the American populace for years, the national effort reached its zenith on May 7, 1958, at 11:00 a.m., when the Federal Civil Defense Administrator, Leo Hoegh (whom Couch worked for), broadcast "the national policy on fallout shelter [*sic*]."[536] Hoegh sent letters to every governor in America. To straddle the line between *informing* and *alarming*, the rollout was done in a "quiet manner."

The FCDA would provide citizens with information on nuclear weapons effects, the construction of shelters, food and water procurement, and the responsibilities of state and local governments. Tiered *response* would be paired with tiered *responsibility*.

Tiered response has been a mainstay of government preparation for generations and remains a key principle today. It simply means local assets will respond to disasters first, then work up to higher levels (county, state, federal, in the case of the US). Related, but far less emphasized, is tiered responsibility. The term has no official definition that I could find, but the notion is either explicit (in the case of countries such as Switzerland) or implied. Tiered responsibility means *everyone* plays a part in preparedness and shares the obligation to be ready. The foundation is individual agency and action, but it also includes businesses, nongovernmental organizations, and informal community ties.

Planning considerations, previously highly classified in the months and years prior to this announcement, were now, in part, made public. The FCDA Administrator's statement ended with an appeal to the logic of extreme disaster preparedness, personal agency mixed with tiered responsibility, and a bit of patriotism:

> Common prudence requires that the Federal government take steps to assist each American to prepare himself—as he would through insurance—against any disaster to meet a possible—although unwanted—eventuality. The national shelter policy is founded upon this principle .... The Administration believes that when the American people fully understand the problem that confronts them, they will rise to meet the challenge, as they have invariably done in the past. This is particularly true, now that the national policy has been declared, backed up with Federal example, Federal leadership, and Federal guidance.[537]

Analysis done by the public affairs team from the FCDA covering the two months after the announcement found editorial commentary was positive and, if anything, a bit stoic. The *Boston Traveler* newspaper printed, "Let the American people have the hard cold facts and let's get started toward doing something about them." The *St. Louis Globe-Democrat* said, "Civil Defense has done a civil service for national sanity .... Civil defense will promote a do-it-yourself shelter policy." And the *Barre Times of Vermont* summarizes what I believe is a timeless message to any national government: "Prudence requires that the government take steps to assist each American to prepare himself against any disaster."[538]

For several years, a blitz of pamphlets, booklets, handbooks, information bulletins, and related materials were poured out on the American populace regarding civil defense. The *Civil Defense Technical Bulletin* of May 1958 provided exquisite detail—including architectural grade renderings, dimensions, and specifications—on various types of home-constructed fallout shelters. This example, and several others of its day, read like a modern *Popular Mechanics* magazine and other do-it-yourself periodicals.

Facts About Fallout Protection instructed people to follow CONELRAD (Control of Electromagnetic Radiation) radio stations so they could know local fallout conditions and when it was safe to emerge. President Eisenhower personally went on the air in May 1960 using one of the CONELRAD radio frequencies to announce the beginning of a "defense exercise against a mock enemy nuclear bomb attack."

Many were published by the successor to the Federal Civil Defense Administration (FCDA), the newly created Office of Civil and Defense Mobilization (OCDM). This new agency was first led by Hoegh. Couch followed him during the transformation.

Financing Your Home Shelter estimated a "do-it-yourself" design would cost just $150 and a professional build by a contractor at $1,500. If you didn't have the money, you could apply for a Veterans Administration loan with an interest rate of 5.25 percent. Of course, once you had improved your home with a shelter, you could expect an additional tax bill of $5.55 per year in the pamphlet's provided example.

The Family Fallout Shelter, produced by OCDM, included updated information gleaned from atomic testing in the Pacific Ocean. It emphasized the vast swath of fallout areas based on prevailing winds. The pamphlet *Survive Nuclear Attack* bluntly stated a "20-megaton explosion ... can kill most people and destroy most buildings within a 5-mile radius of ground zero, a total of about 80 square miles." It informed readers that even though big cities and military centers are likely targets, living in rural areas did not make one safe, and "millions of Americans could save their lives by learning what to do."

Turning up the fear dial, in 1960 OCDM produced *Clay Masonry Family Fallout Shelters*, where Hoegh wrote, "Radioactive fallout respects no person and no place. There is not a home in America that could not be affected by fallout after a nuclear attack." Savvy businessmen took this as an opportunity. For example, a land developer built an entire set of tract housing just north of Hollywood in which every home came with a ten-by-ten-foot fallout shelter under the garage.[539]

OCDM's *Handbook for Emergencies* or their *Home Protection Exercises* handouts give a list of food items, first aid recommendations, and family emergency drills. The latter is introduced by a quote directly from President Eisenhower: "To survive, to be alive after an H-bomb attack, will require that each individual, man, woman, and child, employ to the full every mental and physical resource at his disposal—and these must be trained and equipped resources."

Publications aimed at government officials indicated critical items to stockpile. *Essential Survival Items* listed the following:

- Pharmaceuticals (antibiotics, insulin, anesthetics)
- Blood collection supplies, biologicals (various vaccines and anti-toxins)
- Surgical supplies
- Heavy machinery (bulldozers, five-ton trucks)
- Detection kits and protective items (Geiger counters, dosimeters, protective masks)
- Water purification chemicals (hydrated lime, iodine tablets, chlorine)
- Building materials

If this list were updated to items available in modern inventories, it would make an outstanding checklist for city emergency management.

OCDM took food storage as seriously as it did shelter construction. An early pamphlet on this topic, *Between You and Disaster*, published in November 1958, listed a grocery shopping list for two weeks of survival. OCDM also contracted out to the University of Georgia for a literature review of 735 sources regarding "foods and containers for shelter storage."[540] The report covered publications from January 1959 to January 1960. Which foods would last three years? Five? More than five? What factors could strengthen or weaken longevity? What would it cost, and how nutritious would the selections be? The 1960 report indicated "preference goes to foods that do not require heating," had minimal waste, and contributed to the psychological well-being of the individual.

It may seem striking to us now that the very things preppers are often lambasted for today are listed in official reports as serious items of discussion, which were then broadcast to the public and encouraged in government communications. In the 1960 recommendations, the grocery selections were easily purchased items of the times (including the recommendation to stockpile some cigarettes!), but the government may have overestimated the shelf-life of many suggestions. A modern prepper expert would probably not recommend supplementing with monosodium glutamate (MSG), trusting bacon for more than a year (especially if it was sliced), or white flour for five years.

Our knowledge of emergency food storage safety and health has greatly improved since the 1960s, but even today, there are terrible options sold as emergency foods, a fact I learned the hard way. At one point in my preparedness journey, I stocked up on *years'* worth of emergency food. It was after a rather arduous combat deployment, and I was flush with both cash and the emotional aftermath of a war zone. Several of the items I purchased were "shelf stable" for 10–25 years or more but were laden with junk or sodium. Some of them tasted terrible. My wife and I still joke about how gawd-awful the Pasta Roma packets were. Nowadays, we prepare with pails of staples: rice, sugar, honey, salt, lentils, beans, and so on. This is far cheaper and far healthier. I keep a few cans of dehydrated meals and other items, but only the ones I really like.

An updated version of *Between You and Disaster* called *Family Food Stockpile for Survival* was published by the US Department of Agriculture in cooperation with OCDM. In addition to guidance on how to store food and purify water, it also gave sample meal plans based on limited cooking facilities or no cooking facilities available at all.

Testifying before Congress in March 1959 to a subcommittee under the House Committee on Appropriations, Hoegh was incredibly upbeat.[541] He noted continuity of government programs were moving forward at the state level, emergency communications were improving, and two new federal training centers were established.[542] Marking the administration's shift to tiered responsibility and tiered response from the federal to the local to the individual level, he testified that "the Federal government will give the proper guidance, direction, and example to the States and local governments and the public." Hoegh noted the National Shelter Policy "was based on the oldest American tradition—that every man will protect his family. It defined the government's responsibility to alert the people to their danger and to teach them how to meet it."[543]

Over the next year, Hoegh went on a speaking tour. Portions of his public relations blitz include speeches to the fifteenth annual convention of American Veterans, the International Association of Fire Chiefs, the US Civil Defense Council of Houston, the National Women's Conference on Civil Defense, and the Western Industrial Survival Conference.[544] One theme of his speeches was the intertwining of tiered response and tiered responsibility. In his address to the Department of Defense Conference Group, he stated, "The responsibilities for civil defense in this Nation rest squarely on regularly constituted government at Local, State, and Federal levels, and upon people."[545]

Another theme in his talks is the staunch postulate of good citizenship equaling resilience. In an address to Girls Nation at American University,[546] you can see his appeal to female empowerment, preparedness, and the proper duties of the populace:

> You, in Girls Nation, represent America's greatest asset. You are the leaders of tomorrow. You have been greatly honored. But remember, responsibility is the hand-maiden of honor. Tonight, I will discuss a vital new dimension of citizenship in the Nuclear Age. Under it, you are required to understand, to meet, and to overcome the threat of militant communism. The threat demands that we wage the battle not only with the

material, physical, and economic weapons, but with the mind, the heart, and the spirit.[547]

As we can see by Director Hoegh's official comments and by his OCDM reports and publications, civil defense was an obligation borne by all. As the *Family Food Stockpile for Survival* said, "*Individuals and families will be prepared to exist on personal stocks of survival items in their homes and shelter areas for 2 weeks following attack*" (emphasis original).

Hoegh was not the only advocate from OCDM. In the *Public Affairs Guide for Civil Defense Directors*, senior leaders in OCDM were also directed to engage the citizenry on a "regular basis to keep the public constantly aware of the civil defense program." The effort was a full-court press in all mediums, from radio to television to in-person speeches, as well as the distribution of official publications from OCDM. The message seemed to resonate with a sizable portion of the population.

Virgil Couch engaged with business so often that he also earned the moniker "Mr. Industry Defense." Responding to an inquiry on how to talk to employees, Couch wrote that business leaders' attitudes and encouragement were a "vital service." Workers at factories should be resilient at work and in their communities.[548] Managers in industry should "enlarge their plant protective services such as fire brigades, police, medical and first aid, radiological detection, rescue" and other roles, and each group should "join as reservists or auxiliaries to the appropriate department of local government. In this way the community protective services will have been strengthened, and greater assurance given to continuity of local government leadership and capability for survival in time of disaster."

Couch repeatedly discussed engagement and support of local government and community. He also provided a human and personal touch, noting that his personal home fallout shelter contained a Bible and "additional blankets and clothing," but upon reflection, he chastised himself that he had not yet stocked it with games and a variety of reading materials. Couch encouraged managers to have open conversations with employees and provide them with needed civil defense publications. He noted numerous "manufacturing firms, banks, department stores and other business and commercial firms have done outstanding work in providing such information and education to employees."

One example of this comes from General Electric. That corporation teamed up with OCDM to distribute civil defense packets for their employees. The GE Evendale Plant in Cincinnati, Ohio, circulated the OCDM-approved *Family and Home Survival Kit,* covering preparedness, first aid, stockpiling, and other civil defense motifs. A personal letter—written by N. E. Firestone, the general manager of the plant's flight propulsion division—was addressed to all the employees, emphasizing the importance of individual responsibility. Firestone wrote, "[It] is not my intent to frighten you or to imply in any way that enemy attack is likely. However, by being alert and prepared, you will have a greater sense of security and well-being in the years ahead."

Women were a key demographic in the outreach campaign. In the 1956 Miss America pageant, candidates were asked about civil defense.[549] Several official pamphlets featured women on the cover and seemed to be directed toward housewives. By 1961, the OCDM noted a marked uptick in interest by women after surveying prominent newspaper articles, women's clubs, and parent-teacher associations.[550]

The nation's youth also seemed attuned. A front-page article from July 1960 in the *Chicago Tribune* posted the responses of teenagers when queried if they would "rather acquire a swimming pool for your family or a bomb shelter." All the featured answers indicated a bomb shelter. One student wrote, "There's a probability that the Democrats are going to get in in November. With their appeasement policies, I think we are going to need bomb shelters. Their record always has been war. Chicago would be a prime target."

Another student said, "I'd say, within the next 10 years for sure there will be World War III."[551]

Civil defense was tied to God, guns, and American patriotism. OCDM published the four winning high school student essays from a national competition in *Civil Defense … An American Tradition*. The cover of the pamphlet features a tricorn hat along with a musket and powder horn and was sponsored by the Ladies Auxiliary to the Veterans of Foreign Wars. Girls won first, second, and third place. The first-place essay, from Linda Orsborne of North Wilkesboro, North Carolina, stated:

> I am Civil Defense, an American Tradition. You, my preservers, individuals, and groups … [with] a solid belief in God, have fabricated America, the freest, strongest, most progressive nation on earth.

The essay went on to mention Paul Revere, Molly Pitcher, George Washington Carver, Daniel Boone, Kit Carson, and Johnny Appleseed. The author argued civil defense was inextricably linked to guns, Christian faith, and "the emancipation of the slaves—giving freedom to everyone regardless of skin coloring," the unity of America, and that family participation in building and stocking a fallout shelter would "reduce juvenile delinquency" in an era where there was "lack of unity in the home." The remaining three essays were no less patriotic.[552]

And yet … despite all the reports, despite all the work involved over two administrations, despite the fear, the propaganda, the budgeting, the posturing, the debates within the National Security Council, and all the official publications … no national fallout shelter program ever caught on in high numbers.

What went wrong?

CHAPTER 16

THE PLUMMET OF PREPAREDNESS

The subject of civil defence is unpopular, even distasteful, because it invites an unwanted consideration of the possibility of nuclear war. Talk of it implies that deterrence might 'fail,' and this is a disturbing admission to make, particularly for government leaders of states possessing nuclear weapons. Nuclear civil defence is the embodiment of the most frightful imagery of World War Two. The civil defence shelter jogs the collective unconscious with memories of both terrorising bomb attacks and Nazi death chambers. Civil defence is, literally, unsettling. Whereas the burdens of deterrence are largely intellectual and carried chiefly in the minds of distant statesmen, the burdens of civil defence once implemented are physical and directly influence the daily lives of every citizen. Civil defence is criticised by some for being inadequate while, at the opposite extreme, it is censured by others for representing an excess of state control. One wonders whether a "shelter-centered society" would represent the salvation of humanity in the nuclear age or merely signal the descent into a troglodyte dystopia.

—Lawrence Vale

No one ought to harm another in his life, health, liberty, or possessions: for men being all the workmanship of one omnipotent, and infinitely wise Maker... they are his property, whose workmanship they are, made to last during his, not another's pleasure.

—John Locke

The reason preppers and their forebearers from the 1960s and onward have such a bad reputation originates in the US government's civil defense messaging, the nightmare of the realities of nuclear war, and the protests against omnicide. John F. Kennedy's administration saw the tide go out. Many of his advisers were against public civil defense sheltering plans and messaging. While Kennedy overwhelmingly supported it initially, along with several other proponents, the effort took on an air of government tyranny and overtaxed the American psyche. The blowback was fierce, and the federal authorities retreated to protect only themselves. Internal bickering remained concerning the constitutionality of numerous plans.

Similar to the last chapter, much of my information here came from archival research, this time via the John F. Kennedy library's online database.[553]

FAULT LINES

The presidential administration of John F. Kennedy marked the beginning of the end of the golden age of civil defense, which, as it turns out, was not that golden but merely a fallout shelter façade. Although Kennedy was personally supportive of the effort, festering problems—*some of which were caused or remained unresolved by government planners themselves*—remained. The Kennedy era marks the pivot of national preparedness and public attitudes in the United States that would ripple outward to much of the world for decades, all the way to the present day. Numerous changes came about during his term, which began in January 1961.

Planning updates and reports on civil defense came in from several sources throughout Kennedy's tenure. Not even a month after his inauguration, a formerly Top Secret report was sent to the new national security advisor (NSA), McGeorge Bundy. It gave cost estimates, assessments of probable Soviet attack patterns, and casualty estimations based on a hypothetical nuclear strike set in the future year of 1970. The study's conclusion was 100 million dead initially and another 70 million from fallout out of a total US population of 206 million if no shelter program existed. With a blast and shelter program, at a cost of $30 billion, fatalities could be reduced to 30 million.[554]

Another change was the departure of Leo Hoegh from the Office of Civil and Defense Mobilization (OCDM). Hoegh left government work and went into private business selling . . . fallout shelters.[555] Not all the changes came immediately, and several things stayed roughly the same. Virgil Couch, for example, remained at OCDM.

Hoegh was succeeded by Director Frank Ellis. Ellis was a bulldog of a man. The fifty-four-year-old was once the captain of the Louisiana State University football team in 1929 and played in the tackle position. Immediately before his directorship, he worked as a New Orleans attorney. In the new director's first meeting with the president on March 20, 1961, Kennedy heard the direction Ellis had for civil defense. Ellis wanted "more preparedness training, more bomb shelters, and more funds. As a starter, he asked that OCDM's budget be doubled in fiscal year 1962."[556]

Its current budget in 1961 sat at $104 million. Kennedy "generally speaking" was supportive of this endeavor, and Ellis received only a bit of pushback from Budget Director David Bell, who wanted to increase the OCDM budget a bit slower, an "'easy does it' approach." In his discussion with the president, Ellis wanted to "bring about a great spiritual understanding of the necessity for survival and the re-establishment of a free world should nuclear attack ever occur to ravage this nation." He stated that not preparing was "deliberate suicide."

A week prior to his meeting with the president, and just a week after his confirmation as the new OCDM director, Ellis was interviewed by the *Los Angeles Sunday Times*. Ellis was adamant in his ideology. "We have got to get over the idea of mass suicide." He continued, "As a God-fearing nation, we should condemn the thought that the living would be jealous of the dead in a post-nuclear world. If you don't want to live for yourself you should help others live to rebuild a free world."[557] Education of the masses was one of Ellis's top priorities, including investments in public school programs.

He also wanted to co-opt the 7.5 million federal employees and make them ambassadors of preparedness. At the time he took over OCDM, the office oversaw the "stockpile of strategic materials valued at $6 billion . . . stored at military posts, general services administration warehouses and commercial warehouses throughout the nation." Ellis wanted more. In partnership with the Department of Agriculture, the goal was to increase "storage of surplus foods to be available in an emergency" and locate these foodstuffs across the country. A similar plan was in the works for hospital supplies.[558]

Over time, President Kennedy only increased his support of a fallout shelter program. Part of this may have been due to relative Congressional inaction in terms of budgetary support and criticism by Congress levied against the OCDM. In a staff study report, prepared by the Bureau of the Budget, OCDM was accused "by certain members of Congress as a 'do nothing,' 'boondoggling' organization staffed with incompetent 'political hacks.'"[559] These same congressional members "have suggested that responsibility for civil defense must be borne by the military." The study referenced other sources in support of a shift away from the president and to the military for leading the fallout shelter program and civil defense in general.[560]

Collectively, this may have been a personal swipe against Kennedy himself. Truman was a war president, Eisenhower a former four-star general; Kennedy—who I must add served heroically as a naval officer in World War II and earned the Purple Heart—may have been thought as too junior for the task. Ellis was adamantly opposed to any transfer. In a curt, two-sentence letter to Theodore Sorensen, special counsel to the president, Ellis wrote, "You cannot put civilian leadership and civilian population in a democracy in peacetime under military control."[561]

Three days later, on May 25, 1961, Kennedy addressed a joint session of Congress. After speaking to the issues of strong alliances across the free world, a strong NATO nuclear deterrent, a request for increased funds for military assistance, more money for the military, and an increase to the end strength of the Marine Corps, Kennedy turned to civil defense.

More than 10 percent of his speech was dedicated to this topic. True to Kennedy's oratory skills, this section is remarkable for its lucidity, candor, recognition of limitations, and call for tiered responsibility. It also showed Kennedy was willing to listen to—and work with—those who disagreed with him. I quote him here at length and have italicized key points.

> *One major element of the national security program which this nation has never squarely faced up to is civil defense.* This problem arises not from present trends but from national inaction in which most of us have participated. In the past decade we have intermittently considered a variety of programs, but we have never adopted a consistent policy. *Public considerations have been largely characterized by apathy, indifference and skepticism; while, at the same time, many of the civil defense plans have been so far-reaching and unrealistic that they have not gained essential support.*
>
> This Administration has been looking hard at exactly what civil defense can and cannot do. *It cannot be obtained cheaply. It cannot give an assurance of blast protection that will be proof against surprise attack or guaranteed against obsolescence or destruction. And it cannot deter a nuclear attack.*
>
> We will deter an enemy from making a nuclear attack only if our retaliatory power is so strong and so invulnerable that he knows he would be destroyed by our response. If we have that strength, civil defense is not needed to deter an attack. If

we should ever lack it, civil defense would not be an adequate substitute.

But this deterrent concept assumes rational calculations by rational men. And the history of this planet, and particularly the history of the 20th century, is sufficient to remind us of the possibilities of an irrational attack, a miscalculation, an accidental war, [or a war of escalation in which the stakes by each side gradually increase to the point of maximum danger] which cannot be either foreseen or deterred. It is on this basis that civil defense can be readily justifiable—as *insurance* for the civilian population in case of an enemy miscalculation. It is *insurance* we trust will never be needed—but *insurance* which we could never forgive ourselves for foregoing in the event of catastrophe.

Once the validity of this concept is recognized, there is no point in delaying the initiation of a nation-wide long-range program of identifying present fallout shelter capacity and providing shelter in new and existing structures. Such a program would protect millions of people against the hazards of radioactive fallout in the event of large-scale nuclear attack. Effective performance of the entire program not only requires new legislative authority and more funds, but also sound organizational arrangements....

Federal appropriations for civil defense in fiscal 1962 under this program will in all likelihood be more than triple the pending budget requests; and they will increase sharply in subsequent years. Financial participation will also be required from State and local governments and from private citizens. *But no insurance is cost-free; and every American citizen and his community must decide for themselves whether this form of survival insurance justifies the expenditure of effort, time and money. For myself, I am convinced that it does.*[562]

Much of what Kennedy said remains relevant today. He was right that a civil defense program needs to be realistic; there needs to be a recognition that the state will fail in some way to keep all harm from its citizens. Chance and factors outside of the control of the government will induce certain amounts of risk. Because of that, the proper way to think about preparedness is that it is an insurance plan, not a fail-safe. In hindsight, we know that since the dawn of the nuclear era, America has never been attacked by nuclear weapons nor witnessed a hostile detonation on her shores. The government has a role to play, but that role is not to do everything: The best role the federal government can play is that of recognizing federalism. Finally, preparedness must be rooted in tiered responsibility, from Washington, DC, to the individual citizen.

But his address would not usher in a new era like his "We choose to go to the moon" speech a year later; rather, it was almost a eulogy given *before* a death.

TREMORS

Attempting to identify exactly when the United States turned against civil defense is difficult. However, the period between October 1961 and October 1962 is a reasonable estimate. Civil defense did not nosedive all at once, but the long-term trend was down.

Kennedy was a true believer, and he gave time for his preparedness vision to take shape over the next few months and allow debate and reflection. To keep up the public relations campaign, he planned a televised address to the nation for November 1961 regarding fallout shelters. It would be organized by the Office of Civil Defense (OCD), an organization created as an offshoot of the Office of Civil and Defense Mobilization that same year. OCD would now fall under the Department of Defense, just as Kennedy directed in May. It would be responsible for civil defense planning and would last until 1979, when the Federal Emergency Management Agency (FEMA) was created.

A month prior to his planned November speech, Kennedy penned an open letter to the Civil Defense Committee of the Governor's Conference. In it, he stressed tiered response and tiered responsibility, stating:

> There is a need for a nationwide understanding of what each level of government, each private organization and each citizen can do to bring about and maintain the best attainable protection for the civilian population . . . the goal towards which the federal government, the state governments, industry and other institutions in the United States should work. In simple terms, this goal is to reach for fallout protection for every American as rapidly as possible.[563]

That same day he requested of Congress $100 million to be earmarked for public fallout shelters. Congress soon appropriated $169 million for the effort.[564] Behind the scenes, though, internal battles were heating up. Several advisers to the president stepped up their questioning of the wisdom of the fallout shelter program as envisaged.

One debate was whether a national plan—if fully implemented—would or should increase the bellicosity of foreign policy toward the Soviets. This debate was captured by a now-declassified secret document penned in early October 1961 by Marcus Raskin, who served as the assistant to the NSA. Raskin was no wide-eyed idealist. A lawyer and die-hard progressive liberal, he was a major castigator of government policy and remained so throughout his lifetime.[565] On the one hand, recall that the initial purpose of shelters was to increase the survivability of the population following a surprise nuclear attack, much as the backyard bunkers in Britain were constructed to protect people from German bombs. Civil defense was just that, defensive.

However, some believed that if Fortress America returned, the United States could throw its weight around more on the international scene. Raskin wrote in his letter that civil defense and fallout shelter plans should not embolden policy planners to be more "reckless" because of the safeguard. "Thinking that if we undertake a crash fallout shelter program we can risk nuclear exchange is the height of folly," he wrote. "It is also the height of folly to mold people to believe that because we are preparing spaces, it would be 'not so bad' to have such an exchange."[566]

Another issue that Raskin brought up, and one that resonates heavily in debates surrounding preppers today, is that of preparedness *exclusion*. For years, the government had been hammering the public about the severe shortages that would result from a nuclear exchange, the long duration of recovery, and the paucity of foodstuffs and other goods during this time. Well, the public received that message loud and clear, to deleterious effect.

"We are seeing already the results of a civil defense program," Raskin warned, "people debating whether or not to have guns and to use them against their neighbors in order to keep the fallout shelters for themselves; communities and states discussing the need to have a special militia in order to exclude neighboring communities and states."

Overall, Raskin seemed to personally challenge the strategic logic of a national fallout program. He acknowledged some lives would be saved but that the number was "unknowable." He believed the current civil defense program presented "contradictory instructions" using poor assumptions, especially those based on what the Soviets would, or would not, target in America. In his most frightening (realistic?) analysis, he questioned whether a post-attack America would function under a centralized federal government as envisioned by the writers of *D-Minus* and related plans—

> It is more than likely that after a given attack and knowing of the inter-dependence of the United States, people will be left to their own devices; there will be a breakdown of communications, a pirate system in which those who still have nuclear

> weapons will exercise control by themselves and will use them at their own discretion; there will more than likely be a breakdown of our political system as it is now known and the institution of a system of war lords. During this period it will be necessary to deal with the all encompassing factor of death, bereavement with everyone, hostility against authority, sickness, personal treachery and local dictatorship.[567]

Raskin recommended that President Kennedy should "hold a full scale discussion on civil defense between its proponents and opponents" before Kennedy addressed the nation the following month on the topic. In a previous letter to NSA Bundy, Raskin indicated he personally calculated the odds of thermonuclear war at fifty-fifty—very sobering odds.[568]

At this time, Kennedy's political opponents wanted to paint him as a weak peacenik and a disappointment on the foreign policy scene like his father (and decades later, his nephew Robert F. Kennedy Jr.).[569] Earlier in 1961, Kennedy gave them an opportunity after the Bay of Pigs disaster in Cuba. Kennedy had also campaigned for a nuclear weapons test ban as a "first step to nuclear disarmament."[570] He was successful on this latter front, achieving Senate ratification of the Limited Nuclear Test Ban Treaty in 1963 despite "a fearful public and a divided Senate."[571]

President Kennedy's November speech was to be a full-throated support of a national fallout shelter. In conjunction, sixty million letters signed by Kennedy and fifteen million civil defense booklets endorsed by him would be distributed,[572] a number Raskin (sarcastically?) noted to his boss, NSA Bundy, would be "the most widely distributed piece of literature in man's history outside of the Bible."[573] In a follow-up memorandum, Raskin warned the presidential rollout would "court disaster and create public unrest."[574]

Other interrogations came from Jerome Wiesner. Wiesner functioned as Kennedy's chair of the President's Council of Advisors on Science and Technology and the Director of the Office of Science and

Technology. He would later serve as the president of the Massachusetts Institute of Technology. Wiesner's concerns echoed those of individuals in the Truman and Eisenhower administrations before—namely, cost, policy implications, and public impact. In a note to Bundy, Wiesner asked how exactly funding a $10–50 billion program would work. What would prevent fraud in commercial designs? Would school funds be impacted? "What are the social and political consequences of the fact that a private shelter program will protect only a portion of the population and will favor the better off?"

He indicated disquietude on placing civil defense burdens on citizens, states, and municipalities. If nonfederal entities acted on a shelter program or failed to act, would "dissatisfied" members of the populace "insist" on a federal takeover? "Is it logical for the Federal Government to provide air defense or Nike Zeus missile defense and yet ask the people to provide their own civil defense?" Wiesner believed "state and local organizations are very weak" and counseled that the president should delay his speech until policy matters like these were adequately addressed.[575]

Criticism came in other forms as well and was especially withering against the civil defense pamphlets themselves. One of the many detractors, John Kenneth Galbraith, served in every Democrat administration from Franklin Roosevelt to Lyndon Johnson and frequently taught at Harvard University. Under the Kennedy Administration, Galbraith served as the US ambassador to India. On November 9, 1961, Galbraith penned a letter directly to Kennedy indicating his "grave misgiving" with the pamphlet and the underlying philosophy of the plan behind it.[576]

He was not against a fallout program—and, in fact, greatly supported the underlying principle—but was against the method of its proposed implementation. Galbraith attacked the philosophy of the program in the same way as his contemporaries and in the same blunt manner. First, like Raskin, he struck at the tone, stating the "pamphlet does not make clear that it is American policy to avoid a holocaust." Galbraith, like others, thought the Soviets may get the wrong idea and consider a mass shelter program as an "ostentatious form of war preparation," which would be counterproductive to the very event Kennedy hoped to avoid.

Second, Galbraith seemed circumspect concerning the realities of nuclear war. On the one hand, another great push toward shelter construction felt a bit like doom porn, "likely to set off a certain amount of racketeering on people's fears." On the other hand, he felt the pamphlet did not stress the realities of the apocalyptic landscape survivors would surface to see. Post-strike America "will be a barren and hideous place with no food, no transportation and full of stinking corpses. Perhaps this can't be said but I don't think the people who wrote this pamphlet quite realize this."

His last objection—the topic he spent most of his four-page letter on—was inequality. He brusquely asserted the "present pamphlet is a design for saving Republicans and sacrificing Democrats." Why? Because at home fallout shelters were designed for single-family residences in the suburbs and rural areas, not the cities. This amounted to "social discrimination in survival . . . [w]e don't want to pay the price of deep urban shelters so we are writing off the slum dwellers."[577]

Overall, Galbraith stated he could not support a shelter program as currently designed, with the biggest variables impacting his decision being cost and Soviet perceptions. The combined opposition from Kennedy's advisers had their desired effect. Kennedy would not go on to give a major speech in November 1961.

COLLAPSE

It wasn't just Kennedy's advisers who were souring on the overall concept of civil defense but several portions of the country as well. Kennedy had failed to read the room. Years of public outreach—with positive results—had peaked under Eisenhower, but the climax of the backlash happened under Kennedy.

Anti-civil defense reaction had been building for years. Protesters throughout the country began to push back against preparedness actions, and the civil-military nuclear exercises were viewed by some as morbid drills to normalize omnicide. In New York, a broad coalition of citizens conducted "peace actions" during New York City's "Operation Alert."[578] The drills were a simulation of a nuclear attack, and New Yorkers were mandated by law to participate. Failure to comply came with a $500 fine and up to one year in jail.[579] Some activists who refused were called Communists or murderers and referred by judges for psychological evaluations. One prominent repeat protester, sixty-one-year-old Dorothy Day, was stripped and searched so violently that her vagina was bloodied.[580]

Children were a flashpoint as well. Duck-and-cover drills, made popular under President Truman, were sold to children by Bert the Turtle. Kids in New York City schools were issued dog tags so their bodies could be more easily identified. Parents were encouraged to have their children get tattoos under the armpit since arms might be blown off from shrapnel.[581]

It wasn't just theoretical future fears that got mothers in an uproar. In the late 1950s, moms discovered that nuclear testing had blanketed the earth with a dusting of strontium-90, a nuclear isotope. The strontium was found in cow's milk that children were ingesting and depositing in their bones. The Committee for Nuclear Information (CNI), an antinuclear group, funded the Baby Tooth survey in the late 1950s. Terrified parents could mail baby teeth for testing. Sixty-five thousand samples were gathered, and results indicated strontium in children's teeth was accumulating at an alarming rate. *Consumer Reports* published similar findings in 1961 and 1962.[582] Parents were outraged.

Although not known at the time, 1961 would be the last year for Operation Alert. The nation's political leaders were loath to start accusing protesting mothers and children dressed in their Sunday best as being Communist sympathizers.

While Kennedy did not address the nation in November 1961, as he originally intended, the civil defense pamphlets *Fallout Protection* were distributed by the end of 1961, just around Christmas. Reading the forty-eight-page publication did not put anyone in the holiday spirit.[583] While full of facts and information—including some good advice—it is rather bleak. The booklet was signed and introduced by Secretary of Defense Robert McNamara, a statistical genius whose Pentagon team would catalog, in minute detail, the mass bombing campaign of the early years of the Vietnam War.

Regular citizens had in their hands an official document, *Fallout Protection,* that by itself was no real divergence from previous government pamphlets from the previous decade. But now they were also able to see actual, physical examples. Recall from chapters 10 and 11 the difference between *knowing* about disaster and how you *feel* about it.

The prototypes conceived by NSC 5807 from 1958 were finally on the streets, so to speak. In January 1962, fallout shelter signs appeared in fourteen cities around the country. The signs featured the now-familiar three yellow triangles inscribed in a black circle, which had been designed by Robert W. Blakeley of the Army Corp of Engineers and approved by government psychologists.[584] The insides were as cheerful as mausoleums.

A government mock-up of a fallout shelter[585]

A corrugated steel backyard bunker illustration from the 1961 pamphlet Fallout Protection.

Popular media picked up on the story. The outlets were supportive in their intentions... but destructive in the results. *Life* magazine's front cover for their January 12, 1962, edition introduced the lead story, "New Facts You Must Know About Fallout: The Drive for Mass Shelters." The article captured the zeitgeist and reflected nearly identical concerns as those in Kennedy's administration and the two previous ones by asking "Who should provide shelters? Would they provoke or deter an attack? Were shelters in themselves a bad thing for the nation?"[586] It continued:

> Should every householder think only of himself and his family and prepare his own fallout shield? Should he purchase weapons to repel any of his countrymen who try to intrude? Or should he simply relax and trust in luck and government to protect him? And when the scientists and experts so hotly disagree over matters of fact, which side should he believe?

Life's article quoted everyday citizens who were fatalistic and skeptical against the concept from multiple angles. It also featured proponents and those whose opinions were mixed. Homemaker Florence Ergang said, "I am dismayed at shelter morality. It is natural to protect one's family, but my ethics dictate that my neighbors be protected too."

The January 1962 *Life* article put in everyday language the stark realities of a post-nuclear strike America. It accurately described a hellscape with "rubble for miles" near ground zeroes and several flaws of fallout shelters in certain areas, such as Los Angeles. The realities of *Federal Emergency Plan D-Minus*—including direct radiation poisoning, vector-borne pathogens (e.g., vermin and insect-delivered typhus or plague), low sanitation, irradiated cropland, and removal of the conveniences of modern life—were no longer abstract. They were now on your living room table.

Life quoted nuclear expert Professor Merril Eisenbud: "If we were very lucky we would be back in the 17th Century; if not, we'd be scratching our way back up from the Middle Ages." All of this and more was now wide open for the public to grapple with emotionally and mentally. The mind can take only so much.

There was also the possibility of "disillusioned survivors, scrabbling to stay alive in a chaotic world [who] might form into hostile or battling camps."[587] *TIME* magazine ran an article in its August 18, 1961, edition—under the religion section—titled "Gun Thy Neighbor?" The story opens with a "Chicago urbanite" sounding like the most stereotypically depicted Sentinel:

> When I get my shelter finished, I'm going to mount a machine gun at the hatch to keep the neighbors out if the bomb falls. I'm deadly serious about this. If the stupid American public will not do what they have to to save themselves, I'm not going to run the risk of not being able to use the shelter I've taken the trouble to provide to save my own family.[588]

The article noted, "Relations between Los Angeles and Las Vegas are still recovering from a flap over a speech by Las Vegas Civil Defense Leader J. Carlton Adair, who proposed a 5,000-man militia against the possibility of wartime refugees from California pouring into Nevada 'like a swarm of locusts'" and documented what Christian theology authorized in the nuclear apocalypse.

By early 1962, the personal fallout shelter program was losing steam. Just a few months earlier, Leo Hoegh, the former leader of both the Federal Civil Defense Administration and the Office of Civil and Defense Mobilization, "was selling 200 fallout shelters a week." Just six months later, that number had dropped to ten. Across the fallout shelter industry, per *TIME*, an estimated "600 firms have failed."[589]

The article alleged, "What killed home shelters was the lull in the cold war plus the Kennedy Administration's decision to stress large-scale, community shelters over backyard bunkers."

Life magazine noted this same shift in its pages. Its September 1961 edition stressed family shelters (including a letter from President Kennedy himself), but by January 1962, it was community shelters that were in vogue.[590]

It's one thing to debate, discuss, and even protest against the fallout shelter program. But other than a few people here and there, were households building them?

Not really.

Surveys during 1961 pointed to around 7 percent of the population *planning* on building a bunker, with one estimate indicating that by 1965, only two hundred thousand shelters had been built in all of America.[591] One survey noted that in addition to the practical problem of affordability, many people also had moral scruples about shelters, especially regarding "the moral question of having to exclude others, and whether a life in the aftermath of a nuclear war would be worth living."[592]

Larger community shelters were built, and their remnants were still visible into the early 2000s. The University of California, Berkeley, had sixty shelters.[593] Nearby, Stanford University had twenty-seven shelters on campus with a total capacity of more than 42,000 people. The largest of these had a 5,345-person capacity shelter under Hoover Tower. Stanford's bunker construction began in December 1962 and was controversial from the start, with the program experiencing protests and vandalism.[594] One shelter was occupied as recently as 2013 by a fifth-year student squatter who was soon evicted.

Why were large community shelters an indication of the fall of civil defense? Three factors played a large role—

- **Financial Realities:** Although personal bunkers were not wildly expensive, mass community shelters came with an exorbitant price tag.
- **Annihilation Fatigue:** This refers to the human tendency to avoid thinking about death—and citizens were tired of being forced to think about their demise by nuclear war.
- **Psychological Off-Ramping of Responsibility:** In forcing shelter programs on the public, the government replaced *personal agency* with *political policy*, providing the masses with a psychological off-ramp.

Ultimately, tiered responsibility would yield to *government* responsibility, a return to the comfortable Fortress America mentality. For some members in the federal halls of power and the Pentagon, this was just fine... until it wasn't.

AFTERSHOCKS

While the public was not building fallout shelters en masse, this didn't stop the feds from self-preservation. Continuity of Government (COG) planning endured. Several researchers have commented that the public outreach was done only as a pittance exercise to justify gargantuan sums for senior leaders.[595] Not surprisingly, the military led the pack. In 1961, the North American Aerospace Defense Command's Cheyenne Mountain Complex broke ground in the city of Colorado Springs, Colorado.

Washington, DC, was abuzz with continuity planning. In June 1962, President Kennedy received a Top Secret report from the Emergency

Planning Committee on recommendations as to the protection of selected federal personnel, "physical relocation sites ... and evacuation plans" in the possibility of a nuclear strike or other disasters to maintain a functioning administrative state with military command, control, and communication intact as well.[596] The ability to manage the economy and remaining resources was of top concern.

While efforts had been made previously to spread the burden of catastrophic planning and action responsibilities to other federal agencies, the Office of Emergency Planning (OEP) still shouldered an overwhelming load. In choosing locations, the report noted sites would have to be close enough to Washington, DC, that key personnel could evacuate there in time—but not so close as to be destroyed in a nuclear barrage on the capital. Estimates were that twenty to thirty facilities would suffice. These would include seven regional centers for key federal nodes not in the vicinity of the District of Columbia but spread throughout the United States. The sites would be known as "Relocation Arcs."[597]

State-level COG planning for the executive, legislative, and judicial branches was celebrated and recognized. Funding from the federal government to the states was under debate. Should it be 50 percent—as was the current level—or rise to 90 percent to make it on par with monies contributed to the interstate highway system? Regardless of the amount, states could use these dollars to construct their own "arcs" as well.[598]

The report also opened the door to pushback against several authoritarian assumptions of *Federal Emergency Plan D-Minus* from three years prior in the Eisenhower administration. For example, the very first bullet item in the foreword declared "martial law is not an acceptable planning assumption; martial law as a local proposition is to be avoided wherever possible."

The limits of emergency powers were also broached: "The question of legal authority to perform emergency functions *for which there is no statutory basis* has arisen in the committee's discussion [emphasis added]." What legislation was needed to limit or authorize presidential power was something the OEP stated it would have to revisit. In empowering federalism and respecting the Constitution, the committee recognized the need "to place increasing emphasis on achieving greater assurance of the continuity of State and local governmental authority and operations in a nuclear attack emergency. This objective is not merely a State or local one—it is quite properly a Federal one."[599]

Respect for the Constitution throughout the report ran deep. OEP supported using the constitutional amendment process for "authorizing legislation to provide for lines of succession and such other measures as may be necessary to ensure the postattack continuance of civil government."

Legal disapprobation against dictatorial and unconstitutional powers assumed in *D-Minus* was voiced repeatedly in Kennedy's administration. As I mentioned earlier, references to America becoming a "garrison" state were prolific. Even the director of the Office of Emergency Planning, Edward McDermott, bristled. Writing to the president's aide in October 1962, McDermott indicated President Kennedy had "24 documents approved by President Eisenhower for civil emergency planning purposes," all related to *D-Minus*, but that Kennedy had not "approved any of them."[600]

McDermott believed some were of "doubtful legality." Legal attacks against *D-Minus* continued under President Lyndon Johnson's administration, specifically by his attorney general, who personally "dropped" and "declined to approve" certain unconstitutional emergency powers illegally granted to the president.[601] These documents are known as PEADs: Presidential Emergency Action Documents.

The Continuity of Government plans were also of doubtful reality. In an oral history interview, in part covering the Cuban Missile Crisis, Director McDermott reflected on the challenges of evacuating select federal officials from Washington, DC, to their secure locations.[602] While movements of government officials could reasonably be kept classified in small numbers, a large exodus would be hard to keep quiet.

But family members represented an entirely different problem both to ethics and secrecy. The psychological impact of theory nearing reality is not one to which civilians are accustomed and, for the sake of their mental health, is often rejected or compartmentalized by the brain.

Government bureaucrats, as human beings, spouses, fathers, siblings, and neighbors, need ontological security as well. Director McDermott recalled:

> One of the frustrating things about these responsibilities which are part of this agency is that most people don't want to think about it, talk about it, or hear about it.... We found that these people were then faced with a choice of their responsibility to their Government and responsibility to their families—as heads of a family. In practically every instance, and I'm not so sure we can be critical of this—in practically every instance, the individual felt that his first responsibility was to his family and he had to make some kind of adequate arrangement for them before he was prepared or willing to leave his family in furtherance of his Governmental responsibility.[603]

Director McDermott indicated this was the first time the subject of what to do with families was ever introduced to President Kennedy. The president was, however, previously briefed on how his own family would be escorted to a secure location, should the need arise.

When crises are widespread and overwhelming, the number of bodies for response is often reduced because responders and their families are impacted too. Individuals and governments need to consider this.

The Cuban Missile Crisis was a "shot in the arm" to get US federal agencies to take seriously their Continuity of Government plans. McDermott indicated that before the crisis, only 20 percent of agencies were in compliance with official guidance, but afterward, it was 100 percent.

These plans may have been all for naught. As had been debated by several presidential administrations, full-scale nuclear war—euphemistically known as Mutually Assured Destruction (MAD)—was unwinnable. A 1979 Top Secret memorandum (declassified only in 2013) was addressed to Vice President Walter Mondale by his assistant for national security affairs. It noted the opinion of one senior government official that "the entire PEADs series is obsolete given the total devastation which could be expected from a thermonuclear attack on the US."

Just like the movie *WarGames*, the only winning move was not to play.

TAKEAWAY POINTS

Understanding the key tenets of the last three chapters, one can see why modern government arguments against prepping are nonsensical. Just the nuclear threat alone is far greater today than the era of Truman, Eisenhower, and Kennedy. Take the year 1950 as a baseline. The US government at that time faced only one true major threat. The USSR NSC 68 assumed that by 1954, the Soviets would have two hundred atomic bombs, and in a major war, one hundred of those would hit the United States. By 2023, in contrast, Russia had more than *six thousand* nuclear warheads, China had an estimated three hundred and fifty, and North Korea had fifty.[604] Are we safer today?

What of other factors? Which economy was stronger: that of 1950s America, whose industrial base was rebuilding Europe and Japan, or today's US economy with a debt to GDP ratio well over 100 percent? Was crime worse or better in America in 1950 compared to today? Terrorism? Food availability and cost? Illegal immigration? America was *far* more resilient eighty years ago.

The attitude of Resilient Citizens today, regardless of their home country, and regardless of whether they engage in "extreme" prepping, is just as logical as it was in 1950 or in the time of Hohenwerfen Castle. What changed was not the underlying nature and possibility of threats but rather the government's role in promoting nationwide prepping.

The modern Noah archetype of the Resilient Citizen came about in the nuclear age. Since that age is still upon us, and since federal nuclear shelters still exist, it remains a logical preparedness reaction. And while government preparation for nuclear war is just one aspect of official actions regarding disaster, the politics of disaster are multifaceted.

CHAPTER 17

THE POLITICS OF PREPAREDNESS

The strong do what they can, the weak do what they must.
—Thucydides, Melian Dialogue

When it becomes serious, you have to lie.
—Jean-Claude Juncker, former president of the European Commission

In chapter 13, I listed a few options politicians have in dealing with perils. Overall, there are just four categories: (1) *pretending* to solve the issue, (2) *passing* responsibility to experts or other politicians, (3) amassing *power*, and (4) *prioritizing* and *portioning*. That chapter discussed these options via the concept of elite psychology. Under Presidents Truman, Eisenhower, and Kennedy, we saw examples of all four.

I can now widen the aperture to look at nation-states globally and expand to other disasters beyond a nuclear holocaust. In this chapter, I use the term *state* to refer to an entire nation. This chapter finalizes a discussion on the politics of disaster at the elite levels. It shows how national leaders view real and perceived threats and the responsibility these same leaders feel for their duties coupled with the requirements to stay in office. It illustrates further examples of their interactions with perils and people.

However, I'll note that nothing has changed from my assessment in chapter 13. Control—or the illusion of it—remains the foundational motivation in politics.

WHY GOVERNMENTS ARE INSTITUTED

To understand the politics of disaster, you must first ask two basic questions. First, *what is the primary responsibility of a state*? I am not talking about an ideal state, nor democracies alone, but *all* states from the biggest to the smallest, richest to poorest, most free to least free. Is it to fund schools, protect the freedom of the press, or provide high-speed internet access? No, several states have existed throughout history that have not provided these things. Is it to have a standing army or navy, capable of resisting foreign intervention? No, more than twenty countries in the world presently have no full-time military force, including Iceland, Andorra, Costa Rica, Vatican City, Liechtenstein, and numerous Pacific Ocean states.

The primary responsibility of a state is to provide *security*. Maslow's hierarchy of needs for people has similarities with the needs of states. Security can be performed by a police force, and no country in the world lacks one. But security for whom? The answer *should* be for all its citizens and guests. In reality, states often prioritize the selectorate, those individuals who have the power to select and protect national leadership. All power of a state flows from this security responsibility.

Other tenets of the basics of a state include the rule of law (courts, protection of rights), infrastructure (roads, electrical lines), and governance (taxation, public servants), among others. However, all of these are enforced by the state's monopoly on force. People are taxed and follow the laws of a country under the barrel of a gun. Security undergirds all state functions, whether used properly or for malign purposes. Because states retain the monopoly of force, they can—and often have—used that power against their people. Sadly, disasters are a common trigger for states—even democracies—to abuse their authority.

Several governments have and do use their security responsibility to provide protection. They serve as a barrier against outside hazards, both man-made and natural. Even the worst governments provide some safeguard to the broader citizenry. Proper governments afford aid after a disaster, arrest and detain criminals, protect natural rights, and allow for smooth commerce.

So, again, the first basic question in understanding the politics of disaster is, *What is the primary responsibility of the state?* The second question is related to the first: *What do nations fear above all else*? Nuclear war? Conventional war? The wrath of a deity? Economic contraction? Internal rebellion, conquest, or collapse? We know that individual citizens are guided by ontological security, but so are leaders. While members of the general populace can share many of the same fears as their leaders, it is the burden of government to address, reduce, or eliminate many of these worries, especially those relating to security, as it is fundamental to the state.

Therefore, what nations fear most is summarized in one word: *failure*—specifically, the failure of security. The scope of this failure can be broad, from marginal to existential. Coups are one extreme; wildfires that destroy private property are another. A poor or incompetent response to a hurricane is one level of state failure, having a corrupt police force another, and losing your capital to an invading foe is yet another. The severity of failure rises and falls in proportion to its impact on security. Losing an election is unfortunate if you are in the ruling party of a democracy. But losing your life—as did Muammar Gaddafi (Libya), Saddam Hussein (Iraq), Park Chung-hee (South Korea), and Louis XVI (France)—in more authoritarian structures of government is far worse.

Putting the two questions together, above all else, national leaders fear the failure of providing proper selectorate security. What exactly comprises "state failure" or "security" can therefore be different from state to state. For some states, protecting the elite or the rulers is the prime directive—the citizenry be damned. For other states, protecting ideals, the economy, the culture, or staying out of conflict matters most. Regardless, the general principle remains: Loss of security equals state failure. This has a complex interaction between people and their governments when studying perils.

Catastrophes are, by their very description, destructive. Equally important, people want to be safe. These two truisms become problems for politicians to mitigate and rectify. Actions taken in the wake of calamities can reward politicians or force change. People in need look to their government for support in times of crisis. Rapid and fair response efforts provide tangible and measurable benefits to incumbents. Conversely, failure to provide suitable assistance or reassurance can see politicians voted from office in democracies or the potential for protest and agitation against the government in autocracies.[605]

Failure has the power to alter perceptions of control—of winners and losers—and, in doing so, can change the global order. One example of this is provided by the United States Office of the Director of National Intelligence. Writing in 2024, the office declared, "The world that emerges from this tumultuous period will be shaped by whoever offers the most persuasive arguments for how the world should be governed, how societies should be organized, and which systems are most effective at advancing economic growth and providing benefits for more people, and by the powers—both state and non-state—that are most able and willing to act on solutions to transnational issues and regional crises."[606] Perception is powerful.

It is reasonable that, over time, states will demonstrate a range of responses to various internal catastrophes, and they will learn from their preparedness, recovery, and response. Wealthy, democratic countries should fare the best given their economic resources, allies, and voter feedback mechanisms. If they do not, that could be a sign that a country is slipping closer to autocracy or anarchy. Additionally, in today's age of informational connectedness, citizens in one country can see in real time the events affecting others.

SECURITY AND STATE FAILURE IN CONTEXT

For individuals, the term *human security* is most appropriate in discussing disaster preparedness, but it does not exist in a vacuum. The United Nations Human Development Report of 1994 first introduced the term *human security* and tied it to calamity at its inception. Since this document was written in the early years after the Cold War, the preeminent fears of a nuclear holocaust, a global war between the USSR and the US directly, or smaller regional wars—either proxy or not—were receding from the forefront in the discussion of international security.

In this vein, the document declares, "For most people, a feeling of insecurity arises more from worries about daily life than from the dread of a cataclysmic world event."[607] The report listed several subcomponents of human security, such as economic, environmental, and personal security. Thus, the unit of analysis switched from nations to the smallest level possible: common people. This description provides political scientists a connection point between international security and political economy—which, by nature, concentrates at the nation-state level rather than individuals—just as civil defense is connected to military deterrence and strategy in the nuclear age. Nevertheless, the relation of all these sundry "securities" was opaque. In 2001, Roland Paris published a matrix of security studies to demonstrate the relationship between the source of the security threat and the entity of protection.

Paris reasoned the term *security* had become so malleable that it was losing its meaning.[608] His matrix helps connect multiple threat types, all of which have a bearing on individuals—earthquakes, civil war, conventional war, banking and currency collapses—and politics. It also critically shows states *cannot* prevent all forms of peril. Thus, human security, when approached holistically, has gone full circle. While it still incorporates "worries of daily life," such as hunger or job opportunities, it likewise retains a connection to "cataclysmic" events with death or economic ruin as outcomes.

Hence, this prevention of all harm relates to one of the definitions of state failure, which takes a broader approach in the lexicon. Rather than the term *state failure* equaling *failed state,* it can instead describe the inability to provide basic services. That is a temporary inability of the sovereign state to render goods and services such as electric power, medical assistance, or rule of law *and* a permanent inability to prevent both significant and mundane catastrophes. Disasters of higher impact scale with greater levels of state failure, both in scope and duration. This understanding of state failure acknowledges states cannot provide 100 percent security against disasters.

In summation, *all nations fail* at some point or another. By logical extension, subnational states will also fail at some point. While both can take risk-reduction measures, neither can provide total human security in physical or economic safety. Risk is still prevalent, and some of that risk must be borne by the smallest unit, the individual.

National leaders know this. And yet their levels of concern, or their relative capability to steer change, greatly varies. North Korean leadership cares little about its people. There is mass malnutrition and nonexistent human rights, but only the largest of catastrophic events or regime change could radically alter the ruling class's actions toward the greater populace. While security is challenged, it is not fundamentally challenged in a way that causes modification. The selectorate of North Korea, being a dictatorship, is exceptionally small. They could chart a different course but choose not to as the elites benefit from the current system.

In contrast, the tiny island archipelago nation of Kiribati in the Pacific Ocean is a parliamentary republic, with a score of 93 out of 100 on the Freedom House index.[609] A typhoon or tidal wave could obliterate large swaths of this country overnight. Long-term fears are stark. According to one source, it "is expected to be the first country fully submerged by sea level rise."[610] This is highly politically motivating, as security is fundamentally threatened, and the selectorate is national in size.[611] However, Kiribati's leadership cannot stop rising oceans unilaterally; they must seek outside assistance. Based on this, Taneti Maamau, the country's president, addressed the United Nations in 2022. The highest point in all of Kiribati is only a few feet above sea level, so Maamau had asked rich countries for funds to literally raise his country, elevation-wise.[612]

Let me expound a bit more on how disasters influence national leaders. Chapter 10 showed one way people look at risk through the rubric of scenario, probability, and consequences. Politicians do the same. Two methods to calculate consequences are loss of life and financial toll. The second column of Figure 17.1 shows the global average annual mortality for nine natural disasters from 2003 to 2022 and the third column for the year 2023.[613]

Peril	Average annual deaths '03-'22	Deaths in 2023
Drought	1,157	247
Earthquake	35,124	62,451
Extreme Temperature	11,470	406
Flood	5,518	7,763
Mass Movement (dry)	35	0
Mass Movement (wet)	803	654
Storm	10,017	14,666
Volcanic Activity	80	23
Wildfire	86	264

Figure 17.1: Mortality Rate Annual Average, 2003–2022 and 2023 Yearly Total[614]

The global deaths of 2023 were 86,473, a significant increase from the two-decade annual average of 64,148, much of which was driven by the Turkey and Syria quake. By contrast, Figure 17.2 displays economic losses for these same categories over the same periods.

This database indicates earthquakes and storms are responsible for the highest losses of life and are the most expensive perils globally.

Looking at longer time scales shows the same pattern remains. Isolating the top ten disasters across the world for mortality from 1950 to 2023 shows storms and earthquakes comprised nine of the ten deadliest perils and, for 1900–2023, 100 percent of the worst in terms of

Peril	Average annual economic loss '03-'22	Economic loss in 2023
Drought	9.6	22.1
Earthquake	39.9	51.9
Extreme Temperature	3.4	0.6
Flood	41.1	20.4
Mass Movement (dry)	0	0
Mass Movement (wet)	0.3	0
Storm	95.6	100.8
Volcanic Activity	0.2	0
Wildfire	6.3	6.8

Figure 17.2: Average Annual Economic Loss, 2003–2022 and 2023 Yearly Total (in $ Billions)[615]

economic hit.[616] The data reveal poor or autocratic states bear the brunt of fatalities.[617] Richer or more democratic nations pay dearly at the bank.[618] Writ large, democracies are more casualty-sensitive, whereas autocracies are not. Thankfully for both government structures, deaths from natural disasters are *down* 90 percent as compared to the early 1900s.[619]

POWER TO THE PEOPLE

In democracies, the citizens are the selectorate, so leaders should be highly encouraged to provide rapid response and recovery following an event lest they face wrath at the ballot box. In the US, widely cited studies confirm this for flooding, tornadoes, and droughts.[620] These results are not just for recent events. Shark attacks may have caused President Woodrow Wilson to lose votes in 1916.[621] Herbert Hoover suffered a drop of 10 percentage points during his reelection vote tallies in counties affected by severe flooding in 1927, even though he committed massive resources to respond.[622] His actions were criticized so heavily that Black

Americans, long-time voters of the party of Lincoln, began switching their loyalties from 80+ percent Republican to 80+ percent Democrat voters.[623] Conversely, relief efforts perceived as responsive and fair can provide a boon to incumbents.[624]

Beyond the United States, democracies across the world confirm this leader-led interaction in the framework of disasters. The 2004 Indian Ocean tsunami when Tilly Smith saved one hundred lives in Thailand killed 543 Swedish tourists in the affected region. Not surprisingly, Swedish politics were affected, and the incumbent national party was defeated in the 2006 elections.[625] In contrast, the incumbent party in Thailand not only won the 2005 election but did so in a landslide, gaining more than a hundred seats in the House of Representatives.[626]

Croatian floods in 2014 were so severe that the prime minister, minister of internal affairs, minister of agriculture, and the president of Croatia "were present in the affected areas" and coordinated a major relief effort in an attempt to avoid voter wrath.[627] In 2005, Cyclone Gudrun knocked out power for 8 percent of Swedish households and cost 1 percent of GDP (equivalent to Hurricane Katrina in the US). One study correlated a 3.8 percent drop in support of the ruling Social Democratic Party.[628] In India, one study found a *lack* of rain caused voters to punish incumbents because of the effect on crop yields but was counteracted by relief spending.[629] Furthermore, in Germany, two once-in-a-hundred-year floods struck in 2002 and 2013, leading to small (~.5 percent) but attributable and measurable drops in voter participation in the respective elections, both of which were just a few weeks after the disasters.[630]

Politicians are keenly aware of the intersection of state failure and their political futures.

I SEE WHAT YOU DID THERE

Sometimes, what happens far away can travel to your neck of the woods. In June 1783, the Laki volcano erupted in Iceland. Lava flows and poisonous gas releases continued into the next year. Eighty percent of the island's sheep died from exposure, and more than 20 percent of the human population died from gas and famine. Sulfur dioxide belched high into the upper atmosphere, where it lingered for months and traveled across the globe, wreaking havoc. The eruption caused drought and famine in Egypt, killing six hundred thousand people. Worldwide, upward of six million people died from the eruption's direct or indirect effects.[631]

Modern technology offers another way to look at the interaction among People, Perils, and Politics: exposure to and immediate, firsthand accounts of disasters in other countries. International relations theorists have long posited that not only do domestic politics impact international relations (including the decision to go to war) but international events also reverberate back to domestic politics. The arrow goes both ways. Proximity might be modified by media coverage, locale, or other linkages like race or religion.[632] People "feel" closer to places, even if the distance is much farther in a geographic sense.

For example, when Russia invaded Ukraine in 2022, there was an outpouring of support across the globe. People around the world sported Ukrainian flags in their social media bios and their car windows. Governments provided support by accepting refugees, sending money, or sending arms. Something similar happened in October 2023 when Hamas and Palestinian civilians conducted a raid into Israel, murdered more than a thousand people, and took several hundred hostages. Pro-Palestinian and pro-Israeli activities—and often anti-Palestinian and anti-Israeli activities—were seen in America, Europe, Japan, Australia, Chile, Brazil, and Turkey, for example.[633] States fear failure and the loss of security, so they can see the Ghost of Christmas Future in the tragedies of other nations.

BLAME AND LOSS OF FREEDOMS

Governments of all types have a long legacy of disaster resulting in major changes. Throughout human history, conquerors have vanquished, enslaved, or heavily taxed the conquered. Leaders have also placed these reductions on their citizens. During America's Civil War, Abraham Lincoln suspended habeas corpus and jailed newspaper editors critical of his policies. Franklin D. Roosevelt interned Japanese and German Americans during World War II. After the attacks of 9/11, Congress passed the Patriot Act, enabling a massive increase in citizen surveillance.

Violent foreign events, even below the level of war, also negatively affect domestic politics. In 2015, the Paris terrorist attacks and migrant crisis contributed to stricter border crossings within the Schengen area of Europe. British disaster expert Lucy Easthope termed events like this the "Tombstone Imperative" because governments act when enough bodies stack up.[634]

Catastrophes often *reduce*, rather than expand, freedom. This was certainly true of violent disasters. But it appears even increased *nonviolent* disasters may have the same inhibitive effect on global freedom.[635]

While autocrats have much to fear from disasters, "authoritarian regimes are adept at suppressing post-disaster political unrest."[636] The government of Myanmar used Hurricane Nargis in 2008 as an excuse to uproot Karen[637] rice farmers from fertile lands.[638] Another example of a disaster used to dislocate people comes from "ecological migrants" in China. Hundreds of thousands of civilians were forcibly moved by the government when their lands were declared distressed by "climate change, industrialization, poor policies and human activity."[639] Suspiciously, some were from Muslim populations that the government has been oppressing for some time.

Autocrats also attempt to shift responsibility or claim credit like their more democratic brethren. Linguistic analysis of Chairman Mao Tse-Tung (China), Commander Fidel Castro (Cuba), and President Hosni Mubarak (Egypt) found each of these leaders used strategic language to both assuage citizens and demonstrate regime stability to other countries following natural disasters.[640]

In 2008, when Beijing hosted the summer Olympics, officials were hiding a technological disaster regarding adulterated milk. Several dairy companies had added the compound melamine to baby formula in order to boost the protein content. Melamine is commonly used in household plastics and can leach into your food if you microwave them together. Ingestion causes a host of acute and chronic problems in humans and animals. News finally broke publicly and by November of that year, nearly three hundred thousand infants had been hospitalized due to kidney and urinary tract issues. Chinese dairy exports dropped 92 percent year over year after the scandal, and the United States installed permanent food safety officials.[641] Sixty people were arrested, and Zheng Xiaoyu, the leader of the State Food and Drug Administration, was tried and executed for previous crimes, even though he had no part in the baby formula scandal.[642] Shockingly, just one year earlier, the US Food and Drug Administration discovered melamine had been added to pet food sold in North America.[643] Several hundred dogs and cats died as a result of food poisoning.[644]

Other international impacts were felt in Hong Kong, where local supply was bought out and shipped to the mainland. People in Taiwan used it as an example of why *not* to be close to Beijing, and the World Health Organization issued a critique of China for failing to emphasize breastfeeding.[645]

Governments have evolved to respond to disasters and maintain control. States balance social whims, potentially whipped up by the emotion of a catastrophic event, with other requirements, such as security, the economy, and world opinion. Since it is rare to see large-scale local disasters create long-term policy changes, foreign disaster effects should be more pacified. Much of this is not surprising, especially in the case of autocratic regime survival. In democracies, this is expressed in protecting the selectorate as they often engage in retrospective voting. In either case, Lieutenant General Russel Honoré, commanding general of Joint Task Force Katrina, may have summed it up best: "Everybody wants to be in charge, nobody wants to take the blame."[646]

SUCCESS STORIES

Numerous national governments are working with their people about serious risks beyond just a few days of food and bottled water for a natural disaster. Switzerland has been a multigenerational success story, but there are others. Finland has enough public civil defense shelters to house two-thirds of its population.[647] In 2022, Taiwan issued a pamphlet to ready its citizens for a war with China. Preparedness groups are sprouting up across the island.[648]

Latvia, on the doorstep of Russia, is stridently pushing a "culture of preparedness." Beginning in the 2024–2025 school year, thirty thousand high school students ages fifteen to seventeen will be taught state defense lessons, focusing on "patriotic upbringing, civic awareness, cohesion, leadership, and physical training." The church will have a major role to play, and members of the community must be prepared to "support each other in their private and social circle to give each other more reassurance and build the necessary level of psychological resilience."[649]

Sweden is another exemplar—one that deserves a closer look.

Sweden

Larger scale prepping in Sweden is on an upward trend, thanks in large part to the government. The Swedish Civil Contingencies Agency (MSB, short for the Swedish name, *Myndigheten för samhällsskydd och beredskap*) is roughly analogous to FEMA. It treats preppers with respect and encourages their behavior. MSB openly communicates with the populace, in Swedish and English, on topics ranging from home fires to cybersecurity to climate change, viewing it through the lens of citizen empowerment.[650] They also actively encourage partnerships with researchers to communicate about disasters.

Sweden made waves internationally in 2018 when the MSB released a nationwide pamphlet on disaster preparedness, including war. It was the first time the tract had been updated in nearly sixty years. A full 30 percent of the twenty pages mention or illustrate war or terror attacks, as shown in Figure 17.3.

Total defence

If Sweden is attacked, resistance is required

We must be able to resist various types of attacks directed against our country. Even today, attacks are taking place against our IT systems and attempts are being made to influence us using false information. We may also be affected by conflicts in our region. Potential attacks include:

- Cyberattacks that knock out important IT systems.
- Sabotage of infrastructure (e.g. roads, bridges, airports, railways, electricity cables and nuclear power stations).
- Terror attacks that affect a large number of people or important organisations.
- Attempts to influence Sweden's decision makers or inhabitants.
- Severed transport links that result in a shortage of foodstuffs and other goods.
- Military attack, for example airstrikes, rocket attacks or other acts of war.

If Sweden is attacked by another country, we will never give up. All information to the effect that resistance is to cease is false.

12

Heightened state of alert

The Government can decide to put the country on a heightened state of alert in order to improve Sweden's chances of defending itself. In a heightened state of alert, peacetime laws apply, but other laws may also be used. For example, the state can requisition private property that is of particular importance to Sweden's total defence.

In a heightened state of alert, the whole of society has to gather its collective forces in order to ensure that which is most important functions. In a heightened state of alert, you may be called up to help in various ways.

Information about the heightened state of alert will be broadcast on radio and TV. Sveriges Radio's radio station P4 is the emergency channel.

Total defence

13

Figure 17.3: Excerpt from Sweden's Disaster Pamphlet If Crisis or War Comes

The booklet reminds the populace that war means "total defence." This means that everyone who lives here and is between the ages of sixteen and seventy can be called up to assist in various ways in the event of war or the threat of war. Everyone is obliged to contribute and everyone is needed.[651]

In November 2024, MSB released an updated version and mailed it to every home in the country. Their messaging was blunt and heavily influenced by the war in Ukraine and Sweden's new status as a NATO member:

> The state of the world has worsened drastically in recent years. War is being waged in our vicinity. Extreme weather events are

> becoming increasingly common. Terror threats, cyberattacks, and disinformation campaigns are being used to undermine and influence us. Sweden has even joined the defence alliance NATO. That is why MSB has produced the brochure "In case of crisis or war." To resist these threats, we must stand united and take responsibility for our country. If we are attacked, everyone must help defend Sweden's independence and our democracy. We build resilience every day—together. You are part of Sweden's overall emergency preparedness.[652]

This new pamphlet is twelve pages longer than the one produced in 2018 and details other threats such as organized crime—a major problem due to radical immigration issues—and pathogens.[653] Prepping in Sweden is cultural but varied. It has deep traditional roots, such as *Jantelagen*, a semi-survival practice related to foraging.[654] Some self-identify as preppers (although the name has a stigma), others as "prepared citizens."[655] For some, prepping is done as a part of generational heritage or based on a response to a specific event. For others, it gives a "sense of direction," is "a longing for a less complex life," or is seen as a "responsibility [that] orients one towards the self and one's place in society." For still others, it is an act of regaining agency in a country where too many depend on the government for too much.[656] It is also seen more and more as a communal effort, both at the local level and in partnership with the national state.

> The most resilient communities tend to be those that work together towards a shared purpose. This approach seems to be stronger in the countryside. Furthermore, the actions of preppers can contribute to resilient living conditions and increase a community's resilience as well. But for a community to cope with and adapt to changes, more actors than just individuals such as preppers need to be involved. "Preppers" are an

> important part of increased community resilience, but so are the civil society, the civil defense, businesses, and agencies.[657]

It is likely this overall messaging—*everybody fights and no one quits*—will only increase in the short term.

Civil defense is pushed as a contributor to societal and national resilience. Sweden's special operations forces are working to tie preparedness to the national identity, integrated into every neighborhood. What exactly does that mean? As one study reports:

> A national identity is obtained through promoting measures such as historical and patriotic education consistent with identified cultural values, transparent communication with minority populations to ensure their inclusion in civic and governmental life, separation of politics from national defense policymaking to the greatest degree possible, and national unity messaging to encourage patriotic and civic-minded activity (e.g., youth scouting, camping, sports leagues, and clubs) through nongovernmental organizations (NGOs) or other associations at the local level.[658]

These success stories showcase that threats are real and major national resilience is often justified and therefore required. However, the state is not performing security divorced from the populace, but rather *with* them. These states are requiring tiered responsibility, asking their denizens to be *citizens* while still empowering them and their rights.

I leave the last word to the MSB's 2024 pamphlet: "If Sweden is attacked, we will never surrender. Any suggestion to the contrary is false.

CONCLUSION

THE PORTALS OF PREPAREDNESS

A society grows great when old men plant trees in whose shade they know they shall never sit.

—GREEK PROVERB

The most important thing you need for prepping is community. A cabin in the woods is nuclear war era thinking.

—TUCKER MAX

Beginning your preparedness voyage is like raising boys: You don't know what hellscape, harebrained misadventures they are going to get into next; you just know it's coming. This attitude combines mental resiliency, foresight, planning, personal betterment, an understanding of the past, and tangible action. It is the same core logic that undergirds insurance, fire departments, actuarial tables, Continuity of Government operations, and war planning. Step one is simply the awakening.

For step two, a Resilient Citizen looks at the world and its various threats and asks, "Has this happened before, or does it have the potential to happen in the future?" He or she then localizes this answer, internalizes it, and takes reciprocal actions to mitigate or avoid adverse impacts. In this mid-phase of Resilient Citizenship, the objective is to "do something." It doesn't require perfection or Nostradamus-level prognostication; it requires only an inkling and urge to make a change given a rational observation of the state of the world.

Resilient Citizens in this phase do not entirely escape the rational fear motivation of potential catastrophe, but they do learn to give agency a front seat to drive life actions. Some start a garden, others buy preps, and others buy guns. Some move out of the big city; others plan their escape from the city either by foot or by private jet to their bolt-hole location in New Zealand. Some get into conspiracy theories... and then find out some of those conspiracies are true.

The overwhelming number of Resilient Citizens I encounter are on this second step. There is, however, a third step—one that very, very few ever take, especially in America. But I am getting ahead of myself.

SPIES

Many years ago, I participated in a missionary trip to Eastern Europe. During one of the sermons, the pastor stated that people are composed of five components:

- **S**piritual
- **P**hysical
- **I**ntellectual
- **E**motional
- **S**ocial.[659]

This spells out the acronym SPIES. Each of us has varying manifestations of our SPIES, including strengths and weaknesses. I've thought about this concept often when studying Resilient Citizens and my own actions regarding perils. Those who have a healthy understanding of their SPIES makeup and integrate these elements into their preparedness seem to possess more agency and ontological security.

Overall—and there are exceptions—Resilient Citizens seem to be far more content with life than others. This does not mean Resilient Citizens don't have fears or that they live perfect lives or never make mistakes or have regrets. They just come off as stronger, more vibrant, more *alive*. I have noticed the two bookend variables—spiritual and social—seem to tower above the rest regarding levels of resiliency and mental well-being. Those with deeper connections to their deity and neighborhoods have more hope and, not surprisingly, tend to have more children. People procreate more when they think the world will be a good place for kids.

I have also observed—and experienced in my journey—that the more prepping is akin to a hobby or a lifestyle and deeply integrated into one's habitual activities rather than a sequestered activity, the more "normal" the Resilient Citizen seems. This is particularly common among farmer and rancher types, especially those in a multigenerational endeavor, which brings us back to the social component.

The people I've spoken with who would balk at being described as preppers or even Resilient Citizens had this attitude:

> I wouldn't consider myself a prepper. I just grew up living in the mountains. Of course I own guns; there are coyotes and wolves. Of course I have three months of food at home and a backup generator; it's called "winter." Of course my twelve-year-old can field dress a deer; his grandfather and I both taught him. Of course my sister cans jam and bakes sourdough; it's called homemaking.

These individuals give the impression that what they are doing is perfectly normal, that *not* possessing these skills is the outlier.

In chapters 5–9, I gave five archetypes of Resilient Citizens. The groupings are conceptual and not written in stone. More important is the concept of generalized resilience and the psychology of managing perils. I now move to how you can get better, be more resilient, be more secure, and be more *alive* while becoming a better citizen in the process.

I will provide examples of how to take control of your agency using the SPIES construct mapped to one of the Resilient Citizen groupings. Every person's journey will be different, and I'll share a bit of my life as touchpoints. Some of these will resonate with you, and others may seem far-fetched or unobtainable. Some you can do on your own, and others will require a group effort, including a change of laws or regulations. And, just like the five types of Resilient Citizens, the SPIES blend and compound. It's not the specifics that are important, as everyone's ontological security is unique. What is essential is the *directional system* that aims at improvement and contentment. It's a concept our Founding Fathers called "life, liberty, and the pursuit of happiness."

Spiritual: Hope Springs Eternal

I learned several things from my childhood. I started my Resilient Citizen journey as one of the Faithful, a sinner in the hands of an angry God. *Theodicy* is the discussion of why bad things happen to good people or why—if God is so good—He allows evil. The answer I received from an early age was the duality of suffering and hope. The same God who allows miscarriages allows adoption. The wise were to build their houses on the rock, not because perils would never come but precisely because they *would*. A strong foundation went beyond flesh and bone. Our body is one of brokenness, our soul one of completeness. The Faithful retain an unattainable yearning aspect in their composition, a desire for perfection that will not be met in this life. Therefore, death was not the end, but a portal. Much of Western society has lost this understanding.

Overcoming mortal fear is daunting. Formally known as *thanatophobia* (fear of death or death anxiety), we dread the end and refuse to face it. Given our material blessings, high levels of freedom, and relatively low chances of demise by childbirth, wildlife, or war as compared to our ancestors, the fact that death is still a part of life is incredibly unsettling for many. I think part of it is both the randomness that abounds and the intrusion of fate into our comfortable, Amazon Prime way of life. Death seems . . . unfair.

Droughts, terrorism, economic collapse, interstate conflict, pollution, and other natural and man-made calamities have a multinational impact, even in rich, Westernized countries. Supernatural fears play a part, as many belief systems prophesy the end of the world. Disasters can be regional as well. Droughts, floods, civil war, and heat waves may all lie within a single country's borders. *But shouldn't those calamities only impact others?* we ask.

Scaling down, calamities can be solely individual. A tornado can obliterate one home and leave others unscathed; a lightning strike could kill a hiker yet spare her companion; and, of course, one's eternal soul may reside in the hands of an angry—or merciful—deity. Add to this a mix of crime, civil unrest, or even accidents like chemical spills or massive wildfires sparked by a smoke machine at a gender reveal party,[660] and a sense of general unease creeps in. This is bothersome in this world of control we have created. We don't like talking about it, and even Barbie, in her perfect community, struggled with thoughts of her limited mortality and someone with whom to share those feelings.[661]

In the modern world, death is often "sequestered" because people are torn between a "Victorian romanticism which makes the loss of a loved one unbearable, and the twentieth-century denial that 'forbids' or at least hides death."[662] Philip Mellor and Chris Shilling surmise we attempt "to establish a reliable 'sense of self' in the context of a seemingly hostile and threatening world" and yet avoid the topic of our mortality because it makes us feel "insecure." Death has the power to "shatter ontological security." When faced with this situation, people engage in "survival strategies . . . projects geared towards ensuring their survival and the health of their bodies."[663]

Religion often plays a part in this as well. Christianity, for example, focuses on the immortality of the soul and the resurrection of the body. But many in the Western world have scorned religion in general and Christianity specifically. They ignore the fact that irreligion is both a historical *and* contemporary anomaly.[664] As recently as the 1970s, the number of Americans with no religious affiliation was less than 5 percent.[665] This rise of the religious "nones" crested as high as 21–28 percent of the population in 2022 but may have flatlined.[666] Young men may be the vanguard of a renewed interest in Christianity.[667] Perhaps when thoughts of our mortal coil are retied to thoughts of the eternal, we may lose our thanatophobia.

Christianity also guided America's Founding Fathers in their ideas of government. If the primary purpose of a state is to provide security, what exactly is it securing? Our Founders' answer was *natural rights*. Alexander Hamilton said, "The sacred rights of mankind are not to be rummaged for, among old parchments, or musty records. They are written, as with a sun beam, in the whole volume of human nature, by the hand of the divinity itself; and can never be erased or obscured by mortal power."[668]

No emergency, no peril, no threat was ever to be too big to take away what God provided each of us intrinsically.

Even if you are not a Christian, the tenets of purpose, forgiveness, belonging, and tradition ring through several religions and much of humanity. Harvard Medical School touts the benefits of forgiveness, noting it is "associated with lower levels of depression, anxiety, and hostility; reduced substance abuse; higher self-esteem; and greater life satisfaction."[669] Viktor Frankl, a survivor of Nazi death camps, found that even in the darkest of circumstances, a belief that your life had meaning was a key determinant of your psychological well-being. With meaning came not happiness but purpose, and with purpose came hope . . . and responsibility.[670] This is what we can learn from the Faithful.

Physical: Deep Roots

Many of the Homesteaders in this book have a connection to the land they explained via their faith. For the Christians, it is the stewardship of creation, the responsibility to be guardians of property that was not theirs to pollute, but to caretake and till and partake of the bounty. Many secularists also want to protect the earth. I know several and financially support one organization that does conservation work. I have twice now enjoyed a weekend retreat with Paul Kingsnorth, a strident radical environmentalist in his youth who converted to Christianity in 2020. The

Venn diagram of interests is larger than our divided society realizes, and we have—pardon the pun—common ground.

Michael Shellenberger devoted the entirety of the final chapter of his best-selling disaster book, *Apocalypse Never,* to the tension inherent in the spiritual-secular debate regarding our imperfect world. If purpose is central to our sense of self, as Frankl wrote, then Shellenberger finds "apocalyptic environmentalism gives people a purpose."[671] The "prospects of utopia" are replaced by "climate Armageddon." If thanatophobia and despair are consequences of rejecting Judeo-Christianity, a new religion would have to arise... and it did. Just as Joel Salatin noted that there are Christians who did not care about the Earth because "it's all going to burn," Shellenberger found secularists with the same fervor directed *against* solutions, a mentality of "we are all going down with the ship." Either way, "humankind had lost its connection to nature." It does not have to be this way.

My grandfather was a small-time farmer. He grew up as a child in the Great Depression. Every meal was a blessing, every day a gift. He had an old-time wood-fired stove and would talk about how his mother would make biscuits for breakfast nearly every day. It would be those same biscuits for lunch. He was grateful just to have something to eat. In adulthood, his farm was modest: a few rows of corn, some fruit trees, and a handful of livestock. At harvest time, he was generous with friends and neighbors.

Wendell Berry spoke of the difference between a farmer who exploits and a farmer who nurtures. The former's goal is profit and efficiency, and the latter's is "health—his land's health, his own, his family's, his community's, his country's." In 1977, Berry noted, "The good of the whole of Creation, the world and all of its creatures together, is never a consideration because it is never thought of; our culture now simply lacks the means for thinking of it."[672]

Berry excoriated the way we divorce ourselves from creation. Dominion was remembered, stewardship forgotten. He noted that health was not the "absence of disease" but is "rooted in the concept of wholeness." Wholeness includes all five components of SPIES. "The body cannot be whole alone. Persons cannot be whole alone.... Intellectually, we know that these patterns of interdependence exist... yet modern social and cultural patterns contradict them and make it difficult or impossible to honor them in practice."[673]

Forty years later, Berry saw little had changed. We have embraced a rugged individualism that destroys both people and creation. Berry viewed the root cause as the same for the left and right, just in different manifestations. Both sides, even the right-of-center crowd, ended up rejecting God.

> The tragic version of rugged individualism is in the presumptive "right" of individuals to do as they please, as if there were no God, no legitimate government, no community, no neighbors, and no posterity. This is most frequently understood as the right to do whatever one pleases with one's property.... [T]his kind has cost us dearly in lost topsoil, in destroyed forests, in the increasing toxicity of the world, and in annihilated species. When property rights become absolute they are invariably destructive.

In contrast, the:

> [The] rugged individualism of the left believes that an individual's body is a property belonging to that individual absolutely: the owners of bodies may, by right, use them as they please, as if there were no God, no legitimate government, no community, no neighbors, and no posterity. This supposed right is manifested in the democratizing of "sexual liberation"; in the popular assumption that marriage has been "privatized" and so made subordinate to the wishes of individuals; in the proposition that the individual is "autonomous"; in the legitimation of abortion

> as birth control—in the denial, that is to say, that the community, the family, one's spouse, or even one's own soul might exercise a legitimate proprietary interest in the use one makes of one's body. And this too is tragic, for it sets us "free" from responsibility and thus from the possibility of meaning.[674]

This is not sustainable for the land, our bodies, or our souls.[675]

Half the children in America are vitamin D deficient, a problem that could be solved by spending just twenty minutes a day outside in sunlight. The University of Texas found 85 percent "of kids who needed surgery for fractured or broken bones" lacked sufficient levels of the vitamin.[676] Type 1 diabetes and depression are common in those with low vitamin D.[677] It appears a backlash is reaching a crescendo.

In 2024, Robert F. Kennedy Jr. joined Donald Trump's presidential campaign, declaring he wanted to "Make America Healthy Again." He is now the Secretary of Health and Human Services under President Trump and is yet another example of how motivations that drive Homesteaders are far more ideologically ecumenical. We will still have disagreements over raw milk, Generation IV nuclear reactors, ADHD medications for eight-year-olds, and vaccines, but at least—at the base level—we are getting serious about the problem of our health, much of which comes from our divorce from nature/creation.

In the meantime, start something small to increase your resilience and that of your community. Maybe it is a garden in the backyard. Maybe it is a walk around the block on your lunch break. Maybe you take up beekeeping (my wife did this recently and we love it). Or maybe you start meeting the people who produce your food, perhaps your local rancher. At the very least, can we all agree that farmers' markets are a net good for the community, our land, and our health?

Intellectual: Dungeons and Dragons and Disasters

Sentinels know a few things that can help in your resiliency journey. One is that practice makes perfect. There is a dictum that states "amateurs practice until they get it right; professionals practice until they can't get it wrong." Training under duress is a form of antifragility. The military version of this principle is that "the more you sweat in training, the less you bleed in war."

When my children were younger, I would place them in situations where their normal risk calculations would prevent them from acting, the common reaction of freezing. For example, at a *very* young age, I put them on the high dive at the pool and made them jump. The first leap or two was terrifying, and then it became fun; Dad was right there to guide and protect them.

Resiliency is rooted in *habits of mind*.[678] Habits can be changed. Our brains are remarkably elastic, especially when young, and stretching them is healthy. One of the quickest ways to rewire our minds is through action, simply *doing* something. As Robert Heinlein, author of *Starship Troopers*, wrote:

> A human being should be able to change a diaper, plan an invasion, butcher a hog, conn a ship, design a building, write a sonnet, balance accounts, build a wall, set a bone, comfort the dying, take orders, give orders, cooperate, act alone, solve equations, analyze a new problem, pitch manure, program a computer, cook a tasty meal, fight efficiently, die gallantly. Specialization is for insects.[679]

Camping, ammo reloading, raising goats, making yogurt, knitting, going to the gym, meditation, carpentry—the list is endless. As a Resilient Citizen, you do not have to master, or even practice, all of these, but you will reap the benefits of pushing past your perceived limitations.

Repetition also enhances performance, and you can make your mind resilient via training. Eustress—literally "good stress"—functions much the same as antifragility. I'm talking about small or even moderate shocks that increase your overall resilience. As your resilience and abilities grow, so does your confidence. Highly confident and even overconfident people are statistically *far* more likely to manage through disasters.[680]

This concept—known as the eustress curve, the anxiety-performance curve, the arousal curve, or by its formal original name, the Yerkes-Dodson Law—is incredibly powerful for high levels of agency and success. The original curve is the bottom solid line. It indicates that as arousal (good stress) grows, so does performance. To a point, more *is* better. But then, arousal reaches a peak; from then on, more stress starts to *decrease* performance, leaving you sliding down the other side of the curve.

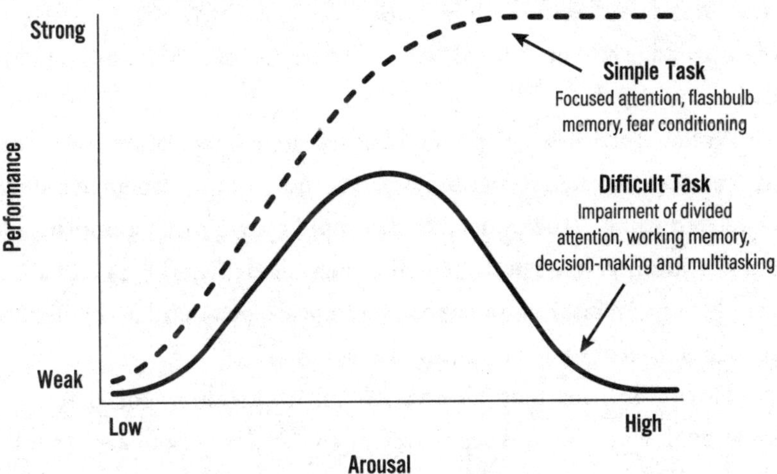

Figure 18.1: The Yerkes-Dodson Curve[681]

However, just like we can use strength conditioning to increase our max squat or bench press weight, repetition and training can raise both performance *and* how much stress we can take before our activity level starts to go down. Paradoxically, what many of us probably need is *more* stress and suffering in our lives, not less.

A related Sentinel insight is that of simulations. It would be a bad idea to gather twenty of your best friends, head out to the woods, and play cops and robbers with live ammunition. But you *can* go paintballing. I never grew up practicing how to react to an incoming artillery strike with live rounds, but I was taught how to do so in ROTC using simulators.

Simulations do not have to be exact replications; in fact, they can be . . . very different. Academic research found that fans of horror movies had lower psychological distress during COVID-19, and those who enjoyed films in the alien invasion and zombie genre were more prepared for the pandemic. Relatedly, individuals who were "morbidly curious"—defined as "motivated to learn about dangerous situations"—had far higher levels of psychological resilience. The researchers conjectured this was due to these individuals possessing "a larger repertoire of knowledge and emotional coping strategies that would be useful in dangerous situations."[682]

A related article supplemented this research. Imagination and fiction help us work through scenarios without a full-cost investment in the real or related thing. "The undead in a zombie movie may be implausible, but the interpersonal and societal upheavals depicted may still allow people to glean information about ecological, social, and psychological consequences of societal turmoil and collapse."

Horror movies may allow fans "an opportunity for practicing emotional regulation to keep their fear and anxiety responses at a tolerable level."[683] In other words, even scary movies can adjust your eustress curve . . . to a point. The authors noted too much "rumination" could increase anxiety to the point of freezing again.

Governments and militaries throughout the world engage in war games, tabletop exercises, and simulations. Asteroid strikes, pandemics, wars, earthquakes, wildfires, and more all have official participation from an assortment of actors. The purpose is to get better at things participants have already encountered or have never encountered.

Military exercise specialists purposefully design games to draw in participants.[684] The *Kriegsspiel*—German for *war game*—has been used for more than two hundred years. Probabilities, dice, game theory such as those regarding negotiations, and artificial intelligence all trace back to elaborate and turn-based play.[685] This is "adaptive simulation," or fluid play. It relates to real-time or near-real-time feedback, whether you're a gamer playing Dungeons and Dragons or a psychologist trying to cure someone of their arachnophobia. Injects—a military term used in exercises to represent stimulus options—can be modulated up and down based on where the player or patient is on the eustress curve.

Games help us work through the "what might" possibilities rather than just the "what will" predictions. One of the reasons that gaming and simulations are so powerful is that we often get engaged emotionally. We can be surprised, *and we can fail*—being wrong has a long-lasting effect. Interactive games can be story-like, and our brains are hardwired for stories, plot, and cause and effect. In fact, the desire for causality is so innate that we often ascribe it power even when reality proves otherwise. We do not like chance... it goes back to the control argument.

Emotional: There Is More to the Story

Resilience is not all brains and no heart. Social psychologist Jonathan Haidt described our mental conscious self as a rider sitting atop an emotionally unconscious elephant. The rider thinks it is in charge, but when the elephant wants something . . . watch out.[686] Emotions are powerful, and you should harness their positive power in your disaster resilience journey, not oppose them.

The reason I chose the term *Noah* to depict one motivational heuristic of Resilient Citizens is because it brings with it a *story*. The storytelling tradition is thousands of years old. Cave drawings, oral traditions, parables, and the writings of Homer and Moses stretch back to antiquity. Relatively modern tales continue, such as "Hansel and Gretel," "The Tortoise and the Hare," "For Want of a Nail," and even *Green Eggs and Ham* and provide moral precepts to the next generation.

Stories are powerful; they stick, they teach, they warn.

We read to our children at bedtime or tell tales around the campfire.

We tell of heroes, villains, and victims.

We tell stories to remember and to warn.

In February 2021, just a month shy of the tenth Tohoku earthquake anniversary I discussed in this book's introduction, a 7.1 earthquake triggered off the coast of Fukushima, Japan. Just forty miles north of Kamaishi lies the town of Miyako. The 2011 tsunami obliterated the town, destroying or damaging four thousand buildings. Yet in the ridgelines above are old stone markers hundreds of years old, one of which bears the following engraving: "High dwellings are the peace and harmony of our descendants. Remember the calamity of the great tsunamis. Do not build any homes below this point."[687] These remembrance stones are scattered throughout Japan. The Japanese are not outliers; our myopia is a human condition. We are slow learners. As Samuel Johnson wrote, "People need to be reminded more often than they need to be instructed."[688]

Noah is depicted in the Bible, warts and all. He is surrounded by wickedness and impending doom; he is almost isolated. But Noah experiences what Aristotle calls the *peripeteia,* a turning point, a flip from either good to bad or bad to good. Disaster becomes the portal for redemption, not the ending. The redemptive arc can be individual or collective. Cities and societies that have undergone major disasters usually follow one of three options: via one pathway, there is the progressive narrative, a hero arc. New York City after 9/11 is an example. A second option is a redemptive route, often religious in nature. The people rededicate themselves to God. The third is the toxic narrative; people are overcome by grief and despair and do not rebuild.[689] All three are more emotion than intellect.

Doomerism—the extremely pessimistic view about the state of the world and a term that pops up in certain *the end is nigh* circles—can be a trap, contributing to the learned helplessness of so many. But emotions, properly channeled, can be an escape. *Tenacity plus anger* was a key combined resource for adults who suffered through childhood adversity. A "self-reported... 'fighting spirit was their most important asset.'"[690] Anger can trump fear. Sometimes, to *get 'er done* means you need to *get 'er mad.*

Another way is to feel good—or at least better—about bad things because of your power to change or improve the circumstances or results. Fear does not make us dumb, but it does activate our System 1 (thinking fast) processing and suppresses our System 2 (thinking slow). Thankfully, the same eustress curve can be modified because our brain manages both rationality *and* emotion, and we can train it to function differently.

Paul Slovic, who has given us so much psychological insight already, researched the phenomenon of the affect heuristic, which is a cognitive bias of using feelings to impact intellectual choices. When used in training for a crisis, the affect heuristic helps us lower the fears of risk and increases the reward of benefit.[691]

For example, say an emergency medical technician (EMT) shows up on the scene of a nasty car accident. There is a risk of injury from fire, sharp objects, other cars still on the road, and so on. However, the EMT knows her skills can save a life or many lives, so she acts *through* the fear. This goes to the very heart of Nelson Mandela's famous quote, "I learned that courage was not the absence of fear, but the triumph over it. The brave man is not he who does not feel afraid, but he who conquers that fear."[692] Courage is not a mental endeavor, but a matter of the heart.

Research has found resilient people possess three key traits: "a belief they can influence life events; a tendency to find meaningful purpose in life's turmoil; and a conviction they can learn from positive and negative experiences."[693] Their "healthy, proactive worldview" is built on high levels of confidence and self-worth.[694] Stated another way, they have an internal locus of control with high agency.

Each of these findings regarding the escape from doomerism are incredible because they are closely related to the profile of heroes. What makes a hero? It is not religion, genetics, politics, or chance. Only three things matter: empathy, agency, and duty.[695]

Empathy should not be confused with sympathy. *Sympathy* is when someone else is hurting and you have concern for them. Maybe you send them a get-well card, give them a call, or offer a hug. But *empathy* is when you have active participation in their suffering; you can see yourself in their shoes and choose to join them.

Agency is a trait I have already covered extensively. It is both the ability and will to act.

Duty is a real kicker. It is not an attitude of doing something "because that's what heroes do." Rather, it is doing something because of how you know you'll feel if you do nothing. Heroes feel they *must* act because they feel committed to their morals and their community.[696] They did not set out to save the world, just the neighborhood.

Social: I'm Coming Home

At the beginning of this chapter, I stated there was a third step in the journey of the Resilient Citizen, one that few ever attain. I have met some incredibly resilient people from all walks of life, genders, races, and income levels. One characteristic stood out above the rest: They placed the *Citizen* component at an equal level of the *Resilient* component. This is the greatest lesson the Interdependent give us.

This involvement of the community is an inescapable conclusion. My greatest criticism of preppers is not that they aim for self-sufficiency—an exceptionally common goal—but that they treat it as an end state, even though they know deep down this is a false summit. The Faithful look to heaven or paradise, a place of *shalom* peace that Earth can offer only in snippets. Sentinels know strength comes in numbers and working together. Homesteaders still need veterinarians and a market to sell their goods. Even the Noahs, bless their hearts, desire at least a maintenance and wait staff to cater to their needs. Only the Interdependent seemed to have embraced the best—and most difficult—step.

A *community* of Resilient Citizens must be formed. It doesn't require everyone to participate, but it does take a coalition of neighbors and core government officials willing to make both the commons and the populace hardy to various shocks. They learn self-sufficiency is paradoxically a *collective* trait. They also understand self-sufficiency is an aspirational goal, not a specific finish line where no more work is required. *This is one of the critical discoveries of my research and experience.* Resilient Citizens engage the administrative state to ensure maximum freedom balanced with appropriate legislation and regulation geared toward flourishing.

For example, at the city and county level, they petition to ensure households can raise chickens in their backyard, support building codes to mandate structures are resistant to earthquake damage, limit or prohibit building in flood-prone areas, and fund protected pathways so that families can safely walk or bike to school, church, or work. Zoning rules encourage high-population-density central hubs where buildings have storefronts on the ground level and two- or three-stories above them for homes designed for multigenerational families. And yet, within ten minutes of biking, these denizens can be in their private or community garden, the gun range, or a protected nature preserve to soak in the sounds of creation. If you think what I have just written is some sort of crazy pipe dream, I can assure you this is attainable. I have lived in such towns and visited several others. At the national level, the goal is retaining natural rights and maximizing control and agency down to the individual level.

Mature Resilient Citizens in this final phase have a deeper understanding of other seeming contradictions and combinations. They inhabit a world of both engineering *and* ecology. They understand we can design systems to reduce the impacts of disaster but that some events are cyclical, habitual, or at least unavoidable. Our actions must be done in concert and stewardship with nature rather than in conquest of it.

Throughout my career, we have been blessed to live in some amazing places. As I write this chapter, I live in Colorado Springs on Peterson Space Force Base. Three hundred and sixty-five days a year, I can bike to the gym, then to work, and then home. The commute is about seven minutes to each destination by pedal power. Traffic is calm, and outside my home office window is Pikes Peak's purple mountain majesty.[697]

Previously, I was stationed in Hawaii. We were deeply integrated with the base chapel. Our neighbors were our best friends. Their children were in our backyard on our rope climb constantly. We parents would spend evenings together talking about issues and life—*real life,* not the *how-are-you-doing-I'm-fine-how's-the-weather* surface-level discussions.

Years before that, I lived in Germany. It was common to go to the local baker almost daily. Sundays were culturally for families. Children and the elderly could walk or bike in the area in near perfect safety. My kids went to German schools, and they dressed and acted (and swore!) like Germans. My daughter's German friends cried when we left.

Notice a theme? While my work was almost always a place of high stress and sometimes mortal danger, home was home. *Comforting, inviting, warm, safe.* What does this have to do with disaster preparedness? *Everything.*

Do you feel like you have a home? I am not talking about a domicile; I am talking about a *home.*

We are a product and a contributor to the ecosystem around us. We crave friendship, togetherness, belonging, and rich relationships. Our modern world provides the exact opposite: isolation, division, fear, and swiping right.

It starts with our kids; heaven forbid you let your children out of your sight. If they walk to the store, you may face arrest.[698] If they head to the park, you risk an investigation by Child Protective Services.[699] If they are on the playground a hundred and twenty feet from your house or in the backyard shooting hoops while you are away, that is grounds for a felony charge.[700] In 2018, Utah actually had to pass a law just so kids could ride their bikes or play in a fenced-in backyard unsupervised.[701]

Contrast this to Japan. A Japanese reality television show thirty years in the running made its way onto Netflix in 2022. *Old Enough!* follows children well before the age of kindergarten on their "first errand." One episode showed a three-year-old—in a city the size of Cincinnati—cross a five-lane street.[702] Toddlers in Japan have more freedom than some American middle-schoolers.

A British public health specialist looked at four generations of "roaming" freedom. The great-grandfather could travel six miles to go fishing without an adult. His great-grandson? Three hundred yards.[703] The doctor's published work argued that this divorce from the outdoors was harming kids' mental health:

> If children haven't had contact with nature, they never develop a relationship with [the] natural environment and they are unable to use it to cope with stress. Studies have shown that people deprived of contact with nature were at greater risk of depression and anxiety. Children are getting less and less unsupervised time in the natural environment. They need time playing in the countryside, in parks and in gardens where they can explore, dig up the ground and build dens.

Instead, we keep our kids indoors and on screens. They burn fewer calories, have vitamin D deficiency from a lack of sunlight, have worse immune systems, and are terrified of using a smartphone to (gulp!) call another human being. If a child is raised in a hypersanitized way, with all possible dangers eliminated, how can they grow? What happens when a real shock comes? We already know the answer: They can't handle it.

Is it any surprise so many of them are physically and psychologically suffering? The Centers for Disease Control and Prevention's 2011–2021 biannual Youth Risk Behavior Survey found almost 60 percent of teen girls "experience persistent sadness or hopelessness" and 30 percent "have seriously considered suicide."[704] During the COVID-19 pandemic, more than 20 percent of twelve- to seventeen-year-olds had "experienced a depressive episode."[705]

We build a car-dependent, cloistered infrastructure that separates us from nature, our neighbors, and our families. Too many of us get in our car in the garage, drive our kids to school, then drive to work alone. It's a giant asphalt hell. We need to engage our civil engineers and city managers to fix this.

We then retreat into our dry-walled enclave at night. There's even a fancy term for it: *tessellated neoliberalism*. Basically, we build a domestic fortress. The creators of the term argue:

> Social anxiety, inequality, and profound economic changes have connected with housing tenure to produce a defensive and physically bolstered form of home ownership, an archipelago of domestic fortresses in a social environment that celebrates private ownership, retreat, and fortification.[706]

Do we feel safe in these garrisons? No. There is the ever-present threat of home invasion or even cyberbullying on our devices.[707] We feel atomized even with five thousand "friends" on social media. What to do?

I have adopted a motto that I try to live by: *Fight Local, Win Local.* Strong communities are curated and maintained by run-of-the-mill individuals just like you. The benefits are staggering. You are who you surround yourself with.

I wrote previously about how we are herd creatures, and we do things because we see others doing them. The term *meme* originally did not describe humorous images but rather came from evolutionary biologist Richard Dawkins to describe how ideas, fashions, or behaviors are transmitted via the social milieu, much like a gene would in DNA. The renowned behavioral economist Robert Cialdini showed how we process these cues in society. His work demonstrated that our neighbors' activities and mannerisms influence us more than any other input studied.[708]

Other research found happiness worked like a social contagion. A Harvard University study, in continuous operation since 1948, found for every "contented person you know, your likelihood of being contented rises 2 percent. Unfortunately, for each discontented person you know, your chances of being discontented rise 4 percent." However, the happiness "infections" lasted twice as long.[709]

Several confirmatory studies find contagion at play in other venues of our lives. Having wealthy friends, for example, can positively impact your finances.[710] We observe the same thing in weight gain or loss. Fit friends lead to a fitter you. Our built environment impacts this. NinjaFit Playgrounds designs parks in neighborhoods based on the American Ninja Warrior TV show geared toward teen and adult fitness. They recognize a key variable is not the individual but the community; therefore, the company invests heavily in community involvement.[711]

Earlier in this chapter, I wrote that habits of mind are alterable. Another area where this has been demonstrated is in the phenomenon of "Blue Zones," or areas around the world in which people have not just extraordinary longevity but health and activity deep into old age. It wasn't just diet and exercise that led to long life, but social bonding.[712]

Therefore, what is the one preparedness item you must buy, the "thing" above all others to work toward the goal of true resilience? The answer is the humble dining room table. Invite your neighbors over, share a meal, and share *life*. Expand your home beyond just the four walls. Learn what others have to offer and recognize what brings us together and what we hold in common. What we truly need is community involvement. This is hard because we must engage with others who are fundamentally imperfect and hold their values and biases. We need sheepdog trainers, dentists, blacksmiths, physical therapists, naturopaths, chemists, sewer engineers, and midwives. We need kids on rollerblades in the streets, and sometimes we need to *not* know where our kids even are. We need to be ready to lend a helping hand. This is life to the fullest.

Become a Resilient Citizen.

Save the neighborhood, save the world.

ACKNOWLEDGMENTS

The dedication of my wife, **Kimberly**, as a military spouse and loving mother during my over a quarter-of-a-century service to America has not been without sacrifices. Taking nearly two years on a project of this size, while still in uniform, has sucked away numerous weekends we could have spent having fun, but I was cloistered in my office. Her constant prayers and support were instrumental. Kim, thank you so much for all the walks and talks where you let me verbalize concepts and structure and gave the necessary feedback. To my children **Tiffani** and **Matthew**, apologies for not calling as much as I should have while I was writing, editing, and then writing and editing some more.

I shared my dissertation with **Ashley Colby-Fitzgerald** and asked if she wanted to expand the interviews with real people and coauthor this book with me. Ashley readily agreed and wrote a few stories that are now contained in chapters 5–9. However, after hearing me present the book's concepts during a speech, Ashley thought I should go solo and make this book my own. She stayed on to provide guidance and assistance, and I am grateful for her suggestions.

Bradley Garrett was of tremendous encouragement, and I am thankful for his contribution. **Nic Rowan**, my editor before we even had a publisher, tore my first draft to shreds, but that is his job. He made the final product better. **John Ramey**, thanks, man. Whenever I thought I was a bit crazy, you reminded me that this discussion is not only needed but also completely sane.

To the Forefront Books team of **Jill Smith, Jen Gingerich, Jacqueline Grace, Allen Harris, Caroline Pierce, Lauren Ward, Aria Fisher, Billie Brownell,** and **Andrew Buss**, thank you so much. You were all helpful guides.

And finally, I want to thank a collection of friends who offered support throughout the process. When you are surrounded by such talent, inspiration, and gentle ribbing, it keeps you going. In alphabetical order, I would like to thank: **Roxanne Ahern, Peter Allen, Jon Askonas, Jeremy Carl, Josh Centers, Patrick Fitzgerald, Nathan Gates, Andy and Keturah Hickman, Andrew Hock, Joseph Keegin, Paul Kingsnorth, Geoffrey Long, Gordon Magill, Paul McNeil, Micah Meadowcroft, Kate Parsons, James Pogue, Santi Ruiz, Seneca Scott,** and **Suzy Weiss.** All of you are such talented writers and intellects in your respective fields.

NOTES AND REFERENCES

Foreword

1 L. Annaeus Seneca, *Tranquility of Mind,* translated by William Langsdorf (New York and London: G. P. Putnam and Sons, 1900), 64.

2 Bradley Garrett, *Bunker: What It Takes to Survive the Apocalypse* (New York: Simon & Schuster, 2021).

Chapter 1: People, Perils, and Politics

3 This story is from my personal conversation with Lauren and her recounting of the event.

4 National Oceanic and Atmospheric Administration, "Japan's 'Harbor Wave'. The Tsunami One Year Later," March 14, 2012, https://web.archive.org/web/20131218045116/http://www.noaa.gov/features/03_protecting/japantsunami_oneyearlater.html.

5 National Police Agency of Japan, "Police Countermeasures and Damage Situation Associated with 2011 Tohoku Distric—Off the Pacific Ocean Earthquake" (Tokyo: National Police Agency of Japan Emergency Disaster Countermeasures Headquarters, September 10, 2019), https://www.npa.go.jp/news/other/earthquake2011/pdf/higaijokyo_e.pdf.

6 World Nuclear Association, "Fukushima Daiichi Accident," October 2018, https://www.world-nuclear.org/information-library/safety-and-security/safety-of-plants/fukushima-accident.aspx.

7 Jane Braxton Little, "Fukushima Residents Return Despite Radiation," *Scientific American,* January 16, 2019, https://www.scientificamerican.com/article/fukushima-residents-return-despite-radiation/.

8 Zoë Schlanger, "The UN Says Japan May Be Violating Human Rights by Returning Families to Fukushima," Quartz, October 26, 2018, https://qz.com/1439696/families-are-returning-to-fukushima-and-japan-may-be-violating-their-human-rights-says-the-un/.

9 Ryusei Takahashi, "Eight Years after Triple Nuclear Meltdown, Fukushima No. 1's Water Woes Show No Signs of Ebbing," *The Japan Times Online,* March 7, 2019, https://www.japantimes.co.jp/news/2019/03/07/national/eight-years-triple-meltdown-fukushima-no-1s-water-woes-slow-recede/.

10 "Tepco Estimates 44 Years to Decommission Fukushima No. 2 Nuclear Plant," *The Japan Times,* January 23, 2020, https://www.japantimes.co.jp/news/2020/01/23/national/tepco-fukushima-decommissioning/.

11 Mari Yamaguchi, "A Robot Retrieves the First Melted Fuel from Fukushima Nuclear Reactor," AP News, November 4, 2024, https://apnews.com/article/japan-fukushima-nuclear-melted-fuel-robot-d4bbfb543a0bbf9839ed2b33ea5ea969.

12 Shih-Chieh Hsu et al., "Hemispheric Dispersion of Radioactive Plume Laced with Fission Nuclides from the Fukushima Nuclear Event," *Geophysical Research Letters* 39 (January 12, 2012), https://doi.org/10.1029/2011GL049986@10.1002/(ISSN)1944-8007.MEGAQUAKE1.

13 Joseph Mangano and Janette Sherman, "Elevated Airborne Beta Levels in Pacific/West Coast

US States and Trends in Hypothyroidism among Newborns after the Fukushima Nuclear Meltdown," *Open Journal of Pediatrics* 3, no. 1 (March 2013): 1–9, https://doi.org/10.4236/ojped.2013.31001.

14 Lucy Jones, *The Big Ones: How Natural Disasters Have Shaped Us and What We Can Do About Them* (New York: Doubleday, 2018).

15 Dave Roos, "The 2004 Tsunami Wiped Away Towns with 'Mind-Boggling' Destruction," HISTORY, September 18, 2020, https://www.history.com/news/deadliest-tsunami-2004-indian-ocean.

16 Jones, *The Big Ones: How Natural Disasters Have Shaped Us and What We Can Do About Them.*

17 Olivier Rubin, "The Political Dynamics of Voter Retrospection and Disaster Responses," *Disasters* 44, no. 2 (April 2020): 239–61, https://doi.org/10.1111/disa.12376.

18 Robert Muir-Wood, *The Cure for Catastrophe: How We Can Stop Manufacturing Natural Disasters* (New York: Basic Books, 2016).

19 Katada's actions here are a summary from Muir-Wood's book.

20 Variations of the identical concept substitute "frequency" or "chance" for probability and "impact" for consequence. This book uses multiple versions, but the meaning is the same.

21 World Economic Forum, "The Global Risks Report 2023: 18th Edition" (Geneva, Switzerland, January 2023), https://www.weforum.org/reports/globalrisks- report-2023/.

22 Michael Lawrence et al., "Global Polycrisis: The Causal Mechanisms of Crisis Entanglement," *Global Sustainability* 7 (January 2024): e6, https://doi.org/10.1017/sus.2024.1.

23 Caroline Hickman et al., "Climate Anxiety in Children and Young People and Their Beliefs about Government Responses to Climate Change: A Global Survey," *The Lancet Planetary Health* 5, no. 12 (December 1, 2021): e863–73, https://doi.org/10.1016/S2542-5196(21)00278-3.

24 National Institute of Mental Health, "Mental Illness," Mental Health Information, September 2024, https://www.nimh.nih.gov/health/statistics/mental-illness.

25 Zach Goldberg (@ZachG932), "16/n Some of you asked for it, so here is the last chart broken down by gender. Biggest gap within age x ideological groups is . . ." Twitter (now X), April 13, 2020, https://x.com/ZachG932/status/1249764370458062850.

26 "9 Out Of 10 Phone Users Have Low-Battery Anxiety," Electron-to-Go,accessed January 11, 2025, https://electrontogo.com/blog/9-out-of-10-phone-users-have-low-battery-anxiety.

27 Charlotte Nickerson, "Learned Helplessness: Seligman's Theory of Depression," Simply Psychology, May 2, 2024, https://www.simplypsychology.org/learned-helplessness.html.

28 Chad Huddleston, "'Prepper' as Resilient Citizen: What Preppers Can Teach Us about Surviving Disasters," in *Responses to Disasters and Climate Change.*, ed. Michele Companion and Miriam Chaiken (Boca Raton, Florida: CRC Press, 2016), https://www.researchgate.net/publication/315957699_Prepper_as_resilient_citizen_what_preppers_can_teach_us_about_surviving_disasters.

29 Years ago when I was at Cornell, I reached out to Chad to let him know I would be expanding on that concept for my dissertation. (Thanks, Chad!) Since then, I have seen multiple references to the connection between resilience and citizenship, but never in the context of preppers.

30 I define these in-depth in chapter 4.

31 United Nations Office for Disaster Risk Reduction, "Sendai Framework for Disaster Risk Reduction 2015–2030" (United Nations Office for Disaster Risk Reduction, 2015).

32 I hate the term *race*. Biblically, we are all one race: human. However, I do recognize the current

political and scientific climate regarding the term and use it, grudgingly, later in this book in its common use.

33 "Joseph Stalin, 1879-1953," *Oxford Reference*, Oxford University Press, accessed May 1, 2025, https://www.oxfordreference.com/display/10.1093/acref/9780191826719.001.0001/q-oro-ed4-00010383.

Chapter 2: The Portrayals of Preparedness

34 Kurt Saxon, "What Is a Survivalist?," 1980, https://web.archive.org/web/20150421050124/http://www.aussurvivalist.com/whatissurvivalismsaxon.htm.

35 "prepper, survivalist," Google Books Ngram Viewer, accessed April 28, 2025, https://books.google.com/ngrams/graph?corpus=26&content=prepper%2C+survivalist&smoothing=3&year_start=1800&year_end=2019&direct_url=t1%3B%2Cprepper%3B%2Cc0%3B.t1%3B%2Csurvivalist%3B%2Cc0#t1%3B%2Cprepper%3B%2Cc0%3B.t1%3B%2Csurvivalist%3B%2Cc0.

36 Saxon, "What Is a Survivalist?"

37 James Coates, *Armed and Dangerous: The Rise of the Survivalist Right* (New York: Hill and Wang, 1987); Carmen Nicole Gonowon, "Just in Case: An Empirical-Phenomenological Analysis of the Lived Experience of Modern Survivalists" (PsyD diss., Chicago School of Professional Psychology, 2011), http://search.proquest.com/pqdtglobal/docview/1040724340/abstract/6B0051B97C5C4FABPQ/7; Philip Lamy, *Millennium Rage: Survivalists, White Supremacists, and the Doomsday Prophecy* (Boston, MA: Springer US, 1996), https://doi.org/10.1007/978-1-4899-6076-4.

38 Dr. Nina Tannenwald coined this "the nuclear taboo" to describe the world's overall reluctance to use nuclear weapons, post–World War II. Her political and psychological observations and claims are complementary to my work in subsequent chapters. You can read about her theory in her book *The Nuclear Taboo* published by Cambridge University Press.

39 Kezia Barker, "How to Survive the End of the Future: Preppers, Pathology, and the Everyday Crisis of Insecurity," *Transactions of the Institute of British Geographers*, December 2, 2019, https://doi.org/10.1111/tran.12362; Michael F. Mills, "Preparing for the Unknown… Unknowns: 'Doomsday' Prepping and Disaster Risk Anxiety in the United States," *Journal of Risk Research* 22, no. 10 (October 3, 2019): 1267–79, https://doi.org/10.1080/13669877.2018.1466825.

40 Tiffany Anne Christian, "Apocalypse and the Utopian Impulse: Gendered Narratives of Survival and Wounded Masculinities in Contemporary Popular Culture" (PhD diss., Washington State University, 2017), http://search.proquest.com/pqdtglobal/docview/1931812828/abstract/6B0051B97C5C4FABPQ/8.

41 Barker, "How to Survive the End of the Future"; Mills, "Preparing for the Unknown… Unknowns."

42 In no way do I dismiss the work of qualitative scholars. Indeed, I feature qualitative methods prominently in this book. However, larger scale and quantitative (mathematical) inquiry, mixed with qualitative data, paints a more accurate picture.

43 Barker, "How to Survive the End of the Future"; Bradley Garrett, "Doomsday Preppers and the Architecture of Dread," *Geoforum*, April 10, 2020, https://doi.org/10.1016/j.geoforum.2020.03.014; Mills, "Preparing for the Unknown… Unknowns."

44 Gwendolyn Audrey Foster, *Hoarders, Doomsday Preppers, and the Culture of Apocalypse* (New

York: Palgrave Macmillan, 2014).

45 Lee'Ann D. Imel-Hartford, "The Preppers: A Multiple Case Study of Individuals Who Choose a Moderate Survivalist Lifestyle" (DBA diss., Northcentral University, 2013), http://search.proquest.com/pqdtglobal/docview/1319955476/abstract/60A03E9D15A940ECPQ/1; "Assessing the Threat from Accelerationists and Militia Extremists" (Government Printing Office, July 16, 2020), https://www.congress.gov/event/116th-congress/house-event/LC65904/text.July 16, 2020.

46 Norah Campbell, Gary Sinclair, and Sarah Browne, "Preparing for a World without Markets: Legitimising Strategies of Preppers," *Journal of Marketing Management* 35, no. 9–10 (June 13, 2019): 798–817, https://doi.org/10.1080/0267257X.2019.1631875.

47 Barker, "How to Survive the End of the Future."

48 Amy Green, "Far Cry 5, American Right-Wing Terrorism, and Doomsday Prepper Culture—Amy M. Green, 2022," *Game and Culture* 17, nos. 7–8 (2022): 1015–35; Mark O'Connell, *Notes from the Apocalypse: A Personal Journey to the End of the World and Back* (New York: Doubleday, 2020); Alison Ford, "'They Will Be like a Swarm of Locusts': Race, Rurality, and Settler Colonialism in American Prepping Culture," *Rural Sociology* 86, no. 3 (2021).

49 Jordan McKenzie, "Millennial Utopians and Prepper Subcultures: Contemporary Utopianism on the Left and Right," *Futures* 126 (December 24, 2020); James Hughes, "A Socialist Approach to Disaster Preparedness: A Leftist Guide for the Coming Catastrophes," Medium, March 27, 2021, https://medium.com/after-the-storm/the-coming-catastrophes-a-socialist-approach-to-disaster-preparedness-46e66705ac97.

50 Juli Gittinger, "Liberal Prepping as Apocalyptic Eco-Religion," *The Journal of Religion and Popular Culture* 35, no. 1 (2023): 1-20, https://doi.org/10.3138/jrpc.2020-0026.

51 Julianna Marilyn Lindsay, "The Living Heritage of Prepping" (PhD diss., Arkansas State University, 2015), http://search.proquest.com/pqdtglobal/docview/1712373754/abstract/60A03E9D15A940ECPQ/3.

52 Mills, "Preparing for the Unknown… Unknowns"; Huddleston, "'Prepper' as Resilient Citizen: What Preppers Can Teach Us about Surviving Disasters"; Chad Huddleston, "For Preppers, the Apocalypse Is Just Another Disaster," SAPIENS, March 14, 2018, https://www.sapiens.org/culture/prepping-anthropology/; Anna Maria Bounds, *Bracing for the Apocalypse: An Ethnographic Study of New York's "Prepper" Subculture* (New York: Routledge, 2021).

53 Coates, *Armed and Dangerous: The Rise of the Survivalist Right.*

54 If you really want a deep dive into the Dominant and Challenger literature, I included several pages of quotes in previous research. Chris Ellis, "Are You Ready for It? Examining Security in Contemporary Disaster Preparedness, From Normal to Noahchian" (Proquest, 2021), https://t.co/RqgohGZStV.

55 Michael F. Mills, "Obamageddon: Fear, the Far Right, and the Rise of 'Doomsday' Prepping in Obama's America," *Journal of American Studies*, June 13, 2019, 1–30, https://doi.org/10.1017/S0021875819000501.

56 Richard Laycock, "Doomsday Preppers: How Many Are Preparing for the End?," *Finder*, 2020, https://www.finder.com/doomsday-prepper-statistics.

57 Richard Laycock, "74 Million Americans Prepping for Disaster," *Finder*, April 11, 2023, https://www.finder.com/doomsday-prepper-statistics.

58 Jon C. Ogg, "Industries Making the Most Money on Doomsday Preppers," *24/7 Wall St.*, 2013, https://247wallst.com/special-report/2013/08/19/industries-making-the-most-money-on-doomsday-preppers/.

59 Of note, he updated this posting in March of 2020.

60 The link provided by Mills for Lawson was dead. The citation was K. Lawson, "Why Survivalist Preppers Make the Best Spouses," accessed July 6, 2017, http://www.brides.com/story/whysurvivalist-preppers-make-the-best-spouses.

61 Lacey N. Wallace, "Responses to Perceived Terrorism Risk by Self-Identified Survivalists: An Exploratory Study," *The Social Science Journal*, April 20, 2020, 1–14, https://doi.org/10.1080/03623319.2020.1744950.

62 Wallace hinted these latter two reasons might be a factor. For example, she stated, "Crime victims were significantly more likely to identify as survivalists."

63 Benjamin Webb, "Mapping North America's Top Doomsday Prepper Hotspots," Survival of the Fittest: Mapping North America's Prepper Hotspots, January 16, 2024, https://www.bestcasinosites.net/blog/north-america-prepper-hotspots.php.

64 Richard Mitchell, *Dancing at Armageddon: Survivalism and Chaos in Modern Times* (Chicago, IL: The University of Chicago Press, 2002).

Chapter 3: The Prominence of Preparedness

65 For any readers who are seriously interested in a deeper understanding of my methodology or more advanced statistical analysis, you can freely access my Cornell dissertation, "Are You Ready for It?," which provides the baseline, at https://ecommons.cornell.edu/items/68463d92-ac1c-475c-9983-c5781be6da18.

66 I suspect that these individuals interpret the question as to *publicly* provided power, water, and transportation. My guess is that many Resilient Citizens, especially those who say they can last two to three months or more, have well water and off-grid power-generation capability.

67 The year 2018 had a better national profile than the 2017 National Household Survey, so I use it often in this chapter as a base year comparison.

68 Based on a 2018 US adult population of 253,768,092. US Census Bureau, "Annual Estimates of the Resident Population for Selected Age Groups by Sex for the United States, States, Counties, and Puerto Rico Commonwealth and Municipios: April 1, 2010 to July 1, 2018," October 8, 2019, https://www2.census.gov/programs-surveys/popest/tables/2010-2018/state/asrh/PEPAGESEX.pdf.. Calculations based on the number of households in America yield a similar answer.

69 Geddes warns that one potential failure of large-N studies is that the value of a variable does not really match what the proposed measurement is. Here, though, the FEMA data are directly a measurement of perceived or actual resilience, exactly what I am trying to ascertain. And clearly, depictions of gender, income, race, and other descriptive statistics are exact (or near exact) representations. See Barbara Geddes, *Paradigms and Sand Castles: Theory Building and Research Design in Comparative Politics* (Ann Arbor: University of Michigan Press, 2003).

70 Wealthy individuals are often categorized as High-Net-Worth Individuals and Ultra-High-Net-Worth Individuals. Therefore, these alternative terms could also be used to describe "normal" Resilient Citizens.

71 A word of caution: I have done my best to accurately represent the data shown here. However, even though the survey samples are roughly five thousand people per year, the number of Resilient Citizens is low. When adding additional variables such as gender or race, the numbers shrink even further. I attempt to play my cards as transparently as possible.

72 See footnote 32 on this term from chapter 1.

73 Ellis, "Are You Ready for It?"

74 Gwendolyn Audrey Foster, "Consuming the Apocalypse, Marketing Bunker Materiality," *Quarterly Review of Film and Video* 33, no. 4 (May 18, 2016): 285–302, https://doi.org/10.1080/10509208.2016.1144017; O'Connell, *Notes from the Apocalypse: A Personal Journey to the End of the World and Back.*

75 Craig Fulgate, "Are Disabled Still at Risk in Disasters?," CNN.com, July 26, 2010, http://www.cnn.com/2010/OPINION/07/26/fugate.disabled.disasters/index.html.

76 FEMA classified disabilities involving "a mobility, hearing, vision, cognitive, or intellectual disability or physical, mental, or health condition."

77 Patrice Lewis, "Are Preppers Responsible for the Unprepared?," WorldNetDaily, December 7, 2012, https://www.wnd.com/2012/12/are-preppers-responsible-for-the-unprepared/.

78 Muir-Wood, *The Cure for Catastrophe: How We Can Stop Manufacturing Natural Disasters.*

79 The jumps on the scale were unequal, and potential valued monthly income answers were: Under $60, $60 to $499, $500 to $999, $1,000 to $1,999, $2,000 to $2,999, $3,000 to $3,999, $4,000 to $4,999, $5,000 to $7,499, $7,500 to $9,999, $10,000 to $14,999, $15,000 to $19,999, and $20,000 and over.

80 Abdullah A. Aldousari, "Exploring Consumer Behavior under Perceived Threat" (Rutgers University, 2015), https://doi.org/10.7282/T31V5GN7.

81 Laycock, "Doomsday Preppers."

82 Emelie Olsson, "Understanding Swedish Prepping—A Mixed-Method Study on Resilience, Trust, and Incentives to Prepare for Crises" (Uppsala, Swedish University of Agricultural Sciences, 2021).

83 Kevin Kohler et al., "Measuring Individual Disaster Preparedness" (Zurich, Switzerland: Center for Security Studies, September 2020).

84 John Cromartie, "Rural-Urban Commuting Area Codes," Economic Research Service, updated January 6, 2025, https://www.ers.usda.gov/data-products/rural-urban-commuting-area-codes/.

85 Codes two and three were Metropolitan Areas that flowed into Urbanized Areas. Codes 4–6 were large Urbanized Clusters (10,000–49,999 residents) or places that flowed into them. Codes 7–9 were small Urban Clusters (2,500–9,999 residents) or places that flowed into them.

86 US Census Bureau, "Urban and Rural Populations Shift Following 2020 Census," Census.gov, December 29, 2022, https://www.census.gov/newsroom/press-releases/2022/urban-rural-populations.html.

87 Research by Anna Bounds finds preppers to be more common than anticipated in New York City. See Anna Maria Bounds, "New Yorkers' Street Smarts and Survival Smarts during the Pandemic: Preppers, Community Resilience and Local Citizenship," *Urbana: Urban Affairs & Public Policy*, November 15, 2020, 65–86, https://doi.org/10.47785/urbana.5.2020.

88 FEMA has added a new disclaimer for their datasets: "FEMA and the Federal Government cannot vouch for the data or analyses derived from these data after the data have been retrieved from the Agency's website."

89 This answer option was not available for the "How long will the supplies that you have assembled last?" question but only for the power and running water questions.

90 This is not a criticism against FEMA; they have a different aim in their surveys than I do, and I understand their reasoning for changing course.

91 Had I counted only Resilient Citizens who answered more than one month and three months for all three questions of supplies, power, and running water, the number of Resilient Citizens would drop precipitously to roughly 4.6 percent (2021) and 5.2 percent (2023). This is not

what I am seeing either anecdotally or via the research of others. The number of people taking enhanced preparedness measures seems to be on the rise.

92 For US population counts for 2021 to 2023, I used data from the US Census Bureau, which can be found here: https://www2.census.gov/programs-surveys/popest/tables/2020-2023/national/asrh/nc-est2023-agesex.xlsx.

93 US Census Bureau.

94 For real world examples, see Tom Luongo, "Crossing the 16% Chasm Is AfD's Goal in Merkel Fight," Gold Goats 'n Guns, June 18, 2018, http://tomluongo.me/2018/06/18/crossing-chasm-afd-goal-merkel/; "The Secret to Accelerating Diffusion of Innovation: The 16% Rule Explained," *Innovate or Die* (blog), May 9, 2010, https://innovateordie.com.au/

95 A word of caution: Women are more likely to participate in online surveys, so gender parity in enhanced preparedness may be an illusion.

96 I also attempted a different strategy to count the number of Hispanics. For the 2021–2023 datasets, I counted as Hispanic those who said yes to the question, "Are you of Hispanic, Latino, or Spanish origin?" In my previous work, I stripped out from this tally those who also marked another race in the "primary race" question from FEMA. Therefore, my 2021–2023 analysis includes far more Hispanic responses.

Chapter 5: The Homesteaders

97 Amanda Sims, "Survival of the Preppers: An Exploration into the Culture of Prepping" (PhD diss., University of Missouri, 2017).

98 Lindsay, "The Living Heritage of Prepping."

99 Kira Bre Clingen, *TEOTWAWKI: A Designer's Guide to Prepping* (Boston, MA: Harvard University, 2021).

100 Alex Turner-Cohen, "Australia's 'Doom Boom': COVID-19 Inspires City-Slickers to Prepare for the End of the World," NewsComAu, December 20, 2020, https://www.news.com.au/finance/australias-doom-boom-covid19-inspires-cityslickers-to-prepare-for-the-end-of-the-world/news-story/bcfc357e996c5fbfe998ceab1dc2ab8e#.4qe9s|s5i5f.

101 Robert Strassler, ed., *The Landmark Thucydides: A Comprehensive Guide to the Peloponnesian War* (New York: Free Press, 1996).

102 Niall Ferguson, *Doom: The Politics of Catastrophe* (New York: Penguin Press, 2021).

103 Laurie Garrett, *The Coming Plague: Newly Emerging Diseases in a World Out of Balance* (New York: Penguin Books, 1994).

104 Garrett.

105 Garrett.

106 Emma Newburger, "Disasters Caused $210 Billion in Damage in 2020, Showing Growing Cost of Climate Change," CNBC, January 7, 2021, https://www.cnbc.com/2021/01/07/climate-change-disasters-cause-210-billion-in-damage-in-2020.html.

107 "What Is the Economic Cost of Covid-19?," *The Economist*, January 9, 2021, http://www.economist.com/finance-and-economics/2021/01/09/what-is-the-economic-cost-of-covid-19.

108 Larry Elliott, "IMF Estimates Global Covid Cost at $28tn in Lost Output," *The Guardian*, October 13, 2020, https://www.theguardian.com/business/2020/oct/13/imf-covid-cost-world-economic-outlook.

109 Tyler Durden, "UK Economy Crashed 9.9% in 2020, Biggest Drop in 311 Years," *ZeroHedge* (blog), February 12, 2021, https://www.zerohedge.com/markets/uk-economy-crashed-99-2020-biggest-drop-311-years.

110 United Nations Meetings Coverage and Press Releases, "Amid Threat of Catastrophic Global Famine, COVID-19 Response Must Prioritize Food Security, Humanitarian Needs, Experts Tell General Assembly," December 4, 2020, https://www.un.org/press/en/2020/ga12294.doc.htm.

111 *Office of the Director of National Intelligence*, 2024 Annual Threat Assessment Director of National Intelligence, (February 5, 2024 , https://www.dni.gov/index.php/newsroom/reports-publications/reports-publications-2024/3787-2024-annual -threat -assessment-of-the-u-s-intelligence-community.

112 Robert F. Kennedy Jr., *The Wuhan Cover-Up: And the Terrifying Bioweapons Arms Race* (New York: Skyhorse, 2023); Select Subcommittee on the Coronavirus Pandemic, "After Action Review of the COVID-19 Pandemic: The Lessons Learned and a Path Forward" (Washington, DC: US House of Representatives, December 4, 2024).

113 Elaheh Eslami et al., "Pattern of Bioterrorism in Ancient Times: Lessons to Be Learned from the Microbial and Toxicological Aspects," *Wiener Medizinische Wochenschrift* 174, no. 13 (October 1, 2024): 288–98, https://doi.org/10.1007/s10354-023-01029-1; Ken Alibek, *Biohazard: The Chilling True Story of the Largest Covert Biological Weapons Program in the World—Told from Inside by the Man Who Ran It* (New York: Dell Publishing, 1999); Vincent Barras and Gilbert Greub, "History of Biological Warfare and Bioterrorism," *Clinical Microbiology and Infection* 20, no. 6 (June 1, 2014): 497–502, https://doi.org/10.1111/1469-0691.12706.

114 Alibek, *Biohazard: The Chilling True Story of the Largest Covert Biological Weapons Program in the World—Told from Inside by the Man Who Ran It.*

115 Alibek.

116 Matt Wilkinson, "Novichok Nerve Agent Attack in Salisbury Cost Taxpayers a Staggering £30million," *The Sun*, August 27, 2019, https://www.thesun.co.uk/news/9809896/novichok-attack-salisbury-taxpayers-30million/.

117 Sarah Knapton and Joe Pinkstone, "Lab Leaks and Accidents up 50pc as Fears Grow Dangerous Viruses and Bacteria Could Escape," *The Telegraph*, January 6, 2024, https://www.telegraph.co.uk/news/2024/01/06/lab-leaks-accidents-pandemic-viruses-bacteria-wuhan/.

118 The White House, "National Biodefense Strategy and Implementation Plan for Countering Biological Threats, Enhancing Pandemic Preparedness, and Achieving Global Health Security" (Washington, DC, October 2022).

119 Bletchley Park, "The World Wants to Regulate AI, but Does Not Quite Know How," *The Economist*, October 24, 2023, https://www.economist.com/business/2023/10/24/the-world-wants-to-regulate-ai-but-does-not-quite-know-how; Bill Drexel and Caleb Withers, "AI and the Evolution of Biological National Security Risks," Center for a New American Security, August 13, 2024, https://www.cnas.org/publications/reports/ai-and-the-evolution-of-biological-national-security-risks.

120 Personal conversation between Roxanne and Dr. Ashley Colby, as are the rest of Roxanne's quotes.

121 John Klar, *Small Farm Republic: Why Conservatives Must Embrace Local Agriculture, Reject Climate Alarmism, and Lead an Environmental Revival* (White River Junction, VT: Chelsea Green Publishing, 2023).

122 Lindsay, "The Living Heritage of Prepping," uses this designation, *Homesteader*, as well as several others.

123 Laura He, "Dumplings without Pork? Swine Fever Is Hitting Chinese Consumers," CNN, October 16, 2019, https://www.cnn.com/2019/10/16/business/african-swine-fever-china-

pork-pigs/index.html.

124 Anna Fleck, "Concern over Food & Water Supply Grows among Europeans," Statista Daily Data, March 22, 2024, https://www.statista.com/chart/28675/survey-on-concern-over-food-and-water-supply.

125 As I mentioned in the acknowledgments, Dr. Colby was an original collaborator with me on this book.

126 Samantha Fields, "44% of Americans Fear They Won't Be Able to Afford Food, Poll Finds," Marketplace, May 7, 2020, https://www.marketplace.org/2020/05/07/44-of-americans-fear-they-wont-be-able-to-afford-food-poll-finds/; Tracey Tully and Bryan Anselm, "Food Lines a Mile Long in America's Second-Wealthiest State," *The New York Times*, April 30, 2020, https://www.nytimes.com/2020/04/30/nyregion/coronavirus-nj-hunger.html; Luke Kenton, "Thousands Line Up outside Drive-Thru Texas Food Bank Where 600,000 Pounds of Food Was Given Away," *Daily Mail Online*, November 16, 2020, https://www.dailymail.co.uk/news/article-8953859/Thousands-line-outside-drive-Texas-food-bank-600-000-pounds-food-given-away.html.

127 Gerson Freitas Jr., "Trump Won't Be Able to Save the Struggling US Beef Industry," Bloomberg.com, December 9, 2024, https://www.bloomberg.com/news/articles/2024-12-09/will-trump-bring-down-meat-prices-why-beef-inflation-isn-t-over.

128 The Centers for Disease Control tracks domestic and international cases and posts them here: https://www.cdc.gov/outbreaks/index.html.

129 Bill Chappell and Allison Aubrey, "Yes, the Number of Food Recalls Has Been Rising. Here's What You Need to Know," National Public Radio, December 9, 2024, https://www.npr.org/2024/12/09/nx-s1-5215713/food-recalls-foodborne-illness-outbreaks-safety-tips.

130 Chris Smaje, *Saying No to a Farm-Free Future* (London, UK: Chelsea Green Publishing, 2023).

131 Klar, *Small Farm Republic: Why Conservatives Must Embrace Local Agriculture, Reject Climate Alarmism, and Lead an Environmental Revival.*

132 I talk about American debt in chapter 8. If you need to be radicalized on soil preservation, read David R. Montgomery's book *Dirt: The Erosion of Civilization.* I don't think I've read a more depressing work.

133 Clingen, "TEOTWAWKI: A Designer's Guide to Prepping."

134 Katie Mayers, "Gardening Statistics in 2024 (Incl. Covid & Millennials) | Garden Pals," January 15, 2024, https://gardenpals.com/gardening-statistics/.

135 Lindsay, "The Living Heritage of Prepping."

136 Paul Hoggett, "Climate Change and the Apocalyptic Imagination," *Psychoanalysis, Culture & Society* 16, no. 3 (September 1, 2011): 261–75, https://doi.org/10.1057/pcs.2011.1.

137 Alec Tyson, Cary Funk, and Brian Kennedy, "What the Data Says about Americans' Views of Climate Change," *Pew Research Center* (blog), August 9, 2023, https://www.pewresearch.org/short-reads/2023/08/09/what-the-data-says-about-americans-views-of-climate-change/.

138 Although political ideology is widely varied. See, for example, N. Rosen, *Off the Grid: Inside the Movement for More Space, Less Government, and True Independence in Modern America* (London: Penguin Books, 2010).

139 Oona Morrow, "Urban Homesteading: Diverse Economies and Ecologies of Provisioning in Greater Boston" (PhD diss., Clark University, 2014), http://search.proquest.com/pqdtglobal/docview/1640884908/abstract/6B0051B97C5C4FABPQ/18.

140 Bounds, "New Yorkers' Street Smarts and Survival Smarts during the Pandemic."

141 Ashley Colby, *Subsistence Agriculture in the US: Reconnecting to Work, Nature and Community*

(New York: Routledge, 2022).

142 The documentary *Tomorrow* (available at https://www.tomorrow-documentary.com/) illustrates several examples of this, including Detroit urban gardens.

143 Martha E. James, "Beyond the Current: A Case Study of Intentional Off-Gridders" (MA thesis, Northern Arizona University, 2013), http://search.proquest.com/pqdtglobal/docview/1433074993/abstract/6B0051B97C5C4FABPQ/14.

144 Josef Nguyen, "How Makers and Preppers Converge in Premodern and Post-Apocalyptic Ruin," *Lateral* 7, no. 2 (June 2018), https://doi.org/10.25158/L7.2.7.

145 *Life Off Grid*, documentary (Royal Roads University, 2016).

Chapter 6: The Sentinels

146 Jamie Ballard, "Most Americans Think There Will Be Another World War within the Next Decade," YouGov, March 21, 2024, https://today.yougov.com/politics/articles/48981-most-americans-think-another-world-war-within-the-next-decade.

147 Brad Lendon and Sooyeon Kim, "South Korea Sets Nationwide Civil Defense Drill, Citing North's 'Provocations,'" CNN, August 4, 2023, https://www.cnn.com/2023/08/04/asia/south-korea-civil-defense-drill-intl-hnk/index.html.

148 Scott Neuman and Eleanor Beardsley, "Israel Is Trying to Arm More Citizens with Guns since the Hamas Attack," National Public Radio, December 6, 2023, https://www.npr.org/2023/12/06/1216088371/guns-israel-hamas-gaza.

149 World Population Review, "Gun Ownership by Country 2025," https://worldpopulationreview.com/country-rankings/gun-ownership-by-country.

150 Matthew Giblin et al., "Self-Protection in Rural America: A Risk Interpretation Model of Household Protective Measures," *Criminal Justice Policy Review* 23, no. 4 (2012): 493–517.

151 Personal conversation between David, Abigail, and Dr. Colby.

152 Lucy Jones, *The Big Ones: How Natural Disasters Have Shaped Us and What We Can Do about Them* (New York: Doubleday, 2018).

153 FBI, "FBI Releases 2020 Crime Statistics," September 27, 2021, https://www.fbi.gov/news/press-releases/fbi-releases-2020-crime-statistics.

154 Tucker Max, "Doomer Optimism: What I See Coming & How I'm Preparing," *Tucker Max* (blog), December 29, 2021, https://www.tuckermax.com/doomer-optimism-what-i-see-coming-how-im-preparing/.

155 Tucker Max, "Doomer Optimism."

156 FBI, "NICS Firearm Checks: Month/Year," https://www.fbi.gov/file-repository/nics_firearm_checks_-_month_year.pdf/view.

157 Lois Beckett, "Americans Have Bought Record 17m Guns in Year of Unrest, Analysis Finds," *The Guardian*, October 30, 2020, http://www.theguardian.com/us-news/2020/oct/29/coronavirus-pandemic-americans-gun-sales.

158 Chauncey Alcorn, "First-Time Buyers Fuel Pandemic-Related Surge in Gun Sales," CNN, October 24, 2020, https://www.cnn.com/2020/10/24/business/gun-sales-surge-black-americans-women/index.html.

159 David Dent, "These Terrified Black Americans Are Packing Heat," *The Daily Beast*, June 8, 2020, sec. us-news, https://www.thedailybeast.com/more-and-more-terrified-black-americans-are-learning-to-use-guns; Tyler Durden, "Black Gun Ownership Soars as Nation's Inner Cities Burn," *ZeroHedge* (blog), June 8, 2020, https://www.zerohedge.com/political/black-gun-ownership-soars-nations-inner-cities-burn.

160 Durden, "Black Gun Ownership Soars as Nation's Inner Cities Burn."

161 Nellie Bowles, "I Used to Make Fun of Silicon Valley Preppers. Then I Became One," *The New York Times*, April 24, 2020, https://www.nytimes.com/2020/04/24/technology/coronavirus-preppers.html.

162 Katherine Rosenberg-Douglas, "'Guns Are Flying off the Shelf.' Permit Applications up More Than 500% amid Coronavirus Pandemic and George Floyd Fallout," chicagotribune.com, June 25, 2020, https://www.chicagotribune.com/news/breaking/ct-chicago-illinois-foid-gun-ammo-sales-uncertainty-20200625-pkve27352jagnp4y5dbaubkyoy-story.html.

163 Hailey Branson-Potts, "Going against the Grain after Orlando Shooting, LGBT Group Embraces Guns," *Los Angeles Times*, September 9, 2016, https://www.latimes.com/local/lanow/la-me-ln-lgbt-guns-pink-pistols-20200809-snap-story.html; Jim Urquhart, "U.S. Gay Gun Group's Membership Surges after Orlando Killings," Reuters, July 12, 2016, https://www.reuters.com/article/us-usa-guns-lgbt-idUSKCN0ZS25B.

164 Gary Kleck et al., "The Effect of Perceived Risk and Victimization on Plans to Purchase a Gun for Self-Protection," *Journal of Criminal Justice* 39, no. 4 (July 2011): 312–19, https://doi.org/10.1016/j.jcrimjus.2011.03.002.

165 Ayaan Hirsi Ali, "When Europe Ignored the Sex Crimes of Immigrants, All Women Suffered," *New York Post*, February 13, 2021, https://nypost.com/2021/02/13/when-europe-ignored-sex-crimes-of-immigrants-all-women-suffered/; Julie Bindel, "The UK's Grooming Gangs and the Lessons Never Learned," Al Jazeera, February 23, 2024, https://www.aljazeera.com/opinions/2024/2/23/the-uks-grooming-gangs-and-the-lessons-never-learned.

166 Daniel Chirot, *You Say You Want a Revolution: Radical Idealism and Its Tragic Consequences* (Princeton, NJ: Princeton University Press, 2020).

167 Chirot.

168 Tyler Durden, "South Korea's Top Cops Arrested, Ex-Defense Chief Tries Suicide as Failed Martial Law Bid Rocks Country," *ZeroHedge* (blog), December 11, 2024, https://www.zerohedge.com/geopolitical/south-koreas-top-cops-arrested-ex-defense-chief-tries-suicide-failed-martial-law-bid.

169 Rasmussen Reports, "37% of Voters Fear the Federal Government," April 18, 2014, https://www.rasmussenreports.com/public_content/politics/general_politics/april_2014/37_of_voters_fear_the_federal_government.

170 Scott Rasmussen, "58% See Federal Government as Threat to Freedom and Liberty; 24% Disagree," *ScottRasmussen.com* (blog), October 2, 2021, https://scottrasmussen.com/58-see-federal-government-as-threat-to-freedom-and-liberty-24-disagree/.

171 Shreya Sheth, "America's Top Fears 2019," Irvine, CA, Chapman University, 2019, https://www.chapman.edu/wilkinson/research-centers/babbie-center/_files/americas-top-fears-2019.pdf.

172 "Busted Trust," *The Economist*, April 20, 2024.

173 "Is America Dictator Proof?," *The Economist*, March 18, 2024.

174 Laura Lington, "32% Believe Democracy Very Likely to End within Generation; Republicans Are More Worried Than Democrats; Dems Seen as Bigger Threat," *ScottRasmussen.com* (blog), December 16, 2021, https://scottrasmussen.com/32-believe-democracy-very-likely-to-end-within-generation-republicans-are-more-worried-than-democrats-dems-seen-as-bigger-threat/.

175 World Economic Forum, "The Global Risks Report 2023: 18th Edition."

176 Tyler Durden, "Germany Hired Koch Institute and Other Scientists to Justify

Unconstitutional Lockdowns: Die Welt," *ZeroHedge* (blog), February 9, 2021, https://www.zerohedge.com/geopolitical/germany-hired-koch-institute-and-other-scientists-justify-strict-lockdowns-die-welt.

177 Lee Brown, "German Quarantine Breakers to Be Held in Refugee Camps, Detention Centers," *New York Post*, January 18, 2021, https://nypost.com/2021/01/18/german-quarantine-breakers-to-be-held-in-refugee-camps/.

178 Cristina Laila, "'How Do You Deprogram 75 Million People?' California Democrat Calls for 'Post WWII' Reeducation for Trump Supporters," *The Gateway Pundit* (blog), November 19, 2020, https://www.thegatewaypundit.com/2020/11/deprogram-75-million-people-california-democrat-calls-post-wwii-reeducation-trump-supporters/.

179 Joseph Wulfsohn, "PBS Lawyer Suggested Sending Children of Trump Voters to 'Reeducation Camps' Where 'They Watch PBS All Day,'" Fox News, January 12, 2021, https://www.foxnews.com/media/pbs-lawyer-michael-beller-project-veritas-trump-voters-children.

180 Sheena Chestnut Greitens, "Surveillance, Security, and Liberal Democracy in the Post-COVID World," *International Organization* 74, Supplement 2020 (November 18, 2020): 1–22, https://doi.org/10.1017/S0020818320000417; Stephen Thomson and Eric C Ip, "COVID-19 Emergency Measures and the Impending Authoritarian Pandemic," *Journal of Law and the Biosciences* 7, no. 1 (July 25, 2020): lsaa064, https://doi.org/10.1093/jlb/lsaa064.

181 Kersten Knipp, "Amid Concerns over Public Safety, Germans Are Buying More Weapons," DW.COM, January 2, 2018, https://www.dw.com/en/amid-concerns-over-public-safety-germans-are-buying-more-weapons/a-42417652.

182 Chris Ellis, "Personal Disaster Preparedness Levels in the National Guard," monograph (Fort Leavenworth, School of Advanced Military Studies, 2016).

183 William Blackstone, *Blackstone's Commentaries: With Notes of Reference to the Constitution and Laws of the Federal Government of the United States and of the Commonwealth of Virginia (Reprint)*, vol. 5 (South Hackensack, NJ: Rothman Reprints, 1969).

Chapter 7: The Interdependent

184 *Merriam-Webster.com Dictionary, s.v.* "interdependent," accessed April 29, 2025, https://www.merriam-webster.com/dictionary/interdependent.

185 All of Jonathan's quotes are from a personal conversation between Jonathan and Dr. Colby.

186 Huddleston, "Chapter 22: 'Prepper' as Resilient Citizen: What Preppers Can Teach Us about Surviving Disasters."

187 Bounds, "New Yorkers' Street Smarts and Survival Smarts during the Pandemic."

188 This is based on anecdotal conversations the author has participated in with those of Hong Kong citizenship and videos such as https://www.youtube.com/watch?v=FpSKb-xrGzg&ab_channel=%E6%9E%9C%E7%B1%BD.

189 Chris Buckley, Vivian Wang, and Austin Ramzy, "Crossing the Red Line: Behind China's Takeover of Hong Kong," *The New York Times*, June 28, 2021, https://www.nytimes.com/2021/06/28/world/asia/china-hong-kong-security-law.html.

190 W. Neil Adger et al., "Social-Ecological Resilience to Coastal Disasters," *Science* 309, no. 5737 (August 12, 2005): 1036–39, https://doi.org/10.1126/science.1112122; Virginia Gil-Rivas and Ryan P. Kilmer, "Building Community Capacity and Fostering Disaster Resilience: Building Capacity and Fostering Community Resilience," *Journal of Clinical Psychology* 72, no. 12 (December 2016): 1318–32, https://doi.org/10.1002/jclp.22281; Fran H. Norris et al., "Community Resilience as a Metaphor, Theory, Set of Capacities, and Strategy for Disaster

Readiness," *American Journal of Community Psychology* 41, no. 1 (March 1, 2008): 127–50, https://doi.org/10.1007/s10464-007-9156-6.

191 Robert Freitag et al., "Whole Community Resilience: An Asset-Based Approach to Enhancing Adaptive Capacity Before a Disruption," *Journal of the American Planning Association* 80, no. 4 (Autumn 2014).

192 I would consider Nassim to be closest to the Interdependent Resilient Citizen archetype, but he does not fit neatly into any of my categories. His books are not "prepper" books, but the philosophies contained in several of his writings are exceptionally complementary to the premises here in my book.

193 Nassim Nicholas Taleb, *Antifragile: Things That Gain from Disorder* (New York: Random House, 2014).

194 American Red Cross, "Home Fires: America's Biggest Disaster Threat," accessed February 2, 2021, https://www.redcross.org/content/dam/redcross/atg/PDF_s/Preparedness___Disaster_Recovery/Disaster_Preparedness/Home_Fire/FireFAQs.pdf; American Red Cross, "New Red Cross Survey Shows Many Americans Overconfident and Underprepared for Home Fires," April 3, 2018, https://www.redcross.org/about-us/news-and-events/press-release/New-Red-Cross-Survey-Shows-Many-Americans-Overconfident-and-Underprepared-for-Home-Fires.html.

195 American Red Cross, "Cooking Leading Cause of US Home Fires; Responsible for Thousands of Injuries Every Year," October 5, 2023, https://www.redcross.org/about-us/news-and-events/press-release/2023/cooking-leading-cause-of-u-s—home-fires.html.

196 Interested in becoming CERT trained? Start here: https://community.fema.gov/PreparednessCommunity/s/welcome-to-cert?language=en_US.

197 James MacCarthy et al., "The Latest Data Confirms: Forest Fires Are Getting Worse," World Resources Institute, August 13, 2024, https://www.wri.org/insights/global-trends-forest-fires.

198 Philip Higuera et al., "Western Wildfires Destroyed 246% More Homes and Buildings over the Past Decade—Fire Scientists Explain What's Changing," The Conversation, February 1, 2023, http://theconversation.com/western-wildfires-destroyed-246-more-homes-and-buildings-over-the-past-decade-fire-scientists-explain-whats-changing-197384.

199 Alanne Orjoux, "PG&E Settles with Insurance Companies for $11 Billion in California Wildfires, Utility Says," CNN, September 13, 2019, https://www.cnn.com/2019/09/13/us/pge-california-wildfires-settlement/index.html.

200 Western Fire Chiefs Association, *After-Action Report: Maui Wildfires* (Maui, Hawaii: County of Maui Department of Fire and Public Safety, April 18, 2024).

201 USGS, "Which Country Has the Most Earthquakes?", updated February 25, 2020, https://www.usgs.gov/faqs/which-country-has-most-earthquakes. This article notes there are several ways of measuring frequency of earthquakes. By sheer volume, Indonesia leads the list. If your metric is "earthquakes per unit area," then Tonga, Fiji, and Indonesia are highest.

202 Judith Covey et al., "Community Perceptions of Protective Practices to Prevent Ash Exposures around Sakurajima Volcano, Japan," *International Journal of Disaster Risk Reduction* 46 (June 1, 2020): 101525, https://doi.org/10.1016/j.ijdrr.2020.101525.

203 Douglas Paton and David Johnston, eds., *Disaster Resilience: An Integrated Approach* (Springfield, IL: Charles C. Thomas, 2006).

204 Covey et al., "Community Perceptions of Protective Practices to Prevent Ash Exposures around Sakurajima Volcano, Japan."

205 Wendell Berry, "Manifesto: The Mad Farmer Liberation Front," lines 1–11, https://allpoetry.

com/poem/12622463-Manifesto—The-Mad-Farmer-Liberation-Front-by-Wendell-Berry.

206 Wendell Berry, "Manifesto," lines 31–45.

207 John Hannigan, *Disasters Without Borders* (Malden, MA: Polity Press, 2012).

208 Stephen Flynn, *The Edge of Disaster* (New York: Random House, 2007).

209 Paton and Johnston, *Disaster Resilience: An Integrated Approach.*

210 Bradley Garrett, *Bunker: Building for the End Times* (New York: Scribner, 2020). See also "List of Major Brushfires in Australia," Wikipedia, accessed July 8, 2025, https://en.wikipedia.org/wiki/List_of_major_bushfires_in_Australia.

211 Brian Sullivan, "The U.S. Has Had 500 Tornadoes in 30 Days," Bloomberg.com, May 29, 2019, https://www.bloomberg.com/news/articles/2019-05-29/500-tornadoes-in-30-days-rival-u-s-records-from-seven-decades.

212 Christopher Burt, "The Blizzard of 1888: America's Greatest Snow Disaster," Weather Underground, March 12, 2020, https://www.wunderground.com/cat6/the-blizzard-of-1888-americas-greatest-snow-disaster; Nick Austin, "How Deadly 1888 Blizzard Transformed US Public Transportation," FreightWaves, March 12, 2020, https://www.freightwaves.com/news/how-deadly-1888-blizzard-transformed-us-public-transportation.

213 CRED, *2023 Disasters in Numbers: A Significant Year of Disaster Impact* (Brussels, Belgium: Centre for Research on the Epidemiology of Disasters, 2024), https://www.emdat.be/categories/adsr/.

214 Ragip Soylu, "Turkey's Slow Earthquake Reconstruction Marred with Infighting and Confusion," Middle East Eye, February 5, 2024, https://www.middleeasteye.net/news/turkey-earthquake-reconstruction-slow-marred-infighting-confusion.

215 Ted Koppel, *Lights Out: A Cyberattack, a Nation Unprepared, Surviving the Aftermath* (New York: Broadway Books, 2015).

216 Kathryn Schulz, "The Really Big One," *The New Yorker*, July 13, 2015, https://www.newyorker.com/magazine/2015/07/20/the-really-big-one.

217 Other disaster planning events along the US West Coast have used a 9.0 earthquake; see Freitag et al., "Whole Community Resilience: An Asset-Based Approach to Enhancing Adaptive Capacity Before a Disruption."

218 Oregon Seismic Safety Policy and Advisory Commission, "The Oregon Resilience Plan," Report to the 77th Legislative Assembly (Salem, OR, February 2013), https://www.oregon.gov/oem/documents/oregon_resilience_plan_final.pdf.

219 Flynn, *The Edge of Disaster*.

220 Oliver Milman and Vivian Ho, "California Wildfires Spawn First 'Gigafire' in Modern History," *The Guardian*, October 6, 2020, http://www.theguardian.com/us-news/2020/oct/06/california-wildfires-gigafire-first.

221 Jones, *The Big Ones: How Natural Disasters Have Shaped Us and What We Can Do about Them.*

222 Klar, *Small Farm Republic: Why Conservatives Must Embrace Local Agriculture, Reject Climate Alarmism, and Lead an Environmental Revival.*

Chapter 8: The Noahs

223 Douglas Rushkoff, *Survival of the Richest: Escape Fantasies of the Tech Billionaires* (New York: W. W. Norton, 2022).

224 One of the benefits of joining the military is the chance to live all over the world. When I was stationed in Bavaria, Germany, I lived just a few hours away from Hohenwerfen and hundreds of other historical sites. Several were built for pure evil. The hundreds of slave labor and

concentration camps, which stretched from France to Latvia, bore witness to some of the greatest atrocities mankind has ever witnessed from the Nazi ruling regime.

225 That's according to my memory and the audio tour I took nearly twenty years ago.

226 To survey the beauty of this area, see Salzburg Burgen and Schlösser Betriebsführung, "Fortress Hohenwerfen," accessed May 1, 2025, https://www.salzburg-burgen.at/en/hohenwerfen-castle/.

227 This is from my memory of the audio tour.

228 Victor Davis Hanson, *The End of Everything: How Wars Descend into Annihilation* (New York: Basic Books, 2024).

229 Chris Ellis, "Nowhere to Run to, Nowhere to Hide: Disasters, Preparedness, and the Shadow of State Failure on U.S. Islands," *Homeland Security Affairs* 19 (September 28, 2023), https://www.hsaj.org/articles/22412.

230 Rick White, Arthur Simental, and John Holst, *21st Century Homeland Defense & Civil Defense: An Analytical Study* (Colorado Springs, CO: United States Air Force Academy, May 2, 2023).

231 Center for Puerto Rican Studies, "Enduring Disasters: Puerto Rico, Three Years after Hurricane María" (New York: Hunter College, City University of New York, September 2020), https://centropr.hunter.cuny.edu/app/uploads/2022/02/centro_3yr_maria_20206.pdf.

232 Ben Fox, "Only 20% in Puerto Rico Have Electricity a Month after Hurricane," CBC News, October 20, 2017, https://www.cbc.ca/news/world/puerto-rico-power-grid-maria-1.4364046; Bianca DiJulio, Cailey Muñana, and Mollyann Brodie, "Views and Experiences of Puerto Ricans One Year after Hurricane Maria" (San Francisco: KFF, September 12, 2018), https://www.kff.org/report-section/views-and-experiences-of-puerto-ricans-one-year-after-hurricane-maria-section-1-quantifying-hurricane-marias-wide-ranging-impacts/.

233 Center for Puerto Rican Studies, "Enduring Disasters: Puerto Rico, Three Years after Hurricane María"; White, Simental, and Holst, "21st Century Homeland Defense & Civil Defense: An Analytical Study."

234 As I was updating this chapter, Cuba, a country of ten million people, had faced its sixth grid collapse in two months at the end of 2024.

235 "On the Endorsement of 'One Second After' by William R. Forstchen," *Congressional Record*, 155, no. 70 (2009), https://www.congress.gov/congressional-record/2009/5/7/extensions-of-remarks-section/article/E1103-1.

236 Patrick Kiger, "'American Blackout': Four Major Real-Life Threats to the Electric Grid," National Geographic, October 25, 2013, https://www.nationalgeographic.com/environment/article/american-blackout-four-major-real-life-threats-to-the-electric-grid.

237 White, Simental, and Holst, "21st Century Homeland Defense & Civil Defense: An Analytical Study" (emphasis added).

238 Electricity Information Sharing and Analysis Center, "2023 E-ISAC End-of-Year Report" (Washington, DC, February 15, 2024), https://nerc123.my.salesforce.com/sfc/p/#2E0000012tgy/a/Pm000000Mfir/nZtc69DSjM7r2UMKlqL8OAoeIPRDxzbu0lAawu9VaCs.

239 Electricity Information Sharing and Analysis Center, "GridEx VII: Lessons Learned Report" (Washington, DC, April 2024), https://www.nerc.com/pa/CI/ESISAC/GridEx/GridEx%20VII%20Report.pdf.

240 Task Force on National and Homeland Security, and Secure the Grid Coalition, "A Call to Action for America," January 17, 2023.

241 Task Force on National and Homeland Security, and Secure the Grid Coalition.

242 Craig Hooper, "With Electrical Grids under Assault, U.S. and Ukraine Seek Scarce Transmission Gear," *Forbes*, January 4, 2023, https://www.forbes.com/sites/craighooper/2023/01/04/with-electrical-grids-under-assault-us-and-ukraine-seek-scarce-transmission-gear/.

243 FRED, "Real Disposable Personal Income," updated March 28, 2025, https://fred.stlouisfed.org/series/DSPIC96.

244 Board of Governors of the Federal Reserve System, "Survey of Household Economics and Decisionmaking Interactive Charts," updated December 20, 2024, https://www.federalreserve.gov/consumerscommunities/sheddataviz.htm.

245 "What Should the U.S. Do about Rising Student Loan Debt?," Council on Foreign Relations, April 16, 2024, https://www.cfr.org/backgrounder/us-student-loan-debt-trends-economic-impact; Giulia Carbonaro, "America's Credit Card Debt Crisis," *Newsweek*, January 8, 2024, https://www.newsweek.com/america-credit-card-debt-crisis-1858160.

246 Amy Fontinelle, "American Debt: Mortgage Debt Reaches $12.25 Trillion in Q4 2023," Investopedia, June 26, 2024, https://www.investopedia.com/personal-finance/american-debt-mortgage-debt/.

247 I'm using data from the US Census for counts: https://www.census.gov/data/tables/time-series/demo/popest/2020s-national-detail.html.

248 Truth in Accounting, "2024 Financial State of the Cities" (Chicago, IL, 2024), https://www.truthinaccounting.org/library/doclib/Financial-State-of-the-Cities-2024.pdf.

249 FRED, "Median Personal Income in the United States," updated September 10, 2024, https://fred.stlouisfed.org/series/MEPAINUSA646N.

250 According to their own records, they start to go bankrupt no later than 2035.

251 Benjamin Roth, *The Great Depression: A Diary*, ed. James Ledbetter and Daniel Roth (New York:PublicAffairs, 2010).

252 Carmen Reinhart and Kenneth Rogoff, *This Time Is Different: Eight Centuries of Financial Folly* (Princeton, NJ: Princeton University Press, 2009); Adam Fergusson, *When Money Dies: The Nightmare of Deficit Spending, Devaluation, and Hyperinflation in Weimar Germany* (New York: PublicAffairs, 2010); Ludwig von Mises, *Human Action: A Treaties on Economics* (Indianapolis, Indiana: Liberty Fund, 2007); F. A. Hayek, *The Road to Serfdom: The Definitive Edition*, ed. Bruce Caldwell (Chicago: University of Chicago Press, 2007); Graham Summers, *Into the Abyss: Life after the Bubble* (n.p.:Summers Capital Press, 2024).

253 In this economic section, I ran out of room to discuss malicious actors that deliberately enslave countries via debt. For more on that, read *Confessions of an Economic Hitman* by John Perkins to see how the US (and now China) seeks to economically conquer or Carol Roth's *You Will Own Nothing* for her take on the World Economic Forum's diabolical strategy.

254 Beacon Research and Shaw and Company Research, "U.S. National Survey on Foreign Policy Attitudes on Behalf of the Ronald Reagan Institute" (Washington, DC: Ronald Reagan Institute, November 2024).

255 American Psychological Association, "Stress in America: Money, Inflation, War Pile On to Nation Stuck in Covid-19 Survival Mode," March 2022, https://www.apa.org/news/press/releases/stress/2022/march-2022-survival-mode.

256 Besides nuclear war, the other top threats were climate change, biological threats, and disruptive technologies (aka artificial intelligence). See "2025 Doomsday Clock Statement," Bulletin of the Atomic Scientists, January 28, 2025, https://thebulletin.org/doomsday-clock/current-time/nuclear-risk/.

257 Bridget Williams et al., "Can Humanity Achieve a Century of Nuclear Peace? Expert Forecasts of Nuclear Risk" (Forecasting Research Institute, October 29, 2024).

258 White, Simental, and Holst, "21st Century Homeland Defense & Civil Defense: An Analytical Study."

259 Brendan Cole, "Four Changes in Russia's Nuclear Doctrine Raise Alarm," *Newsweek*, November 20, 2024, https://www.newsweek.com/russia-putin-nuclear-doctrine-1988843.

260 Gerrard Kaonga, "World War 3: Pakistan Launch Nuclear-Capable Ballistic Missile in Warning to India," Express.co.uk, November 18, 2019, https://www.express.co.uk/news/world/1205916/world-war-3-Pakistan-India-news-nuclear-military-missile-test-update-latest-ww3; Aparna Pande, "Pakistan's Moderates Threatening Nuclear War over Kashmir Is a Sign It's Losing the Argument," *ThePrint* (blog), December 5, 2019, https://theprint.in/opinion/pakistan-moderates-threatening-nuclear-war-over-kashmir-sign-losing-argument/330615/.

261 Katharina Buchholz, "The Rise of North Korean Missile Tests," Statista, August 29, 2024, https://www.statista.com/chart/9172/north-korea-missile-tests-timeline.

262 Martin Armstrong, "Nuclear Weapon Spending on the Rise," Statista, June 17, 2024, https://www.statista.com/chart/32449/global-nuclear-weapon-spending-change.

263 White, Simental, and Holst, "21st Century Homeland Defense & Civil Defense: An Analytical Study"; Garrett Graff, *Raven Rock: The Story of the U.S. Government's Secret Plan to Save Itself—While the Rest of Us Die* (New York: Simon & Schuster, 2018).

264 Alicia Sanders-Zakre, Michaela de Verdier, and Josefin Lind, *No Place to Hide: Nuclear Weapons and the Collapse of Health Care Systems* (Geneva, Switzerland: International Campaign to Abolish Nuclear Weapons, February 2022).

265 World Health Organization, *National Stockpiles for Radiological and Nuclear Emergencies: Policy Advice* (Geneva, Switzerland, 2023).

266 Guthrie Scrimgeour, "Inside Mark Zuckerberg's Top-Secret Hawaii Compound," *Wired*, December 14, 2023, https://www.wired.com/story/mark-zuckerberg-inside-hawaii-compound/; "Inside Plans for Mark Zuckerberg Massive $260M Bunker on Secluded Hawaiian Island," News.com.au, March 4, 2024, https://www.news.com.au/finance/business/billionaire-facebook-founder-mark-zuckerberg-building-enormous-secretive-underground-bunker/news-story/717b98c50292ff01f82adc6ab53758b8.

267 Evan Osnos, "Survival of the Richest," *The New Yorker*, January 23, 2017, https://www.newyorker.com/magazine/2017/01/30/doomsday-prep-for-the-super-rich.

268 Garrett, "Doomsday Preppers and the Architecture of Dread."

269 Sarah Hooper and Josh Milton, "Doomsday Community Wants People to Live in Bunkers 'When All Hell Breaks Loose,'" *Metro* (blog), April 5, 2024, https://metro.co.uk/2024/04/05/doomsday-community-wants-people-live-575-bunkers-2-20585400/; O'Connell, *Notes from the Apocalypse: A Personal Journey to the End of the World and Back.*

270 Nassim Nicholas Taleb, *Skin in the Game: Hidden Asymetries in Daily Life* (New York: Random House, 2018).

271 Osnos, "Survival of the Richest."

272 Rowland Atkinson and Sarah Blandy, *Domestic Fortress: Fear and the New Home Front, Domestic Fortress* (Manchester, UK:Manchester University Press, 2016), http://www.manchesterhive.com/view/9781526108166/9781526108166.xml.

273 Bowles, "I Used to Make Fun of Silicon Valley Preppers. Then I Became One"; Tyler Durden, "Rich Americans Flee to Luxury 'Doomsday Resort' Shelters in New Zealand as Panic Grows,"

ZeroHedge (blog), April 21, 2020, https://www.zerohedge.com/economics/rich-americans-escaped-luxury-doomsday-resort-shelters-new-zealand-panic-grew; Shirin Ghaffary, "'No Handshakes, Please': The Tech Industry Is Terrified of the Coronavirus," Vox, February 13, 2020, https://www.vox.com/recode/2020/2/13/21128209/coronavirus-fears-contagion-how-infection-spreads; O'Connell, "Why Silicon Valley Billionaires Are Prepping for the Apocalypse in New Zealand."

274 Kim might fail my third criterion of extremism. I have not dug deeply into his life, but I know he has been convicted of several crimes. Based on my ignorance, I'll give him the benefit of the doubt for now.

275 O'Connell, *Notes from the Apocalypse: A Personal Journey to the End of the World and Back*; Garrett, *Bunker: Building for the End Times*.

276 See Vivos Global Shelter Network, https://www.terravivos.com/; or Fortitude Ranch, https://fortituderanch.com/.

277 Jacqui Goddard, "Why Jeff Bezos Bought Three Homes in Florida's 'Billionaire Bunker,'" *The Times UK*, April 5, 2024, https://www.thetimes.co.uk/article/jeff-bezos-miami-mansion-billionaire-bunker-jnwq5nzk3; James Powel and Jennifer Sangalang, "Bezos Bunker: Amazon Founder Buys Third Property in Florida's Wealthy Hideaway, Reports Say," April 3, 2024, https://www.msn.com/en-us/money/companies/bezos-bunker-amazon-founder-buys-third-property-in-floridas-wealthy-hideaway-reports-say/ar-BB1kXZWJ.

278 Tyler Durden, "'Parameters of Paranoia Are Changing' as Doomsday-Bunker-Builders Boom in Post-COVID Normal," *ZeroHedge* (blog), June 26, 2020, https://www.zerohedge.com/personal-finance/parameters-paranoia-are-changing-doomsday-bunker-builders-boom-post-covid-normal; Jon Lockett, "Super-Rich Buying Underground Bunkers with SHOOTING RANGES over Fears Coronavirus Will Spark Social Meltdown," *The US Sun*, May 15, 2020, https://www.the-sun.com/news/833092/super-rich-underground-bunkers-shooting-ranges/; "Emergency Preparedness: Tips for Troglodytes," *The Economist*, October 19, 2019; Anna Desmarais, "Going Underground: Behind the Growing Demand for Luxury Doomsday Bunkers," Yahoo News, April 6, 2024, https://www.yahoo.com/news/going-underground-behind-growing-demand-070053465.html.

279 Garrett, "Doomsday Preppers and the Architecture of Dread."

280 Matan Shapiro and Nurit Bird-David, "Routinergency: Domestic Securitization in Contemporary Israel," *Environment and Planning D: Society and Space* 35, no. 4 (August 2017): 637–55, https://doi.org/10.1177/0263775816677550.

281 Anderson Shelters, "History," https://www.andersonshelters.org.uk/history.html.

282 May Warren, "Preppers Becoming Mainstream in the Trump Age?," *Toronto Star*, February 15, 2017, https://www.thestar.com/news/gta/2017/02/15/preppers-becoming-mainstream-in-the-trump-age.html.

Chapter 9: The Faithful

283 In an interesting note, in the dedication or acknowledgment section of several dissertations on disaster preparedness, multiple academics (e.g., Shalae De Jarnatt, Lee'Ann Imel-Hartford, Ahmed Al-Otaibi) indicated a thankfulness to God or Allah. There are several academics in this field who left their personal beliefs unmentioned or professed atheism as well, though.

284 Hanson, *The End of Everything: How Wars Descend into Annihilation*.

285 Not everybody would agree with this assessment. The founder of Answers in Genesis, Ken Ham, once debated "Bill Nye the Science Guy." The latter sees the former as a religious loon

and dismisses creation science as baseless and false.
286 All of Caleb's quotes are from a personal conversation between Caleb and Dr. Colby..
287 J. Oliver Conroy, "We Mocked Preppers and Survivalists—until the Pandemic Hit," *The Guardian*, April 30, 2020, https://www.theguardian.com/global/2020/apr/30/preppers-survivalists-disasters-lessons.
288 Koppel, *Lights Out: A Cyberattack, a Nation Unprepared, Surviving the Aftermath.*
289 You can find free pdf copies on numerous prepper websites or purchase the book on Amazon. This manual is commonly referenced by non-Mormon preppers and is a collection of lists, how-to-guides, and other sundry disaster information.
290 Christopher Parrett, *LDS Preparedness Manual: Book Two, Temporal Preparedness, General Member Edition*, Version 8.0, 15th Anniversary Edition (Rigby, ID: Another Voice of Warning, 2012).
291 Skip the seed oils; better options are olive and coconut oil.
292 Shalae De Jarnatt, "Disaster Preparedness Levels: Traditional First Responder Roles and Affiliation with the Church" (PhD diss., Capella University, June 2019), http://search.proquest.com/docview/2288850147?accountid=10267&pq-origsite=summon.
293 "Off the Grid with Thomass Massie," posted September 26, 2018, YouTube, 35 min., 30 sec., https://www.youtube.com/watch?v=18_yXt1s2yc.
294 Thomas Massie (@RepThomasMassie), "There's an explanation for why the U.S. government pushed the false narrative that COVD came from the wild and not a lab: COVID was created with U.S. funded technology. They were playing god with new viruses to create new vaccines. They gave us both. Stop funding the madness," Twitter (now X), March 11, 2024, https://x.com/RepThomasMassie/status/1767215668301041710.

Chapter 10: The Psychology of Perils Processing

295 John-Paul Mulilis and Richard Lippa, "Behavioral Change in Earthquake Preparedness Due to Negative Threat Appeals: A Test of Protection Motivation Theory," *Journal of Applied Social Psychology* 20, no. 8 (1990): 619–38, https://doi.org/10.1111/j.1559-1816.1990.tb00429.x; Torsten Grothmann and Fritz Reusswig, "People at Risk of Flooding: Why Some Residents Take Precautionary Action while Others Do Not," *Natural Hazards* 38, no. 1 (May 1, 2006): 101–20, https://doi.org/10.1007/s11069-005-8604-6.
296 This term and its related complements are also known as low-frequency/high-harm (e.g., Cass R. Sunstein, "Irreversible and Catastrophic," SSRN Scholarly Paper (Rochester, NY: Social Science Research Network, March 1, 2005), https://doi.org/10.2139/ssrn.707128.
297 Grothmann and Reusswig, "People at Risk of Flooding."
298 Floyd, Prentice-Dunn, and Rogers, "A Meta-Analysis of Research on Protection Motivation Theory"; Grothmann and Reusswig, "People at Risk of Flooding"; Mulilis and Lippa, "Behavioral Change in Earthquake Preparedness Due to Negative Threat Appeals."
299 See also Ronald C. Plotnikoff and Linda Trinh, "Protection Motivation Theory: Is This a Worthwhile Theory for Physical Activity Promotion?," *Exercise and Sport Sciences Reviews* 38, no. 2 (April 2010): 91–98, https://doi.org/10.1097/JES.0b013e3181d49612.
300 Lacey N. Wallace, "Responses to Perceived Terrorism Risk by Self-Identified Survivalists: An Exploratory Study," *The Social Science Journal*, April 20, 2020, 1–14, https://doi.org/10.1080/03623319.2020.1744950.
301 Robert Meyer and Howard Kunreuther, *The Ostrich Paradox: Why We Underprepare for Disasters* (Philadelphia, PA: Wharton Digital Press, 2017).

302 Or what Nassim Taleb has deemed "ensemble risk." Taleb describes this as repeat play of risk for a single person, not a collection of people (see his book *Skin in the Game*).

303 Clearly none of these six biases is new, not just for disaster literature but for many other fields. However, those seeking further reading regarding these psychological predispositions in relation to risk can refer to several other books. See, for example, Nassim Taleb's *Incerto* series, *Worst Cases* by Lee Clarke, *The Edge of Disaster* by Stephen Flynn, *Foolproof* by Greg Ip, *The Logic of Failure* by Dietrich Dörner, and *Learning from Catastrophe* by Howard Kunreuther and Michael Useem.

304 Several poisons and toxins have a bitter taste.

305 Meg Jay, *Supernormal: The Untold Story of Adversity and Resilience* (New York: Twelve, 2017).

306 Daniel Kahneman, *Thinking, Fast and Slow* (New York: Farrar, Straus, and Giroux, 2011).

307 Emma Bryce, "How Many Calories Can the Brain Burn by Thinking?," livescience.com, November 9, 2019, https://www.livescience.com/burn-calories-brain.html.

308 Paul Slovic, "Perception of Risk," *Science* 236, no. 4799 (April 17, 1987): 280–85, https://doi.org/10.1126/science.3563507.

309 Slovic.

310 Slovic.

311 Although Slovic's data indicate at least a 70 percent overlap in the top ten riskiest items between experts and any of his three groups of laypeople.

312 Of note, the specter of Three Mile Island still figures prominently over four decades later in discussions of the next generation of nuclear power.

313 Christy Bieber, "Car Accident Statistics for 2024," *Forbes Advisor*, January 23, 2023, https://www.forbes.com/advisor/legal/auto-accident/car-accident-statistics/.

314 Howard Kunreuther and Michael Useem, *Learning from Catastrophes: Strategies for Reaction and Response* (Upper Saddle River,NJ: Wharton School Publishing, 2010).

315 Chip Heath and Dan Heath, *Switch: How to Change Things When Change Is Hard* (New York: Broadway Books, 2010).

316 Heath and Heath.

317 Lee Clarke, *Worst Cases: Terror and Catastrophe in the Popular Imagination* (Chicago: University of Chicago Press, 2006).

318 Clarke.

319 Clarke.

320 Nassim Nicholas Taleb, *Skin in the Game: Hidden Asymetries in Daily Life* (New York: Random House, 2018).

321 Taleb.

322 United Nations Office for Disaster Risk Reduction, *Global Assessment Report on Disaster Risk Reduction: Our World at Risk: Transforming Governance for a Resilient Future* (Geneva, Switzerland, 2022), www.undrr.org/GAR2022.

323 United Nations Office for Disaster Risk Reduction (emphasis added).

Chapter 11: The Psychology of Perils Personalization

324 William Ernest Henley, "Invictus," Poetry Foundation, accessed July 8, 2025, https://www.poetryfoundation.org/poems/51642/invictus.

325 In chapter 3, I used the very simplistic heuristic of thirty-one days of survival.

326 Previous research of mine has tickled at the math a bit but is statistically rudimentary.

327 Jay, *Supernormal: The Untold Story of Adversity and Resilience.*

328 See a chart of this here: https://www.simplypsychology.org/maslow.html.

329 Anthony Giddens, *Modernity and Self-Identity: Self and Society in the Late Modern Age* (Cambridge: Polity, 1991).

330 Trine Flockhart, "Is This the End? Resilience, Ontological Security, and the Crisis of the Liberal International Order," *Contemporary Security Policy* 41, no. 2 (April 2, 2020): 215–40, https://doi.org/10.1080/13523260.2020.1723966.

331 Jennifer Mitzen, "Ontological Security in World Politics: State Identity and the Security Dilemma," *European Journal of International Relations* 12, no. 3 (September 2006): 341–70, https://doi.org/10.1177/1354066106067346 (emphasis added).

332 Giddens, *Modernity and Self-Identity: Self and Society in the Late Modern Age*; Mitzen, "Ontological Security in World Politics."

333 Heath and Heath, *Switch: How to Change Things When Change Is Hard.*

334 J. Paul Goode, David R. Stroup, and Elizaveta Gaufman, "Everyday Nationalism in Unsettled Times: In Search of Normality during Pandemic," *Nationalities Papers*, May 22, 2020, 1–25, https://doi.org/10.1017/nps.2020.40.

335 Goode, Stroup, and Gaufman; "Do You Speak Corona? A Guide to Covid-19 Slang," *1843 Magazine*, April 8, 2020, http://www.economist.com/1843/2020/04/08/do-you-speak-corona-a-guide-to-covid-19-slang.

336 Goode, Stroup, and Gaufman, "Everyday Nationalism in Unsettled Times."

337 Lisa Garbe, Richard Rau, and Theo Toppe, "Influence of Perceived Threat of Covid-19 and HEXACO Personality Traits on Toilet Paper Stockpiling," *PLOS ONE* 15, no. 6 (June 12, 2020): e0234232, https://doi.org/10.1371/journal.pone.0234232.

338 Rob McMillan, "Some SoCal Stores Seeing Shortages of Toilet Paper Again," ABC7 Los Angeles, November 4, 2020, https://abc7.com/hoarding-toilet-paper-shortage-towel-state-bros/7649903/.

339 Siladitya Ray, "Germans Are Panic Buying Toilet Paper and Disinfectants as Covid-19 Surges Again," *Forbes*, October 22, 2020, https://www.forbes.com/sites/siladityaray/2020/10/22/germans-are-panic-buying-toilet-paper-and-disinfectants-as-covid-19-surges-again/?sh=ec3533817f07.

340 Holly Bancroft and Alex Lawson, "National Lockdown: UK Shoppers Strip Shelves of Toilet Paper AGAIN," *Daily Mail Online*, October 31, 2020, https://www.dailymail.co.uk/news/article-8901407/Shoppers-strip-shelves-toilet-paper-household-essentials-ahead-national-lockdown.html.

341 Charles Bethea, "The Americans Prepping for a Second Civil War," *The New Yorker*, November 4, 2024, https://www.newyorker.com/magazine/2024/11/11/among-the-civil-war-preppers.

342 Katie Hawkinson, "More Than 5,000 Requests for Abortion Pills Made in 12 Hours after Trump's Win," *The Independent*, November 8, 2024, https://www.independent.co.uk/news/world/americas/us-politics/donald-trump-abortion-medication-access-b2643847.html; Katie Dangerfield, "'Huge Surge' in U.S. Abortion Pill Demand after Trump's Election Win," Global News, November 7, 2024, https://globalnews.ca/news/10857921/abortion-pills-surge-demand-trump-election-win/.

343 Heath and Heath, *Switch: How to Change Things When Change Is Hard*; Amanda Ripley, *The Unthinkable: Who Survives When Disaster Strikes and Why* (New York: Three Rivers Press, 2009).

344 Ripley, *The Unthinkable: Who Survives When Disaster Strikes and Why.*

345 US Federal Emergency Management Agency, "2018 National Household Survey Results," Executive Summary (Washington, DC: FEMA, January 2, 2020), https://www.fema.gov/

media-library/assets/documents/182373; Wallace, "Responses to Perceived Terrorism Risk by Self-Identified Survivalists."

346 Anna Maria Bounds, *Bracing for the Apocalypse: An Ethnographic Study of New York's "Prepper" Subculture* (New York: Routledge, 2021), 9, emphasis original.

347 Elias Mellander, "Dread Expectations? Prepping, Culture, and Fear in Late Modernity," *Ethnologia Scandinavica* 53 (September 1, 2023).

348 Ellis, "Personal Disaster Preparedness Levels in the National Guard."

349 Kaitlin Vogel, "Antidepressant Use on the Rise among Young Adults, Adolescents," Healthline, February 27, 2024, https://www.healthline.com/health-news/antidepressant-prescriptions-increasing-young-people.

350 Greg Lukianoff and Jonathan Haidt, *The Coddling of the American Mind: How Good Intentions and Bad Ideas Are Setting Up a Generation for Failure* (New York: Penguin Press, 2018).

351 Ripley, *The Unthinkable: Who Survives When Disaster Strikes and Why*.

352 Michael F. Mills, "Preparing for the Unknown… Unknowns: 'Doomsday' Prepping and Disaster Risk Anxiety in the United States," *Journal of Risk Research* 22, no. 10 (October 3, 2019): 1267–79, https://doi.org/10.1080/13669877.2018.1466825.

353 In this quote, she cites Catarina Kinnvall, Ian Manners, and Jennifer Mitzen, "Introduction to 2018 Special Issue of European Security: 'Ontological (in)Security in the European Union,'" European Security 27, no. 3 (July 3, 2018): 249–65, https://doi.org/10.1080/09662839.2018.1497977. Trine Flockhart, "Is This the End? Resilience, Ontological Security, and the Crisis of the Liberal International Order," *Contemporary Security Policy* 41, no. 2 (April 2, 2020): 215–40, https://doi.org/10.1080/13523260.2020.1723966 (emphasis added).

354 "Charting the News: The Trump Bump," *The Economist*, December 21, 2019.

355 Tyler Durden, "These Were the Top News Stories of 2023 Based on Google Search Trends," *ZeroHedge* (blog), January 6, 2024, https://www.zerohedge.com/geopolitical/these-were-top-news-stories-2023-based-google-search-trends.

356 Kahneman, *Thinking, Fast and Slow*.

357 Phillip Lipscy, "COVID-19 and the Politics of Crisis," *International Organization* 74, no. Supplement (2020), https://doi.org/10.1017/S0020818320000375.

358 Ashley Nellis and Joanne Savage, "Does Watching the News Affect Fear of Terrorism? The Importance of Media Exposure on Terrorism Fear," *Crime and Delinquency* 58, no. 5 (September 2012): 748–68, https://doi.org/10.1177/0011128712452961; Douglas A. Van Belle, "New York Times and Network TV News Coverage of Foreign Disasters: The Significance of the Insignificant Variables," *Journalism & Mass Communication Quarterly* 77, no. 1 (March 1, 2000): 50–70, https://doi.org/10.1177/107769900007700105.

359 Brian Resnick, "A Psychologist Explains the Limits of Human Compassion," Vox, July 19, 2017, https://www.vox.com/explainers/2017/7/19/15925506/psychic-numbing-paul-slovic-apathy.

360 Resnick.

361 Mitzen, "Ontological Security in World Politics."

362 Ronald D. Laing, *The Divided Self: An Existential Study in Sanity and Madness* (London:Penguin Books, 1965).

363 Karl Gustafsson and Nina C. Krickel-Choi, "Returning to the Roots of Ontological Security: Insights from the Existentialist Anxiety Literature," *European Journal of International Relations* 26, no. 3 (September 1, 2020): 875–95, https://doi.org/10.1177/1354066120927073.

364 Lloyd's Register Foundation, "World Risk Poll 2021: A Resilient World?," 2022, https://

wrp.lrfoundation.org.uk/publications/a-resilient-world-understanding-vulnerability-in-a-changing-climate.

365 Ipsos, "Positivity about How This Year Has Gone Highest Since Before the Pandemic," December 10, 2024, https://www.ipsos.com/en/ipsos-predictions-2025#towards2025.

366 Tsukasa Nishida, "Anxiety Uncertainty Management Theory," in *The International Encyclopedia of Communication* (American Cancer Society, 2008), https://doi.org/10.1002/9781405186407.wbieca046.

367 Mitzen, "Ontological Security in World Politics."

368 Flockhart, "Is This the End?"

Chapter 12: The Parameters of Perils

369 If you think I'm lying, see Amy M. Green, "Far Cry 5, American Right-Wing Terrorism, and Doomsday Prepper Culture," *Games and Culture* 17, nos. 7-8 (2022): 1015-35, https://doi.org/10.1177/15554120211073379. You can also search for articles relating to the video game *Mr. Prepper* for additional examples.

370 United Nations Office for Disaster Risk Reduction, "Sendai Framework for Disaster Risk Reduction, 2015–2030."

371 Bounds, *Bracing for the Apocalypse: An Ethnographic Study of New York's "Prepper" Subculture.*

372 E. L. Quarantelli, "Catastrophes Are Different from Disasters: Some Implications for Crisis Planning and Managing Drawn from Katrina," Items, June 11, 2006, https://items.ssrc.org/understanding-katrina/catastrophes-are-different-from-disasters-some-implications-for-crisis-planning-and-managing-drawn-from-katrina/; Kathleen Tierney, *Disasters: A Sociological Approach* (Medford, MA: Polity Press, 2019).

373 Howard Kunreuther and Michael Useem, *Learning from Catastrophes: Strategies for Reaction and Response* (Upper Saddle River: NJ: Wharton School Publishing, 2010), 177.

374 Flynn, *The Edge of Disaster.*

375 Centre for Research on the Epidemiology of Disasters (CRED), "EM-DAT," EM-DAT. The International Disaster Database, 2019, https://www.emdat.be/.

376 Md Zahid Arefin Choudhury, "Politics of Natural Disaster: How Governments Maintain Legitimacy in the Wake of Major Disasters, 1990–2010" (PhD diss., University of Iowa, 2013).

377 Arizona State University—SHELDUS, https://cemhs.asu.edu/sheldus.

378 CEMHS, "Spatial Hazard Events and Losses Database for the United States, Version 17.0. [Online Database]," Metadata, Center for Emergency Management and Homeland Security, Arizona State University, 2018, https://cemhs.asu.edu/sheldus/metadata#sheldus-data.

379 CEMHS, "Spatial Hazard Events and Losses Database for the United States, Version 17.0. [Online Database]," Community, Center for Emergency Management and Homeland Security, Arizona State University, 2018, https://cemhs.asu.edu/sheldus/applications.

380 Recreated from SHELDUS.

381 FEMA, "Disaster Declarations for States and Counties: May 2, 1953–April 29, 2025," https://www.fema.gov/data-visualization/disaster-declarations-states-and-counties.

382 For the process by which these occur and the assistance available, see "How a Disaster Gets Declared," FEMA, last updated July 22, 2024, https://www.fema.gov/disaster/how-declared.

383 See "Fire Management Assistance Grants," FEMA, last updated July 23, 2024, https://www.fema.gov/assistance/public/fire-management-assistance.

384 FEMA, "National Risk Index," https://hazards.fema.gov/nri/map.

385 My search was performed in late 2019. Scores are ever evolving.

386 International Federation of Red Cross and Red Crescent, "What Is a Disaster?," accessed March 30, 2020, https://www.ifrc.org/en/what-we-do/disaster-management/about-disasters/what-is-a-disaster/.

387 United Nations Office for Disaster Risk Reduction, "Sendai Framework for Disaster Risk Reduction, 2015–2030."

388 United Nations Office for Disaster Risk Reduction (UNDRR), "The Sendai Framework Terminology on Disaster Risk Reduction," 2017, accessed April 29, 2025, https://www.preventionweb.net/terminology/view/7831.

389 Louise Comfort, Arjen Boin, and Chris Demchack, eds., *Designing Resilience: Preparing for Extreme Events* (Pittsburgh, PA: University of Pittsburgh Press, 2010).

390 United Nations Office for Disaster Risk Reduction (UNDRR), "The Sendai Framework Terminology on Disaster Risk Reduction," 2017, accessed April 29, 2025, https://www.undrr.org/terminology/preparedness.

391 American Red Cross, "What Is the Red Cross Global Network?," September 16, 2022, https://www.redcross.org/about-us/news-and-events/news/2022/what-is-the-red-cross-global-network.html.

392 Department of Homeland Security, "National Response Framework: Fourth Edition," October 28, 2019, https://www.fema.gov/sites/default/files/2020-04/NRF_FINALApproved_2011028.pdf.

393 Department of the Army, *Army Doctrine Publication (ADP) 3-28: Defense Support of Civil Authorities* (Washington, DC: Department of the Army 2019).

394 Alexander McFarlane and Fran H. Norris, *Methods for Disaster Mental Health Research*, ed. Fran H. Norris et al. (New York: Guilford Press, 2006).

395 Wallace, "Responses to Perceived Terrorism Risk by Self-Identified Survivalists."

396 Disaster databases rarely contain all three, so the issue of counting disasters to use as an independent variable is a challenge, even in the United States where data are abundant. For example, EM-DAT tracks only natural and technological disasters. SHELDUS, as noted, counts only natural disasters. FEMA's Disaster Declarations Summary data visualization website has some, but not all, technological or man-made events. Presidential disaster declarations are problematic as well.

397 Daya Somasundaram et al., "Natural and Technological Disasters," in *Trauma Interventions in War and Peace: Prevention, Practice, and Policy*, ed. Bonnie L. Green et al., International and Cultural Psychology Series (Boston, MA: Springer US, 2003), 291–318.

398 Kayleigh Lewis, "Radioactive Reindeer in Norway Are a Stark Reminder of the Chernobyl Legacy," *The Independent*, March 1, 2016, https://www.independent.co.uk/news/world/europe/chernobyl-radioactive-reindeer-norway-a6903571.html.

399 Flynn, *The Edge of Disaster*.

400 Zach Wichter, "California's Largest Utility Says It Is Bankrupt. Here's What You Need to Know," *The New York Times*, January 29, 2019, https://www.nytimes.com/2019/01/29/business/pge-bankruptcy.html.

401 Alejandra Reyes-Velarde, "California's Camp Fire Was the Costliest Global Disaster Last Year, Insurance Report Shows," *Los Angeles Times*, January 12, 2019, https://www.latimes.com/local/lanow/la-me-ln-camp-fire-insured-losses-20190111-story.html; Doyle Rice, "USA Had World's 3 Costliest Natural Disasters in 2018, and Camp Fire Was the Worst," *USA TODAY*, January 8, 2019, https://www.usatoday.com/story/news/2019/01/08/natural-disasters-camp-fire-worlds-costliest-catastrophe-2018/2504865002/.

402 I use the term *vaccination* in its pre-COVID definition, which is the administration of a vaccine that provided *immunity* to a disease. This is the same way Louis Pasteur, the father of microbiology and developer of some of the world's first vaccines, would have used the term.

403 One fascinating study argued that while natural disasters follow the logic of political survival, pandemic flu, as in the case of the 2009 swine influenza outbreak, did not. Those authors argue that citizens in the nine Western democracies they studied treated this epidemic more as a technical matter for scientific experts rather than a political issue. Erik Baekkeskov and Olivier Rubin, "Why Pandemic Response Is Unique: Powerful Experts and Hands-off Political Leaders," *Disaster Prevention and Management; Bradford* 23, no. 1 (2014): 81–93, http://dx.doi.org.proxy.library.cornell.edu/10.1108/DPM-05-2012-0060.

404 Seren Morris, "How Many People Died in Hiroshima and Nagasaki," *Newsweek*, August 3, 2020, https://www.newsweek.com/how-many-people-died-hiroshima-nagasaki-japan-second-world-war-1522276. Additional deaths attributed to fallout and succumbing to injuries put the final death toll at over two hundred thousand. For a fascinating explanation of methodology in estimation, see Alex Wellerstein, "Counting the Dead at Hiroshima and Nagasaki," Bulletin of Atomic Scientists, August 4, 2020, https://thebulletin.org/2020/08/counting-the-dead-at-hiroshima-and-nagasaki/.

405 Aaron O'Neill, "Number of Casualties and Fatalities during the Battle of the Somme in 1916," Statista, August 12, 2024, https://www.statista.com/statistics/1022625/casualty-fatalities-statistics-battle-somme-1916/.

406 Marijke Verpoorten, "The Death Toll of the Rwandan Genocide: A Detailed Analysis for Gikongoro Province," *Cairn.info* 60, no. 4 (2005), accessed April 29, 2025, https://www.cairn-int.info/article-E_POPU_504_0401—the-death-toll-of-the-rwandan-genocide-a.htm; and Survivors Fund SURF, "Statistics," https://survivors-fund.org.uk/learn/statistics/.

407 Our World in Data, "Causes of Death, World, 2021," https://ourworldindata.org/grapher/annual-number-of-deaths-by-cause.

408 Amy Novotney, "How Does Climate Change Affect Mental Health?," American Psychological Association, April 21, 2023, https://www.apa.org/topics/climate-change/mental-health-effects; Michael Shellenberger, "Why Climate Alarmism Hurts Us All," *Forbes*, December 4, 2019, https://www.forbes.com/sites/michaelshellenberger/2019/12/04/why-climate-alarmism-hurts-us-all/.

409 Christine Emba, "The Real Reason People Aren't Having Kids," *The Atlantic*, August 1, 2024, https://www.theatlantic.com/family/archive/2024/08/fertility-crisis/679319/; Ross Douthat, "Is It Weird to Care about the Birthrate?," *The New York Times*, August 2, 2024, https://www.nytimes.com/2024/08/02/opinion/birthrate-jd-vance.html.

410 Alan Yuhas, "They Prepared for the Worst. Now Everyone's a Prepper," *The New York Times*, March 17, 2020, https://www.nytimes.com/2020/03/17/us/coronavirus-preppers.html.

411 Autism Capital (@AutismCapital), "ELON MUSK TALKS ABOUT PEANUT THE SQUIRREL," Twitter (now X), November 4, 2024, https://x.com/AutismCapital/status/1853619010526720401.

412 Tyler Durden, "'This Is the Wildest Market I've Ever Seen': Druckenmiller's Must-See Goldman Interview," *ZeroHedge* (blog), February 8, 2021, https://www.zerohedge.com/markets/wildest-market-ive-ever-seen-druckenmillers-must-see-goldman-interview.

413 A disease that can jump from animals to humans.

Chapter 13: The Probing of Perils

414 Nassim Nicholas Taleb, *Statistical Consequences of Fat Tails: Real World Preasymptotics, Epistemology, and Applications* (n.p.: STEM Academic Press, 2020). Nassim was a former instructor of mine, and I learned quite a bit about how to think about disasters from him. I am exceptionally grateful.

415 "Transdisciplinary Discovery and Practice," Center for Emergency Management and Homeland Security, Arizona State University, https://cemhs.asu.edu/content/welcome.

416 Columbia Climate School National Center for Disaster Preparedness, https://ncdp.columbia.edu/wp-content/uploads/2023/04/NCDP_About_Us.pdf.

417 Risk Management and Decision Processes Center, *Annual Report 2018* (University of Pennsylvania Wharton School, 2018), https://esg.wharton.upenn.edu/wp-content/uploads/2023/07/Wharton-Risk-Center-Annual-Report-2018_Web.pdf (emphasis added).

418 Sadly, there are not. My anecdotal experience was that high preparedness levels clustered in public administration departments or emergency management, where more practitioners abounded. Those in more theoretical domains or those with little real-world experience had little in terms of preparedness. I found it highly disconcerting that so many bright minds could not make the connection between what they were teaching in class versus what they should have been doing at a household and community level to prepare for the very events they used as historical examples or future potentials.

419 Hannah Ritchie, "There Have Been Five Mass Extinctions in Earth's History," Our World in Data, November 30, 2022, https://ourworldindata.org/mass-extinctions.

420 Hannah Ritchie, "Five Mass Extinctions"; and Michael R. House, "Devonian Extinctions," *Encyclopedia Britannica*, accessed May 1, 2025, https://www.britannica.com/science/Devonian-extinctions.

421 Avi Melamed et al., "Popular Impact: Public Opinion and Planetary Defense Planning," *Acta Astronautica* 214 (November 13, 2023): 505–25.

422 Nahum Melamed and Avi Melamed, *Planetary Defense against Asteroid Strikes: Risks, Options, and Costs* (Arlington, VA: Center for Space Policy and Strategy, January 2018).

423 European Space Agency (ESA), "Lessons Learnt from Simulated Strike," April 30, 2021, https://www.esa.int/Space_Safety/Lessons_learnt_from_simulated_strike.

424 Michael Prasad, "Global Pandemics Are Extinction-Level Events and Should Not Be Coordinated Solely through National or Jurisdictional Emergency Management," *Homeland Security Affairs,* Pracademic Affairs 3 (August 2023), www.hsaj.org/articles/22285.

425 Office of the Director of National Intelligence, "2024 Annual Threat Assessment Director of National Intelligence."

426 "Worldwide Threats to the Homeland," *Congressional Record*, November 15, 2022, https://www.congress.gov/event/117th-congress/house-event/115183/text.

427 Federal Emergency Management Agency, *2022–2026 FEMA Strategic Plan* (Federal Emergency Management Agency, February 6, 2024).

428 Susan Elizabeth Turek, "FEMA Reveals Devastating Reason Disaster Recovery Projects Have Come to a Halt: 'It's Crippled Us Right Now,'" Yahoo News, November 11, 2023, https://www.yahoo.com/news/fema-reveals-devastating-reason-disaster-111510644.html.

429 Anders Hagstrom, "DHS Sec. Mayorkas Says FEMA 'Will Need Additional Funds' after Hurricanes Helene, Milton," Yahoo News, October 10, 2024, https://www.yahoo.com/news/dhs-sec-mayorkas-says-fema-175536847.html.

430 Ella Nilsen, "How Did FEMA Spend $9 Billion So Quickly? Back-to-Back Disasters," CNN,

October 10, 2024, https://www.cnn.com/2024/10/10/politics/fema-disaster-funding-congress-explainer/index.html.

431 Henry H. Willis et al., "Global Catastrophic Risk Assessment" (Santa Monica, CA: RAND Corporation, October 30, 2024), https://www.rand.org/pubs/research_reports/RRA2981-1.html.

432 Noelani Revina, "Vibrant Response Reaches New Heights with Emergency Deployment Readiness Exercises," US Army Reserve, May 11, 2023, https://www.usar.army.mil/News/News-Display/Article/3392243/vibrant-response-reaches-new-heights-with-emergency-deployment-readiness-exerci/; Jake Draugelis, "Task Force 46: The Lansing-Based Soldiers in Charge of Responding to Nuclear Disaster," https://www.wilx.com, May 14, 2022, https://www.wilx.com/2022/05/14/task-force-46-lansing-based-soldiers-charge-responding-nuclear-disaster/.

433 Carlos Fantauzzi, "Vibrant Response Tests Army Response Capabilities on Home Turf," US Army, May 20, 2019, https://www.army.mil/article/222057/vibrant_response_tests_army_response_capabilities_on_home_turf.

434 Sometimes it is also referred to as CBRNE, with the "E" standing for explosives.

435 Walter Ham IV, "20th CBRNE Command Marks 20 Years of Defeating World's Most Dangerous Hazards," US Army, October 16, 2024, https://www.army.mil/article/280533/20th_cbrne_command_marks_20_years_of_defeating_worlds_most_dangerous_hazards.

436 JTF-CS Public Affairs and DCRF Public Affairs, "Members of JTF-CS and the DCRF Participate in Exercise Vibrant Response-Guardian Response," Joint Task Force Civil Support, May 15, 2019, https://www.jtfcs.northcom.mil/MEDIA/NEWS-ARTICLES/Article/1849151/members-of-jtf-cs-and-the-dcrf-participate-in-exercise-vibrant-response-guardia.

437 "Muscatatuck Training Center,"Indiana National Guard, accessed July 8, 2025, https://www.in.gov/indiana-national-guard/muscatatuck-urban-training-center/.

438 United States Senate Committee on Armed Services, March 14, 2024, https://www.armed-services.senate.gov/hearings/to-receive-testimony-on-posture-of-united-states-northern-command-and-united-states-southern-command-in-review-of-the-defense-authorization-request-for-fiscal-year-2025-and-the-future-years-defense-program.

439 World Health Organization, "Our Work,"accessed April 29, 2025, https://www.who.int/our-work.

440 "What We Do: Our Goals for 2030," The Nature Conservancy, accessed April 29, 2025, https://www.nature.org/en-us/what-we-do/our-priorities/.

441 USU National Center for Disaster Medicine and Public Health, https://ncdmph.usuhs.edu/about.

442 "Plum Island Animal Disease Center," US Department of Homeland Security, https://www.dhs.gov/science-and-technology/plum-island-animal-disease-center.

443 Donald McNeil, *The Wisdom of Plagues: Lessons from 25 Years of Covering Pandemics* (New York: Simon & Schuster, 2024).

444 Madison Muller, "A Mysterious Lab Is Shutting Down. It's the End of an Era for Biosecurity," *Stars and Stripes*, September 16, 2023, https://www.stripes.com/theaters/us/2023-09-16/ny-plum-island-biosecurity-lab-closure-11398754.html.

445 "National Bio and Agro-Defense Facility," US Department of Agriculture, https://www.usda.gov/nbaf.

446 Center for Excellence in Disaster Management & Humanitarian Assistance, https://www.cfe-dmha.org/.

447 US Drought Monitor, "This Week's Drought Summary," April 22, 2025, https://droughtmonitor.unl.edu/CurrentMap.aspx.

448 HazardAware, "Know Your Risk. Be Risk Ready," https://www.hazardaware.org/.

449 "World's Top Asset Management Firms," ADV Ratings, accessed July 8, 2025, https://www.advratings.com/top-asset-management-firms.

450 BlackRock Investment Institute, "2024 Global Outlook," 2023, https://d1e00ek4ebabms.cloudfront.net/production/uploaded-files/bii-global-outlook-2024-d0bb6652-6a08-4661-b3a0-002e424abd69.pdf.

451 Jeff Cox, "U.S. Deficit Tops $1.8 Trillion in 2024 as Interest on Debt Surpasses Trillion-Dollar Mark," CNBC, October 18, 2024, https://www.cnbc.com/2024/10/18/us-deficit-tops-1point8-trillion-in-2024-as-interest-on-debt-surpasses-trillion-dollar-mark.html; Diccon Hyatt, "A Record $1.2 Trillion Interest Payments Are Blowing Up the Federal Budget," Investopedia, September 13, 2024, https://www.investopedia.com/why-interest-payments-are-blowing-up-the-federal-budget-8712197; USAFacts, "How Much Does the Government Spend on Medicare?," August 1, 2024, https://usafacts.org/articles/how-much-does-the-government-spend-on-medicare/.

452 BlackRock Investment Institute, "2024 Global Outlook."

453 World Economic Forum, *The Global Risks Report 2024: 19th Edition* (Geneva, Switzerland, January 10, 2024), https://www.weforum.org/publications/global-risks-report-2024/.

454 World Economic Forum.

455 The national risk list contained thirty-six categories and slightly different wording of some terms (e.g., "inequality" in this list but "Lack of economic opportunity" in Table 13.1).

456 Graff, *Raven Rock: The Story of the U.S. Government's Secret Plan to Save Itself—While the Rest of Us Die*; Ben Garrison, *Bracing for Armageddon: Why Civil Defense Never Worked* (Oxford: Oxford University Press, 2006); Bounds, *Bracing for the Apocalypse: An Ethnographic Study of New York's "Prepper" Subculture*; Mike Lauder, *In Pursuit of Foresight: Disaster Incubation Theory Re-imagined* (New York: Gower Publishing, 2017); Clarke, *Worst Cases: Terror and Catastrophe in the Popular Imagination.*

457 Graff, *Raven Rock: The Story of the U.S. Government's Secret Plan to Save Itself—While the Rest of Us Die.*

458 Muir-Wood, *The Cure for Catastrophe: How We Can Stop Manufacturing Natural Disasters.*

459 You can go to your online search engine and type in "is eating/drinking (grapefruit, eggs, milk, meat, chocolate, ice cream, etc.) good/bad for you?" There is no consensus.

460 Within reason. I'm not defending witchcraft or astrology. Stay with me, folks.

461 William Wilson, "Scientific Regress," *First Things*, May 1, 2016, https://www.firstthings.com/article/2016/05/scientific-regress.

462 Task Force on National and Homeland Security, and Secure the Grid Coalition, "A Call to Action for America."

463 "Presidential Approval Ratings—George W. Bush," Gallup, https://news.gallup.com/poll/116500/presidential-approval-ratings-george-bush.aspx.

464 Katie Notopoulos, "Mark Zuckerberg Calls Donald Trump a 'Badass' after the Former President Threatened Him with Prison," *Business Insider*, July 19, 2024, https://www.businessinsider.com/zuckerberg-calls-trump-badass-assassination-attempt-shooting-endorsement-prison-2024-7.

465 Witness the treatment of free-range parents, gun manufacturers, skeptics, people who pray at abortion clinics, those opposed to genetically modified organisms, homeschoolers, etc.

466 Falsely attributed to Thomas Jefferson. Thomas Jefferson Foundation, "Government Big Enough to Give You Everything You Want... (Spurious Quotation)," *Thomas Jefferson Encyclopedia*, accessed May 1, 2025, https://www.monticello.org/research-education/thomas-jefferson-encyclopedia/government-big-enough-give-you-everything-you-wantspurious-quotation/.

467 World Economic Forum, "The Global Risks Report 2024: 19th Edition."

468 World Economic Forum; World Economic Forum, "The Global Risks Report 2023: 18th Edition."

469 Jacob Mchangama, "Evidence Is Growing That Free Speech Is Declining," *Foreign Policy*, December 4, 2023, https://foreignpolicy.com/2023/12/04/evidence-is-growing-that-free-speech-is-declining/.

470 Thomas Brooke, "Three-Quarters of Germans Believe Fear of Repercussion Is Silencing Free Speech," *Remix News* (blog), November 28, 2024, https://rmx.news/article/three-quarters-of-germans-believe-fear-of-repercussion-is-silencing-free-speech/.

471 Philip Magness and David Waugh, "The Hyperpoliticization of Higher Ed: Trends in Faculty Political Ideology, 1969-Present," *The Independent Institute* 27, no. 3 (Winter 2022/2023), https://www.independent.org/publications/tir/article.asp?id=1782.

472 Lee Jussim, "Political Biases in Academia," *Psychology Today*, May 29, 2020, https://www.psychologytoday.com/us/blog/rabble-rouser/202005/political-biases-in-academia.

473 Meimei Xu, "More Than 80 Percent of Surveyed Harvard Faculty Identify as Liberal," *The Harvard Crimson*, July 13, 2022, https://www.thecrimson.com/article/2022/7/13/faculty-survey-political-leaning/.

474 McNeil, *The Wisdom of Plagues: Lessons from 25 Years of Covering Pandemics.*

475 Garrett, "Doomsday Preppers and the Architecture of Dread"; Paul Joseph Watson, "Mega Rich Are Forcing Out Millionaires on 'Billionaires Bunker' Island," Modernity, January 9, 2024, https://modernity.news/2024/01/09/mega-rich-are-forcing-out-millionaires-on-billionaires-bunker-island/; Douglas Rushkoff, "Survival of the Richest," Medium, September 1, 2020, https://onezero.medium.com/survival-of-the-richest-9ef6cddd0cc1.

476 Lee Clarke and Caron Chess, "Elites and Panic: More to Fear Than Fear Itself," *Social Forces* 87, no. 2 (December 2008).

477 Clarke and Chess.

Chapter 14: The Preliminaries of Preparedness

478 For an easy-to-read PDF version, see *NSC 68: United States Objectives and Programs for National Security*, April 14, 1950, https://www.citizensource.com/History/20thCen/NSC68.PDF (hereafter NSC 68).

479 US Army, "Department of National Security and Strategy," https://ssl.armywarcollege.edu/DNSS/index.cfm; Tami Davis Biddle, "NSC-68: The Policy Document That Shaped the Cold War," *War Room Online Journal*, December 8, 2017, https://warroom.armywarcollege.edu/podcasts/nsc-68-policy-document-shaped-cold-war-dusty-shelves/.

480 NSC 68.

481 NSC 68.

482 The 2024 US presidential election saw several accusations that President Donald Trump and his supporters were attempting to enshrine Christianity as the supreme law of the land.

See, for example, Terry Gross, "Tracing the Rise of Christian Nationalism, from Trump to the Ala. Supreme Court," National Public Radio, February 29, 2024, https://www.npr.org/2024/02/29/1234843874/tracing-the-rise-of-christian-nationalism-from-trump-to-the-ala-supreme-court.

483 NSC 68. Spelling from original.

484 NSC 68.

485 NSC 68.

486 Sadly, one of the fatal flaws in NSC 68 was the conflation of two terms: *Divine Providence* and *Manifest Destiny.* The Founding Fathers of America believed in Divine Providence, that God had chosen America out of His beneficence. In the Founders' understanding, America was good because of God's blessing. Manifest Destiny, which emerged in the 1800s, flipped this on its head. In Manifest Destiny, God was a red-blooded American and a supporter of the American cause. In Christian theology, this is akin to the doctrine of works earning salvation, with people in charge of their eternity rather than God's grace.

487 NSC 68.

488 "Overseas Military Bases by Country 2025," World Population Review, https://worldpopulationreview.com/country-rankings/overseas-military-bases-by-country.

489 Patrick J. Garrity, "The Long Twilight Struggle," *Claremont Review of Books* 6, no. 3 (Summer 2006), https://claremontreviewofbooks.com/the-long-twilight-struggle/. If you wish to know more about the legacy of containment and decades of American policy as shaped by NSC 68, this short paper is an excellent overview.

490 NSC 68.

491 NSC 68.

492 "President Truman Receives NSC-68 Report, Calling for 'Containing' Soviet Expansion," History.com, January 31, 2025, https://www.history.com/this-day-in-history/president-truman-receives-nsc-68.

493 Consult a copy of this note on page 2 of the Truman Library declassified version. See "'A Report to the National Security Council—NSC 68,' April 12, 1950," Harry S. Truman Library and Museum, accessed July 8, 2025, https://www.trumanlibrary.gov/library/research-files/report-national-security-council-nsc-68?documentid=NA&pagenumber=2.

494 Mitzen, "Ontological Security in World Politics."

495 "Executive Order 10186—Establishing the Federal Civil Defense Administration in the Office for Emergency Management of the Executive Office of the President," The American Presidency Project, December 1, 1950, https://www.presidency.ucsb.edu/documents/executive-order-10186-establishing-the-federal-civil-defense-administration-the-office-for.

496 Homeland Security Digital Library, https://www.hsdl.org/c/tl/federal-civil-defense-act-1950/.

497 The basement of the Truman Library contains the White House Decision Center. Here, both high school and college students, as well as adults, are led through assorted simulations of actual events President Truman encountered during his executive tenure. Proctors guide participants in recreations of the events and actors surrounding issues such as civil rights in the armed forces, the re-creation of Israel in 1948, and the Soviet blockade of Berlin. See "The White House Decision Center," Harry S. Truman Library and Museum, accessed July 8, 2025, https://www.trumanlibrary.gov/education/white-house-decision-center. As part of a military education field trip, I was there to act as a presidential cabinet member, advising President Truman on whether to drop nuclear weapons on Japan. My group overwhelmingly

recommended in the affirmative. Curious about this outcome, I asked one of the staff at the library how often teams came to the same conclusion as the historical record. The answer: almost always.

498 See *A Report to the National Security Council by the Executive Secretary on Basic National Security Policy*, October 30, 1953, https://irp.fas.org/offdocs/nsc-hst/nsc-162-2.pdf (hereafter NSC 162/2).

499 NSC 162/2.

500 NSC 162/2.

501 *Mobilization Plan D-Minus*, 1957.

502 "MOBILIZATION PLAN *D-MINUS* is based on an assumed international situation involving *surprise attacks* with atomic weapons so crippling in their effects that military strength would be seriously reduced, the national economy would come to a virtual standstill, Government would be disrupted and millions of casualties would result. However remaining population and resources [*sic*] would be adequate to rebuild the nation. Maximum military action would be required to conduct offensive and defensive operations. . . . *Drastic Governmental actions would be required* to sustain life, to continue the prosecution of the war, to maintain Government and the cooperation of the free world, and to restore the economy of the nation. Maximum effective use of the residual capabilities of the United States and its Allies would be necessary. *This would require that the remaining human and material resources be organized and directed toward concerted action* against the enemy and toward equally concerted action to preserve life, to restore the nation and to maintain a cooperative international community" (emphasis added).

503 US Bureau of the Census, *Statistical Abstract of the United States: 1958*, 79th ed. (Washington, DC: US Government Printing Office, 1958), https://www2.census.gov/library/publications/1958/compendia/statab/79ed/1958_02.pdf.

504 Office of Civil and Defense Mobilization, *Federal Emergency Plan D-Minus*, April 1, 1959, https://www.brennancenter.org/sites/default/files/2021-11/Federal%20Emergency%20Plan%20D-Minus%20%28Apr.%201959%29.pdf.

505 *Federal Emergency Plan D-Minus*, 1959.

506 *Federal Emergency Plan D-Minus*, 1959.

507 *Report of the NET Evaluation Subcommittee*, 1958.

508 *Report of the NET Evaluation Subcommittee*, 1958.

509 Megan Pagaduan, "America's Epidemic of Antidepressants," *Berkeley Political Review*, November 7, 2021, https://bpr.studentorg.berkeley.edu/2021/11/07/americas-epidemic-of-antidepressants/.

510 National Institute on Drug Abuse, "What Is the Scope of Tobacco, Nicotine, and E-Cigarette Use in the United States?," *Tobacco, Nicotine, and E-Cigarettes Research Report*, January 1, 2020, https://nida.nih.gov/publications/research-reports/tobacco-nicotine-e-cigarettes/what-scope-tobacco-use-its-cost-to-society.

511 Centers for Disease Control and Prevention, "FastStats: Illicit Drug Use," *National Center for Health Statistics*, last reviewed July 26, 2024, https://www.cdc.gov/nchs/fastats/drug-use-illicit.htm.

512 Centers for Disease Control and Prevention, *National Diabetes Statistics Report: Estimates of Diabetes and Its Burden in the United States*, Atlanta, US Department of Health and Human Services, Centers for Disease Control and Prevention, 2023, https://www.cdc.gov/diabetes/data/statistics-report/index.html.

513 Mallory Locklear, "Insulin Is an Extreme Financial Burden for over 14% of Americans Who Use It," Yale News, July 5, 2022, https://news.yale.edu/2022/07/05/insulin-extreme-financial-burden-over-14-americans-who-use-it.

514 Naomi Thomas, "Insulin: 1.3 Million Americans with Diabetes Rationed Their Supply in the Past Year, Study Finds," CNN Health, October 17, 2022, https://www.cnn.com/2022/10/17/health/insulin-rationing-diabetes-study/index.html.

515 Linda Wang, "Closing the COVID-Induced Cancer Screening Gap," National Cancer Institute, May 17, 2022, https://www.cancer.gov/news-events/cancer-currents-blog/2022/covid-increasing-cancer-screening.

516 Elizabeth Pegg Frates, "Did We Really Gain Weight during the Pandemic?," Harvard Health Publishing, October 5, 2021, https://www.health.harvard.edu/blog/did-we-really-gain-weight-during-the-pandemic-202110052606.

517 Kirsten Weir, "The Extra Weight of COVID-19," American Psychological Association, July 1, 2021, https://www.apa.org/monitor/2021/07/extra-weight-covid.

518 *Report of the NET Evaluation Subcommittee*, 1958.

Chapter 15: The Pinnacle of Preparedness

519 Dwight D. Eisenhower Presidential Library, *Virgil L. Couch: Papers, 1951–1980*, Accession A91-19, 96-4, processed February 1994, https://www.eisenhowerlibrary.gov/sites/default/files/finding-aids/pdf/couch-virgil-papers.pdf. This summation of Virgil Couch's life comes directly from the online version of the Virgil Couch Papers stored at the Eisenhower Library.

520 Dwight D. Eisenhower Presidential Library, *Virgil L. Couch: Papers, 1951–1980*, Accession A91-19, 96-4, processed February 1994, accessed May 1, 2025, https://www.eisenhowerlibrary.gov/sites/default/files/finding-aids/pdf/couch-virgil-papers.pdf. In my archival research in the library, I perused a mere fraction of the collection. While the Virgil Couch Papers focused on the period in which civil defense was at its pinnacle (the 1950s and 1960s), overlapping with Virgil's time in the FCDA, the full collection spans civil defense and disaster preparedness data in America from 1916 to 1980. The Couch Papers also contain several works on "industrial survival" and "industrial mutual aid, and the vulnerability of the food industries" as well as two foreign civil defense entries, one Canadian and one from NATO. There is also "an Agriculture Department report on radioactive fallout on the farm, a Navy study on biological warfare, a civil defense manual for the city of San Diego, California, a civil defense survival plan for St. Louis City and County, and a facilities self-protection manual for the State of Wisconsin."

521 Quotes and data from this report were taken from my archival research in the Eisenhower Library.

522 *Federal Emergency Plan D-Minus*, 1959.

523 "The Interstate Highway System," History.com, originally published May 27, 2010, last updated February 27, 2025, https://www.history.com/topics/us-states/interstate-highway-system.

524 If you would like a second opinion, Stanford University's Research Institute prepared a Top Secret (now declassified) report for the National Security Council titled *Survival of Population Following a Massive Nuclear Exchange*. The report's assumptions were of a 1965 Soviet attack using 1,082 nuclear weapons in an 8,450-megaton assault. Ninety-eight million Americans (out of a population of 192 million) would die, even if a national fallout shelter program were initiated, and 165 million would die if there were no fallout shelter program. Estimates put the

pre-attack ratio at one doctor for every thirteen patients, but the post-attack national average at thirty-four patients per doctor. Stanford predicted the loss of 54 percent of all doctors, 68 percent of US engineers, and 56 percent of all skilled laborers. The report goes into heavy analysis of contamination, fatalities, and lives saved. It also looks at impacts across various sectors (food, water, power, industrial base, transportation, etc.), much like *D-Minus* did. The findings are not identical but paint an analogous picture of widespread devastation. Data from this report were taken from my archival research in the Eisenhower Library.

525 For a modern comparison, countries like Finland and Switzerland primarily have fallout shelters. Israel has a version of blast shelters, but those are built for the specifications of incoming Palestinian rockets and mortars, not nuclear missiles.

526 National Security Council, *Economic Implications of Alternative Shelter Programs* (Executive Office of the President, August 14, 1957).

527 Report to the National Security Council by the Special Committee on Shelter Programs, 1957.

528 Economic Implications of Alternative Shelter Programs, 1957.

529 See *Deterrence & Survival in the Nuclear Age*, Security Resources Panel of the Science Advisory Committee, November 7, 1957, https://www.documentcloud.org/documents/2995999-1957-Gaither-Report (hereafter referred to as Gaither Report).

530 To get a smaller scale sense of the public concern (panic?) Sputnik caused, recall main street and media coverage of the Chinese high-altitude balloons in 2023.

531 Gaither Report.

532 Highly classified (now declassified) notes from these meetings include the *Active and Passive Measures to Protect the Civil Population* (November 6, 1957), *NSC 5724/1* (December 17, 1957), and the January 16, 1958, NSC meeting.

533 US Congress, Joint Committee on Defense Production, *Deterrence and Survival in the Nuclear Age: The "Gaither Report" of 1957* (Washington, DC: US Government Printing Office, 1976), https://ia803201.us.archive.org/34/items/deteviv00unit/deteviv00unit.pdf.

534 Gaither Report.

535 *NSC 5807: Measures to Carry Out the Concept of Shelter*, 1958.

536 *Report on the Status of Shelter Measures*, 1958.

537 Federal Civil Defense Administration, "Public Affairs: For Your Information. Hoegh Announces National Policy on Shelters," May 7, 1958.

538 Federal Civil Defense Administration.

539 "Weekly News Digest," Office of Civil and Defense Mobilization, February 17, 1961.

540 A literature review in academia is a large sampling of professional writings (sometimes with popular references as well) to summarize what has been said on a particular topic. Since they can be heavily skewed by bias in many instances, the best include contrary opinions on a topic. This report was called *Foods for Shelter Storage* and was found in the Virgil Couch Papers at the Eisenhower Library.

541 "Information Bulletin: Statement of the Director," Office of Civil and Defense Mobilization, March 30, 1959.

542 And here I mean the fifty US states.

543 Information Bulletin No. 68.

544 Quotes and data from these references were taken from my archival research notes in the Eisenhower Library. The text of these speeches was recorded in "Information Bulletins" and published by the Office of Civil and Defense Mobilization.

545 "Information Bulletin: Address of Leo A. Hoegh to Department of Defense Conference

Group," Office of Civil and Defense Mobilization, August 10, 1960.

546 A one-week conference to Washington, DC, and sponsored by the American Legion, which is still active as of 2023.

547 "Information Bulletin: Address by Leo A. Hoegh to Girls Nation," Office of Civil and Defense Mobilization, July 21, 1960.

548 *Informing and Educating Employees in Civil Defense Methods for Personal and Home Protection* (no date). From the Virgil Couch Papers at the Eisenhower Library.

549 Garrison, *Bracing for Armageddon: Why Civil Defense Never Worked.*

550 "Weekly News Digest," Office of Civil and Defense Mobilization, February 17, 1961.

551 "Information Bulletin: Inquiring Camera Girl," Office of Civil and Defense Mobilization, July 29, 1960.

552 "Civil Defense . . . . An American Tradition: Four National Award Winning Essays," Office of Civil and Defense Mobilization, 1960.

Chapter 16: The Plummet of Preparedness

553 If you are interested in reading these yourself, see "Papers of John F. Kennedy. Presidential Papers. National Security Files," John F. Kennedy Presidential Library and Museum, accessed July 8, 2025, https://www.jfklibrary.org/asset-viewer/archives/jfknsf#overview. Search for Box 295, which primarily covers civil defense from Kennedy's inauguration to his assassination. Using a key word search on this web page will also yield other civil defense sources, but not all are digitally archived.

554 John F. Kennedy Presidential Library and Museum, *Civil Defense: General, 1962, Part I*, National Security Files, Box 295, Folder 1, accessed May 1, 2025, https://www.jfklibrary.org/asset-viewer/archives/jfknsf-295-001#?image_identifier=JFKNSF-295-001-p0002.

555 "Civil Defense: Boom to Bust," *TIME*, May 18, 1962, https://web.archive.org/web/20101207065853/http:/www.time.com/time/magazine/article/0,9171,896157,00.html.

556 "Weekly News Digest," Office of Civil and Defense Mobilization, March 24, 1961.

557 "Weekly News Digest," March 24, 1961.

558 "Weekly News Digest," March 24, 1961.

559 John F. Kennedy Presidential Library and Museum, *Civil Defense: General, 1962, Part I*, National Security Files, Box 295, Folder 1, accessed May 1, 2025, https://www.jfklibrary.org/asset-viewer/archives/jfknsf-295-001#?image_identifier=JFKNSF-295-001-p0010.

560 For sake of brevity, I did not list other sources from the JFK archives that also supported moving Civil Defense to the active-duty military, or at least the National Guard or Reserves.

561 John F. Kennedy, *National Security Files, 1961–1963*, box 295, folder 3, John F. Kennedy Presidential Library and Museum, accessed May 1, 2025, https://www.jfklibrary.org/asset-viewer/archives/jfknsf-295-003#?image_identifier=JFKNSF-295-003-p0022.

562 John F. Kennedy, "Special Message to the Congress on Urgent National Needs," May 25, 1961, *John F. Kennedy Presidential Library and Museum*, accessed May 1, 2025, https://www.jfklibrary.org/archives/other-resources/john-f-kennedy-speeches/united-states-congress-special-message-19610525.

563 See "Civil Defense: General, October 1961: 1-27," John F. Kennedy Presidential Library and Museum, accessed July 8, 2025, https://www.jfklibrary.org/asset-viewer/archives/jfknsf-295-006#?image_identifier=JFKNSF-295-006-p0002.

564 "A Look Back at America's Fallout Shelter Fatuation," CBS News, October 7, 2010, accessed May 1, 2025, https://www.cbsnews.com/news/a-look-back-at-americas-fallout-shelter-

fatuation/.

565 Hillel Italie, "Vietnam-Era Whistleblower Daniel Ellsberg, Who Leaked Pentagon Papers, Dies at 92," AP News, June 16, 2023, accessed May 1, 2025, https://apnews.com/article/daniel-ellsberg-vietnam-war-pentagon-papers-12f57b417c372c1b8760a21d447cb502. Interestingly, Raskin was one of the people whom Daniel Ellsberg leaked the Pentagon Papers to in 1971.

566 John F. Kennedy, *National Security Files, 1961–1963*, box 295, folder 6, John F. Kennedy Presidential Library and Museum, accessed May 1, 2025, https://www.jfklibrary.org/asset-viewer/archives/jfknsf-295-006#?image_identifier=JFKNSF-295-006-p0003. Further quotes from Raskin come from the same source.

567 John F. Kennedy, *National Security Files*.

568 John F. Kennedy, *National Security Files*, 1961–1963, box 295, folder 3, John F. Kennedy Presidential Library and Museum, accessed May 1, 2025, https://www.jfklibrary.org/asset-viewer/archives/jfknsf-295-003#?image_identifier=JFKNSF-295-003-p0016. Raskin wrote, "This means to me that we have to judge every action that we undertake and that others undertake in a way which will help us ascertain whether or not the odds for war decrease or increase. This in turn should help us know what to do. We have also to decide whether or not we are building a world which is safe for democracy—or one only finitely safe even for a garrison state. I have great fears for this civil defense program. I do not think that it will decrease the probabilities of war." "The Anti-interventionist Tradition: Leadership and Perceptions," Libertarianism.org, accessed July 8, 2025, https://www.libertarianism.org/publications/essays/anti-interventionist-tradition-leadership-perceptions.

569 Justus Doenecke, "The Anti-Interventionist Tradition: Leadership and Perceptions," *Literature of Liberty* 4, no. 2 (Summer 1981), accessed May 1, 2025, https://www.libertarianism.org/publications/essays/anti-interventionist-tradition-leadership-perceptions. Critics of Robert F. Kennedy's 2024 presidential election bid accuse him of the same anti-interventionism. See Derek Beres, Matthew Remski, and Julian Walker, "The Conspirituality of Robert F. Kennedy Jr.," *TIME*, July 5, 2023, https://time.com/6292191/robert-f-kennedy-jr-conspiracy-theory-vaccines-essay/.

570 John F. Kennedy Presidential Library and Museum, "Nuclear Test Ban Treaty," November 7, 2024, https://www.jfklibrary.org/learn/about-jfk/jfk-in-history/nuclear-test-ban-treaty.

571 "Nuclear Test Ban Treaty."

572 John F. Kennedy, *National Security Files, 1961–1963*, box 295, folder 6, John F. Kennedy Presidential Library and Museum, accessed May 1, 2025, https://www.jfklibrary.org/asset-viewer/archives/jfknsf-295-006#?image_identifier=JFKNSF-295-006-p0014.

573 John F. Kennedy, *National Security Files*.

574 John F. Kennedy, *National Security Files*.

575 John F. Kennedy, *National Security Files*.

576 John F. Kennedy, *National Security Files*.

577 John F. Kennedy, *National Security Files*. I have personally heard versions of this argument from several sources, including government officials. When asked why the federal government does not issue guidance for higher levels of preparedness for those who can or want to achieve higher levels of resilience, the responses I've received are a mixture of fear (panic) avoidance, the fairness of such guidance, and issues of legality.

578 Garrison, *Bracing for Armageddon: Why Civil Defense Never Worked.*

579 Garrison.

580 Garrison.

581 Graff, *Raven Rock: The Story of the U.S. Government's Secret Plan to Save Itself—While the Rest of Us Die.*

582 Garrison, *Bracing for Armageddon: Why Civil Defense Never Worked.*

583 *Fallout Protection: What to Know and Do about Nuclear Attack* (Washington, DC: US Department of Defense, Office of Civil Defense, December 1961), https://www.dahp.wa.gov/sites/default/files/Fallout%20Protection%20What%20to%20Know%20and%20Do.pdf.

584 Robert Klara, "Nuclear Fallout Shelters Were Never Going to Work," History.com, October 16, 2017, https://www.history.com/news/nuclear-fallout-shelters-were-never-going-to-work.

585 Library of Congress digital image number LC-DIG-ds-07442. Archived at: https://www.loc.gov/pictures/resource/ds.07442/.

586 D. D. Teoli Jr., "Drive for Mass Shelters," *Life*, January 12, 1962, https://archive.org/details/drive-for-mass-shelters-life-1.12.62-d.-d.-teoli-jr.-a.-c.-11.

587 D. D. Teoli Jr., "Drive for Mass Shelters."

588 "Religion: Gun Thy Neighbor?," *TIME*, August 18, 1961, https://content.time.com/time/subscriber/article/0,33009,872694,00.html.

589 "Civil Defense: Boom to Bust," *TIME*, May 18, 1962, https://web.archive.org/web/20101207065853/http:/www.time.com/time/magazine/article/0,9171,896157,00.html.

590 Robert Klara, "Nuclear Fallout Shelters Were Never Going to Work."

591 Naomi Kroll Hassebroek, "Historic Structure Report: Mansion and Belvedere Nuclear Bomb Shelters," Marsh-Billings-Rockefeller National Historical Park, Woodstock, VT, September 2018. For a synopsis, see "Kennedy, Rockefeller, and Civil Defense," National Park Service, accessed July 8, 2025, https://www.nps.gov/articles/coldwar_civildefense_kennedyrockefellerandcd.htm.

592 Hassebroek.

593 Patrick Monreal, "Inside Stanford's Last Fallout Shelter: A Time Capsule to Cold War Politics and Protests," *The Stanford Daily*, September 25, 2019, https://stanforddaily.com/2019/09/25/inside-stanfords-last-fallout-shelter/.

594 Monreal.

595 Garrison, *Bracing for Armageddon: Why Civil Defense Never Worked*; Graff, *Raven Rock: The Story of the U.S. Government's Secret Plan to Save Itself—While the Rest of Us Die.*

596 Emergency Planning Committee. *On a Re-examination of Federal Policy with Respect to Emergency Plans and Continuity of Government in the Event of a Nuclear Attack on the United States.* June 11, 1968, https://www.brennancenter.org/sites/default/files/2021-11/Federal%20Policy%20with%20Respect%20to%20Emergency%20Plans%20%28Jun.%201962%29.pdf.

597 Yes, that is arcs with a "c" and not arks.

598 Emergency Planning Committee.

599 Emergency Planning Committee, 35.

600 Edward A. McDermott, memorandum to Captain Tazewell T. Shepard, "Civil Emergency Action Documents," with attachments, October 29, 1962, declassified, https://www.brennancenter.org/sites/default/files/2023-09/Memorandum%20from%20Edward%20A.%20McDermott%20to%20Captain%20Tazewell%20Shepard%2C%20%E2%80%9CCivil%20Emergency%20Action%20Documents%2C%E2%80%9D%20with%20attachments%2C%20October%2029%2C%201962%2C%20Top%20Secret.pdf.

601 Department of Justice, *Staff Memorandum of Office of Legal Council: Review of Presidential Emergency Documents*, December 22, 1967, 10, https://www.brennancenter.org/sites/default/files/2020-05/2%29%20Office%20of%20Legal%20Counsel-%20Review%20of%20PEADS.pdf.

602 Edward A. McDermott, recorded interview by Charles Daly, June 4, 1964. Archived at the John F. Kennedy Library Oral History Program: https://www.jfklibrary.org/asset-viewer/archives/jfkoh-eam-03.

603 Edward A. McDermott, recorded interview by Charles Daly, June 4, 1964.

604 World Population Review, "Nuclear Weapons by Country 2025," accessed May 1, 2025, https://worldpopulationreview.com/country-rankings/nuclear-weapons-by-country.

Chapter 17: The Politics of Preparedness

605 An autocracy is a form of government in which one person holds near total power. Dictatorships are an example, but so are monarchies if the royalty truly rules and is not just a titular figurehead like Sweden or the United Kingdom. Some countries are autocratic in nature (e.g., China and Russia), even though technically the ruler does not have absolute government authority.

606 Office of the Director of National Intelligence, "2024 Annual Threat Assessment Director of National Intelligence."

607 United Nations Development Programme, ed., *Human Development Report: New Dimensions of Human Security* (New York: Oxford University Press, 1994).

608 For example, he cites the large gap between Japan and Canada's definitions of human security.

609 Freedom House, "Kiribati: Freedom in the World 2022 Country Report," *Freedom in the World 2022*, accessed May 1, 2025, https://freedomhouse.org/country/kiribati/freedom-world/2022.

610 Owen Mulhern, "Sea Level Rise Projection Map—Kiribati," Earth.Org, August 6, 2020, https://earth.org/data_visualization/sea-level-rise-by-2100-kiribati/.

611 "Why Are Hundreds of Pacific Islands Getting Bigger?," ABC News, January 8, 2021, https://www.abc.net.au/news/2021-01-08/why-are-hundreds-of-pacific-islands-getting-bigger/13038430. Interestingly, one University of Auckland study shows that some Pacific Island states are growing, not shrinking.

612 Oliver Milman, "'No Safe Place': Kiribati Seeks Donors to Raise Islands from Encroaching Seas," *The Guardian*, November 18, 2022, https://www.theguardian.com/environment/2022/nov/18/cop27-kiribati-donors-raise-islands-sea-level-rise.

613 Based on EM-DAT's calculation of what qualifies as a disaster.

614 CRED, "2023 Disasters in Numbers: A Significant Year of Disaster Impact."

615 CRED.

616 Statista, "Natural Disasters by Death Toll Worldwide since 1980," accessed May 1, 2025, https://www.statista.com/statistics/268029/natural-disasters-by-death-toll-since-1980/. https://www.statista.com/statistics/268126/biggest-natural-disasters-by-economic-damage-since-1980/. Finding sources that agreed on death tolls or costs is a fool's errand based on how tabulations are made. The two sources I include here from CRED and Statista should not be seen as irrefutable. However, they present their data in a crisp fashion and are respectable from an academic viewpoint as a source. For other examples, see "Economic Damage by Natural Disaster Type," Our World in Data, accessed July 8, 2025, https://ourworldindata.org/grapher/economic-damage-from-natural-disasters; and "Climate and Weather Related Disasters Surge Five-Fold over 50 Years, but Early Warnings Save Lives--WMO Report," United Nations, September 1, 2021, https://news.un.org/en/story/2021/09/1098662#:~:text=Three%20of%20the%20costliest%2010%20disasters%2C%20all%20hurricanes,billion%2C%20and%20Irma%20%2458.2%20billion%20i-

n%20Cape%20Verde.

617 For comparison, the US had 47,000 battle deaths in Vietnam and 292,000 battle deaths in World War II, https://www.va.gov/opa/publications/factsheets/fs_americas_wars.pdf.

618 One way to reconcile these statistics is the composition of infrastructure and population density patterns in various countries. Hydrological and geological catastrophes destroy flimsily built shantytowns in poor countries, killing tens of thousands, but destroy fewer (but far more expensive) homes in the West.

619 Michael Shellenberger, *Apocalypse Never: Why Environmental Alarmism Hurts Us All* (New York: HarperCollins, 2020).

620 Kevin Arceneaux and Robert M. Stein, "Who Is Held Responsible When Disaster Strikes? The Attribution of Responsibility for a Natural Disaster in an Urban Election," *Journal of Urban Affairs* 28, no. 1 (January 1, 2006): 43–53, https://doi.org/10.1111/j.0735-2166.2006.00258.x; Andrew Healy and Neil Malhotra, "Random Events, Economic Losses, and Retrospective Voting: Implications for Democratic Competence," *Quarterly Journal of Political Science* 5, no. 2 (August 11, 2010): 193–208, https://doi.org/10.1561/100.00009057; Christopher H. Achen and Larry M. Bartels, *Democracy for Realists: Why Elections Do Not Produce Responsive Government* (Princeton, NJ: Princeton University Press, 2016).

621 Christopher H. Achen and Larry M. Bartels, "Blind Retrospection: Electoral Responses to Drought, Flu, and Shark Attacks" (Unpublished working paper, Princeton, June 2004).

622 Boris Heersink, Brenton D. Peterson, and Jeffery A. Jenkins, "Disasters and Elections: Estimating the Net Effect of Damage and Relief in Historical Perspective," *Political Analysis; Oxford* 25, no. 2 (April 2017): 260–68, http://dx.doi.org.proxy.library.cornell.edu/10.1017/pan.2017.7.

623 Jones, *The Big Ones: How Natural Disasters Have Shaped Us and What We Can Do about Them.*

624 Joshua Hart, "Did Hurricane Sandy Influence the 2012 US Presidential Election?," *Social Science Research* 46 (July 1, 2014): 1–8, https://doi.org/10.1016/j.ssresearch.2014.02.005; Narayani Lasala-Blanco, Robert Y. Shapiro, and Viviana Rivera-Burgos, "Turnout and Weather Disruptions: Survey Evidence from the 2012 Presidential Elections in the Aftermath of Hurricane Sandy," *Electoral Studies* 45 (February 1, 2017): 141–52, https://doi.org/10.1016/j.electstud.2016.11.004; Robert M. Stein, "Election Administration during Natural Disasters and Emergencies: Hurricane Sandy and the 2012 Election," *Election Law Journal: Rules, Politics, and Policy* 14, no. 1 (March 2015): 66–73, https://doi.org/10.1089/elj.2014.0271; Laurie A. Rudman, Meghan C. McLean, and Martin Bunzl, "When Truth Is Personally Inconvenient, Attitudes Change: The Impact of Extreme Weather on Implicit Support for Green Politicians and Explicit Climate-Change Beliefs," *Psychological Science* 24, no. 11 (November 1, 2013): 2290–96, https://doi.org/10.1177/0956797613492775; Kevin J. Coleman and Eric A. Fischer, "Elections in States Affected by Hurricanes Katrina and Rita," May 26, 2006, https://www.hsdl.org/?abstract&did=; Betsy Sinclair, Thad E. Hall, and R. Michael Alvarez, "Flooding the Vote: Hurricane Katrina and Voter Participation in New Orleans," *American Politics Research* 39, no. 5 (September 1, 2011): 921–57, https://doi.org/10.1177/1532673X10386709.

625 Rubin, "The Political Dynamics of Voter Retrospection and Disaster Responses."

626 "2005 Thai General Election," Wikipedia, accessed July 8, 2025, https://en.wikipedia.org/wiki/2005_Thai_general_election.

627 Kosta Bovan, Benjamin Banai, and Irena Pavela Banai, "Do Natural Disasters Affect Voting Behavior? Evidence from Croatian Floods," *PLOS* 10 (April 6, 2018), https://doi.

org/10.1371/currents.dis.cbf57c8ac3b239ba51ccc801d3362c07.

628 Lina M. Eriksson, "Winds of Change: Voter Blame and Storm Gudrun in the 2006 Swedish Parliamentary Election," *Electoral Studies* 41 (March 1, 2016): 129–42, https://doi.org/10.1016/j.electstud.2015.12.003.

629 Shawn Cole, Andrew Healy, and Eric Werker, "Do Voters Demand Responsive Governments? Evidence from Indian Disaster Relief," *Journal of Development Economics* 97, no. 2 (March 1, 2012): 167–81, https://doi.org/10.1016/j.jdeveco.2011.05.005.

630 Lukas Rudolph and Patrick M. Kuhn, "Natural Disasters and Political Participation: Evidence from the 2002 and 2013 Floods in Germany," *German Politics* 27, no. 1 (January 2, 2018): 1–24, https://doi.org/10.1080/09644008.2017.1287900.

631 Jones, *The Big Ones: How Natural Disasters Have Shaped Us and What We Can Do About Them*; Hannigan, *Disasters Without Borders*.

632 Van Belle's research found that after controlling for casualties, the only variable to affect media coverage in US markets was the distance from America to the effected state. See Van Belle, "New York Times and Network TV News Coverage."

633 "Tens of Thousands Rally around the World in Support of Israel and Palestinians," *The Guardian*, October 13, 2023, https://www.theguardian.com/world/2023/oct/14/tens-of-thousands-rally-around-the-world-in-support-of-israel-and-palestinians; Patricia Garip, "Gaza War: Why Latin American Countries Are Joining South Africa's ICJ Genocide Case against Israel," *Foreign Policy*, January 29, 2024, https://foreignpolicy.com/2024/01/29/israel-hamas-gaza-war-latin-america-chile-argentina-colombia-mexico-genocide/.

634 Lucy Easthope, *When the Dust Settles: Stories of Love, Loss and Hope from an Expert in Disaster* (London, UK: Hodder & Stoughton, 2022).

635 One paper, studying 150 countries around the world, found mixed results as to the relationship among natural disasters, pathogens, and climatic events on one side and economic, individual, political, and media freedom on the other (Kodai Kusano and Markus Kemmelmeier, "Ecology of Freedom: Competitive Tests of the Role of Pathogens, Climate, and Natural Disasters in the Development of Socio-Political Freedom," *Frontiers in Psychology* 9 (2018), https://doi.org/10.3389/fpsyg.2018.00954.). Some inhibited freedom, some did not, but no trend *expanded* freedom.

636 Mark Pelling and Kathleen Dill, "Disaster Politics: Tipping Points for Change in the Adaptation of Sociopolitical Regimes," *Progress in Human Geography* 34, no. 1 (February 2010): 21–37, https://doi.org/10.1177/0309132509105004.

637 An undesirable ethnic group in this country.

638 Pelling and Dill, "Disaster Politics."

639 Edward Wong, "Resettling China's 'Ecological Migrants,'" *The New York Times*, October 25, 2016, https://www.nytimes.com/interactive/2016/10/25/world/asia/china-climate-changeresettlement. html?mcubz=0&_r=0.

640 Leah C. Windsor, Nia Dowell, and Art Graesser, "The Language of Autocrats: Leaders' Language in Natural Disaster Crises," *Risk, Hazards & Crisis in Public Policy* 5, no. 4 (2014): 446–67, https://doi.org/10.1002/rhc3.12068.

641 Ruijia Yang et al., "Milk Adulteration with Melamine in China: Crisis and Response," *Quality Assurance and Safety of Crops & Foods* 1, no. 2 (2009): 111–16, https://doi.org/10.1111/j.1757-837X.2009.00018.x.

642 "Melamine and Food Safety in China," *The Lancet* 373, no. 9661 (January 31, 2009): 353, https://doi.org/10.1016/S0140-6736(09)60114-8.

643 US Food and Drug Administration, "Melamine Pet Food Recall of 2007," last modified February 6, 2008, https://www.fda.gov/animal-veterinary/recalls-withdrawals/melamine-pet-food-recall-2007.

644 Food and Agriculture Organization of the United Nations, "Melamine," accessed April 29, 2025, https://www.fao.org/food/food-safety-quality/a-z-index/melamine/en/.

645 Stephen McGlinchey, ed., *International Relations* (Bristol, England: E-International Relations Publishing, 2017).

646 Russel Honoré, *Survival: How Being Prepared Can Keep You and Your Family Safe* (New York: Atria Books, 2010).

647 Finland Ministry of the Interior, "Civil Defence Shelters Would Be Used during Military Threat," accessed November 17, 2019, https://intermin.fi/en/rescue-services/preparedness/civil-defence-shelters.

648 Wen Liu, "The Mundane Politics of War in Taiwan: Psychological Preparedness, Civil Defense, and Permanent War," *Security Dialogue* 55, no. 1 (September 12, 2023), https://doi.org/10.1177/09670106231194908.

649 Ministry of Defence of the Republic of Latvia, *The State Defense Concept* (Riga, September 24, 2020).

650 Swedish Civil Contingencies Agency (MSB), "Empowering Citizens through Research and Innovation," accessed April 29, 2025, https://www.msb.se/en/about-msb/research-and-statistics/empowering-citizens-through-research-and-innovation/.

651 Swedish Civil Contingencies Agency, "If Crisis or War Comes" (Stibo Graphic A/S, 2019), https://www.dinsakerhet.se/siteassets/dinsakerhet.se/broschyren-om-krisen-eller-kriget-kommer/om-krisen-eller-kriget-kommer—-engelska.pdf.

652 Swedish Civil Contingencies Agency (MSB), "Download or Order the Brochure in Case of Crisis or War," last modified January 9, 2025, https://www.msb.se/en/advice-for-individuals/the-brochure-in-case-of-crisis-or-war/download-and-order-the-brochure-in-case-of-crisis-or-war/.

653 Swedish Civil Contingencies Agency, "In Case of Crisis or War," 2024, https://rib.msb.se/filer/pdf/30874.pdf.

654 Lindsay, "The Living Heritage of Prepping."

655 Olsson, "Understanding Swedish Prepping—A Mixed-Method Study on Resilience, Trust, and Incentives to Prepare for Crises"; Mellander, "Dread Expectations? Prepping, Culture, and Fear in Late Modernity."

656 Mellander, "Dread Expectations? Prepping, Culture, and Fear in Late Modernity."

657 Olsson, "Understanding Swedish Prepping—A Mixed-Method Study on Resilience, Trust, and Incentives to Prepare for Crises."

658 Otto Fiala, *Resistance Operating Concept* (MacDill Air Force Base, FL: Joint Special Operations University Press, 2020).

Conclusion: The Portals of Preparedness

659 Sadly, I cannot remember the pastor's name. His five components, however, stuck with me.

660 Christina Morales and Allyson Waller, "A Gender-Reveal Celebration Is Blamed for a Wildfire. It Isn't the First Time," *The New York Times*, September 18, 2020, https://www.nytimes.com/2020/09/07/us/gender-reveal-party-wildfire.html.

661 Beth Greenfield, "Barbie Has Death Anxiety. Here's What It Means," Yahoo Life, July 25, 2023, https://www.yahoo.com/lifestyle/barbie-death-anxiety-heres-means-230211814.html.

662 Philip Mellor and Chris Shilling, "Modernity, Self-Identity and the Sequestration of Death," *Sociology* 27, no. 3 (August 1993): 411–31.

663 Mellor and Shilling, "Modernity, Self-Identity and the Sequestration of Death."

664 "Major Religious Groups," Wikipedia, last modified April 28, 2025, https://en.wikipedia.org/wiki/Major_religious_groups.

665 Frank Newport, "Slowdown in the Rise of Religious Nones," Gallup.com, December 9, 2022, https://news.gallup.com/opinion/polling-matters/406544/slowdown-rise-religious-nones.aspx.

666 Newport; Gregory A. Smith and Alan Cooperman, "Has the Rise of Religious 'Nones' Come to an End in the U.S.?," Pew Research Center, January 24, 2024, https://www.pewresearch.org/short-reads/2024/01/24/has-the-rise-of-religious-nones-come-to-an-end-in-the-us/.

667 Anna Fleck, "More Young Men Are Now Religious Than Women in the U.S.," Statista Daily Data, November 14, 2024, https://www.statista.com/chart/33484/share-of-us-male-and-female-respondents-who-say-they-are-religious-by-generation.

668 Hillsdale College Politics Faculty, ed., *The U.S. Constitution: A Reader* (Hillsdale, MI: Hillsdale College Press, 2012).

669 "The Power of Forgiveness," Harvard Health, May 1, 2019, https://www.health.harvard.edu/mind-and-mood/the-power-of-forgiveness.

670 Viktor Frankl, *Man's Search For Meaning* (Boston, MA: Beacon Press, 2006).

671 Shellenberger, *Apocalypse Never: Why Environmental Alarmism Hurts Us All.*

672 Wendell Berry, *The Unsettling of America: Culture and Agriculture* (San Francisco, CA: Sierra Club Books, 1996).

673 Berry.

674 Wendell Berry, *The World-Ending Fire: The Essential Wendell Berry* (Berkeley, CA: Counterpoint, 2017).

675 As all things are connected, Paul Kingsnorth wrote the foreword to *World-Ending Fire.*

676 Erica Pandey, "Soak Up the Sun," Axios, June 1, 2022, https://www.axios.com/2022/06/01/sun-vitamin-d-deficiency-american-adults-kids.

677 Chloe Garnham, "42% of Americans Are Deficient in Vitamin D. Are You at Risk? If So, What Can You Do about It?," HealthMatch, November 30, 2022, https://healthmatch.io/blog/42-of-americans-are-deficient-in-vitamin-d-are-you-at-risk-if-so-what-can.

678 Andrew Zolli and Anne Marie Healy, *Resilience: Why Things Bounce Back* (New York: Simon & Schuster, 2012).

679 Robert Heinlein, *Time Enough for Love* (New York: G. P. Putnam's Sons, 1973).

680 Ripley, *The Unthinkable: Who Survives When Disaster Strikes and Why.*

681 "The Yerkes-Dodson Curve," Wikimedia Commons, accessed July 9, 2025, https://commons.wikimedia.org/wiki/File:OriginalYerkesDodson.svg.

682 Coltan Scrivner et al., "Pandemic Practice: Horror Fans and Morbidly Curious Individuals Are More Psychologically Resilient during the COVID-19 Pandemic," *Personality and Individual Differences* 168 (January 1, 2021): 110397, https://doi.org/10.1016/j.paid.2020.110397.

683 Valerie van Mulukom and Mathias Clasen, "The Evolutionary Functions of Imagination and Fiction and How They May Contribute to Psychological Wellbeing during a Pandemic," PsyArXiv, May 7, 2025, https://doi.org/10.31234/osf.io/wj4zg.

684 Peter Perla and Ed McGrady, "Why Wargaming Works," *Naval War College Review* 64, no. 3 (2011).

685 "Everything to Play For: How Games Changed the World," *The Economist*, June 22, 2024.

686 Jonathan Haidt, *The Happiness Hypothesis: Finding Modern Truth in Ancient Wisdom* (New York: Basic Books, 2006).

687 Meyer and Kunreuther, *The Ostrich Paradox: Why We Underprepare For Disasters.*

688 "Quote Origin: People More Frequently Require to Be Reminded Than Informed," *Quote Investigator*, June 18, 2024, https://quoteinvestigator.com/2024/06/18/require-remind/.

689 Lawrence Vale and Thomas Campanella, eds., *The Resilient City: How Modern Cities Recover from Disaster* (Oxford: Oxford University Press, 2005).

690 Jay, *Supernormal: The Untold Story of Adversity and Resilience.*

691 Paul Slovic et al., "The Affect Heuristic," in *Heuristics and Biases: The Psychology of Intuitive Judgment* (Cambridge, UK: Cambridge University Press, 2002).

692 Encyclopedia Britannica, "15 Nelson Mandela Quotes," accessed April 29, 2025, https://www.britannica.com/list/nelson-mandela-quotes.

693 Ripley, *The Unthinkable: Who Survives When Disaster Strikes and Why.*

694 Ripley.

695 Ripley.

696 Ripley.

697 The poem "America the Beautiful" was inspired by Katharine Lee Bates's summiting of the mountain.

698 Sally Hawkins et al., "Georgia Mom's Arrest Puts Free-Range Parenting Back into Spotlight," ABC News, November 21, 2024, https://abcnews.go.com/US/georgia-moms-arrest-puts-free-range-parenting-back/story?id=116004039.

699 National Public Radio Staff, "What Kind of Parent Are You? The Debate over 'Free-Range' Parenting," National Public Radio, April 26, 2015, https://www.npr.org/2015/04/26/402226053/what-kind-of-parent-are-you-the-debate-over-free-range-parenting.

700 Matthew Cooke, "Is 'Free-Range' Parenting a Crime?," *Seattle*, February 22, 2016, https://seattlemag.com/free-range-parenting-crime/.

701 Steph Montgomery, "Here's When You Can Let Your Child Play Unsupervised, According to Experts," Romper, August 23, 2019, https://www.romper.com/p/when-can-you-let-your-child-play-unsupervised-experts-explain-18568803.

702 Henry Grabar, "How Japan Built Cities Where You Could Send Your Toddler on an Errand," *Slate*, April 11, 2022, https://slate.com/business/2022/04/old-enough-netflix-do-japanese-parents-really-send-toddlers-on-errands.html.

703 David Derbyshire, "How Children Lost the Right to Roam in Four Generations," *Daily Mail*, June 15, 2007, https://www.dailymail.co.uk/news/article-462091/How-children-lost-right-roam-generations.html.

704 Jon Haidt, "Social Media Is a Major Cause of the Mental Illness Epidemic in Teen Girls. Here's the Evidence: Journalists Should Stop Saying That the Evidence Is Just Correlational," After Babel, February 22, 2023, https://www.afterbabel.com/p/social-media-mental-illness-epidemic.

705 Anna Fleck, "Nearly One in Five U.S. Teens Experienced Depression in 2023," Statista Daily Data, December 2, 2024, https://www.statista.com/chart/33610/share-of-us-teenagers—12-17-y-o—who-have-experienced-a-major-depressive-episode.

706 Atkinson and Blandy, *Domestic Fortress.*

707 Atkinson and Blandy.

708 Zolli and Healy, *Resilience: Why Things Bounce Back.*

709 Zolli and Healy.

710 Colin Lodewick, "Having Rich Friends Growing Up Can Help People Escape Poverty, New Study Says," *Fortune*, August 1, 2022, https://fortune.com/2022/08/01/poverty-social-mobility-high-income-friends-study/.

711 Neighborhood Ninjas, "Scholarship, Mentorship, Community, Connection," accessed April 29, 2025, https://www.neighborhoodninjas.org/.

712 Blue Zones, "Live Better, Longer," accessed April 29, 2025 https://www.bluezones.com/.